Ready for
FCE

Roy Norris

Coursebook

MACMILLAN

Contents map

Introduction

Welcome to *Ready for First Certificate*, a course which is designed to help you prepare for the Cambridge First Certificate in English examination.

This book contains a wide range of activities aimed at improving your English and developing the language and skills which you will need to pass the examination. As well as providing relevant practice in reading, writing, listening and speaking, each unit of *Ready for First Certificate* includes one or more Language focus sections, which revise the main grammar areas, together with Vocabulary slots which will help you to increase your word store.

A significant feature of the Use of English syllabus in the book is the systematic approach to Word formation. At regular intervals you will find special sections which focus on the most important aspects of word building, ensuring that you are properly prepared for this part of the examination.

At the end of every unit there is a two-page Review section, which enables you to revise and practise the new language you have encountered in the unit.

Throughout the book you will find the following boxes, which are designed to help you when performing the different tasks.
• **What to expect in the exam**: these contain useful information on what you should be prepared to see, hear or do in a particular task in the examination.
• **How to go about it**: these give advice and guidelines on how to deal with different task types and specific questions.
• **Don't forget!**: these provide a reminder of important points to bear in mind when answering a particular question.

Further information and advice is included in the five supplementary 'Ready for…' units, one for each of the five papers in the examination. These are situated after every third unit in the book and can be used at appropriate moments during the course.

At the end of the book you will find detailed explanations of the grammar areas seen in the units in the Grammar reference together with a topic-based Wordlist.

Overview of the examination

The Cambridge First Certificate in English examination consists of five papers, each of which carries 20% of the total marks. A low mark in one paper does not necessarily mean a candidate will fail the examination; it is the overall mark which counts. A, B and C are pass grades; D and E are fail grades.

Paper 1: Reading   1 hour 15 minutes

There are four parts to this paper, with a total of 35 questions. Each question in Parts 1, 2 and 3 carries 2 marks; each question in Part 4 carries 1 mark. Texts are taken from a variety of sources and include newspaper and magazine articles, fiction, advertisements and brochures. For more information and advice on appropriate reading strategies for each part, see the Ready for Reading unit on pages 38 to 41, as well as the relevant sections in the main units of the book.

Part	Task type	Number of questions	Task format
1	Multiple matching (identifying the main ideas)	6 or 7	A text preceded by headings or summary sentences, which must be matched to their corresponding paragraphs.
2	Multiple choice (understanding detail)	7 or 8	A text followed by multiple choice questions with four options A, B, C or D.
3	Gapped text (understanding text structure)	6 or 7	A text from which sentences or paragraphs have been removed. Candidates replace each of these in the appropriate part of the text.
4	Multiple matching (locating specific information)	13 to 15	A text preceded by multiple matching questions which require candidates to find specific information in a text or texts.

Paper 2: Writing   1 hour 30 minutes

There are two parts to this paper, each of which carries the same number of marks. Part 1 is compulsory, so must be answered by all candidates, whereas in Part 2 candidates choose one from four tasks. Candidates are required to write between 120 and 180 words for each part. For more information and advice on the questions in this paper, see the Ready for Writing unit on pages 118 to 121, as well as the relevant sections in the main units of the book.

Part	Task type	Number of questions	Task format
1	Transactional letter: formal or informal	1 (compulsory)	Candidates write a letter in response to a given situation. Prompts are provided in the form of written input material such as a letter, an advertisement and/or notes.

2	4 (candidates choose one)	A situation-based writing task with a clear context, purpose for writing and target reader. Tasks include: – article – composition – report – informal letter – letter of application – short story The last question is always one of the above task types on a background reading text (2 options).	

Paper 3: Use of English   1 hour 15 minutes

This paper consists of five parts with a total of 65 questions, which test grammar and vocabulary. Each question in Part 3 carries two marks; questions in all other parts each carry one mark. For more information on this paper, see the Ready for Use of English unit on pages 78 to 81, as well as the relevant sections in the main units of the book.

Part	Task type	Number of questions	Task format
1	Multiple choice cloze (emphasis on vocabulary)	15	A text with 15 gaps; there is a choice of four answers for each gap.
2	Open cloze (grammar and vocabulary)	15	A text with 15 gaps, each of which must be completed with one word.
3	'Key' word transformations (grammar and vocabulary)	10	Gapped sentences which must be completed using a given word.
4	Error correction (emphasis on grammar)	15	A text with some lines which are correct and others which contain an extra and unnecessary word. The task is to identify the extra words.
5	Word formation (vocabulary)	10	A text containing 10 gaps. The task is to complete each gap with the correct form of a given word.

Paper 4: Listening   about 40 minutes

This paper consists of four parts with a total of 30 questions, each of which carries one mark. Each part contains one or more recorded texts, which are heard twice. Candidates are tested on their ability to understand gist, the main points or specific information, and to deduce meaning. For more information on this paper, see the Ready for Listening unit on pages 158 to 161, as well as the relevant sections in the main units of the book.

Part	Task type	Number of questions	Task format
1	Multiple choice	8	Short unrelated extracts of approximately 30 seconds each with one or two speakers. Multiple choice questions have three options, A, B or C.
2	Note taking or blank filling	10	A monologue or conversation lasting approximately three minutes. Candidates write a word or short phrase to complete notes or sentences, or in response to questions.
3	Multiple matching	5	Five short extracts, each lasting approximately 30 seconds. The extracts are all related to a common theme. Candidates match extracts with prompts.
4	Selecting from 2 or 3 possible answers	7	One or more speakers talking for approximately three minutes. Possible task types include: True/False; Yes/No; three-option multiple choice; matching (eg Who said what?).

Paper 5: Speaking   about 14 minutes

There are four parts to this paper. There are usually two candidates and two examiners. Candidates are given marks for range and correct use of grammar and vocabulary, pronunciation, communication and successful completion of tasks. For more information on this paper, see the Ready for Speaking unit on pages 196 to 199, as well as the relevant sections in the main units of the book.

Part	Task type	Time	Task format
1	Interview	3 minutes	Candidates give personal information in response to questions from the interviewer.
2	Talking about photographs	4 minutes	Each candidate talks about two pictures for about one minute, and comments briefly on the other candidate's pictures.
3	Collaborative task	3 minutes	Candidates are given visual material and then speak to each other about it in order to complete a task.
4	Further discussion	4 minutes	The interviewer leads a discussion which is related to the topic of Part 3.

①Lifestyle

Vocabulary 1: Clothes

1   Find the following items of clothing and accessories in the pictures above. Which item is not there? What other items can you see?

waistcoat	jumper	dungarees	tracksuit bottoms
bracelet	trainers	blazer	dinner jacket
scarf	cardigan	bow tie	high-heeled shoes

2   The following adjectives can be used to describe clothes. Which of them can you match to the pictures above?

tight-fitting	formal	tasteful	trendy
baggy	colourful	unfashionable	shabby
casual	plain	smart	waterproof

3   In exercises A and B, put the correct form of the appropriate verb in each space.

A   *fit*   *suit*   *match*   *go with*

Personally, I don't think those shoes **(1)** _____ that dress. I mean red and blue just don't **(2)** _____ , do they? And as for those earrings, well they really don't **(3)** _____ her – someone with short hair should not be wearing long ones like that. He looks alright though, except perhaps for those trousers. Do you think they **(4)** _____ him properly? They look a little tight on him to me.

B   *wear*   *put on*   *get dressed*

As it was Sunday I got up and had breakfast in my dressing gown. I didn't **(1)** _____ until well after 11 o'clock. I **(2)** _____ a long-sleeved jumper at first, but immediately changed my mind. It was far too hot outside and I spent the whole day **(3)** _____ just a short-sleeved cotton shirt and shorts.

4 Using the vocabulary from exercises 1, 2 and 3, describe what the people are wearing in the photographs on page 2.

 5 Describe the clothes that you most like wearing. Use the vocabulary from exercises 1, 2 and 3 and the Wordlist on page 202 to help you. Say why you like them, when you wear them and when you wouldn't wear them.

 Reading:
FCE Part 3

Gapped text

1 You are going to read a text written by a woman whose job it once was to 'care for and protect' teenage models, such as those in the photographs.

What do you imagine the lifestyle of teenage fashion models is like?
How do you think they spend a typical week?
What do they need protection from?

2 Read the article on the next page quite quickly. Do you think the writer would recommend this lifestyle to teenagers?

3 Read the following instructions for this Part 3 Reading task.

Eight sentences have been removed from the article. Choose from the sentences **A–I** the one which fits each space (**1–7**). There is one extra sentence which you do not need to use. There is an example at the beginning (**0**).

How to go about it

- Check that the whole sentence fits in with the meaning of the text before and after the space.
- To help you do this, parts of the text are written in **bold**. These show connections between the language in the text and the language in the missing sentences.
- In addition, connections between pronouns and other words are shown in *italics*.
- Now look at space number **1** and answer the following questions.

a What pronouns could be used in the missing sentence to refer to 'our girls'?
b Which sentence (**A–I**) contains one of these pronouns *and* mentions 'talking' and 'getting a job'?
c When you think you have found the sentence, read the whole paragraph again to check that it fits.
- Now complete the rest of the spaces with an appropriate sentence.

Handle with care

After recent news stories of drug-taking amongst teenage models in the care of their model agencies, the catwalk world has once again come under public scrutiny. Jess Hallett used to be a booker, taking bookings for models, organizing their itineraries and generally running their lives. She talks about what she had to do in order to protect her girls.

While bad behaviour in the modelling world evidently exists, there are many people in the fashion industry who work very hard to try and make sure it doesn't. **With all my experience I should know.** [0 | *I*] I left because I didn't have the energy to be a kind of substitute mother to yet another beautiful teenager. Bookers care for and protect these young models to such a point that they are often too tired at the end of the day even to go home.

We did all kinds of things for **our girls.** [1 ⬚] Sometimes **we had to talk to them** and cheer them up **even when they did get the job they wanted**; such as the cover of Italian 'Vogue' or the Chanel show in Paris. They were terrified they were going to do it badly and the booker would reassure them and tell them they looked fantastic.

The trend of using girls as young as 14 or 15 means a lot of responsibility. **The consequences of not taking good care of them** are too huge for any agency to consider. [2 ⬚] Backstage at any show in New York, Paris or Milan, you see bookers from all over the world, there to support their girls and make sure that another agency doesn't try to attract them with a better contract.

[3 ⬚] I'll never forget the time when Charles de Gaulle airport was closed down because of a strike and **Kate Moss had to get to Paris** for a very important job. The Channel Tunnel hadn't been built then, so I flew with her to Brussels **with the idea of getting the train** from there. [4 ⬚] **The whole journey took 12 hours,** but with a studio full of people waiting for her at the other end, we had no choice.

One danger we had to protect models from was **their parents.** [5 ⬚] It was quite clear that **she** was humiliated by **his behaviour** and wasn't at all interested in being a model.

There were **some parents** who would let their daughter go **alone** to fashion shoots if it meant fame and fortune. [6 ⬚] At the model agency where I worked, parents were usually encouraged to get involved in their daughters' careers and travelled with them whenever they could.

The fact is that **the majority of girls love the lifestyle.** [7 ⬚] The Russian model Lida Egorova told me recently how happy she was, working with creative and talented people. She was wealthy and living in Paris; and the night before she had met Madonna at a party. What more could any girl want?

A *One father* insisted that *his daughter* was better-looking than anyone in 'Vogue' and **complained about me** to my boss because I wouldn't employ *her*.

B **If you don't look after *them* properly**, then someone else will.

C *Others* never allowed them to go anywhere **unaccompanied**.

D Whether it was because *they* were having a hard time at school, had split up with their boyfriend, or **hadn't got a job *they* really wanted, their booker was the one *they* talked to.**

E And considering how many of *them* there are nowadays, **you don't hear many complaints**.

F However, it seemed that the rest of Europe had the **same idea**, so we had to persuade a taxi driver to take us **all the way to Paris**.

G *She* said *she* was **having a wonderful time** and couldn't imagine doing any other job.

H **Models tend to travel a lot** and whenever necessary a booker will accompany them on a trip.

I *I* **spent almost ten years as a booker** and became emotionally involved with almost every girl in my care.

When you have finished, check that the sentence which you have not used does not fit into any of the spaces.

Reacting to the text ⬤

Do you think that children who are encouraged to step into adult roles, such as catwalk modelling, are being exploited?

At what age do you think teenagers should be allowed to work for adult agencies?

Do you think it is right that models should be so highly paid?

Language focus 1: Habitual behaviour

A General tendencies

1 Which of the alternatives in this sentence is not possible?
Models <u>tend to/use to/usually</u> travel a lot.

🔍 Look in the Grammar reference on page 206 to see how *tend to* is used.

2 Make three general statements about the habits of the following groups of people in your country using *tend to*.

- pop stars
- teenagers
- old people
- teachers
- people in big cities

Example:
Pop stars in my country tend to arrive late for concerts and interviews. It's very irritating, especially as you have to pay so much to go and see them perform.

B Frequency adverbs

1 Look at the following extracts from the text.

*They are **often** too tired at the end of the day even to go home.*
***Sometimes** we had to talk to them and cheer them up even when they did get the job they wanted.*
*I'll **never** forget the time when Charles de Gaulle airport was closed down...*
*Parents were **usually** encouraged to get involved in their daughters' careers...*
*Others **never** allowed them to go anywhere unaccompanied.*

2 What is the normal position in the sentence for frequency adverbs with the following?

a main verbs   **b** the verb *to be*   **c** auxiliary verbs

Practice

1 For sentences **1–6**, decide if the position of the adverb is possible. If it is not possible, correct the sentence.

1. I hardly ever get clothes for my birthday or for Christmas.
2. I have sometimes breakfast in my pyjamas.
3. Always I fold my clothes up before I go to bed.
4. Someone in my family is always borrowing my clothes – it's so irritating!
5. When I go shopping for clothes, I rarely can find jeans which fit me perfectly.
6. Occasionally I wash my own clothes, but normally my mum or dad does it.

🔍 Check your ideas on page 206 of the Grammar reference.

2 💬 Say whether or not the sentences in exercise 1 are true for you. Use frequency adverbs and *tend to*.

Example:
Well, unfortunately number 1 is not true for me. My aunt often buys me clothes but they're usually not very tasteful or fashionable, so I don't tend to wear them often.

C *Used to* and *would*

1 *Used to* and *would* can be used to talk about past habits. Look at these sentences from the reading text.
   a *The booker **would** reassure them and tell them they looked fantastic.*
   b *There were some parents who **would** let their daughter go alone to fashion shoots.*
   c *Jess Hallett **used to** be a booker.*

2 In sentences **a** and **b** *used to* is also possible. In sentence **c** *would* is not possible. Why is this?

🔍 Check your ideas on page 206 of the Grammar reference.

Practice

1 In the following paragraph, decide whether the underlined verbs can be used with:
   a both *used to* and *would*
   b only *used to*
   c neither *used to* nor *would*

From a very early age I often **(1)** <u>looked</u> at models in catalogues and **(2)** <u>said</u>: 'I'd like to do that.' I **(3)** <u>was</u> a very small child so one day my mum **(4)** <u>gave</u> me one of her tops to wear as a dress and on sunny days I **(5)** <u>walked</u> up and down the garden path as if I was modelling it on the catwalk. I **(6)** <u>loved</u> that top and I really **(7)** <u>believed</u> that one day I'd be a model. I **(8)** <u>found</u> it recently when I was cleaning the house and I **(9)** <u>smiled</u> to myself.

2 Write six sentences comparing your life now with your life five years ago. Write about things which have changed.

Example:
I didn't use to have a job, but now I work on Saturdays so I have more money.

Vocabulary 2: *Get*

A Expressions with *get*

The following sentences all contain phrasal verbs or expressions with *get*. Decide which answer **A**, **B**, **C** or **D** best fits each space and underline it. There is an example at the beginning **(0)**.

0 That jumper looks so old and dirty. When are you going to get _____ of it?

    A away   **B** throw   **C** waste   **D** <u>rid</u>

1 Here's my telephone number. If you have any problems, just get in _____ with me.

    A talk   **B** speak   **C** touch   **D** tact

2 I heard she was a lovely woman. Unfortunately, I never got the _____ to meet her.

    A occasion   **B** opportunities   **C** possibilities   **D** chance

3 I asked him how much he got _____ but he refused to tell me.

    A paid   **B** earned   **C** money   **D** salary

4 Come on, hurry up and get _____ ! Your bus leaves in five minutes.

    A ready   **B** ordered   **C** fit   **D** prepare

5 His parents are worried about his behaviour. He's always getting into _____ at school.

    A problems   **B** trouble   **C** difficulty   **D** punishment

6 His girlfriend left him in March and he still hasn't got _____ it.

    A by   **B** over   **C** off   **D** past

7 I can't speak French very well, but I always manage to get _____ with a dictionary and a few gestures.

    A by   **B** over   **C** across   **D** through

8 He wanted to get to the town centre but he got _____ the wrong bus and ended up at the station.

    A in   **B** out of   **C** on   **D** off

B Meanings of *get*

1 *Get* can have many different meanings. Look at the uses of *get* (**1–8**) and match each one with an appropriate equivalent (**a–h**). The first one has been done for you.

1 *get* better	**a** receive
2 *get* the bus	**b** ask
3 *get* to the station	**c** become
4 *get* a headache	**d** become ill with
5 *get* somebody to do something	**e** catch
6 *get* something for Christmas	**f** arrive at/reach
7 *get* a newspaper	**g** go out
8 *get* out of the house	**h** buy

2 Look back at the text on teenage models and find examples of *get*. Decide on the meaning in each case.

3 Discuss the following questions.
- How long does it take you to *get* to work/school?
- When did you last *get* away for the weekend?
- What presents did you *get* for your last birthday?
- Do you often *get* angry?
- Where do you usually *get* your clothes?

Multiple matching

You will hear five people talking about occasions when a person's clothes and appearance caused surprise or concern. Match the speaker to the correct occasion in the list **A–F**. Use the letters only once. There is one extra letter which you do not need to use.

Before you do the task...

What to expect in the exam

- You will have 30 seconds to read the descriptions. Use this time to try to predict some of the ideas and language you might hear (see below).
- You are not expected to understand everything you hear.

- Some of the extracts may contain distractors (key words or expressions which could cause you to make the wrong decision).
- Pay close attention the second time you hear the recording. You may discover that you need to change your answers.

Prediction

guest
spectator
audience
competitor
witness
star
candidate
host
invigilator
opponent

1 Match each of the people in the box to the appropriate occasion **A–F** in the listening activity below. More than one word may be used for each occasion and some words may be used twice.

eg A wedding: *guest, witness*

What other people might you also find in each of the situations?

eg *At a wedding the people who get married are the bride and groom.*

2 Where does each occasion take place?

eg *A wedding usually takes place in a church or a registry office.*

3 What clothes would you wear on the occasions **A–F** mentioned in the listening task below?

eg *If I was going to a wedding I would buy an expensive dress. I would probably wear high-heeled shoes.*

Now you are ready to do the task.

A a wedding   Speaker 1 ☐

B a birthday party   Speaker 2 ☐

C a job interview   Speaker 3 ☐

D a sporting event   Speaker 4 ☐

E a film premiere   Speaker 5 ☐

F an examination

 Have you ever been in a situation where someone's appearance caused surprise?

7

Language focus 2: *Be used to, get used to* and *used to*

1 Look at the following sentences from the listening. In which of them does *used to*

a mean 'accustomed to'?
b refer to a past state which has now finished?

1 *Her unconventional, yet practical clothing shocked spectators, who **were used to** seeing women play in the long, heavy dresses which were typical of that period.*
2 *And he **used to** live in France, which means he probably wouldn't mind changing countries if we needed him to.*
3 *...he will have to **get used to** wearing something a little more formal.*

2 What is the difference in meaning between *be used to* and *get used to*?

3 What form of the verb is used after *be used to* and *get used to*?

Ⓖ Check your answers on page 206 of the Grammar reference.

Practice

1 ⬤ Talk about all the things you have to *get used to* in the following situations.

- you get your first job
- you become famous
- you go on a diet
- you get married
- you have children
- you retire

Example:
In a new job, you might have to get used to working together with other people.

2 a If you went to live in Britain, what aspects of life there would you find it difficult to *get used to*?

b Read the following text about Juan, who moved from Spain to live in England. Ignore the spaces for the moment. How many of the things which you spoke about in **a** are mentioned?

Now that Juan has been living in England for five years he **(0)** *is used to doing* (do) things differently, but it hasn't always been the case. When he first moved there he couldn't **(1)** _____ (have) lunch at 1pm, so he often **(2)** _____ (cook) for himself in his flat and eat at 3pm, as his family does in Spain. Even now I don't think he **(3)** _____ (eat) English food, because when he comes home to Madrid, he buys Spanish 'delicacies' to take back with him.
I remember how he **(4)** _____ (write) to me and complain about the shop closing times. It took him a long time to **(5)** _____ the fact that you can't buy anything after about five o'clock. Most shops in Spain close at eight in the evening.
He bought an English car a year ago, so he should **(6)** _____ (drive) on the left by now. I wonder if he'll ever be able to **(7)** _____ (drive) on the right again when, or if, he comes back to live in Spain!

c Read the text again and complete each of the spaces using the correct form of *used to*, *be used to* or *get used to*. If a verb is given in brackets, you should write the appropriate form. There is an example at the beginning **(0)**.

d ⬤ What do you think a British person coming to your country might find it difficult to *get used to*?

⬤ **Speaking:**
FCE Part 2

Talking about photos ⬤

Look at the four photographs on page 9. They show people who have different lifestyles. Before you do the speaking task, read the How to go about it box below.

How to go about it

Student A
- You are not asked to describe the photographs in detail, but to comment on the similarities and differences.
  Similarities: *'Both pictures show ...'*
  Differences: *'In the first picture... whereas in the second one...'*
- When talking about what kind of lives the people lead, comment on some of the following:

daily routine	working hours	leisure time
eating habits	health	travel
family life	type of home	clothes

- Useful language for speculating:
  I get the impression *it's a stressful life.*
  I expect/imagine *he travels a lot.*
  He probably *spends a lot of time working.*
  Perhaps *she doesn't have her own home.*
  She might/may *have a wide circle of friends.*
- Don't forget the second part of the instructions, giving your reasons.

Student B
When you say which person you would prefer to change with, don't forget to give your reasons.

Student A: Compare and contrast photographs **1** and **2** and say what kind of lives you think these people lead.

Student B: When your partner has finished, say which person you would prefer to change places with for a month if you had to choose.

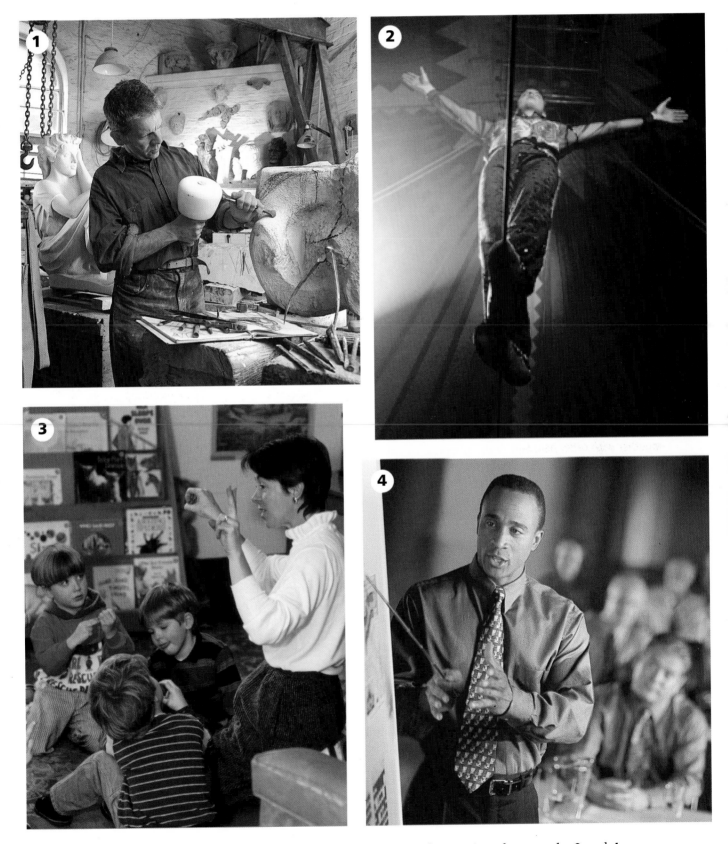

Now change roles. Follow the instructions above using photographs **3** and **4**.

Informal letters

1   Read the following letter, which you have received from your English penfriend, Mark. What two things does he ask you to tell him?
What would *you* accept Mark's invitation? Why/Why not?

Dear _____,

a) <u>Many thanks for your last letter</u>. The new house sounds brilliant – how are you settling in? b) <u>I'm sorry I haven't written sooner</u>, but I've been really busy helping my parents out on the farm.

It's great fun, though I still haven't got used to getting up at six every morning to milk the cows! We often have the radio on while we're doing it, so it's not too bad. Then, once we've had breakfast, we tend to spend the rest of the day outside, either in the fields or looking after the sheep.

c) <u>That reminds me</u>, do you remember Lady, our oldest sheepdog? Well, she's just had puppies! If you're free in the summer, you could come and see them all and help with the harvest as well. d) <u>Let me know</u> if you can make it – we'd love to see you again.

Anyway, e) <u>I must go</u>, as it's getting late and tomorrow we've got another early start. f) <u>Can't wait to hear from you</u>.

g) <u>Best wishes</u>
    Mark

2   What is the purpose of each of the four paragraphs?
Example:
Paragraph 1: *To say thank you for the letter and to apologize for not writing before.*

3   Match each underlined expression **a–g** from Mark's letter with an appropriate alternative from **1–10**. Which three phrases cannot be used and why are they inappropriate?
Example: 1 e)

1 I'd better close now
2 Thanks a lot for the letter
3 Yours sincerely
4 By the way
5 All the best

6 I would be most grateful if you could inform me
7 I look forward to your prompt reply
8 Please write and tell me
9 I'm sorry it's taken me so long to write to you
10 I'm looking forward to hearing from you

Notice the use of contractions in Mark's letter: *I'm, it's* and *haven't*. These are typical of informal writing.

4   Find and circle the following linking words in Mark's letter. Then use an appropriate linker from the box to complete the spaces in sentences **1–6**. Each linker can be used more than once.

but	while	so	and	as well	as

1 You'll never guess what happened to me _____ I was shopping in the centre of town the other day!
2 I'm writing to ask you to do me a favour _____ I've got myself into trouble.

3 We're having a party next Saturday _____ we were wondering if you'd like to come. Bring a friend _____ .

4 I'd love to accept your invitation, _____ I'm afraid I'm going to be busy.

5 I haven't got any plans _____ I'll certainly be able to go.

6 I'm very sorry, _____ I'm afraid I lost your camera _____ I was in the disco on Friday.

5   Match each of the following six reasons for writing with an appropriate sentence **1–6** from exercise **4**.

inviting	accepting an invitation
giving news	asking for help
apologizing	refusing an invitation

6   Read the following Writing Part 2 instructions.

Six months ago you moved to a new house in another part of your country. Write a reply to Mark's letter giving news about how you are settling in to your new surroundings and what a typical day is like. You should also say whether or not you can accept his invitation to go and stay on his farm in the summer.

Write your **letter**. You should write **120–180** words.

Before you write your letter…

Planning

Look at the following paragraph plan. In each paragraph decide which points would be relevant in your letter. Tick (✓) those which are relevant and put a cross (✗) next to those which are not. The first one has been done for you.

Paragraph 1
- Thank Mark for his letter. ✓
- Make a friendly comment about his life on the farm.
- Tell him you have moved.
- Give a detailed description of the house.

Paragraph 2
- Mention what you have/haven't got used to.
- Say whether you have made any friends.
- Give details of their names, ages and jobs.
- Say two or three things about your daily routine.
- Mention how long it takes to get to school/work.
- Describe your school/workplace in detail.

Paragraph 3
- Refuse the invitation but don't say why.
- Accept or refuse the invitation and give a reason.

Paragraph 4
- Talk about what you did last Christmas.
- Explain why you have to finish the letter.
- Refer to a possible future meeting/letter.

Not all of the points that you ticked have to be included in the letter and you may also add relevant points of your own.

Don't forget!

- Organize your letter into paragraphs using the plan above.
- The language of your letter should be informal. Use some of the informal language and linkers that you have just studied.
- Your answer must be relevant to the question.
- Write between 120 and 180 words.

Use of English:

FCE Part 3

Transformations

For questions **1–9**, complete the second sentence so that it has a similar meaning to the first sentence, using the word given. **Do not change the word given.** You must use between two and five words, including the word given. There is an example at the beginning **(0)**.

0 How long was your journey from London to Manchester?
take
How long *did it take you to* get from London to Manchester?

1 Rick is making a slow recovery from his illness.
getting
Rick _____ his illness.

2 Why don't you throw away that old blouse?
rid
How about _____ that old blouse?

3 We usually buy our food from the local market.
tend
We _____ our food from the local market.

4 He never asks when he borrows my things!
always
He is _____ asking!

5 When I was younger we often used to go on holiday abroad.
would
When I was younger _____ on holiday abroad.

6 I'm sure I won't have any problems sharing a flat after a couple of weeks.
get
I'm sure I'll _____ a flat after a couple of weeks.

7 I still find it difficult to work with a computer.
used
I still haven't _____ with a computer.

8 I can't wait to see you again.
forward
I'm really _____ you again.

9 I ought to phone my dad to tell him I've arrived safely.
better
I _____ my dad to tell him I've arrived safely.

Vocabulary

A **Clothes**

For questions **1–6,** decide which of the three words is not normally used with the word in capitals at the end of the line. The first one has been done for you.

1 evening	<u>afternoon</u>	fancy	DRESS
2 colourful	smart	baggy	BOW-TIE
3 waterproof	expensive	tasteful	NECKLACE
4 shabby	plain	tight-fitting	SCARF
5 high-heeled	long-sleeved	trendy	SHOES
6 dinner	casual	waist	JACKET

B Expressions crossword

Expressions for use in informal letters

Across

1 Many _____ for your letter.
5 I'm looking _____ to hearing from you.
8 By the _____ , how did the exam go?
9 Write back soon.

_____ ,
Susie
12 I'm sorry it's _____ me so long to write to you.

Down

2 Let me _____ if you can make it.
7 Anyway, I'd _____ close now.
11 Can't wait to _____ from you.

Expressions with *get*

Across

3 Chewing gum is forbidden in class – get _____ of it now!
4 If you don't get _____ the train now, it'll leave without you!
10 They said they'd get in _____ with me, but so far they haven't written or phoned.
13 How much do you get _____ a week in your job?

Down

1 He's always getting into _____ with the police.
3 Turn off your PlayStation now and get _____ for school.
6 I had a shower, got _____ and then went out for a walk.

C People

Each of the words for people **1–6** has a relationship of some kind with one of the words **a–f**. Match the words and then use them to complete the sentences below. You may need to use plural forms.

1 invigilator   **a** groom
2 host   **b** spectator
3 bride   **c** patient
4 competitor   **d** audience
5 performer   **e** candidate
6 doctor   **f** guest

1 The youngest _____ in the stadium surprised the _____ by winning the 400 metres in record time.

2 The only person I recognized at the party was the _____ ; I didn't know any of the other _____ .

3 The _____ and _____ looked very happy as they walked back down the aisle after the ceremony.

4 Many members of the _____ left the theatre before the end of the play, disappointed at the acting of some of the _____ .

5 After a thorough examination the _____ could find nothing wrong with his _____ .

6 One of the _____ was caught cheating in the exam by the _____ .

2 High energy

Vocabulary 1: Music

1 Would you go to see any of these groups or singers perform?
What would be the ingredients of the ideal concert for you?
Who would you see? Where would the concert be? What would you wear?

2 **a** How many of the musical instruments in the photographs can you name?

b All the words in each of the groups below can be used in combination with one of the words in the box. Write an appropriate word from the box in each of the spaces. There is an example at the beginning **(0)**.

play (v)
~~rock~~
lead (adj)
on
in
instrument
live (adj)
a song
musician

0 _rock_ band singer star	**3** talented rock session _____	**6** _____ album performance music
1 _____ vocalist singer guitarist	**4** _____ tour stage the radio	**7** _____ the charts concert tune
2 sing perform mime _____	**5** _____ a track a tune a record	**8** musical wind stringed _____

3 Study the word combinations in exercise 2 for two minutes. Then look at the words in the box and cover the exercise. How many word combinations can you remember?

4 Imagine that you are the organizing committee for a charity and you want to make a CD to raise money. Try to agree what the title of the CD will be, which musicians you will include and which tracks would be best. Where would you advertise it?

Listening 1:
FCE Part 2

Blank filling

1 Do you enjoy going to discos?
What type of music do you prefer to dance to?
How important is the DJ?

2 You will hear a radio interview with Brad Andrews, a club DJ. For questions **1–10**, complete the sentences which summarize what he says.

Before you do the task...

What to expect in the exam

- You don't normally need to write more than three words for each answer.
- You hear the answers in the same order as the questions.
- The words you *read* in the question may not be the same as the words you *hear* in the recording, eg Question 1:
  You *read*: DJ-ing isn't the same as it was in…
  You *hear*: 'DJ-ing has changed an awful lot since…'
- However, the word or words you need to write are actually spoken on the cassette.
- You will hear the recording twice.
- You usually have 30–45 seconds to read the questions before you listen. Use this time to try to predict the type of information you might hear.

Example:
Question 1: *We might hear the name of a town or country. The present and past tenses in the question make me think it might be comparing DJ-ing now with DJ-ing in the past, so perhaps it's a year.*

3 Look at the other questions and try to predict the information you might hear for each one. Then listen to the recording and complete the sentences.

1 DJ-ing isn't the same as it was in _____ .
2 DJs often use _____ turntables at the same time.
3 Many DJs are also _____ .
4 Their job consists mainly of _____ .
5 They can earn as much as _____ pounds for a performance.
6 Fans can see their favourite DJs perform every _____ .
7 For Brad, performing a gig is like taking people _____ .
8 To prepare himself mentally, Brad practises _____ before a gig.
9 In the future DJs may use _____ instead of vinyl records.
10 DJs are employed by famous groups to help them attract _____ .

4 Is DJ-ing something you would like to try?
What do you think are the positive and negative aspects of the job?

15

Language focus 1: Indirect questions

1 Look at four of the questions which the interviewer asked Brad Andrews in the listening. Which are direct and which are indirect questions?

a *Why are club DJs so popular these days?*
b *Do you really need that much skill to put on a few records?*
c *Would you mind telling us how much you earn for a single gig?*
d *Could you tell us what the future of dance music is?*

2 Underline the expressions in exercise 1 which make the questions indirect.

Asking questions in this way can make them sound more polite.

3 **a** How are indirect questions formed?

Think about:
• word order
• auxiliary verbs

b What happens when there is no question word such as *when, how, what, where* etc?

Rewrite the following question to make it indirect. Does a gig require much preparation?
I'd like to know _____ ?

 Check your ideas on page 206 of the Grammar reference.

Practice

Rewrite the following questions to make them indirect. Choose an appropriate phrase from the box to begin each question.

> I'd be interested to know…   Could you explain…
> Would you mind telling us…   We'd like to know…
> I was wondering if you could tell me…   Could you tell us…

1 Why is dance music so popular?
_____

2 What does a clubber have to pay to see you perform?
_____

3 When did you do your first gig?
_____

4 Do you plan to work with any famous groups?
_____

5 What do you like most about DJ-ing?
_____

6 How did you become a DJ?
_____

7 Has anything ever gone wrong at a gig?
_____

 Writing 1: FCE Part 1

Transactional letters: Asking for information

1 Read the following Writing Part 1 instructions.

You are interested in going to England to study music in the summer and you have seen this advertisement in a magazine. Using the notes you have made, write to Charlesworth House asking for more information.

transport available?

STUDY MUSIC IN STYLE

If you play a musical instrument and would like to benefit from expert tuition in an English-speaking environment, come and spend the summer at Charlesworth House.
— *Situated in the beautiful Suffolk countryside close to the delightful town of Ipswich, the school offers peace, tranquillity and inspiration.*

• *Accommodation available*   *included in price?*
• *Weekly excursions to London (including trips to concerts)*   *ask!*

For more information and details of costs, write to:
Charlesworth House, Hadleigh, IP7 8RJ, Suffolk

Charlesworth House – tailor-made music courses since 1953

Dates:
July 16th – August 15th

Classes:
hours?
individual or groups?

Ask for publicity materials

Write a **letter** of between **120 and 180** words in an appropriate style. Do not write any addresses.

2   Would it be more appropriate to write the letter using formal or informal language? Read the example letter below and for questions **1–10**, underline the most appropriate word or phase. There is an example at the beginning **(0)**.

Dear Sir/Madam,

    (0) I'm writing about/<u>I am writing in response to</u> your advertisement, which appeared in last week's edition of 'International Musician'. I am interested in having violin lessons at your school in the summer and I **(1) would like/want** further information about your courses.

    Firstly, **(2) you could give me a few/I would be grateful for** details about the classes. **(3) I would/I'd** be interested to know how many hours of lessons there are each day and whether tuition is individual or in groups.

    Your advertisement **(4) says something about/mentions** the proximity of the school to Ipswich. Since I would **(5) appreciate/love to have** the opportunity to go shopping or visit a museum, could you tell me if there is a regular public transport service into the town?

    I also have **(6) a couple of questions/some queries** regarding costs. In particular, I would like to know the price of a one-month course from July 16th to August 15th. Could you also **(7) let me know/indicate** whether the cost of excursions and accommodation is included?

    If you have a brochure with photographs of the school, **(8) send me/I would be pleased to receive** a copy. Thank you in advance for your assistance. **(9) I look/I'm looking** forward to **(10) getting your answer/receiving your reply**.

    Yours faithfully,
    Marianna Ilyina

---

3   **a**   You will lose marks if you do not answer the question fully. Does this example answer cover all the notes in the question?

    b   Candidates who write good answers build on the information given and add relevant points of their own. Find examples of this in the model.

    c   Avoid copying phrases or sentences from the input material. Find examples of how the writer of the model has rephrased language from the notes in the question.

4   Now do the following Writing Part 1 task.

You and two of your friends would like to go to a rock music festival in July and you have seen this advertisement in a magazine. Using the notes you have made, write a letter to Melody Tours and ask for more information.

what bands?

Spend a weekend of summer fun at the

THE BENNINGTON ROCK FESTIVAL

at Bennington Park, near Oxford. 15th – 17th July

'Melody Tours' will organize everything for you.

Our package includes:
- Entrance tickets for all three days
- Transport to and from London's Heathrow airport
- Accommodation for two nights
- Sightseeing tour of Oxford

Total cost: £150

For further information write to:
Melody Tours,
PO Box 43,
Selby, N. Yorks.

Last flight back on 17th: 9.15pm

Room for three if possible

Write a **letter** of between **120 and 180** words in an appropriate style. Do not write any addresses.

meals included?   *times?*

Don't forget!

- Write in a formal style and try to use indirect rather than direct questions.
- Cover all the notes in the question.
- Good answers build on the information given in the notes and other materials.
- You should not copy phrases or sentences from the question.
- Write between 120 and 180 words.

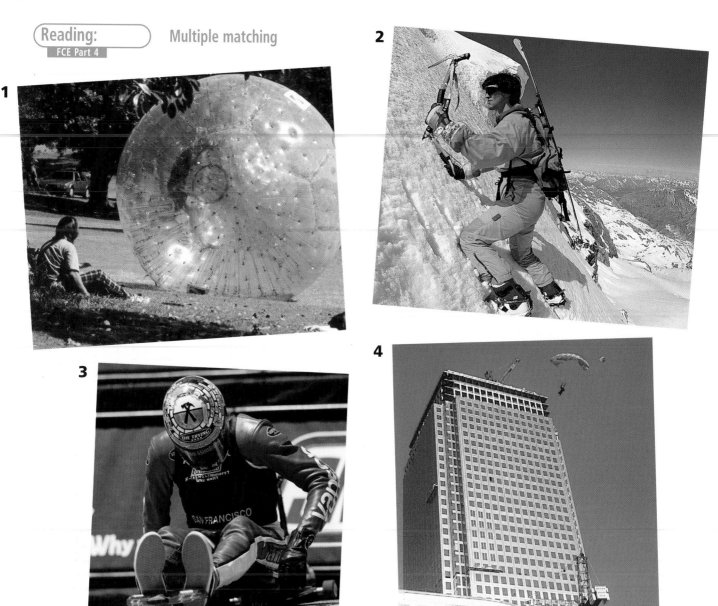

1 The pictures above all show extreme or dangerous sports.

Student A: Compare and contrast two of the sports and say which of them you think is more enjoyable.

Student B: Compare and contrast the remaining two sports and say which sport you think is more difficult to learn.

2 Read the magazine article about extreme sports on page 19 quite quickly and match each paragraph to a picture. Have you changed your ideas about each sport?

3 You are going to read the article again. For questions **1–12**, choose from the sports **(A–D)**. Each sport may be chosen more than once. When more than one answer is required, these may be given in any order. There is an example at the beginning **(0)**.

How to go about it

● To help you with some of the questions, certain parts of each paragraph have been underlined. For example, the clue to the example **(0)** can be found in paragraph **D**.

0: *You do not need to have any special abilities.*

D: *... no more skill than a hamster running in its wheel.*

A Street luge   C Base-jumping
B Ice-climbing   D Zorbing

Of which of the sports A–D are the following true?

You do not need to have any special abilities.	**0** D
The equipment and clothes are specially made for the participant.	**1**
You need to co-operate with a group of people.	**2**
It was started by the inventors of another extreme sport.	**3**
You can hurt yourself while trying to stop.	**4**
It demands previous experience in another sport.	**5**
You need to be both strong and psychologically prepared.	**6**
It offers reasonably good protection from injury.	**7**
It could get you into trouble with the police.	**8**
It has caused deaths.	**9** **10**
You can make your own protection for your feet.	**11**
You need to be able to react quickly.	**12**

The Thrill of it all

As our lives become safer, danger is being marketed as more and more desirable. Here is an armchair guide to some of the sports which can make skydiving seem about as 'extreme' as dominoes.

A Street luge

Ice luge is an adolescent but established Olympic sport, but street luge, the pavement version is its undisciplined younger brother. Both involve lying flat on your back and steering a luge not much bigger than a skateboard, with your head just inches off the ground. Street luge started off in southern California, where groups of riders first began flying down steep, winding roads for thrills. A complete lack of fear is an essential requirement for this sport, as well as a thick piece of rubber, <u>preferably from car tyres</u>, for your footwear. Top lugers can reach speeds of 145 kilometres per hour, yet their only way of braking is to use their feet, often causing painful injuries. But it is not only the element of risk which prevents many people from taking up this sport. Not everyone can afford to pay $1500 for a skin-tight, <u>tailor-made</u> leather race suit and the luge, which is also <u>built to fit the athlete</u>, is equally expensive.

B Ice-climbing

As the name suggests, practitioners of this activity clamber up glaciers with the aid of an ice axe and a great deal of other specialist equipment. It was inspired by American climber Yvonne Chouinard who, in the 1970s, introduced ice picks and crampons (metal spikes which are attached to the bottom of the climber's boots) to the UK. As well as all the equipment, incredible physical and mental toughness are essential, together with an ability to <u>work closely with other team members</u> in the most dangerous circumstances. Extreme ascents are as famous for the climbers who died trying to conquer them as for those who made it to the top.

C Base-jumping

This sport began way back in 1978, when parachutists started jumping off El Capitán, a 100-metre-high cliff in Yosemite National Park, California. BASE is an acronym for Buildings, Antenna, Span, Earth and participants have to freefall from an object in each case. Being able to make split-second decisions is essential as these objects are not very high off the ground and you need to open your parachute at just the right moment. Before even contemplating your first jump you should have done <u>at least 100 skydives</u>. You are at the mercy of gusts of wind during the descent and must know exactly how to steer yourself away from danger. Illegal in some countries, this sport has claimed the lives of 20 jumpers since it was invented and many more have been severely injured.

D Zorbing

Brought to us by the same people who gave us bungee-jumping, zorbing is the latest adventure experience from New Zealand. It involves rolling around in a three-metre ball, or zorb, made out of PVC. It requires <u>no more skill than a hamster running in its wheel</u>, because centrifugal force will keep you pinned inside the zorb. Although zorbonauts have hurtled downhill at speeds of 50 kilometres per hour, the air cushioning inside means you don't risk hurting yourself too seriously. Having said this, co-inventor Andrew Akers broke his collar bone the first time he tried it.

Reacting to the text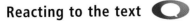

Which of these extreme sports would you most and least like to do? Give reasons for your answers.
Have you ever tried any unusual sports?

Language focus 2: Gerunds and infinitives A

1 Look at the following sentences from the reading text. Do you remember which sport each one refers to?

   a It involves **rolling** around in a three-metre ball.
   b **Being** able to make split-second decisions is essential as these objects are not very high off the ground…
   c Before even **contemplating** your first jump you should have done at least 100 skydives.

2 The words written in **bold** in exercise 1 are all gerunds. Match each of these gerunds with the appropriate explanation for its use, **1–3**.

   1 as the subject of a clause or sentence
   2 after prepositions
   3 after certain verbs

3 Look at the following sentences from the text. What verb form follows each of the verbs in **bold**?

   a Not everyone can **afford** to pay $1500 for a skin-tight, tailor-made leather race suit.
   b This sport began way back in 1978, when parachutists **started** jumping off El Capitán.
   c The air cushioning inside means you don't **risk** hurting yourself too seriously.

4 Certain verbs are usually followed by either the gerund or the infinitive. Which of the verbs in **bold** in exercise 3 can be used with either the gerund or infinitive without a change in meaning?

Practice

1 Complete each of the following sentences using the gerund or the infinitive of the verbs in brackets. One verb will be in the gerund and the other in the infinitive.

   1 When I *suggested* _____ (go) skiing she was extremely enthusiastic and we *arranged* _____ (meet) at seven o'clock on Saturday morning.

   2 I *can't help* _____ (smile) when I see my dad playing tennis. He's had hundreds of lessons but he still hasn't *learnt* _____ (hit) the ball properly.

   3 Playing with golfers better than myself has certainly *helped* _____ (improve) my game. Now I'm even *considering* _____ (take) golf up professionally.

   4 One of my cousins has *promised* _____ (take) me windsurfing with him as soon as I've *finished* _____ (study).

   5 At first my parents *refused* _____ (let) me go to karate lessons, but I *kept* _____ (ask) and eventually they agreed.

   Check your answers on page 206 of the Grammar reference.

2 The verbs in the box can be used to talk about our likes and dislikes. They are all usually followed by the gerund. Write each verb in an appropriate place on the line below according to the strength of its meaning.

really enjoy	don't mind	quite like
detest	can't stand	don't like
love	absolutely adore	hate

STRONG DISLIKE   **STRONG LIKE**

detest   *absolutely adore*

3 Certain adjectives followed by a preposition and the gerund can also be used to talk about what does and doesn't interest you. Study the following table and complete each space with a preposition from the box. The first one has been done for you.

at	in	~~on~~	about	with	of

	adjective + preposition	noun or gerund
I'm (really)	keen *on*	sport/cinema etc
I'm not (really)	interested _____	listening to… etc
I've never been	fond _____	watching…
I've always been	good/bad _____	playing…
I get (really)	bored _____	doing…
I never get	excited _____	going…

4 Write eight sentences about your likes and dislikes using the language you have just studied.

Examples:

Preposition + gerund:	I never get excited about going to the cinema.
Verb + gerund:	I quite like listening to jazz.
Gerund as subject:	Collecting postcards is one of my favourite pastimes.

5 Compare your sentences with your partner's. Ask questions about each other's likes and dislikes.

Example:

A: I've always been keen on going to the cinema.
B: How often do you go?
A: I tend to go once every two weeks or so.
B: And what are your favourite films?
A: Well, I really enjoy watching science fiction, but I don't like films with a lot of violence. I get bored very easily if there are lots of deaths.

You may be asked to talk about your interests in Part 1 of the Speaking Test. Make sure you develop your answers, explaining and justifying your opinions.

Listening 2:
FCE Part 4

Multiple choice

1 How popular is snowboarding in your country? Have you ever done it?
What are the potential dangers of snowboarding?
What are sponsors? How do you think they might help snowboarders?

2 Read the following Listening Part 4 instructions.

You will hear an interview about snowboarding. For questions **1–7**, choose the best answer **A**, **B** or **C**.

What to expect in the exam

- Look at question 1 below and the following extract from the tapescript. The underlined words all appear in the possible answers **A**, **B** and **C**, but only one of these answers fits the question. The other words are distractors. Decide which is the correct answer and say why the others are incorrect.

Tapescript:
I first did it when I was on holiday with my parents. When I was younger I used to go skiing <u>every year</u> with them and then <u>one year</u> I tried snowboarding and I haven't skied since then. That was <u>five years</u> ago.

1 How long has Liz been snowboarding?
  A one year
  B five years
  C every year since she was a child

2 According to Liz, if you want to be a snowboarder
  A you have to be naturally sporty.
  B you need to be born with good co-ordination and balance.
  C you don't need long to acquire the skills.

3 What injuries has Liz suffered?
  A She broke her back.
  B She broke an arm.
  C She fell badly on her back.

4 What does Liz say about the ratio of male to female snowboarders?
  A There are nearly the same number of girls as boys.
  B You almost never see girls who snowboard.
  C There are a lot more girls than boys.

5 What does Liz say about money?
  A Girls don't get paid as much as boys.
  B Her sponsors don't give her any money.
  C She doesn't have to pay for her equipment.

6 What does she recommend to girls who want to snowboard?
  A They should have lessons on an artificial slope.
  B They should buy lots of warm clothing.
  C They should go to a place where it snows.

7 Why does Liz do modelling work?
  A She earns money to finance her snowboarding.
  B It will improve her job prospects.
  C She has always wanted to be a model.

Don't forget!

- Pay close attention the second time you hear the recording. You may discover that you need to change your answers.

Is there any sport which you would like to take up?
What qualities or strengths would you need to have?
Are there any dangers involved?

Word formation: Affixes

1 **1–7** show different suffixes which can be used to form the words for people. Add an appropriate suffix from the box to the root words **8–14** to form the words for the corresponding people. You may need to make changes to the root word.

-er -ist -eer -or -ant -ee -ian	Root word		Person	Root word		Person
	1 snowboard	→	snowboard**er**	8 instruct	→	_____
	2 spectate	→	spectat**or**	9 economic	→	_____
	3 parachute	→	parachut**ist**	10 mountain	→	_____
	4 participate	→	particip**ant**	11 electric	→	_____
	5 engine	→	engin**eer**	12 entertain	→	_____
	6 employ	→	employ**er**/employ**ee**	13 assist	→	_____
	7 politics	→	politic**ian**	14 interview	→	_____

2 The prefixes in the box can be added to some nouns, verbs and adjectives to make them negative. In **1–7** below, the same prefix can be used with all three adjectives to make them negative. Choose the appropriate prefix for each group and write the negative forms. The first one has been done for you.

dis- un- in- ir- il- im-	Adjectives	Negative
	1 lucky/pleasant/reliable	*unlucky/**un**pleasant/**un**reliable*
	2 experienced/competent/tolerant	_____
	3 legal/logical/legible	_____
	4 moral/mature/modest	_____
	5 practical/patient/perfect	_____
	6 regular/responsible/relevant	_____
	7 honest/obedient/satisfied	_____

Note that *in-* is not normally used with words beginning with *l, m, p* or *r*. What happens instead?

3 What meaning do the affixes in bold have in the following words?

undercook	**over**eat	**pre**historic	**post**graduate	**hyper**market
microelectronics	**mis**spell	**re**write	**ex**-wife	manager**ess**

Language focus 3: Gerunds and infinitives B

1 Look at the following extracts from the listening and answer the questions below.

1 Liz: *I came first in the Big Air event and won some money.*

Interviewer: *Let's hope you can go on winning!*

2 Liz: *... and any part-time modelling work now could be useful for the future.*

Interviewer: *You mean, you might go on to become a full-time model?*

In which sentence does *go on* mean
a continue to do the same activity?
b change to a different activity?

2 Meaning is also affected when using either the gerund or the infinitive with the following verbs:

remember   forget   stop   regret   mean   try

Decide what the difference in meaning is between the two uses of each verb in the following pairs of sentences.

1 a I remember studying this piece of grammar last year.
   b I must remember to study my notes on gerunds and infinitives tonight.

2 a We regret to announce that all trains to York will experience delays of up to two hours.
   b I regret catching the train to York. I got to the meeting two hours late.

3 a I stopped to buy a newspaper on my way home from the office.
   b I've stopped buying newspapers. You can't believe a word you read in them.

4 a I tried having tennis lessons, but they didn't make much difference to my game.
   b I tried to have tennis lessons, but none of the teachers was available in the evening.

5 a I'm glad I took the exam. It meant doing a lot more studying, but it was worth it in the end.
   b I meant to do some studying last night, but Tom called and we spent an hour on the phone.

Vocabulary 2: Sports

1 Can you name all the sports in the pictures? Write the name of each sport next to the verb which it is used with. The first one has been done for you.

do   *athletics* _____

go   _____

play   _____

2 Where do each of the sports in exercise 1 take place? Use the words in the box.

court	slopes	track	gym	pitch	pool

Example: You do athletics on an indoor or an outdoor track.

3 What are the people who do each sport called?

Example: A person who does athletics is called an athlete.

4 In **1–4** write each word in **bold** on the appropriate line.

1 to take place or **to take part**
_____ (= to participate) in a competition/sporting event
_____ (= to happen) on a court/in a gym

2 to win or **to beat**
_____ a competition/a sporting event/a game/a medal
_____ an opponent/another team

3 to play or **to practise**
_____ a sport
_____ serving the ball/a particular shot (in order to improve)

4 the audience or **the spectators**
_____ at a football match/a sporting event/an athletics meeting
_____ in a cinema/in a theatre/at a concert

Writing 2:
FCE Part 2

Articles

1 Read the following Writing Part 2 instructions.

You have just seen the following advertisement.

Write your **article** for International Sports Weekly magazine. You should write **120–180** words.

INTERNATIONAL SPORTS WEEKLY

➤ What is your favourite sport?
➤ Why do you like it?
➤ What advice would you give to someone who wants to take it up?

We are looking for short articles answering these questions and we will publish some of the best articles next month.

How to go about it

- Before you write your article, read the model and analysis on page 200.
- To help you plan your article, answer the following questions and make notes.

Paragraph 1:
What is your favourite sport?
What is special about it?

Paragraph 2:
Why do you like it?
What are the benefits of doing it?

Paragraph 3:
What advice can you give to people who want to take it up?
Are any special qualities, equipment or clothes needed?

Paragraph 4:
What final encouragement can you give?

- Give your article a title and include some of the features of style from page 200.

Word formation

1 In **1–6** below, one of the four words is not normally used. Underline the word.

1 undercook	undercharge	underestimate	undersleep
2 overgrown	overweight	overlittle	overcrowded
3 overeat	oversing	oversleep	overwork
4 misbehave	misunderstand	misspell	missucceed
5 dislove	dishonesty	disappearance	disobedience
6 manageress	doctoress	actress	waitress

2 For questions **1–6**, complete each of the spaces with the correct form of one of the words from exercise 1.

1 These jeans should have cost £30, but the assistant made a mistake and _____ me. I only paid £20 for them.

2 The house has been abandoned for years. That's why the garden is looking so _____ .

3 I'm sorry I'm late. My alarm didn't go off, so I _____ .

4 You've _____ my surname. There are two 't's in Hutton, not one.

5 Police are investigating the _____ of confidential documents from the Prime Minister's office.

6 Shall I ask the _____ for the bill?

3 Now write five sentences of your own using some of the other words from exercise 1. Leave a space in each sentence where the word should be and ask another student to complete them.

Use of English:
FCE Part 5

Word formation
Read the following text about the sport of free-diving. Use the word given in capitals at the end of each line to form a word that fits the space in the same line. There is an example at the beginning **(0)**.

Former swimming **(0)** _instructor_ Tanya Streeter, 26, has achieved what many	INSTRUCT
thought was **(1)** _____ and dived to 370 feet below the sea on a single	POSSIBLE
lungful of air. **(2)** _____ in free-diving take a deep breath before	COMPETE
(3) _____ into the depths of the ocean. Rigorous training has helped	APPEAR
Tanya to go deeper than male **(4)** _____ and break one of the most	DIVE
difficult diving records.	
Free-diving is a dangerous sport. Deaths are frequent and it is not	
(5) _____ to pass out or have a nose bleed on the descent. Tanya, who	COMMON
can hold her breath for five minutes **(6)** _____ , says that many men tried	WATER
to **(7)** _____ her from attempting to break the record. 'They all said	COURAGE
it was **(8)** _____ that a woman could reach such depths without breathing	LIKELY
equipment. They **(9)** _____ my abilities and I proved them wrong.' In 1988	JUDGE
the French film **(10)** _____ Luc Besson made a film about free-diving,	DIRECT
Le Grand Bleu, which became the biggest box-office hit in France of all time.	

How long can you hold your breath for?
How far can you swim underwater?

Gerunds and infinitives

1 Complete each of the spaces below with the correct form of the verb in brackets.

1 I've been meaning _____ (write) to you for ages but I just haven't had the time.

2 If we go skiing tomorrow, it'll mean _____ (get) up early. The slopes get crowded very quickly.

3 I wish you'd stop _____ (tap) your foot!

4 These long car journeys make me really hungry. Can we stop _____ (have) lunch soon?

5 When I tell you to be quiet, why must you always go on _____ (talk)?

6 After looking at verbs which take the gerund, we went on _____ (study) those which are followed by the infinitive.

7 I tried hard _____ (open) the window, but I couldn't move it. It was stuck.

8 These plants look as if they need a lot more light. Try _____ (put) them a little closer to the window.

2 In each of the groups below, one of the verbs is grammatically different from the other three. Decide whether the verbs take the gerund, the infinitive or both, in order to discover which verb is the odd one out. The first one has been done for you.

Example: admit *takes the gerund, whereas the others take the infinitive*

0 expect	**2** remember	**4** keen on
hope	begin	interested in
<u>admit</u>	forget	tend to
agree	regret	fond of
1 promise	**3** want	**5** can't afford
offer	would like	can't imagine
refuse	feel like	can't help
finish	decide	can't stand

3 Now look at the verb lists on pages 206 and 207 of the Grammar reference and make two groups of your own like those in exercise 2. Then give them to another student, who will try to find the odd one out.

Vocabulary: Music

Complete each of the spaces below with an appropriate word combination from page 14 of this unit. You may need to use nouns in the plural. There is an example at the beginning **(0)**.

0 I never buy *live albums* . You don't get the same quality of sound as you do with a studio recording.

1 Ricky Martin's latest album sounds great. I heard a couple of tracks _____ _____ last night.

2 I spend all my time in piano lessons practising the scales. I still haven't learnt to _____ .

3 Her last record only got as far as number ten _____ .

4 When groups make a record they often have to employ _____ to play some of the instruments.

5 That guitar sounds awful! Are you sure it's _____ ?

6 I hate it when they _____ on the TV. It's so obvious they aren't really singing.

7 The band is going _____ again next year. They'll be playing in nine European countries in three months.

8 Next on Capital Radio we're going to _____ from the latest 'Sidewinder' album. It's called *Ready for love* – I hope you like it.

A change for the better?

Vocabulary: Machines and devices

Here are three words which are often used to talk about everyday inventions.

a domestic appliance:

A machine, usually an electrical one, which is used in the house to do a job such as cooking or cleaning.
Examples: a vacuum cleaner, a cooker, a dishwasher

a device:

A word for a useful machine or instrument.
Example: We've just bought a useful little device for peeling oranges.

a gadget:

Another word for a useful machine or instrument. (It can sometimes be used to suggest that a device or appliance is unnecessary.)
Example: Our kitchen is so full of gadgets you can hardly move.

1 Make a list of appliances, devices and gadgets that you have at home.

How useful is each one? Use the following adjectives, giving reasons for your ideas.

| handy | labour-saving | useless | clever | unusual | complicated | simple |

Which of the objects would you find it difficult to live without?

2 Look at the pictures at the side of the reading text.

Do they show 'appliances', 'devices' or 'gadgets'?
Which adjectives would you use to describe these objects?

Reading:

FCE Part 2

Multiple choice

1 The following text was written by Bill Bryson, an American who writes about his fellow Americans, mainly for a British audience. Read through the text quickly and choose the best answer **A**, **B**, **C** or **D**, to the following question.

1 What is the author's opinion of everyday inventions?

  A On the whole they make life easier.

  B Some people do not know how to use them very well.

  C They cause more problems than they solve.

  D He likes them now more than he used to.

2 Now read the text by Bill Bryson again and for questions **2–7** on page 28, choose the best answer **A**, **B**, **C** or **D**.

How to go about it

- Find the part of the text which relates to the particular questions you are answering. As in the exam, the questions follow the same order as the text.

- Eliminate the answers which are obviously wrong, then check the answer or answers which you have not eliminated.
- If you still cannot decide, make an intelligent guess. Do not leave questions unanswered.

The Convenience Society, or con for short

The other day I took my younger children to a Burger King for lunch and there was a line of about a dozen cars at the drive-through window. Now, a drive-through window is not a window you drive through, but a window you drive up to and collect your food from, having placed your order over a speakerphone along the way; the idea is to provide quick takeaway
5   food for those in a hurry.

We parked, went in, ordered and ate and came out again, all in about ten minutes. As we departed, I noticed that a white pickup truck that had been last in the queue when we arrived was still four or five cars back from collecting its food. It would have been much quicker if the driver had parked like us and gone in and got his food himself, but he would never have thought
10 that way because the drive-through window is supposed to be speedier and more convenient.

Americans have become so attached to the idea of convenience that they will put up with almost any inconvenience to achieve it. The things that are supposed to speed up and simplify our lives more often than not have the opposite effect and I started wondering why this should be.

15 Americans have always looked for ways to increase comfort. It is an interesting fact that nearly all the everyday inventions that take the difficulties out of life – escalators, automatic doors, passenger lifts, refrigerators, washing machines, frozen food, fast food – were invented in America, or at least first widely used here. Americans grew so used to seeing a constant stream of labour-saving devices, in fact, that by the sixties they had come to expect machines to do
20 almost everything for them.

The moment I first realized that this was not necessarily a good idea was at Christmas of 1961 or '62, when my father was given an electric carving knife. It was an early model and not as light as the ones you can buy today. Perhaps my memory is playing tricks on me, but I have a clear impression of him putting on goggles and heavy rubber gloves before plugging it in. What
25 is certainly true is that when he sank it into the turkey it sent pieces flying everywhere and then the blade hit the plate with a shower of blue sparks and the whole thing flew out of his hands and shot across the table and out of the room, like a creature from a *Gremlins* movie.

My father was always buying gadgets that proved to be disastrous – clothes steamers that failed to take the wrinkles out of suits but caused wallpaper to fall off the walls in whole sheets,
30 or an electric pencil sharpener that could consume an entire pencil (including the tips of your fingers if you weren't quick) in less than a second.

But all of this was nothing compared with the situation today. Americans are now surrounded with items that do things for them to an almost absurd degree – automatic cat-food dispensers, refrigerators that make their own ice cubes, automatic car windows, disposable
35 toothbrushes that come with their own ration of toothpaste. People are so addicted to convenience that they have become trapped in a vicious circle: the more labour-saving devices they buy, the harder they need to work; the harder they work, the more labour-saving appliances they feel they need.

When we moved into our house in New Hampshire it was full of gadgets installed by earlier
40 owners, all of them designed to make life a little easier. Most, however, were completely useless. One of our rooms, for instance, came equipped with automatic curtains. You flicked a switch on the wall and four pairs of curtains effortlessly opened or closed. That, at least, was the idea. In practice what happened was that one opened, one closed, one opened and closed repeatedly and one did nothing at all for five minutes and then started to produce smoke. We didn't go
45 anywhere near them after the first week.

Automatic curtains, electric cat-food dispensers and clothes steamers only *seem* to make life easier. In fact, all they do is add expense and complication to your existence.

2 What point is the author making with the story of his experience at Burger King?
   A Fast food restaurants are not very fast.
   B Some aspects of modern life are not always as convenient as they are intended to be.
   C The driver of the pickup truck had parked in the wrong place.
   D The queues at the drive-through windows are usually very long.

3 What does the author tell us about everyday inventions in America?
   A They were all invented there.
   B They make life less exciting.
   C People assumed they would make life more comfortable.
   D There aren't as many now as there used to be.

4 What does the author mean by 'Perhaps my memory is playing tricks on me' (line 23)?
   A He is sometimes very forgetful.
   B He cannot remember all the details.
   C What he says might not be completely true.
   D He remembers having fun.

5 What does 'the whole thing' in line 26 refer to?
   A the turkey
   B the plate
   C the rubber gloves
   D the carving knife

6 What does the author say about labour-saving devices today?
   A People cannot stop buying them.
   B People try to do ridiculous things with them.
   C They are better than the ones in the sixties.
   D They help people to do more work.

7 What are we told about the automatic curtains?
   A They had been brought from a previous house.
   B Some of them worked as they were supposed to.
   C The room where they were fitted was never used.
   D The author and his family decided not to use them.

What to expect in the exam

In Part 2 of the Reading Paper, the multiple choice questions will test some or all of the following:

- a detailed understanding of the text: *see questions 2, 3, 6 and 7* (the most common type of question).

- a general understanding of the text: *see question 1* (this type of question usually comes last in the exam).
- an understanding of reference words in context: *see question 5* (these are often pronouns such as *it* or *they*).
- the ability to decide meaning from context: *see question 4*.

Reacting to the text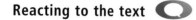

Do you agree with Bill Bryson when he says that 'the things that are supposed to speed up our lives more often than not have the opposite effect'?
Have you ever had a device or appliance which created problems for you?
Are there any devices or appliances you think should or will be invented in the future?

Language focus 1: Comparisons

Complete the following sentences from the text. If a word is given in brackets, write the correct form of that word.

1 It would have been much _____ (quick) if the driver had parked like us.

2 The drive-through window is supposed to be _____ (speedy) and _____ _____ (convenient).

3 The things which are supposed to simplify our lives _____ often _____ not have the opposite effect.

4 The electric carving knife was an early model and not _____ light _____ the ones you can buy today.

5 The electric pencil sharpener could consume an entire pencil in _____ _____ a second.

6 But all of this was nothing compared _____ the situation today.

7 The _____ labour-saving devices they buy, the _____ (hard) they need to work.

8 The gadgets were designed to make life a little _____ (easy).

Now check your answers in the reading text.

A Comparative and superlative adjectives

1 What are the comparative and superlative forms of the adjectives *quick, speedy* and *convenient* in sentences **1** and **2** above?

2 What are the comparative and superlative forms of the following adjectives?

clean	hot	strange	clever
good	bad	far	

3 In sentences **1** and **8** above, Bill Bryson uses *much* to talk about a big difference (*much quicker*) and *a little* to talk about a small one (*a little easier*). Are the following used for big or small differences?

a bit   far   significantly   a lot   slightly

B Other comparative expressions

1 To talk about people or things that are the same in some way we can use *as* + adjective or adverb + *as*.

*They're **just as silly as** each other.*

In negative sentences, which talk about differences, *so* can be used instead of the first *as*.

*She's **not so fit as** she used to be.*

2 *The... , the...*
The structure *the* + comparative is used to talk about things which occur together.

***The more** labour-saving devices they buy, **the harder** they need to work.*

 Read more about comparisons on pages 207 and 208 of the Grammar reference.

Practice

1 Match each sentence **1–6** with a sentence **a–f** which expresses a similar idea. The first one has been done for you.

1 She's far lazier than anyone else.   *c*
2 She works a lot less than she ought to.   ___
3 She's not quite as lazy as she used to be.   ___
4 She doesn't have as many problems as she used to. ___
5 She's the least successful student in the class. ___
6 The more she works, the more success she has. ___

a She doesn't work nearly as much as she should.
b She has fewer difficulties than before.
c Everyone works much harder than her.
d She's more successful when she works harder.
e She's slightly more hardworking than before.
f No one does as badly as she does.

2 Using some of the comparative structures you have just studied, write eight sentences about yourself. Compare yourself with a friend or friends, a member of your family and/or yourself as you used to be.

3 Match each line of dialogue **1–6** with an appropriate response **a–f**. The first one has been done as an example.

1 That's the third time this week. It really needs repairing.   *d*
2 When would you like to discuss this?   ___
3 Where have you been? It's 10 o'clock!   ___
4 It doesn't hurt, but I'll make an appointment. ___
5 It was overbooked? What happened then?   ___
6 Can I bring a friend?   ___

a Better late than never.
b It's better to be safe than sorry.
c The sooner the better.
d No sooner said than done.
e The more the merrier.
f Things went from bad to worse.

4 Complete the second sentence so that it has a similar meaning to the first sentence, using the word in **bold**.

1 The film wasn't nearly as good as I thought it would be. **far**
The film _____
I thought it would be.

2 She's happier than she used to be. **sad**
She isn't _____
was before.

3 I've never had such a boring time on holiday! **enjoyable**
This is _____
holiday I've ever had!

4 If you work harder now, you won't have to do so much later. **the**
The harder _____
you'll have to do later.

5 Kate has slightly more experience than the others. **quite**
The others don't have _____
Kate.

Word formation: Suffixes -*ful* and -*less*

Some adjectives can be formed by adding the suffixes -*ful* or -*less* to nouns or verbs.

USE   *We've just bought a **useful** device for peeling oranges.*
                   *Most of the gadgets were completely **useless**.*

Sometimes only one of the suffixes may be used:

SLEEP   *I've had a few **sleepless** nights, worrying about it.*
                   *I'm going to bed: I feel a little **sleepy**. (**not** sleepful)*

GRATITUDE   *I'd be very **grateful** if you could help me.*
                   *She didn't even say 'thank you'! How **ungrateful**. (**not** grateless)*

1   Which of the suffixes -*ful* and -*less* can be used to form adjectives from the words in
    the box? If either of them cannot be used, is there an alternative?

success	skill	home	cheer	delight	thought
harm	pain	end	power	care	price

    *Example: success → successful → unsuccessful (**not** successless)*

2   Look at the following adjectives formed from the word *taste*.

    TASTE → *tasty, tasteful, tasteless*

    In what way are *tasty* and *tasteful* different?
    a a tastefully decorated room/a tasteless pink shirt
    b very tasty food/a tasteless soup

    Put the correct form of *help* in the sentences below. You may need to use an adjective
    or an adverb, in the positive or the negative.

    1 I'm so pleased I spoke to him. He made several very _____ suggestions.
    2 Her arms tied behind her back, she watched _____ as the thieves got away with
    all her priceless paintings.
    3 The hotel was comfortable but the staff were so _____ . We won't be going
    back there again.

3   For questions **1–10** use the word given in capitals at the end of each line to form a
    word that fits in the space in the same line. You may need to form a noun, an
    adjective or an adverb.

    1 The Prime Minister handled the situation extremely _____
    and managed to avoid a scandal.   **SKILL**
    2 Before Hillary and Tensing reached the peak in 1953 there had
    been several _____ attempts to conquer Everest.   **SUCCESS**
    3 Road accidents are very often caused by drivers' _____ at
    the wheel.   **CARE**
    4 Thank you so much! That's very _____ of you.   **THOUGHT**
    5 Until my eldest brother went to university his life had been
    rather dull and _____ .   **EVENT**
    6 The school banned cigarettes from the premises and warned
    pupils of the _____ effects of smoking.   **HARM**
    7 Despite her initial concerns, she was reassured that the operation
    would be _____ .   **PAIN**
    8 One of her most positive and attractive qualities is her almost
    constant _____ .   **CHEER**
    9 He'll never change his mind. It's absolutely _____ trying
    to argue with him.   **POINT**
    10 The Government announced plans yesterday to tackle the problem
    of _____ .   **HOME**

Multiple matching

1 Read the following Listening Part 3 instructions.

You will hear five people talking about solar-powered gadgets, some of which are shown above. Match the speaker to the correct description in the list **A–F**. There is one extra letter which you do not need to use.

2 Before you do the listening task, look at the solar-powered gadgets **A–F** below and discuss the following questions.

What are the advantages and disadvantages of each of the solar-powered gadgets compared with the more conventional models?
Where might you expect to use each of them?

A a torch	Speaker 1 ☐
B a radio	Speaker 2 ☐
C a digital video camera	Speaker 3 ☐
D path lights	Speaker 4 ☐
E an oven	Speaker 5 ☐
F a refrigerator	

Noticing language

1 Look at the following sentences from the listening. Can you suggest alternative words or expressions in English for the underlined parts? How would you express them in your own language?

1 *They come on <u>as soon as</u> it gets dark.* (Speaker 1)
2 *It'll charge itself in a couple of hours – <u>as long as</u> it's sunny, of course!* (Speaker 2)
3 *<u>As well as</u> a handle to wind it up, it comes equipped with a solar panel.* (Speaker 4)
4 *Cost an arm and a leg, mind you, but <u>as far as I'm concerned</u> it was worth every penny.* (Speaker 5)

2 Complete the following sentences using words from the box.

far   long   much   many   soon   well

1 You can go out, *as _____ as* you do your homework first.
2 *As _____ as* he got home he got changed and went back out again.
3 There are plenty of biscuits. Eat *as _____ as* you want.
4 *As _____ as* being an excellent sportswoman, she's a brilliant scientist.
5 'Are Claire and Mario still going out with each other?'
   'As _____ as I know they are, yes.'
6 That exam was really difficult. I did *as _____ as* I could and left the rest blank.

31

Speaking 1:
FCE Part 3

Collaborative task ⬤

Your class has been doing a project on developments over the last 100 years and you have been asked to write an article. Talk with your partner about some of the changes that have taken place in each of the areas shown in the photos and then decide which theme you will write your article on.

Education

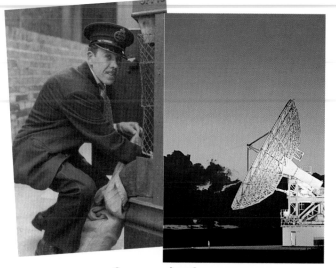

Communication

Travel and transport

Free time

How to go about it

What to say

- The instructions tell you to talk about *each* of the areas. Don't just talk about your favourite!
- The pictures are there to help you, but you can also think of other ideas related to each theme.
  Example: Education:
  Discipline, number of children attending school and university, school leaving age, equipment etc.
- You could discuss whether you think each of the changes has been for the better or for the worse. In some cases you may feel there haven't been any changes!

How to say it

- In the Speaking Test the examiners will give you marks for using a range of structures. Answer the following questions:
  a Which language area can you use to talk about regular past actions or situations?
  b Which language area is useful for expressing present habitual behaviour?
  c Why is the present perfect used in the following sentence?
  There have been a lot of changes in education over the last 100 years.
  d Which language areas can you use to talk about the differences between the past and the present?

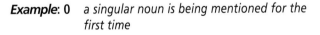

Speaking 2:
FCE Part 4

Further discussion

In Part 4 of the Speaking Test the examiner will ask you questions which are related to the topic in Part 3.

How to go about it

- Answer the questions fully, giving reasons for your opinions.
- You can also talk to your partner, as well as the examiner, during this part.
- Try to keep the conversation going as much as possible. You can ask your partner questions to achieve this:
  What do you think about that?
  Do you agree with me on that?

Discuss the following questions, which are related to Part 3 on page 32, and try to keep the conversation going as much as possible.

- What other changes have there been in the last 100 years?
- Do you think the quality of life in general is better now than it used to be?
- Can computers ever replace teachers?
- Do you agree that there are too many cars?
- In what ways has life changed for you in the last few years?
- What do you think will be the biggest changes in the next 100 years?

Language focus 2: Articles

1 Read the text entitled 'The home computer', ignoring the spaces for the moment, and answer the following questions.

What is the attitude of these people to the educational value of computers?

a parents
b the government
c some educationalists

What are *your* views?

2 Now read the text again and complete each of the spaces with *a*, *an* or *the*, or leave it blank. There is an example at the beginning (0).

3 Read the main rules for the use of articles on page 208 of the Grammar reference. Then use them to give reasons for each of the answers in exercise 2.

Example: 0   *a singular noun is being mentioned for the first time*

The home computer

Many parents believe that having (0) __*a*__ home computer is an investment in (1) _____ future of their children and they often pay more than (2) _____ thousand pounds for a product they do not fully understand.

According to (3) _____ recent survey, over two thirds of parents firmly believe in (4) _____ educational importance of (5) _____ personal computers. But as the pressure on parents to buy (6) _____ extremely sophisticated and expensive equipment increases, (7) _____ concern is growing in (8) _____ Britain over the real educational value of (9) _____ computer.

(10) _____ concern comes as schools are being encouraged by private industry to invest in (11) _____ latest technology. (12) _____ Government also intends to make (13) _____ access to computers easier in schools as (14) _____ best way to win what it calls the 'Knowledge Race' against other nations.

However, according to some educationalists, parents who think of (15) _____ computer as some form of home tutor could be heading for (16) _____ trouble. Dr George Hadley, who is (17) _____ lecturer in educational computing at (18) _____ Oxford University, stresses that (19) _____ educational software can never completely replace (20) _____ teachers.

Matching

1 Look at the following newspaper headlines.
What do you think was the story behind each of the headlines?
Do mobile phones make a positive or a negative contribution to our lives today? Why?

Mobile phones should carry health warnings

Mobile phone ban as pupil chats to girlfriend

Prison for passenger who refused to switch off phone

What to expect in the exam

- Matching is one of four possible task types in Part 4 of the Listening Paper. The other three possible tasks are:
  Multiple choice, which you saw in unit 2.
  True/False or *Yes/No*, which you will see in later units.
- This task involves matching statements or questions to one of three options. You may have to decide, for example:

Which of the hotels offers this facility: Hotel A, Hotel B or neither?
Which holiday is this statement true of: Holiday A, Holiday B or both?
Which person said this: Person A, Person B or Person C?

- In all Part 4 tasks, you will hear the answers in the same order as the questions. There are always seven questions.

---

2 You will hear a conversation about mobile phones, which takes place at home between Helen and her parents. Answer questions **1–7** by writing **H** for Helen, **F** for her father or **M** for her mother in the boxes provided.

How to go about it

- Before you listen, read through all of the statements or questions to get an idea of what you are going to hear.
- The first time you listen get an idea of the general meaning of the recording and write down any answers you feel sure about.

- The second time you listen pay close attention to those questions you have not answered and check those you have.
- Make sure you have not left any question unanswered. Guess the answer if necessary.

Who suggests that someone does not know all the facts?   **1** [ ]
Who mentions that mobile phones can affect memory?   **2** [ ]
Who says that something is not always reliable?   **3** [ ]
Who is worried about cost?   **4** [ ]
Who imposes conditions?   **5** [ ]
Who gives an example of the misuse of a mobile phone?   **6** [ ]
Who complains about noise?   **7** [ ]

Compositions

1 Read the following Writing Part 2 instructions.

Your class has been discussing the role of technology in today's society. For homework your teacher has asked you to write a composition, giving your opinions on the following statement.

The mobile phone has made a positive contribution to our lives today.

Write your **composition**. You should write **120–180** words.

Mobile phones are no longer a luxury item and they clearly have many advantages for those who use them. However, there are also some drawbacks.

On the positive side, they enable us to communicate with other people wherever they may be and at any time of the day. Teenagers who need help can contact their parents immediately and emergency services can be called to the scene of an accident without delay. Another advantage is that recent models are so light and compact that they fit easily into a pocket or handbag.

On the negative side, the mobile phone is thought to be a serious threat to health, particularly in the case of children. Moreover, drivers who use one at the wheel constitute a danger to others and fatal accidents have occurred. Finally, what for many people is a useful device, for others is a nuisance and they object to the constant ringing tones in public places.

In conclusion, cellphones have certainly improved many people's lives, but we need to be careful about when and where we use them.

2 Read the model answer to the instructions above. What is the *purpose* of each of the four paragraphs?

Example: Paragraph 1 – *a general introduction*

3 a The underlined words and expressions in the model can be grouped in the following way:

Expressing contrasts	**Adding information**	**Concluding**
On the positive side/	*Another advantage is*	*In conclusion*
On the negative side	*Moreover*	
	Finally	

b Add the following alternative linking devices to the appropriate group in exercise **a**.

In addition (to this)	*On the one hand*	*What is more*
On the other hand	*Besides this*	*Furthermore*
Some people feel that	*On balance*	*Others argue that*
Another disadvantage is	*To sum up*	

The following linkers can also be used to organize ideas.

First of all.../ To begin with...   Secondly...   Finally...

4 Examiners look for evidence of a good range of structures and vocabulary. Which words has the writer of the model answer used to avoid repeating 'mobile phones'?

5 Read the following Writing Part 2 instructions and the advice in the How to go about it box.

Your class has been discussing the role of technology in today's society. For homework your teacher has asked you to write a composition, giving your opinions on the following statement:

The computer has greatly improved our lives today.

How to go about it

- Read the question carefully. Irrelevant answers lose marks.
- List the positive and negative aspects of computers.
- Select some points from the list for the body of your composition. Note down any supporting reasons and examples.
- Organize your ideas and opinions using:
  a some of the linking devices you saw above
  b paragraphs: 4 is the usual number (introduction, points for the statement, points against the statement, conclusion)

- Check your work for grammar, vocabulary, spelling and punctuation errors. In addition, answer the following questions:
  Have you written a relevant answer to the question?
  Is the style appropriate?
  Is your work the correct length?
  Have you organized your ideas into logical paragraphs?
  Is there a good range of language or are words and expressions repeated?

Now you are ready to write your **composition** in **120–180** words.

③ Review

Vocabulary: Word partnerships

1 Write a noun in each of the spaces below to complete the word partnerships. Try to do the exercise without looking at the nouns, which are given in the box below.

1 takeaway _____
2 an electric carving _____
3 a microwave _____
4 a washing _____
5 an electric pencil _____
6 a clothes _____
7 a remote _____
8 a labour-saving _____
9 a domestic _____
10 a disposable _____

device	machine	appliance	knife	control
oven	food	toothbrush	sharpener	steamer

2 Write down:

a three more adjectives to go with the noun *device*.
b three more adjectives to go with the noun *food*.
c three more nouns for objects which are *disposable*.
d three more devices or appliances which are not mentioned in exercise 1.

Comparisons

1 Match each sentence beginning **1–8** with a suitable ending **a–h**. The first one has been done for you.

1 They can stay   a as soon as we heard.
2 I did it   b as soon as you can.
3 We came   c as long as she pays.
4 Let me know   d as long as they like.
5 She isn't here   e as well as I could.
6 She can come   f as well as a handbag.
7 A purse   g as far as the coast.
8 You can see   h as far as I know.

2 Write a four-line dialogue. The first or last line of the dialogue must be one of the sentences from exercise 1.

3 Complete the following sentences in an appropriate way.

1 The more I study, _____ .
2 The older I get, _____ .
3 The less chocolate he eats, _____ .
4 The more quickly I do my homework, _____ .
5 The more it rains, _____ .
6 The hotter it gets, _____ .

4 Write two sentences making comparisons for each of the following. Try to use a variety of structures.

two actresses	two films	two countries	two types of pet
two sports	two (pop) groups or singers		

Articles: Error correction

1 The text below paints a picture of family life in Britain today. Read the text quite quickly. Is the description also true of your family life?

  0 Personal computers have changed ⌃*the* nature of family life in Britain,   *the*

00 dominating conversations and challenging ~~a~~ television as the most popular   *a̶*

  1 form of entertainment, according to a report published today. A report   _____

  2 reveals how a family members fight to surf the Internet and how   _____

  3 computers have become more popular as a conversation topic than the   _____

  4 relationships, the hobbies and football. With one in four households   _____

  5 owning computer – more than those with a satellite television or a mobile   _____

  6 phone – the home computer has replaced dog as 'man's best friend'.   _____

  7 People spend far more time on their computer than an other domestic   _____

  8 activities and it is not only the preserve of a young: the over-60s are more   _____

  9 addicted to computers than anyone. A word-processing is one of the major   _____

10 uses, but games are also high on the list of favourite activities. The girls   _____

11 are more likely to do their homework electronically than boys and the more   _____

12 and more of their parents are opting to use their machines to work at the   _____

13 home. Jane Audrey, who is computer consultant, said: 'In our family the   _____

14 computer has certainly become main source of entertainment. My eldest   _____

15 son, Graham, is far more likely to spend evening playing computer games   _____
    than watching television'.

2 Each numbered line in the text in exercise 1 has one mistake in the use of articles. You may have to **add**, **change** or **delete** an article. The first two have been done for you.

Use of English:
FCE Part 5

Word formation

Read the following text about the benefits of e-mail. Use the word given in capitals at the end of each line to form a word that fits in the space in the same line. There is an example at the beginning **(0)**.

Don't forget!

- Adjectives or adverbs may be positive or negative.
- Nouns may be in the singular or the plural.
- If you need to form a verb, decide on the correct form.

- Read the whole text at least once before writing your answers. The meaning of the text before and after the spaces will help you make the correct decisions.

E-mail is such a **(0)** _painless_ way to write letters. I've never found it easy to put pen to paper, not even to say 'thank you' for presents sent by **(1)** _____ relatives. They must have thought I was so **(2)** _____ . Now there's no stopping me! I type away **(3)** _____ on my computer, all types of messages to all types of people. E-mail has all the benefits of a word **(4)** _____ and none of the tedious **(5)** _____ of writing by hand. It's better than the letter because you can edit it, quickly and **(6)** _____ , and it's instant like the phone but without the need to talk! And sending an e-mail is so **(7)** _____ fast: just press the button and it's gone. By contrast, the Web is **(8)** _____ overrated and sometimes so slow that it's **(9)** _____ . What's more, Web sites are not updated and a lot of the information is **(10)** _____ . I think it's a joke in that respect – and not a very good one.

PAIN
THOUGHT
GRATITUDE
END
PROCESS
ADVANTAGE
EFFORT
WONDER
EXTREME
PRACTICAL
USE

Reading

Introduction

In Paper 1 you have 1 hour 15 minutes to answer questions on four different texts. Understanding of each of the four texts is tested in a different way with a different type of task each time. In this unit we will look at how to read each of the text types.

Part 1: Multiple matching

1   Part 1 consists of a text from which headings or summary sentences have been removed and placed before the text in a different order. You have to decide which paragraph in the text each of the headings or summary sentences belongs to. This tests your ability to identify the main ideas expressed in each paragraph. You do not necessarily need to understand every word in the text. You should focus on the general idea of each paragraph, without worrying about individual words or phrases.

2   For the text on the opposite page, read the summary sentences first, together with the title and the introductory sentence. This will give you an idea of the main points of the text. Then read through the text quite quickly before you start to make your choices.

What to expect in the exam

Be careful. Looking for words in the text which are the same as the words in a question does not guarantee you will find the correct answer. For example, look again at the example sentence for paragraph **0**:
I *The heat can create serious health problems for walkers.*

The word 'heat' appears in paragraphs 4 and 5, but neither of these paragraphs is the correct answer.
Similarly, the words '*create problems for walkers*' can be seen in paragraph 6, but this is also the wrong answer.

A   Getting wet is one way of keeping temperatures down.
B   Your clothing acts as an important defence against the sun.
C   Water has a number of important advantages.
D   There are several alternatives to just water.
E   The wrong clothing can cause problems.
F   Always protect those parts of your body which are not covered by clothing.
G   One part of your body which can suffer is your feet.
H   Take enough water and drink it sensibly.
I   The heat can create serious health problems for walkers.

Part 2: Multiple choice

1   Part 2 consists of a text followed by seven or eight multiple choice questions. Most of the questions in this task require a detailed understanding of the text.

2   Look back at page 28 to see the different types of questions you can expect to find in the exam. Then look at questions **1–7** on the opposite page and decide which type of question each one is. These questions all refer to the text you have just read for the Part 1 task, but in the exam they will refer to a completely different text.

Example: Question 1 is testing our detailed understanding of the text.

3   Now for questions **1–7** choose the answer which you think fits best according to the text. For questions **3**, **4** and **6** you should first decide on the meaning of the words in *italics* in the paragraphs with the same numbers. Use the context in which each word appears to help you work out the meaning.

A walk in the midday sun
When the heat is on, walkers need to be on their guard.

0   *I*

Hot weather makes your heart pump harder, and if you're not very fit, you start to understand why the majority of mountain rescue statistics are made up from summer walkers suffering heart attacks. Heat exhaustion is quite easy to get when you're
5 making a great physical effort. It happens where your body can't produce enough sweat to keep you cool.

1

The answer is to keep up your water intake. It's a good idea to drink a pint of water for every 10 degrees Fahrenheit every 24 hours. So, if the temperature is in the 70s, and you are doing
10 a five-hour walk, you'll need a minimum of around one and a half pints of water. It's vital that you don't wait until you develop a raging thirst before you stop for a drink – keep taking regular swigs from your water bottle.

2

Many walkers flavour their water with fruit juice, which makes
15 it a lot more palatable. You could even use one of the isotonic drinks made for athletes, which replace the body's salts lost through sweating. Powders such as Dioralyte, which you may have in the house as a treatment for diarrhoea, will do the job just as well, as its main aim is also effective rehydration.

3

20 Given that evaporation is your body's cooling mechanism, you can help things along with an external application of water. Soaking your hat with water is a great way to cool the head, though if the sun is beating down, **it** will probably dry off almost immediately. Better still then if you can plunge into a
25 river or the sea fully-clothed. And if that's not possible, then at least take off your boots and socks and paddle in a cool stream.

4

Walking in the heat increases the rate at which your feet *swell*, which can lead to them feeling tight in your boots. Cool water from a stream reduces any swelling and helps general foot
30 comfort. At the same time, you can check out your feet for signs of *blisters*. Extra sweating makes the skin softer and increases the chance of blisters forming, in the same way as when water *leaks* into your boots and gets to your feet.

5

As for what clothing you wear, this should be lightweight and
35 reasonably loose-fitting. Tight clothing will feel uncomfortable and may even lead to the formation of an irritating *rash* known as 'prickly heat' on your skin. The answer, if this does develop, is to try and stay cool as much as possible. Do this by either keeping in the shade, or washing the affected area
40 with cold water, but without soap. But prevention is by far the best approach, so keep your clothing light.

6

It's understandable to want to remove any extraneous clothing when it's extremely hot, but it doesn't really make much sense to take off T-shirts. The sun's rays can be quite strong, and
45 shoulders are always very sensitive to sunburn. This is the worst place to be red and sore when you are wearing a heavy rucksack on your back. Wearing shorts can also create problems for walkers, as the backs of the legs can catch the sun very easily.

7

50 In fact, those days when an apparently harmless *breeze* is blowing can be the most *deceptive*. It might not feel so hot, so you probably won't notice the damage being done so soon. As on every other day then, a good strong sun cream should therefore be applied to any skin which is exposed. Make the most of the
55 summer, but treat the sun with the respect it deserves.

1 What does the writer say about 'Dioralyte'?
 A It helps to reduce sweating.
 B It prevents the loss of body salts.
 C It will prevent you getting diarrhoea.
 D It works in the same way as an isotonic drink.

2 'it' in line 23 refers to
 A the sun.
 B your hat.
 C the head.
 D water.

3 According to the text, when might your feet suffer?
 A when they cool down
 B if you are wearing tightly-fitting boots
 C when they are wet
 D if you have to walk through water

4 According to the writer, it is better to wear loose-fitting clothing because
 A it keeps you cool.
 B it is very light.
 C it is less likely to create problems for your skin.
 D it lasts longer than tight-fitting clothing.

5 What does the writer mean by 'extraneous' clothing in line 42?
 A clothing which is no longer needed to keep you warm
 B clothing which most people would consider unusual in hot weather
 C clothing which is too tight
 D clothing which is too heavy to wear

6 According to the writer, when are walkers particularly at risk from the effects of the sun?
 A when they are unaware of the heat
 B if their sun cream is not strong enough
 C when there is a strong wind
 D if they have suffered an injury

7 Who has the text been written for?
 A people who go walking in the mountains
 B walkers who are unfit
 C people who go walking in hot weather
 D people who only go walking in summer

Part 3: Gapped text

1   Part 3 consists of a text from which paragraphs or sentences have been removed and placed in a different order after the text. You have to decide which part of the text the paragraphs or sentences have been removed from. This part of the Reading Paper tests your understanding of the way texts are structured, so look carefully at the language both before and after each gap.

2   Read the headline for the following newspaper article and predict what the text is about. Then read through the text (ignoring the questions in blue) and check your predictions.

3   Students who do well in Part 3 also try to predict the general content of each gap before making their choices.

Use the questions in each space as well as the underlined language to help you predict the sentences which have been removed from each gap. Write your predictions for each space on a separate piece of paper. No help is given for spaces 5 and 6.

Internet ends 38-year search

A woman who spent 38 years searching for her brother traced him during a free 90-minute lesson on how to use the Internet. [1]   *The next sentence begins 'After that'. What moment or incident do you think is mentioned in this gap? The next sentence talks about both 'he' and 'she'. Look through the rest of the text and find the full names of these two people: these names will probably be mentioned in this gap.*

<u>After that</u> he moved repeatedly round the world, while she married and settled in the North East. [2]   *Look ahead to the next sentence. Who will be the subject in this gap; the woman or her brother? What did she do in this gap to make her become desperate?*

<u>In desperation</u> she called into a branch of Age Concern near her home in Gateshead and asked for help on their <u>computer</u>. [3]   *The previous sentence to this gap tells us she looked for her brother on a computer. Now look at the next sentence. Which part of the world did she start looking in? Was she immediately successful?*

<u>It was only when the search was extended to include the rest of the United States</u> that Eileen finally located a P. Rider living in Largo, Florida. [4]   *What did Eileen do in this gap? The next sentence will help you. What does the word 'Finally' tell us?* Finally, a woman, who turned out to be her brother Percival's wife, <u>picked up the phone</u> in Florida. [5]   The following week Mrs Stevens flew to Florida, to be reunited with her brother and meet her sister-in-law for the first time. [6]   But thankfully we are back in touch again, thanks to a simple computer lesson.'

4   Turn to page 200 and read the sentences which were removed. Try to match each of the sentences to your own. There is one extra sentence which you do not need to use. Always check that the extra sentence which you have not used does not fit anywhere in the text.

Part 4: Multiple matching

1   Part 4 consists of either one continuous text divided into sections, or a number of smaller texts. Between 13 and 15 questions are placed before the text or texts. For this part of the Reading Paper you are asked to find specific information in the text or texts. Although both Part 1 and Part 4 are both multiple matching tasks, the appropriate reading strategy for each is different.

As we have already seen, Part 1 tasks require you to identify the main ideas in each paragraph. The appropriate technique is known as *skimming*: your eyes *skim* over the surface of the text, picking out the main points as they go.

In Part 4, *scanning* is usually a more appropriate strategy: your eyes *scan* the text, forwards and backwards, until they pick out the specific information you need. We do this, for example, when we look at the TV page in the newspaper. Rather than reading the whole page, we look for the parts which talk specifically about the programme or type of programme we want to watch.

Don't forget!

Look at the title and the introduction first then skim the texts for a general understanding.

2 Read the following Part 4 instructions.

Read this article about different study Web sites. For questions **1–15**, choose from the Web sites **A–F**. The Web sites may be chosen more than once. When more than one answer is required, these may be given in any order. There is an example at the beginning **(0)**.

3 Now look at each question one by one, *scanning* the texts to find the answers.

Which of the Web sites would you consult in the following situations?

You know the date, but not the day of your next exam.	**0** D
You want to check the exact meaning of the verb 'to swell'.	**1** **2**
You are curious to see what problems other students have had.	**3**
You need some advice on how to prepare for your exams.	**4** **5**
You are going to Australia to study English and you need to know the exchange rate for the Australian dollar.	**6**
You want to receive some personal attention from someone.	**7** **8** **9**
You are 16 and your cousin is 13: you both need information about chemistry which is appropriate to your level.	**10** **11**
You want to consult a site which is not too serious.	**12**
You do not want to waste time looking at sites which turn out to be irrelevant to you.	**13**
For geography homework you have been told to find out the capitals of all the countries in south east Asia.	**14**
You are interested to see what the person answering your questions looks like.	**15**

Exploring the Web: Education

Emma Houghton looks at several useful Web sites for students who need information fast. The sites offer links to other Web sites, search engines and the increasingly popular ask-the-expert sites.

A Topmarks   **www.topmarks.co.uk**

An excellent UK site offering links to sites across all subjects, including astronomy, classics, design technology, economics, personal and social education, physical education and religious studies. You can select under subject and age group, and each link has a five-line description so you know exactly where you are going. There is a particularly good section on exam help, with lots of links to help revise different subjects, while the parents' area has a number of useful articles.

B Homework Elephant   **www.homeworkelephant.free-on-line.co.uk**

A UK service with 700 links to some of the best educational sites on the Web, as well as other resources like dictionaries and search engines. You'll also find revision tips for each subject, and a section pointing towards relevant online experts, who may be able to give you more individual help. If you're still stuck, consult the Agony Elephant, which will point you in the right direction. Not to be missed.

C StudyWeb   **www.studyweb.com**

Over 118,000 links across subjects as diverse as agriculture, philosophy, architecture, criminology and medicine, as well as all the usual curriculum subjects. Each link has a US school grade to indicate its approximate age level, while the Study Buddy offers a wide range of online useful extras, including a calculator and currency converter.

D Kid Info School Subjects   **www.kidinfo.com/SchoolSubjects.html**

An easy-to-use site offering links across the full range of subjects, as well as calendars, dictionaries, quotations, atlases, encyclopedias and museums.

E Pitsco's Ask an Expert   **www.askanexpert.com**

Can connect you to hundreds of real live experts, from astronomers to zoologists and plenty in between. You can browse via category or keyword search to find the most likely candidate, then visit their Web site to see if your answer is already there; if not, stick it on e-mail, press send, and wait for your reply. In the Arts/Humanities section, for example, there is a fine art expert, an artist, a classical musician, a composer and even a piano teacher.

F Ask Dr Universe   **www.wsu.edu/DrUniverse/**

A good-looking and appealingly light-hearted site which lets you pose questions to researchers at Washington State University, then follow them up by e-mail if you want to explore further. You can also look up archives of former questions, which are usually accompanied by photos of the answering academic.

4 A good story

For the ride of your life...
All you need for Christmas are your two front seats!

AIRPLANE II
THE SEQUEL

PARAMOUNT PICTURES PRESENTS A HOWARD W KOCH PRODUCTION AIRPLANE II THE SEQUEL ROBERT HAYS
JULIE HAGERTY · LLOYD BRIDGES · CHAD EVERETT · WILLIAM SHATNER · DIRECTOR OF PHOTOGRAPHY JOE BIROC A.S.C.
PRODUCED BY HOWARD W KOCH · WRITTEN AND DIRECTED BY KEN FINKLEMAN A PARAMOUNT PICTURE

FROM OUT OF SPACE.... A WARNING AND AN ULTIMATUM!

THE DAY THE EARTH STOOD STILL

MICHAEL RENNIE · PATRICIA NEAL · HUGH MARLOWE

SHAFT

Hotter than Bond,
Cooler than Bullitt.

SHAFT's his name.
SHAFT's his game.

Vocabulary 1: Films

1 Look at these film posters. Do you know any of these films? What type of film is each one? Choose from the words in the box.

> thriller   horror film   comedy   romance
> historical drama   science fiction   action film   western

2 The words in the box are all related to films. Divide them into three different groups: *story and events*, *people* and *other aspects*.

> cast   plot   soundtrack   main characters   animation   supporting role
> screenplay   photography   special effects   action scenes

3 For exercises **A** and **B**, decide which word best fits each space.
   A   *terrible   terrific   terrifying*

   1 It was a _____ performance, for which he deserves to win an Oscar.
   2 Absolutely _____ ! I 've never been so frightened in all my life.
   3 This was probably the worst film I've seen all year. The plot was non-existent and the acting was _____ .

   B   *review   criticism   critic*

   It seems that every **(1)** _____ I read of this film gives a different opinion. For example, the **(2)** _____ who writes for *The Times* is very enthusiastic about it and has nothing but praise for George Lucas. The same director, however, comes under strong **(3)** _____ in the magazine *Premiere*.

4 Using some of the vocabulary in exercises 1 and 2, talk about:

   • a film you didn't enjoy
   • your favourite film
   • the most frightening film you have ever seen
   • the most exciting film you have ever seen

Reading 1:
FCE Part 1

Multiple matching

1 Which films has Keanu Reeves starred in? What do you know about his private life?

2 Read the following Reading Part 1 instructions.

You are going to read a magazine article about the actor Keanu Reeves. The headings have been removed and placed before the text. Choose the most suitable heading from the list **A–H** for each part (**1–6**) of the article. There is one extra heading which you do not need to use. There is an example at the beginning (**0**).

3 Look at the headings and predict what each one might refer to in relation to Keanu Reeves. Some of the headings may have more than one meaning.

Example:
Settling down: *this usually means 'to lead a more stable life', so the relevant paragraph might talk about Keanu Reeves buying a house or getting married and having children.*

4 Now read the text through quickly before you try to match the headings. Were your ideas in exercise 1 correct?

A Settling down	**E** Contrary to expectations
B The big break	**F** A question of priorities
C Getting started	**G** Taking it seriously
D Life on the move	**H** Roots

He's been a cop, a computer hacker, a muscular hero and Buddha. But who is the real Keanu Reeves?

0 | *H*

With such an unusual name, it was obvious from the start that Keanu's life was going to be different. Born in Beirut on September 2 1964, his name is pronounced 'key-ah-noo' and is Hawaiian for 'cool breeze over the mountains'. His Chinese-Hawaiian father, Samuel, moved away when Keanu was two, leaving his English-born mother Patricia to raise him and his younger sister Kim. They lived in Australia and New York before finally settling in Toronto, Canada.

1

Keanu decided to be an actor at the age of 15, when he had a few acting lessons and became hooked. He spent some time working in a pasta restaurant and sharpening skates at an ice hockey rink in order to pay his way. He went to auditions between shifts and got various parts in local theatre and TV productions, as well as a part in a Coca-Cola advert.

2

At 19 he decided to take a risk and try his luck in Hollywood. Within eight months, he'd got his first major role in *Youngblood*, which, funnily enough, was all about ice hockey. After *Youngblood* Keanu starred in several other films, but it wasn't until 1991, when he was given the part of Ted in *Bill and Ted's Excellent Adventure*, that he started to make a name for himself.

3

Keanu often played troubled, slightly weak characters and he soon gained a reputation for being the same in real life. Trying to shake off his 'dumb and distant' image, Keanu took more challenging parts, like a hired killer in *I Love You to Death* and an FBI agent in *Point Break*, but it was in the box office hit *Speed* in 1994 that he really showed his talent. Producers were desperate to have Keanu back for the sequel, *Speed 2: Cruise Control* but he shocked everyone by rejecting the reported £9 million offer to tour Europe, America and Japan with his band Dogstar, in which he plays bass guitar.

4

So what else does he get up to? In general, Keanu is very guarded about his private life. He keeps a low profile claiming that he's 'a homebody', but in reality he has no home at all! Instead, he lives out of a suitcase and flits from one five star hotel to another. 'I've never really thought about a home,' he says, 'I feel that's a trap.' We do know, however, that he's into motorbikes in a big way and that the reckless rider has had two accidents, one in which he broke an ankle and the other which left him with a 25-centimetre navel-to-chest scar.

5

Keanu likes to do things properly and once he gets a role, he loves getting his teeth into it. For the film *The Matrix* he lost weight and shaved his hair and eyebrows off. 'The first two weeks after I've finished a movie I feel so exhausted that I can't speak about anything,' he confesses.

6

Despite his good looks, a successful career, vast sums of money and even a film-study course at a California University named after him, you would have thought that Keanu Reeves would feel on top of the world. Well, think again. 'My life isn't actually that interesting,' he says. 'I go to work, then I go back to LA, then I go to work. Life isn't a bowl of cherries and I don't consider myself a happy person.'

Reacting to the text

What are the advantages and disadvantages of being famous?
How would you feel if you had fame and fortune? What would you do with your life?
If you could meet a famous person, who would it be and what would you say?

Language focus 1: *So* and *such*

Look at these two sentences from the text.

*With **such** an unusual name, it was obvious from the start that Keanu's life was going to be different.*
*'The first two weeks after I've finished a movie I feel **so** exhausted that I can't speak about anything,' he confesses.*

Why are *so* and *such* used in each of these sentences?
What types of words follow *so* and *such*?

 Check your ideas in the Grammar reference on page 209.

Practice

For questions **1–4** complete the second sentence so that it has a similar meaning to the first sentence, using the word given. **Do not change the word given.** You must use between two and five words, including the word given.

1 We decided to see the film because it got such good reviews.
that
The reviews for the film _____ we decided to see it.

2 The weather was so bad that we decided to come home.
such
It _____ that we decided to come home.

3 I got so bored during the film I fell asleep.
such
It _____ film I fell asleep.

4 The party was so crowded we could hardly move.
so
There _____ people at the party we could hardly move.

Word formation: Adjectives ending in *-ing* and *-ed*

To describe how we feel about something or someone we can use past participles as adjectives.

*I got really **frightened** when I saw the main character being killed.*

To describe the thing or person that produces the feeling we can use present participles as adjectives.

*It was an extremely **frightening** scene.*

Adverbs can be formed from present participle adjectives.

*Not **surprisingly**, we were disappointed that we couldn't get tickets to see the film.*

1 Put the past participle of each of the following regular verbs in the appropriate group, according to how the *-ed* ending is pronounced.

annoy	frustrate	tire	disappoint	disgust	astonish	
amuse	fascinate	bore	impress	frighten	relax	terrify

/d/	/t/	/id/
surprised	*embarrassed*	*excited*

2 The present participle (*-ing*) form of the verbs in exercise 1 can all be used as adjectives, except in the case of one of the verbs. Which one is it and how is the adjective formed?

3 Complete each space with the present or past participle form of an appropriate verb from exercise 1. You may need to use an adverb.

1 Teachers need long holidays. They do a very _____ job.
2 I'm sorry, but I'm just not _____ . I don't find it at all funny.
3 I wish you'd stop whistling. It's extremely _____ !
4 My mark in the exam was _____ low. I thought I had done much better.
5 I find the whole subject of genetic engineering extremely _____ . I really would like to read more about it.
6 I'm not eating that – it smells _____ ! What is it?
7 _____ , she was still alive after spending 20 days buried under a building which had collapsed in the earthquake.

Vocabulary 2: *Take*

A **Expressions with *take***

Like *get*, which you saw in Unit 1, *take* has many different meanings and uses. Look at these two uses of the verb *take* from the text on Keanu Reeves.

*At 19 he decided to **take a risk** and try his luck in Hollywood.*

Taking it seriously

1 Complete each space **1–8** with an appropriate form of the verb *take*.

A 1 My dad used to _____ me to school, but now I have to get the bus.
  2 A pair of shoes should last longer than two months. If I were you, I _____ them back to the shop.

B 3 I lost money on that business deal! Of course I regret _____ his advice!
  4 She criticizes everybody else and refuses _____ any of the blame herself.

C 5 If you _____ more interest in the children, they'd probably respond better!
  6 The stray cat was looking a lot healthier. It was clear that someone _____ pity on it and given it something to eat.

D 7 Street luge _____ a great deal of courage. You wouldn't catch me doing it!
  8 Come on! I can't understand why you _____ so long to do this exercise.

2 In each of the sentences in exercise 1, identify the expression with *take* and underline it.

  Example: *Who is* <u>*taking care of the children*</u> *tonight while you're at the party?*

3 The expressions in exercise 1 are organized into four groups, **A**, **B**, **C** and **D**. Match each of the following general meanings for *take* to an appropriate group.

  1 to express what is needed or required
  2 to talk about the movement of something or someone from one place to another
  3 to talk about the way people feel or react to others
  4 to accept

4 Which group in exercise 1 do the following expressions belong to? Write four sentences, each including one of the expressions.

  to take pride in something   *to be taken to hospital*

  to take a joke   *to take the infinitive*

B **Phrasal verbs with *take***
1 Read the following short story and give it a title.

I **a)** <u>take after</u> my father in many ways, particularly in my love of good food and a tendency to eat more than I need to. However, several years ago the situation had reached crisis point – my clothes no longer fitted me – so I decided to **b)** <u>take up</u> some form of sport. Karate seemed like a good idea, so I signed up for a course at the local sports centre.

I **c)** <u>took to</u> it immediately and by the end of the first class I was hooked. Over the next four years I progressed through the different levels until two years ago I achieved my ambition and qualified as an instructor. And now the same sports centre where I started all those years ago has just **d)** <u>taken me on</u> as a full-time karate teacher. What's more, they needed

someone to **e)** <u>take over from</u> the man who was my very first teacher and who has left to set up his own gym. I am certainly very grateful to him! Now, what with training, competitions and the classes themselves, karate has become my life and **f)** <u>takes up</u> all my time. I still manage to go out for a good meal now and again though!

2 Match each of the underlined phrasal verbs in exercise 1 to one of the meanings in the box below. Use the context of the story to help you.

| employ | start doing | resemble | occupy | start to like | replace |

3 Now write a short story of your own using at least three expressions and three phrasal verbs with *take*.

Speaking: **FCE Part 2**

Talking about photos

What to expect in the exam

- In Part 2 of the Speaking Test you talk on your own for about a minute.
- Start speaking immediately and keep talking throughout the minute to make the most of your time.

In the exam one candidate speaks for a minute and the other has about 20 seconds to answer an additional question. However, as this is a practice you can have a little more time to complete the task, but try to keep speaking all the time.

How to go about it

Student A
- First point out the similarities and differences between the two photographs. Do not describe the photographs in detail.
- Then answer the second part of the question, which begins 'and say...'

Student B
- Your comment should be brief, but you do have time to give reasons for your feelings or opinions.

Student A: The following two photographs show different types of entertainment. Compare and contrast these photographs and say how you think the people are feeling in each of the situations.

Student B: When Student A has finished, say how you would feel in each situation.

Now change roles.

Student A: Compare and contrast the photos again and say what the advantages and disadvantages are of each of these activities.

Student B: When Student A has finished, say which activity you would prefer to do.

Preparing for listening: Focus on distractors

1 Match each sentence beginning **1–5** with an appropriate ending **a–e**.

① My brother was so scared he couldn't watch the film

2 **Although** most critics agreed that the film was her best ever

3 **Although** snow is now unlikely

4 My daughter wanted me to help her with her homework

5 **Whereas** in most of his other films he plays the 'baddie'

a we can expect a certain amount of rain later on.

b in this one he's definitely the good guy.

c **whereas** I didn't find it at all frightening.

d I was rather disappointed by her performance.

e **but** I told her to ask her mother.

2 Now decide on the correct alternative in each of the following interpretations of the sentences in exercise 1. Give reasons for your answers.

The speaker in sentence…

1 **A** was frightened by the film.

2 **A** loved the film.

3 **A** says it will probably rain.

4 **A** helped his daughter.

5 **A** says the actor is the villain.

B was not frightened by the film.

B was not enthusiastic about the film.

B says it will probably snow.

B didn't help his daughter.

B says the actor is the hero in the film.

The incorrect answers in exercise 2 are typical of the distractors you might find in a Part 1 Listening task. The ideas in them are similar to the information in exercise 1 but not the same. Note the use of contrast linkers, written in **bold**.

Listening:
FCE Part 1

Multiple choice 🔈

You will hear people talking in eight different situations. For questions **1–8**, choose the best answer, **A**, **B** or **C**.

Don't forget!

In this Part 1 exercise you will hear distractors of the type you met in the Preparing for listening section.

1 Listen to this woman talking about an actor. What is her opinion of him?

   A He is handsome.

   B He is fashionable.

   C He is rude.

2 You overhear this conversation between two friends. What type of film are they going to see?

   A an historical drama

   B a romance

   C a thriller

3 You hear a conversation in a video hire shop. How long has the customer had the video for?

   A one day

   B two days

   C three days

4 You hear an actress talking about her performance in a play. How does she feel?

   A tired

   B disappointed

   C excited

5 You overhear this man talking on the telephone. Who is he talking to?

   A an old school friend

   B a work colleague

   C a relative

6 You hear a young woman talking to her friend about a film. Why didn't she like it?

   A It was too slow.

   B There was too much violence.

   C It was very predictable.

7 You hear a woman telephoning a bookshop. What is she doing?

   A making a complaint

   B making a suggestion

   C apologizing

8 You hear this young man talking on the phone. What does he have in common with his girlfriend?

   A They were born under the same star sign.

   B They share the same taste in music.

   C They have the same sense of humour.

Reading 2:
FCE Part 3

Gapped text

○ 1 Look at this photo of an examination centre.

How many invigilators can you see?
What different duties does an invigilator have to perform on the day of an exam?
What do you think the job is like?

2 Now read the extract and compare your ideas in exercise 1 with the text.
What exam are they sitting for?

He was invigilating the exam in the *Casa de Cristal*, a huge glass-fronted building on the edge of the city used twice-yearly as an examination centre. It was a cold December day and the heating had broken down. With their coats and scarves pulled tightly round them, the four hundred or so candidates struggled to forget the temperature and focus their attention instead on the four examination papers which would take them most of the day to complete. [0 *H*] However, no obvious improvement was ever made.

The job of invigilator was not one he particularly enjoyed, but it earned him some much-needed cash before the approaching Christmas holidays. As well as patrolling a small part of the large examination room, answering questions and discouraging cheats, he had to carry out a number of administrative duties. [1] And then, of course, there were the question papers to hand out and answers to take in. It was all rather dull, but it made a change from the rigours of teaching.

To relieve the boredom he set himself several simple arithmetical tasks to perform. [2] This helped to pass the time and made the whole thing more bearable. Now and again he would walk up and down the aisles, giving out rough paper, reminding candidates to use pens rather than

pencils and picking up items which had been dropped on the floor.

He was walking back up the exam room in his soft shoes when he caught her. [3] The candidates were now on the third paper, which tested English grammar and vocabulary, and as he neared her desk from behind, he could hardly believe what he saw. He had heard of some ingenious methods of cheating but nothing like this. [4] She was now looking down at the back of her exposed leg, which was covered with several columns of phrasal verbs and their translations, copied out onto her skin in fine blue ink. Suddenly, she felt his presence behind her and she pulled the trouser leg down to her ankle and looked round.

[5] Then she blushed, acutely embarrassed but also uncomfortably aware of the possible consequences of having been found out and she looked away to contemplate her fate. None of the other candidates seemed to have noticed what was happening, which gave him time to decide how best to deal with the situation. [6] But this was not a course of action he had considered and as he asked her to accompany him to the front, he noticed the tears forming in her eyes.

3   Seven sentences have been removed from the text. Choose from the sentences **A–H** the one which fits each space **(1–6)**. There is one extra sentence which you do not need to use. There is an example at the beginning **(0)**.

Don't forget!

- Look carefully at the meaning and the language of the text both *before* and *after* the space. Look at the example sentence, **H**: *The cold was terrible and the caretaker of the building had assured him that a heating engineer was trying to solve the problem.*

Look at the text before the space.
What is 'the building' which is referred to?
Which person does 'him' refer to?
What is 'the problem'?
Look at the text after the space.
What is the result of the engineer's work?

A The girl was wearing loose fitting trousers and had pulled one of the trouser legs up as far as the knee.

B He counted the number of separate window panes (85), worked out the most popular colour for coats (blue) and calculated the ratio of females to males in the room (5:2).

C There were lists of names to make, seating plans to draw and identity papers to check.

D This brief delay gave her hope that he might turn a blind eye and forget he had seen anything.

E She had obviously not heard him approaching.

F They had only been writing for some 20 minutes when he received the first complaint.

G For a brief moment they stared at each other in disbelief, neither one of them quite sure what to do next.

H The cold was terrible and the caretaker of the building had assured him that a heating engineer was trying to solve the problem.

Reacting to the text

Does this method of cheating surprise you?
What do you think happened to the girl next?

Language focus 2: Past tenses

1   Look at the following sentences from the text about cheating and name the underlined past tenses. Choose from:
past simple   past continuous
past perfect simple   past perfect continuous

1 *He was invigilating the exam in the Casa de Cristal.*
2 *It was a cold December day and the heating had broken down.*
3 *He was walking back up the exam room in his soft shoes when he caught her.*
4 *Suddenly she felt his presence behind her and she pulled the trouser leg down to her ankle and looked round.*
5 *They had only been writing for some 20 minutes when he received the first complaint.*

2   In which sentence in exercise 1 is the past tense or combination of tenses used to describe:
a a series of actions following each other in chronological order?
b an event which occurred before the other past actions in the narrative?
c the duration of an action until a specific point in the past?

d a situation which occurred over a period of time and which forms the background to the other past actions in the narrative?
e an action which was in progress when another action occurred?

3   Name the tenses in the following pairs of sentences and explain the difference in meaning between each pair.
1 a When he was taking the exam, he felt ill.
  b When he had taken the exam, he felt ill.
2 a I was listening to the radio when I heard about it.
  b I listened to the radio when I heard about it.
3 a I lived in Oxford for six years.
  b I had been living in Oxford for six years.

4   In which of the sentences in exercise 3 can *while* be used in place of *when*?
In which sentences can *as soon as* be used in place of *when*?
Do these words change the meaning of the sentences in any way?

G   Look at pages 208 and 209 of the Grammar reference for more information about past tenses and time linkers.

Practice

1 For each of sentences **1–6** decide which of the three alternative time expressions fits the space. Pay attention to both grammar and meaning.

1 He wasn't allowed to go home _____ he'd apologized to the teacher.

   A until   **B** afterwards   **C** as soon as

2 _____ she was coming home, she fell over and hurt herself.

   A After   **B** During   **C** As

3 It can get very hot here _____ the summer.

   A while   **B** during   **C** when

4 First of all he won the 100 metres freestyle competition. _____ he went on to break the record for backstroke and crawl at the same distance.

   A After   **B** After it   **C** Afterwards

5 She got so tired of waiting for him that _____ she just went home.

   A at the end   **B** in the end   **C** at last

6 _____ she'd gone, he started to cry.

   A Eventually   **B** Until   **C** As soon as

2 Read the following texts in which two people tell the story of an embarrassing moment. In each of the spaces write the appropriate past form of the verb in brackets. There is an example at the beginning **(0)**.

Bus blush

Something very embarrassing **(0)** _happened_ (happen) to me while I **(1)** _____ (travel) home from school on the bus one day. We **(2)** _____ (have) a laugh at the back of the bus when I **(3)** _____ (see) a friend from school. She **(4)** _____ (sit) at the front, so I **(5)** _____ (run) up and **(6)** _____ (sit) down behind her, pulling her ponytail and shouting, 'Hi there, Rebecca!' I felt so stupid when a man I **(7)** _____ (never/see) before turned round! 'Actually, my name's Andrew,' he **(8)** _____ (smile). I **(9)** _____ (not/stop) blushing until I **(10)** _____ (get) home.

Mobile control

I **(11)** _____ (go on) at my parents for months to let me have a mobile phone and they eventually **(12)** _____ (agree) to buy me one. Keen to show it off, I **(13)** _____ (take) it with me when I **(14)** _____ (go) out with my friends one night. By 10pm no one **(15)** _____ (phone) me, so I thought I'd impress everyone by making a call. As soon as I **(16)** _____ (get) my phone out of the bag, I realized I **(17)** _____ (take) the TV remote control with me instead. As if that wasn't bad enough, when I finally **(18)** _____ (arrive) home my dad **(19)** _____ (keep) going on about the fact that he **(20)** _____ (have) to watch the same TV channel all night!

Writing: (FCE Part 2)   Short stories

1 Read the following Writing Part 2 instructions.

You have decided to enter a short story competition. The rules say that the story must end with the following words:

It was such a relief to see them again.

Write your **story** in **120–180** words.

2 Read the two sample answers on page 51 and decide which is the better entry.

3 The box below shows the criteria which an examiner would use when marking these competition entries. Decide how well each story satisfies the criteria by answering the questions in each category. Give examples from the stories to support your opinions.

Content:	Have the instructions in the question been followed?
Range:	Have a variety of past tenses been used? Is there a wide range of vocabulary?
Organization and cohesion:	Are the ideas and events organized logically? Are linking devices used well?
Style and format:	Is the story written using suitably neutral language? (neither too formal nor too informal)
Target reader:	Would the reader be sufficiently interested to want to read to the end? Would it have a chance of winning the competition?

You may be asked to begin or end with the words in the question.

Don't forget to read the question carefully!

A

It was such a relief to see my glasses again. I lost them when I was at the fairground on one of the rides.

We went there because it was my birthday and I wanted to celebrate it at the fairground. I went there with my friends. We went on all the rides except the ghost train. It's not very frightening. We were walking home when I noticed I didn't have my glasses. 'Where are my glasses?' I asked. 'I don't know,' said my friend. 'Perhaps you lost them on one of the rides.' So we went back and I asked at all the rides we had been on. They didn't have them at the rollercoaster, they didn't have them at the dodgems and what's more no one knew where they were. At last I found them. They were on the ground near the big wheel. What a relief!

B

My sister and I had just been to the cinema and when we came out we were thrilled to see it was snowing. The ground was covered in a sparkling white blanket of snow and although it was getting late, we couldn't resist having a quick snowball fight.

However, by the time we arrived at the bus stop, we had missed the last bus. Unfortunately, we couldn't afford to get a taxi back to our village and our parents had gone away for the weekend, so we had no choice but to set off on foot in the snow.

After we had been walking for nearly an hour we were both freezing cold and exhausted. It was snowing so heavily that we could hardly make out where we were going and we had both fallen over several times in the deep snow.

Just as our situation was becoming desperate, a car pulled up beside us and my mother wound down the window. 'Would you like a lift?' she asked. My parents had had to come home because of the poor weather conditions. It was such a relief to see them again.

4 Your teacher has asked you to write a story for the school's English magazine. It must end with the following words:

I had never been so surprised in all my life.

How to go about it

- First think of a general outline for your story. Choose two of the categories below and think of possible story lines for each one. Remember, your story has to *end* with a surprise.

  a discovering the truth about someone
  b meeting someone you hadn't seen for a long time
  c finding something you thought you had lost forever
  d achieving something you had thought impossible
  e an unexpected birthday surprise

  ***Example: a** applied for a job – went for an interview – car broke down – hitchhiked – wet, cold – got a lift – arrived at interview – interviewer was person who gave lift*

- Make a plan, organizing your ideas into logical paragraphs.

  Opening: Set the scene.
  Main events: One or two paragraphs on what happened. Remember the word limit is 180 words, so do not write about too many events.
  Ending: The surprise. Don't forget to end with the exact words in the question.

- Make sure your story has well organized paragraphs, a variety of past tenses, a wide range of vocabulary and appropriate linking words.
- Remember to write between 120 and 180 words.

Now you are ready to write your **story** in **120–180** words.

4 Review

Transformations

For questions **1–10** complete the second sentence so that it has a similar meaning to the first sentence, using the word given. **Do not change the word given**. You must use between two and five words, including the word given.

1 When the meeting was over, they went out for a drink.
   had
   As _____ finished, they went out for a drink.

2 When we eventually arrived at the party, all the food had been eaten.
   got
   By _____ the party, all the food had been eaten.

3 Immediately after he went, we started to relax.
   once
   We started to relax _____ gone.

4 He put everything back in its place before he left.
   until
   He didn't _____ everything back in its place.

5 I liked him the first time I met him.
   took
   I _____ the first time I saw him.

6 They decided against employing him because of his age.
   take
   They decided _____ because of his age.

7 She is proud of her achievements.
   pride
   She _____ her achievements.

8 She isn't very interested in my work.
   in
   She doesn't _____ my work.

9 His exam mark was such a disappointment.
   so
   He _____ with his exam mark.

10 I was so tired after that walk.
   such
   It _____ walk.

Error correction

In each short text **1–5**, there are two words which should not be there. Find these words and underline them.

1 At first we weren't sure whether we could afford to go on holiday, but in the end we had felt we ought to spend at least during a week on the coast.

2 I was extremely impressed with the special effects and some part of the action scenes. As for as the acting, though, I felt many amateurs could have done better.

3 After that the invigilators had taken in our answers to the reading exam, they handed out of Paper 2, the Writing test.

4 When he had came home from work he was made himself a cup of tea and read the newspaper. It had been an exhausting day.

5 I'm so pleased we took to your advice and went to the new Indian restaurant that's just opened. The service was marvellous and it was such a good food.

Vocabulary: The cinema

1 In the word square below there are ten words related to acting and the cinema. The words are written from left to right, top to bottom or diagonally. Find the words and write them in the spaces on the right.

R	T	U	T	C	E	N	I	N	B
A	O	P	H	O	R	R	O	R	C
C	C	L	O	M	D	I	R	E	H
T	A	R	E	X	T	R	A	H	A
R	W	E	I	A	U	B	N	E	R
E	A	V	M	T	C	E	T	I	A
S	T	I	E	X	I	S	O	O	C
S	N	E	Y	P	A	C	R	T	T
A	C	W	M	C	P	L	O	T	E
S	B	T	H	R	I	L	L	E	R

_____ _____

_____ _____

_____ _____

_____ _____

_____ _____

_____ _____

_____ _____

_____ _____

_____ _____

2 Now write ten more words related to the cinema. The words can be nouns or verbs.

Use of English: FCE Part 5

Word formation

1 Read the following text about special effects, ignoring the spaces for the moment. How many of the films mentioned have you seen?

George Lucas's *Star Wars* transformed 20th-century entertainment and raised audience expectations to **(0)** ___alarming___ heights for film producers. Since *Star Wars* was made in 1977 special effects have become **(1)** _____ important in selling a film. The script of *Jurassic Park*, for example, was rather **(2)** _____ but the film was a box office success because the dinosaurs were so **(3)** _____ realistic. However, special effects do not always guarantee success. **(4)** _____ , when *Lost World* came out the technology was far superior, but people had become **(5)** _____ of dinosaurs and were simply not **(6)** _____ enough to want to go and see them any more. The film was not nearly as successful as its predecessor.
But who is not **(7)** _____ when they see Jar Jar Binks in *The Phantom Menace*, the first ever 3D interactive digital character seen on film? Computer generated actors, or 'synthespians' are certainly the way ahead, but you may be **(8)** _____ to discover that the most expensive special effect was filmed in 1956. The parting of the Red Sea in Cecil B DeMille's *The Ten Commandments* cost an **(9)** _____ £2 million!
But what does the future hold? It is **(10)** _____ to think that with CGI (computer generated imagery) filmmakers may be able to recreate deceased movie stars, such as James Dean or Marilyn Monroe.

ALARM
INCREASE
DISAPPOINT
AMAZE
INTEREST
TIRE
MOTIVATE

IMPRESS

SURPRISE

ASTONISH
FASCINATE

2 Read the text again and use the word given in capitals at the end of each line to form a word that fits in the space in the same line. There is an example at the beginning **(0)**.

5 Doing your duty

Speaking 1:
FCE Part 2

Talking about photos

Compare and contrast these photos and say which learning environment you prefer and why.

Reading:
FCE Part 3

Gapped text

1 In the UK children can be educated by teachers at school or by their parents at home. What do you think are the advantages and disadvantages of education at home?

2 Read this article, ignoring the spaces and the paragraphs on the next page for the moment. Which arguments are given in favour of home education and against education at school?

Home is where the school is

At 8am, when other children have to catch trains or buses to school, 14-year-old Rhiannon Cassell walks into the family living room in Huntly, Aberdeenshire and checks on the day's assignments with her teacher – her father Matthew.

0	H

After a ten-minute tea break at 11am, more maths takes *her* through to lunch at midday. If she is having difficulties, she seeks her father's help. 'He doesn't do the work for us, just helps us to reason it out.'

1	

Matthew, 37, has been supervising his children's education since he retired on health grounds in 1995. He is not anti-school or critical of teachers. 'It's just that I can give the children more time than they'd get in a large class.' Regular tests and careful record-keeping ensure Matthew keeps a check on their progress.

2	

Rhiannon echoes another common reason for parents opting for home education: 'At school I always felt they were holding me back. Now I can learn at my own pace.'

3	

Cassie was also much better than her classmates at reading but the teacher still made her sound out the individual letters of words. Although she rapidly became bored with everything, the school would not let her go up to a higher class.

4	

Soon afterwards, *they* removed Cassie from school and Beverley began supervising her work at home. Now ten, *Cassie* reads voraciously over a wide range of subjects. "Jane Eyre" is my favourite book at the moment,' enthuses *the lively girl*. 'I've read it several times.'

5	

As well as being more fun, home education can be positively beneficial. On average, home-schoolers are two years ahead of their schooled counterparts,' says Roland Meighan, Professor of Special Education at Nottingham University.

6	

Parents do not even need to tell the local authority, although it is necessary for the headteacher to be informed if a child is withdrawn from a state school. In that case, responsibility for ensuring that alternative arrangements are satisfactory does lie with local authorities, which can take parents to court if children's needs are not being met.

3 Seven paragraphs have been removed from the article. Choose the most suitable paragraph from the list **A–H** for each part (**1–6**) of the article. There is one paragraph which you do not need to use. There is an example at the beginning (**0**).

- Look out for the different ways in which the paragraphs are linked together. Look at the example (**0:H**) to see these 'links':

Lexical links
- Paragraph **H** says that after studying science 'Rhiannon... switches to maths.' We are then told in the text that 'more maths takes *her* through to lunch'. To help you, these lexical links (vocabulary from the same topic area) are underlined in the text.

Grammatical links
- We are also helped by the pronoun *her*, which tells us that the previous paragraph must be talking about a girl or a woman. These grammatical links (both nouns and pronouns) are shown in *italics*.

Sequence links
- Look out for words which show the order (or sequence) in which events happen. At the beginning of this article you can see times; *8am* and *11am*. Notice other linking words such as *soon afterwards* and *then*.

A The Cassells are in good company. Home schooling is increasingly popular among parents fed up with bullying, narrow curriculums, rigid timetables, or the lack of proper religious teaching.

B *She and her brother Alexander*, seven, don't follow a fixed timetable and there's no bell to bring studies to an abrupt end. Cassie approves of this flexible regime. 'If it's a nice day I can go for a bike ride with my dad,' she says.

C By 1.15pm Rhiannon is back at work for a practical follow-up on the morning's science lesson: an experiment with balloons and dust. She then reads her current literary classic 'Little Women' until 2.30pm. Although that's the official end of the school day, Rhiannon may carry on with a subject she enjoys or is having problems with.

D Then Cassie contracted an infectious skin disease and had to stay at home for a fortnight, with a package of homework to keep her going. 'She completed it in an hour,' recalls *Beverley*, 35, who is studying for a psychology degree. *Beverley and her husband David* were now seriously thinking of educating their daughter themselves.

E A parent need not be a qualified teacher to be a home educator and children do not have to follow the national curriculum or sit formal tests. It is perfectly legal to keep a child away from school, as long as he or she is being educated.

F Beverley Young became concerned about her daughter Cassandra's progress at school when it became clear that her numerical skills were far more advanced than those of the other four-year-olds in her class. '*Cassie* told me she was doing the type of activity she normally did with her baby brother.'

G However, *she* is not simply allowed to do just what she wants. Her parents ensure that a code of discipline is adhered to in the home, in the same way as it would be in a school. 'She is well aware of what she can and can't do,' explains David. 'A line has to be drawn somewhere and she knows she mustn't overstep it.'

H Then Rhiannon, like her older sisters Tess, 16, and Abigail, 15, heads back to her own room, while their father works with the two youngest children, James, ten and Alicia, eight, who need more individual attention. *Rhiannon* spends an hour and a half studying science then switches to maths.

- When you are asked to give your opinions in the oral exam remember to justify them, saying why you think the way you do.

Reacting to the text

Do you think that home schooling is a good idea?
Would it have worked for you?
Can parents be good teachers?

Recording prepositions

1 Did you notice that the article was full of prepositions? To help learn prepositions these can be recorded in different categories in your notebook. Look for the following prepositions in the reading text. There is an example for each category.

Adjective + preposition	to be good/better __at__ (reading)
	to be/become bored _____
	to be fed up _____
Verb + preposition	to think __of__ (educating their daughter)
	to approve _____ (this flexible regime)
	to study _____ (a degree)
Noun + preposition	a reason __for__ (opting for home education)
	to have responsibility _____ (ensuring that)
	to have problems _____ (a subject)
Preposition + noun	__at__ the moment
	_____ average
	(to learn) _____ your own pace

2 Can you find any more prepositions in the text for each category?

3 Can you remember how the prepositions were used in the text?

Example:
'I think it was Cassie who was better than her classmates at reading.'
'Yes, and because of that she became bored with school.'

Language focus: Obligation, necessity and permission

1 Look at these extracts from the text and answer the questions **1–4** below.

a *At 8am, when other children <u>have to catch</u> trains or buses to school...*
b *Cassie... <u>had to stay</u> at home for a fortnight.*
c *Children <u>do not have to follow</u> the national curriculum.*
d *Parents <u>do not need to tell</u> the local authority.*
e *A parent <u>need not be</u> a qualified teacher.*
f *She <u>mustn't overstep</u> the line.*
g *She is well aware of what she <u>can</u> and <u>can't do</u>.*
h *She <u>is not</u> simply <u>allowed to do</u> just what she wants.*

1 Which underlined forms talk about what is permitted?
2 Which forms talk about what isn't permitted?
3 Which ones express necessity and/or obligation?
4 Which express a lack of necessity and/or obligation?

2 Who might say the following sentences?

a *You must hand in your homework tomorrow.*
b *We have to hand in our homework tomorrow.*

Why is *must* used in the first sentence and *have to* in the second?

3 In the following sentences the forms which express obligation, necessity and permission are all incorrect. Correct the mistakes and then check your answers in the Grammar reference on pages 209 and 210.

1 I have not to tidy my room up today; I did it yesterday.
2 Do you must make such a noise? I'm trying to concentrate!
3 Last week I must went to the hairdresser. Mum said my hair was far too long.
4 Did you be allowed to watch that film on telly last night?
5 They've changed my hours! Now I must start work at 7.30 instead of 8.30!
6 At my school we mustn't wear a tie if we don't want to.
7 You need prepare your bags tonight if your train leaves at 6.30 in the morning.
8 You really should to go and see that film.

4 *Make* (obligation) and *let* (permission)

Note that both of these verbs in the active are followed by the infinitive without *to*.

a Rewrite the following two sentences from the text in the passive.

1 The teacher still made her sound out the individual letters.
She was still _____ out the individual letters.

2 The school would not let her go up to a higher class.
She was not _____ go up to a higher class.

b Complete the following sentences using the correct form of *make*, *let* or *allow*.

1 I wanted to watch the film last night but I wasn't _____ to.

2 I'd love to come but I don't think my boss will _____ me have the day off work.

3 I hate cabbage but my mum _____ me eat it.

5 a Rhiannon is talking about being taught at home by her father. Complete the spaces with a verb from the box.

must	mustn't	have to	don't have to	need to

The best thing about home-schooling is that I
(1) _____ get up very early to go to school. OK, I **(2)** _____ start studying at eight o'clock but my school day's over at 2.30. I can carry on working in the afternoon, but I **(3)** _____ if I don't want to. Well, that's not quite true actually. If my dad feels I **(4)** _____ spend more time on a certain subject, he says, 'Well, I think you'd better carry on, don't you?' He's good like that, my dad; not strict. You know, he doesn't get all bossy and say 'You **(5)** _____ do some extra work this afternoon.' He just tries to persuade us. There is one thing I **(6)** _____ do, though and that's chat to my sisters when we're supposed to be working. Tess, Abigail and I all **(7)** _____ work alone in our own rooms at certain times of the day. James and Alicia, on the other hand, both **(8)** _____ spend more time working together with my dad, because they're a lot younger.

I think you'd better carry on...

b *Be supposed to* and *had better* both appear in the passage. Which one means 'should do because of a rule or because it is expected' and which means 'should do because it is a good idea'?

6 Complete the second sentence so it has a similar meaning to the first sentence, using the word given. **Do not change the word given.** You must use between two and five words, including the word given.

1 When I was young I wasn't allowed to watch much TV.
let
When I was young my parents _____ much TV.

2 She had to wash up before she could go out.
made
She _____ wash up before she could go out.

3 I'm never allowed to do what I want.
can
I _____ what I want.

4 Why can't we go to the party?
allowed
Why _____ go to the party?

5 In my opinion parents ought not to smack their children.
should
I don't think _____ their children.

6 There's no need for you to hand the report in until next week.
need
You _____ in the report until next week.

7 I think you should tell your parents exactly what happened.
better
I think you _____ your parents exactly what happened.

8 Do you know what the homework is?
supposed
Do you know what we _____ for homework?

7 ◐ Talk about the things you *have to, should* or *ought to* do and those things you *don't have to* or *aren't allowed to* do at:

- home
- school/college/work
- the weekend

Example: home:
I ought to tidy my room more often, but I never seem to find the time. I don't have to clean it, though. My mother does that for me.

Word formation: Nouns and adjectives

The adjectives of the nouns *tolerance* and *patience* are *tolerant* and *patient* and the verb form of *tolerant* is to *tolerate*.

1 Put the verb forms in the box below into the table according to whether they follow the pattern of *tolerance* (*-ance* and *-ant* endings) or *patience* (*-ence* and *-ent* endings). Write both the noun and adjective formed from each verb. One of them has been done for you as an example.

~~confide~~	ignore	obey	differ
signify	depend	*appear	*please

Verb	**Noun**	**Adjective**
tolerate	toler**ance**	toler**ant**
–	pati**ence**	pati**ent**
confide	*confidence*	*confident*

*These words do not follow exactly the same pattern as either *tolerant* or *patient*.

2 Where this is possible use the prefixes *un-*, *in-*, *im-*, or *dis-* to form the opposite of the adjectives you formed in exercise 1.

   Example: *in*tolerant

   How are the adverbs of each word formed?

(Use of English 1:) Word formation
FCE Part 5

For questions **1–10**, read the text below. Use the word given in capitals at the end of each line to form a word that fits in the space in the same line. There is an example at the beginning **(0)**.

A changed person

I don't see my teenage godson as **(0)** <u>frequently</u> as I did in the past   FREQUENT
and when I visited him and his family today I was **(1)** _____   PLEASE
surprised. He's changed **(2)** _____ since the last time I saw him.   SIGNIFY
Whereas he used to be such a horrible **(3)** _____ little boy, now   OBEY
he is extremely well-behaved and a **(4)** _____ to be with. He   PLEASE
seems to attach more **(5)** _____ now to what others might be   IMPORTANT
thinking of him and he takes more care over his **(6)** _____ .   APPEAR
He has developed greater **(7)** _____ in himself and his own   CONFIDE
judgement and he puts up stiff **(8)** _____ to his parents' advice   RESIST
and decisions if he feels they are wrong. **(9)** _____ he is   APPEAR
beginning to take an interest in girls and his mum tells me he's got a
girlfriend. These, it seems, are his first steps towards **(10)** _____   DEPEND
and it won't be very many years before he leaves home.

Listening 1:
FCE Part 4

True/False

1 Which of the following jobs or duties do you have to do?
How do you feel about doing them?

2 Richard and Louise are discussing how *they* feel about doing these jobs and which three they both think are the worst. Listen to their conversation and decide whether the following statements are true or false. Write **T** for True or **F** for False.

Richard does most of the washing up in his family.	1
Richard's father makes him clean his shoes.	2
Louise doesn't mind shopping for food.	3
Richard's grandparents are all still alive.	4
Louise prefers to wait for her grandparents to visit her.	5
Louise has to take her dog for a walk every day.	6
Louise's father cleans the car himself.	7

Which three do *you* think are the worst?
Are there any other things you have to do but don't like doing?

Speaking 2:
FCE Part 3

Collaborative task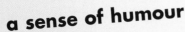

When a mixed group of teenagers and adults was asked what they thought were the qualities of a good parent they came up with the following list. Talk to each other about how necessary it is for a parent to have each of these qualities, and then decide which three are the most important.

a sense of humour   *an interest in pop music*   **good fashion sense**

fairness   *strictness*   **patience**   *tolerance*   energy   *the ability to listen*

How to go about it

- The task says *'Talk to each other about... and then decide...'*. In the exam listen carefully to *both parts* of the instructions. You can ask the examiner to repeat them if you want.
- You have about three minutes to talk, so don't make your decision too soon.
- Ask your partner one or two questions to give him or her the opportunity to speak.
- You can disagree with your partner.

Useful language
Listen to Richard and Louise's conversation again and tick the expressions you hear. You can then use some of the phrases in your discussion.

Starting the conversation
Which one shall we start with?
Let's see. Where shall we begin?
Let's talk about... first.
I think we should start with...

Moving to a new point
Which one now?
Shall we move on?
So, that could be one of our three.
Let's have a look at the next one.

Finishing the discussion
So, what have we decided?
Which ones do we agree on then?
We'll have to agree to disagree.
We both seem to agree on...

Vocabulary: The world of work

1 **a** The following verbs can all be used before the countable noun *job*.

get   *look for*   *apply for*   ~~*be out of*~~   *go for an interview for*

Put the verbs in the boxes below depending on the order they normally occur in. The first one has been done for you.

| be out of a job | → | | → | | → | | → | |

b The following verbs all indicate ways of ending a job. Put each one into an appropriate space below.

sacked   *made redundant*   *resigned*

1 Because of the economic crisis 50 workers were _____ in order to ensure the survival of the company.
2 She had become increasingly bored in her job, so she _____ from the company in order to take up a more challenging post.
3 He was _____ for stealing and he's finding it difficult to get another job.

2 **a** Which of the verbs below is not normally used before the countable noun *career?*

to change   *to give up your*   *to devote yourself to your*   *to study a*   *to start a*

b Which of the nouns below is not normally used after the verb *to earn?*

a high salary   *a weekly wage*   *a good living*   *a competition*   *a lot of money*

3 What is the difference in meaning between the following?

to work shifts   *to work long hours*   *to work overtime*
to work part-time   *to work full-time*   *to work flexitime*

4 Can you identify the jobs in the photographs?

5 Describe the jobs in the pictures in exercise 4, but without saying the name of the job. Your partner has to decide which one you are describing. Use the vocabulary below to help you.

A Skills
telephone   computer   artistic   organizational   language

B Adjectives for personal qualities
patient   confident   intelligent   brave   well-educated   talented
strong   creative   hard-working   polite   cheerful   fit

C Adjectives for jobs
well-paid   responsible   satisfying   challenging
badly-paid   tiring   unpleasant   monotonous

Listening 2:
FCE Part 2

Blank filling 🔲

You will hear a radio interview with Allan Nicholls, station officer at Hove Fire Station. For questions **1–10** on page 61, complete the sentences which summarize what he says.

Don't forget!

Underline the correct alternative in each of the following sentences.

- You **need to/don't need to** write more than three words for each answer.
- You **should/shouldn't** write a word or phrase that you actually hear.

- You **need/don't need** to rephrase.
- Minor spelling errors **can/can't** be made, but the words you write **need/don't need** to be recognizable to the examiner, so you **should/shouldn't** check your spelling.
- You **can/can't** expect to hear the answers in the same order as the questions.

Before you listen to the recording, read through all the questions and try to predict the type of information you will hear for each one.

Potential recruits are not required to have any [1].

They do not have to satisfy any [2] requirements.

However, there are tests to measure the strength of their [3].

Hove Fire Station currently employs [4] women.

After working a series of day and night shifts firefighters have [5].

At the Watch Parade they have to [6].

Then they carry out a thorough inspection of the [7] as well as the equipment.

Most call-outs occur during [8].

Firefighters can spend [9] clearing up after a fire.

Being a firefighter is a [10] job.

Use of English 2: Multiple choice cloze
FCE Part 1

For questions **1–15**, read the text below and underline which answer **A, B, C** or **D** best fits each space. There is an example at the beginning **(0)**.

Before you do the task, make sure you read the whole text through first. As you read, answer the following question:
How does Roger Press feel about his decision to change career?

A more commercial tune

Roger Press, 40, has **(0)** ___*B*___ his career. After spending five years **(1)** _____ a concert pianist he has gone into business, recently **(2)** _____ up his own company.

'After leaving university I decided to **(3)** _____ myself to a career in music. I loved performing but it was very hard **(4)** _____ . I played at concerts in Europe and America, made recordings and got good **(5)** _____ . But after a while I felt I had gone as **(6)** _____ as I could. Unless you're one of the world's top pianists, it's difficult to earn a good **(7)** _____ and I wasn't one of the greatest.

I have always thought that it's important to be commercial, to participate and compete in the modern world. So although **(8)** _____ on was a difficult decision, having reached it I felt relieved in many **(9)** _____ . When I **(10)** _____ up my performing career, people around me were more sad and disappointed than I was. But I felt free and **(11)** _____ I knew I was getting serious about life.

After getting a **(12)** _____ in business administration I **(13)** _____ the recording company EMI and started their classical video division, producing programmes about famous artists. A year ago I left EMI and formed a new company, New Media Systems, which **(14)** _____ in multimedia programmes.

Now that I run my own business I am in control of my life and I can feel proud of my achievements. Although the stress is high and I work **(15)** _____ hours, the stress involved in piano playing was much worse. It took physical, emotional and mental skills. I prefer the pressures I live with now.'

0 A moved	B changed	C adjusted	D stopped
1 A like	B working	C how	D as
2 A giving	B setting	C forming	D bringing
3 A devote	B take	C assign	D employ
4 A job	B effort	C work	D career
5 A reviews	B critics	C reports	D praise
6 A soon	B often	C far	D much
7 A life	B living	C money	D payment
8 A changing	B getting	C continuing	D moving
9 A factors	B forms	C manners	D ways
10 A took	B brought	C gave	D put
11 A lastly	B at last	C at the end	D lately
12 A qualification	B title	C graduate	D grade
13 A enrolled	B applied	C attended	D joined
14 A specializes	B focuses	C concentrates	D dedicates
15 A overtime	B large	C long	D bonus

Writing:
FCE Part 2

Letters: An application

1 Read the following Writing Part 2 instructions.

You have seen the following advertisement in an international newspaper.
Write a **letter of application**, giving your reasons for applying and saying why you think you would be suitable for the job.

You should write between **120 and 180** words in an appropriate style. Do not write any addresses.

2 Read this model letter of application for the job. Do you think the applicant would be suitable? Give reasons for your answer.

Camp GB,
Wargrave,
Wokingham
RG11 9PA

Dear Sir or Madam,
I would like to apply for the job of Camp Helper as advertised in this month's issue of Recruitment International.

I like working with children very much and I would enjoy the challenge of organizing activities for them on one of your camps. Moreover, I have just finished school and in October I will be starting a degree course in English. I am therefore very keen to improve my language skills in an English-speaking country before I go to university.

My interests include basketball, tennis and orienteering and I can also play the guitar. For the past seven years I have attended summer camps in my country with the scouts and last year I helped to run a number of events, including an orienteering competition and a kite-making workshop.

I feel I have the necessary patience and energy to make a positive and enthusiastic contribution to your camps and I hope you will consider my application favourably.

I am available for interview at any time and look forward to hearing from you soon.

Yours faithfully
Costas Stergis

We are looking for

CAMP HELPERS

to work in the UK on one of our International Summer Camps

Applicants should be hard-working, energetic and able to organize activities for young children in the following areas:

▲ workshops
▲ sports
▲ outdoor pursuits
▲ indoor and outdoor games

Minimum age: 18
Some knowledge of English essential
Previous experience preferred

Write in English stating relevant skills and experience to:
Camp GB, Wargrave, Wokingham RG11 9PA

3 Read the letter again and find the sentence or sentences which cover each of the following points.

a reasons for writing the letter   *I would like to apply for the job of Camp Helper*

b reasons for applying for the job

c suitability for the job

d experience

e language skills

f other relevant skills/interests

g age

h closing comments

4 Read the following Writing Part 2 question. You have just read this job advertisement.

Coastal Campsites require

- Reception Assistants
- Bar and Restaurant Staff
- Shop Staff
- Gardeners
- Swimming Pool Attendants

to work in the UK on our busy, five-star campsites this summer.

Applicants must have a reasonable command of English and be willing to work hard.

- Relevant skills and experience an advantage
- Good pay and conditions
- Free board and accommodation

Apply in writing to:
Coastal Campsites, 79 North Road, Brighton BN1 6TF

Write a **letter of application** in **120–180** words to Coastal Campsites applying for one of the jobs. Say why you would be suitable for the job and ask for more details about the working hours and the length of contract. Do not write any addresses.

5 Look at pages 200 and 201. You will find one student's answer to question 4, together with further work on using formal expressions in letters of application.

6 Now write your own letter, applying for one of the other jobs available at Coastal Campsites. Say why you would be suitable for the job and ask for more details about the pay and the accommodation.

Don't forget!

- Write in a formal style using some of the expressions in the model letter and in exercise 2 on page 201.
- Do not use contractions.
- Try to use indirect rather than direct questions in formal letters.
- Organize your letter into logical paragraphs.

(5) Review

Open cloze: Prepositions

For questions **1–15**, read the text below and think of the word which best fits each space. Use only **one** word in each space. In this exercise, each missing word is a preposition. There is an example at the beginning **(0)**.

Don't forget!

● Always read the text through once before you start to complete the spaces in order to gain an overall understanding of the passage. For this text, answer the following two questions:

How does talking to babies and young children benefit them?
What is one of the main obstacles to a child's progress, according to the text?

Gift of the gab

Chatting to babies in a particular way boosts their intelligence and gives them a head start **(0)** _in_ life, a new study has found. Speech and language therapist Dr Sally Ward selected 140 nine-month-old children from Manchester. She then gave 70 of the parents detailed advice **(1)** _____ the best way to communicate **(2)** _____ their child and left the other 70 without guidance. The 'communicating' parents were told to spend at least 30 minutes every day talking to their child, **(3)** _____ any background noise, about subjects which their infant might take an interest **(4)** _____ . More than six years later, and after regular checks had been kept **(5)** _____ their progress, the children had IQ tests. Those in the talking group were, **(6)** _____ average, a year and three months ahead **(7)** _____ the other group. Nine children had IQs in the gifted category, whereas none in the non-talking group was as bright.

In a separate study at the American Academy of Paediatrics, experts have warned **(8)** _____ the dangers of children under the age of two watching television. Research has shown that exposure to television is responsible **(9)** _____ anything from delayed speech to Attention Deficit Hyperactivity Disorder. The problem **(10)** _____ television is that it confuses infants, who block out the background noise coming **(11)** _____ it. They consequently learn to ignore all noise and this includes speech. Paediatric and language specialists also disapprove **(12)** _____ radio, which has much the same effect **(13)** _____ a child's language development.

The main finding of the report was that **(14)** _____ very early ages children should not be allowed to watch any television at all. Parents have good reasons **(15)** _____ ignoring their youngsters' protests and simply switching off.

Word formation

Write down as many forms as possible of the words below.

Example: depend (v) *dependent (adj), independent (adj), independently (adv), dependence (n), independence (n), dependant (n), dependable (adj), dependably (adv), dependability (n)*

1 differ   (n)   _____
2 appear   (v)   _____
3 frequent (adj) _____
4 please   (v)   _____
5 tolerate (v)   _____

Vocabulary: The world of work

Use the clues to help you complete the grid. When you have all the answers you will find an extra item of vocabulary for number 12 down. Write your own clue for number 12 down in the space provided.

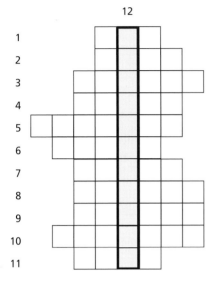

1 It's a good job but I don't _____ paid very much.
2 We had to _____ him. He was stealing money from the cash till.
3 After 20 years as a teacher she decided to change _____ and become a social worker.
4 You don't have to have a _____ of humour to work here but it certainly helps.
5 I didn't like working for someone else, so I decided to set up my own _____ .
6 This job sounds good. Why don't you _____ for it? You've got nothing to lose.
7 Don't phone her during the day. She's working the night _____ at the hospital so she'll be asleep.
8 He gave up his job in order to _____ himself to his painting.
9 To get to the top in this profession you need to have good organizational _____ .
10 There's a lot of stress involved in _____ your own business.
11 The people who work for me get a weekly _____ of £315.
12 _____

Use of English: FCE Part 4

Error correction

For questions **1–15**, read the text below and look carefully at each line. Some of the lines are correct and some have a word which should not be there. If a line is correct, put a tick (✔) in the space at the end of the line. If a line has a word which should not be there, write the extra word in the space. There are two examples at the beginning (**0** and **00**).

Maternal patience

0	I can now understand perfectly why people say you need to have	✔
00	had limitless patience when you have children. The child is no problem;	*had*
1	it's the relatives and other adults that make me to feel like screaming and shouting	_____
2	in despair. Why does everyone think they know better than you do? Advice is	_____
3	given in all forms and the most of it is either mildly irritating or downright	_____
4	lunatic. I've been told that my daughter looks like a boy and I should to put	_____
5	some pink clothes on her; that in temperatures as high as 30°C she ought to have	_____
6	socks on; that she's thirsty and needs drink a little fruit juice (at two weeks	_____
7	old it probably would have to killed her!). When changing my daughter's	_____
8	nappy I have received disapproving looks because I don't can use talcum powder,	_____
9	and this advice came from a man whose last child he was born 40 years ago	_____
10	and was brought up by a nanny. One interfering relative even went so far as to say	_____
11	that no mother of a small baby should not have long hair: for some unknown reason	_____
12	she wanted me to have my hair cut! Unfortunately, all new mothers have to	_____
13	go through this stage and some may be find it difficult to cope with the relentless	_____
14	and seemingly pointless advice. If you have suffer the same situation as I do,	_____
15	remember that no matter how angry you get you shouldn't never smack your	_____
	relatives. It only makes them worse.	

Multiple matching

You are going to read an article about family mealtimes. For questions **1–13**, choose from the people (**A–E**). The people may be chosen more than once. When more than one answer is required, these may be given in any order. There is an example at the beginning (**0**).

How to go about it

- Look at the title and introductory sentence and try to predict what the text will say. Read the text quite quickly and check your predictions.

- The key words in the example question (**0**) have been underlined. Underline the key words in the other questions.

- Now read the text again and try to find the answers, thinking about the key words in the questions. Underline the part of the text which you think gives the answer. This has been done for you for the part of the text which relates to the example question (**0**).

A The writer   **B** Gerry   **C** Andrew   **D** James   **E** Ben

Which of the people A–E

sees the <u>positive side of arguments</u> at the meal table?	**0**	*A*
is influenced by past experiences?	**1**	
doesn't let his children watch television at mealtimes?	**2**	
doesn't mind what his children talk about?	**3**	
says his family argues at mealtimes?	**4**	**5**
doesn't see as much of his children as he used to?	**6**	
rarely eats with his children?	**7**	
says his family eat all together only on certain days?	**8**	**9**
sees family meals as preparation for eating in other situations?	**10**	
organizes his working day to be with his family for meals?	**11**	
has children who complain about what they have to eat?	**12**	**13**

Family Feuds
— or just lunch?

If you find family meals tense and unpleasant, you're not alone. Alan Jefferson explains.

The nation's eating habits have changed and many families no longer eat together on a regular basis. To be honest, this doesn't strike me as particularly surprising. Lunchtime last Sunday in my own home consisted of my two-year-old son happily throwing his food on the floor whilst – yet again – his older brother and sister protested loudly about the vegetables they were being made to eat.

Despite the noise and chaos, though, we still prefer to have meals as a family. On weekdays that's difficult as there are too many things going on and there just isn't enough time for me and my wife to sit with the children at breakfast. Only our youngest is with his mother for lunch and the children's supper is too early for me to participate. But we do our best at weekends.

If, as some research shows, parents now talk to their children for an average of just 12 minutes a day, then our decision to eat together as much as possible is more than justified. Whilst the quality of the kitchen table chat is not particularly high – a mixture of bad jokes, song lyrics and gossip – we are at least communicating, which is the main thing, so it doesn't matter to me what the topic of conversation is.

Of course, family meals can be tense and we don't always see eye to eye. But for me, arguing together is an essential part of family life and all part of learning to get on with each other.

Gerry, a 35-year-old father of two young girls, would not agree. He had enough of stressful family meals as a child and now sees them as both impractical and undesirable.

'I hardly ever get home early enough to eat with my kids, but I don't particularly mind that. It has a lot to do with my own childhood memories. Mealtimes were very formal occasions, and they provided my parents with the opportunity to interrogate me about everything I'd done that day. I used to feel very uncomfortable. Later, during my teenage years, the meal table became the scene of terrible rows. Of course, I'd like to spend less time rushing around and more time with my family, but I don't miss family meals at all.'

Andrew finds family meals difficult, but necessary. 'We're always having rows, particularly when the kids start moaning about what's on their plate,' he says. 'Trying to keep everyone happy isn't easy, especially with three children under nine who all have different tastes and a teenage stepdaughter who would much rather be eating her dinner on the sofa in front of the TV. But eating with others is an important social skill. I want my

children to get used to doing it in the home so that they will know how to eat in public.'

James, the father of two teenage boys, says: 'The older my kids become, the less contact I have with them and the more important family meals become. They're often the only opportunity we get to talk.'

As a travelling sales representative, James is responsible for his own time management and he tries to organize his appointments in such a way that he can return to his Liverpool home in time for dinner with his family at 7.00 pm. 'I've made it a priority,' he says, 'because I feel that mealtimes are an important point of family contact.'

So have **Ben** and Angela, who manage to get their four children aged 5 to 16 around the table for weekend family meals. 'We try to keep everyone at the table for at least half an hour on Saturdays and Sundays. We have a telly in the kitchen but the kids aren't allowed to have it on when we are eating there – that would make the whole thing rather pointless,' says Ben.

He recalls a recent trip to the States, where his American friends had the television on all day. 'Different members of the family would wander in at different times, grab something from the fridge and eat alone, always in front of the TV. I think it's a shame that Britain is becoming much more like that now.'

Reacting to the text

How often do you eat with all your family?
Do you have the television on when you eat?
Are mealtimes in your country becoming more like those described in the last paragraph?
Which way of eating do you prefer? Why?

Language focus 1: *Too* and *enough*

1 Look at these sentences from the reading text.

*On weekdays... there are **too** many things going on and there just isn't **enough** time for me and my wife to sit with the children at breakfast.*
*...the children's supper is **too** early for me to participate.*
*I hardly ever get home early **enough** to eat with my kids.*

2 Choose the correct alternative in each of these sentences.
   a *Too* is followed by **nouns/adjectives and adverbs**.
   b *Too much* or *too many* is followed by **nouns/adjectives and adverbs**.
   c *Enough* is used **before/after** nouns.
   d *Enough* is used **before/after** adjectives and adverbs.

3 Look at the sentences in exercise 1. What do you notice about the structure of the sentence after *too* and *enough*?

For a summary of the rules for using *too* and *enough* read the Grammar reference on page 210.

Practice

1 Write six sentences of your own using the phrases in the box below.

Example: enough time – *I didn't have enough time to do all my homework last night.*

| enough money | too difficult | strong enough |
| too much noise | old enough | too many people |

2 Complete the second sentence so that it has a similar meaning to the first sentence, using the word given. **Do not change the word given.** You must use between two and five words, including the word given.

1 I couldn't hear what they were saying because they were speaking so quietly.
too
They were speaking _____ hear what they were saying.

2 He couldn't see over the wall because he was so small.
enough
He was _____ see over the wall.

3 We'll need more eggs if we want to make an omelette.
enough
There _____ make an omelette.

4 I can't drink this tea because it's too sweet.
sugar
There _____ in this tea for me to drink it.

5 I didn't go into the bar because it was too crowded.
too
I didn't go into the bar because _____ _____ people.

Vocabulary 1: Phrasal verbs

A Romance

1 The following sentences tell the unhappy love story of a young couple. Match a sentence beginning **1–6** with an ending **a–f**. The first one has been done for you.

① It would be our first 'anniversary' today. We started **going**
2 It was her smile which first attracted me and I **fell**
3 We were in a disco. Someone told me she had just **split**
4 We shared the same sense of humour and we **got**
5 Unfortunately, we had an argument last week and we **fell**
6 I think about her a lot, so I suppose I haven't **got**

a up with her boyfriend, so I asked her to dance.
b on with each other really well, always laughing and joking together.
c out with each other exactly one year ago.
d over her yet. I miss her very much.
e for her immediately. It was love at first sight.
f out with each other. We haven't spoken since.

2 Write the infinitive of each of the phrasal verbs from exercise 1 next to its meaning.

   1 to argue and stop being friendly with someone _____
   2 to end a relationship with someone _____
   3 to have a romantic relationship with someone _____
   4 to have a good relationship with someone _____
   5 to fall in love with someone _____
   6 to recover after the end of a relationship with someone _____

B Family

1 Work out the meaning of the phrasal verbs in **bold** in the following sentences. Use the context of the sentence to help you.

   1 Her parents died when she was very young, so her grandparents **brought** her **up** as if she was their own daughter.

   2 I was born in England but I **grew up** in France; I lived in Paris until I was 18.

   3 My brother was very naughty as a child. He **got up to** all sorts of things he knew he shouldn't, just to annoy my parents.

   4 His mother **told** him **off** for breaking the plate and he started crying. He didn't like it when she was angry.

   5 My father is an important figure to me. I have always **looked up to** him because of his patience and calmness.

   6 They felt they had been badly **let down**. They had given their son so much freedom and he had 'thanked' them by becoming a thief.

2 What is the infinitive form of each of the phrasal verbs in exercise 1?

3 Write six sentences, each containing one of the phrasal verbs from Vocabulary 1. Leave a space instead of writing the phrasal verb and ask your partner to complete the sentences with the correct phrasal verb.

Speaking 1:
FCE Part 3

Collaborative task

Marriage

Parents and children

Team games

Bosses and employees

People and animals

Here are some pictures of different types of relationships. Talk with your partner about the positive and negative aspects of each relationship and then decide which two are the most important to you.

   1 Write down at least three of the phrasal verbs from the Vocabulary exercises which you think might be useful.

   2 Now add three expressions from the Useful language section on page 59 of Unit 5.

   3 Try to use all of this language in your conversation.

Listening 1:
FCE Part 3 **Multiple matching** 😀

1 Look at these photographs of sisters.

Which photograph shows twins?
What type of relationship do you think the sisters have with each other?

2 You will hear five of the people in the photos talking about their sisters. For questions **1–5**, choose from the list **A–F** what each speaker says about her relationship with her sister. Use the letters only once. There is one extra letter you do not need to use.

How to go about it

● The key words in the questions have been underlined. However, if you hear one of these words or phrases do not assume that the question which contains those words is the answer.

● Listen carefully both times before making your final decision.

A Her sister <u>teased</u> her.   Speaker 1 ☐
B They <u>don't get on</u> with each other.   Speaker 2 ☐
C They <u>compete</u> with each other.   Speaker 3 ☐
D They have always led very <u>different lives</u>.   Speaker 4 ☐
E They were <u>treated differently</u> by other people.   Speaker 5 ☐
F She <u>protected</u> her sister.

3 Can you match any of the speakers to the women in the photographs?

Speaking 2:
FCE Part 1 **Interview** ⬤

In Speaking Part 1 you may be asked to talk about your family. Talk to your partner, answering the following questions.

Don't forget!

Say as much as possible about each question. One word answers are not enough!

• Do you have a large family?
• How many brothers and sisters have you got?
• If you don't have any brothers or sisters, what are the advantages of being an only child?
• Do you have many cousins? Do you get on well with them?
• Describe the relationship you have with one of your family members.
• Do you take after your mother or your father? In what ways?
• Do you see your grandparents very often?

Language focus 2: Defining relative clauses

Defining relative clauses contain information which is essential for our understanding of the whole sentence.

1 Look at the following extracts from the listening exercise and answer the questions.

I moved into a flat with a boy <u>who</u> played drums in a punk band.
I wore clothes <u>that</u> got all the neighbours talking.

The underlined words are relative pronouns. What alternative pronouns can be used?

Can the relative pronoun be omitted from these two sentences? Why/Why not?

2 *She'd come home with blackberries she'd picked and tales of wild rabbits she'd seen.*

Two relative pronouns have been omitted from this sentence. Where could they be inserted and which ones could be used? Why is it possible to leave them out in this case?

3 *The woman <u>to whom</u> I spoke had no idea what was going on.*
The woman <u>who</u> I spoke <u>to</u> had no idea what was going on.

Which of these sentences is more formal?

Can the relative pronoun be omitted in either of them?

4 Complete these sentences using *when, where, why* or *whose*.
   a What's the name of the place _____ we had that accident last year?
   b The reason _____ people from Mediterranean countries live so long is because they eat so well.
   c I'll always remember the day _____ I got my first job.
   d That's the woman _____ husband you spoke to on the phone.

Ⓖ Check your answers and read more about defining relative clauses on pages 210 and 211 of the Grammar reference.

Practice

Complete each of the spaces below with an appropriate relative pronoun or relative adverb. Decide in which sentences there is more than one possibility and whether the word can be left out.

1 I'd like to go back to the restaurant _____ we celebrated your birthday last year.
2 Have you been to the new cyber café _____ has just opened in the town centre?
3 Ironic, really. The person _____ car they stole had just finished a three-year prison sentence for car theft.
4 Have you finished the book _____ I lent you?
5 I wish I could remember the name of the man _____ sold me this computer.
6 The only thing _____ worries me is the cost. Will we be able to afford it?
7 Here's that phone number _____ you wanted.
8 I was born in 1969. That was the year _____ the first man landed on the Moon.

Reading

Read the following text about a type of club and answer the following questions. Who goes to these clubs and what do they do there? What are the benefits according to
a Ben Sassen, aged 17?   **b** his father?

Rock of ages

It may sound surprising, given that you'd imagine the average child wouldn't be seen dead near his or her parents on a disco floor, but there is an amazing new trend towards families going clubbing together. Child-friendly venues are appearing everywhere, the main difference being that they are predominantly alcohol- and smoke-free zones and parents and their children actually get up on the dance floor together to have a bop.

The Whirl-Y-Gig club, which held its first family club nights over 15 years ago, is currently one of the most popular places for different generations to let their hair down together. It plays credible music, there's a cool atmosphere and children under 12 are allowed in free. Ben Sassen, 17, first started going there with his father, Michael, 36, when he was just six years old. His parents were separated and he was then living with his mother, so it was a good opportunity for father and son to have some fun together.

'Occasionally I was embarrassed that my father was there,' says Ben. 'But usually friends thought it was great because of the relationship I had with him. It's one thing to get on well with your parents, but another to have something specific in common, that you can sit down and talk to them about.'

For Michael, who dances with every bit as much energy and enthusiasm as his teenage son, the experience brought back memories of his own youth. 'It was certainly an interesting experience watching someone go through the same stages as I did growing up and to have a unique insight into what he was doing and thinking about.'

 Would you consider going to a club like the Whirl-Y-Gig? Why/Why not?
Is there a big generation gap between children and parents in your country?

Vocabulary 2: *Have*

A Expressions with *have*

1 In the text on page 71 the expression 'to have a bop' is an informal way of saying 'to have a dance' or 'to dance'. Look at the text and find four more expressions with have.

to have _____   to have _____
to have _____   to have _____

2 Talk to your partner about the following:

- something that you have difficulty doing
- someone who has had a strong influence on you
- somewhere you go to have a good time
- something you would like to have more time to do
- something you would like to have the power to change
- something you have in common with a brother, sister or friend

3 What does 'it' refer to in each of the following sentences? Match each item in the box to an appropriate sentence **1–6**. There may be more than one possible answer.

a headache   hair   a scarf   a tooth   something private   a book

1 Can I have it back next week, please?
2 You had it on this morning when we left the house.
3 I'm afraid you'll have to have it taken out.
4 That's nice; where did you have it done?
5 It's got nothing to do with you – mind your own business!
6 I see, and how long have you had it?

Can you think of any other possible meanings for *it* in each of the sentences?

4 With your partner make up a short dialogue which includes one of the sentences from exercise 3. Compare your dialogue with those of other students in the class.

B Causative *have*

1 In **1** and **2** below, explain the difference in meaning between the two sentences.

1 a She wants to dye her hair red.
   b She wants to have her hair dyed red.
2 a He took a photo of his daughter.
   b He had a photo taken of his daughter.

1 b and **2 b** contain the causative use of *have*. Complete the following sentence:

To use this structure we need the appropriate form of the verb *to* _____ + the object + the _____ of the main verb.

Read more about causative *have* on page 210 of the Grammar reference.

2 In questions **1–6**, write a suitable form of *have* in the first space and the correct form of the verb in brackets in the second. The first one has been done for you.

1 Do you think it would be interesting _to have_ your head completely _shaved_ (shave)?
2 Do you like _____ your photo _____ (take)?
3 Would you like _____ any part of your body _____ (pierce)?
4 When was the last time you _____ a tooth _____ (fill)?
5 When are you next _____ your hair _____ (cut)?
6 Do you know anyone who _____ their house _____ (break) into?

3 Ask and answer questions **1–6** in exercise 2.
   Example:
   A: Do you think it would be interesting to have your head completely shaved?
   B: Well, I think it would be OK in summer, but not very practical in winter. I suppose one important advantage is that you wouldn't have to dry your hair after a shower.

Language focus 3: Non-defining relative clauses

1 Look at the following two sentences from the reading text.

a *The Whirl-Y-Gig club, which held its first family club nights over 15 years ago, is currently one of the most popular places for different generations to let their hair down together.*

b *For Michael, who dances with every bit as much energy and enthusiasm as his teenage son, the experience brought back memories of his own youth.*

Each of these sentences contains two separate ideas.

a **Main idea:** The Whirl-Y-Gig club is currently one of the most popular places for different generations to let their hair down together.

Second idea: The Whirl-Y-Gig club held its first family club nights over 15 years ago.

b **Main idea:** For Michael the experience brought back memories of his own youth.

Second idea: Michael dances with every bit as much energy and enthusiasm as his teenage son.

The information contained in the second idea is not essential to our understanding of the meaning of the main idea. A relative clause which contains non-essential information is called a *non*-defining relative clause.

2 Underline the correct alternative in the following rules for non-defining relative clauses.
a *who* or *which* **can/cannot** be replaced by *that*
b the relative pronoun **can/cannot** be omitted
c commas **are/are not** used

Practice

For **1–5** below, link the ideas contained in the two sentences to form one sentence. Use an appropriate relative pronoun (*who, which, whose*) or relative adverb (*when, where*) and make any other necessary changes. Don't forget to add commas.

Example:
Main idea: Michael has always enjoyed the mixed-generation nights.
Second idea: Michael first took Ben to the club when he was six.

Michael, who first took Ben to the club when he was six, has always enjoyed the mixed-generation nights.

1 **Main idea:** We spent the weekend in York.
Second idea: My mother was born in York.

2 **Main idea:** My best friend has just got married.
Second idea: My best friend always said she wanted to stay single.

3 **Main idea:** My oldest sister lives in Thessaloniki.
Second idea: My oldest sister's husband is Greek.

4 **Main idea:** We're having our holiday in September.
Second idea: Everywhere is a lot less crowded in September.

5 **Main idea:** His daughter borrowed the car.
Second idea: He wasn't very happy about the fact that his daughter borrowed the car.

Open cloze: Relative clauses

For questions **1–8** read the text below, which is the continuation of the text on mixed-generation clubs. Complete each of the spaces with either a relative pronoun (*who, which, that, whose*) or a relative adverb (*when, where*). If there is more than one possibility, or the word can be left out, you should also indicate this. There is an example at the beginning **(0)**.

Unfortunately, those clubs (0) *which/that* depend on serving alcohol to make a profit are less keen on the idea of allowing youngsters in. But places such as Whirl-Y-Gig, (1) _____ opens from 9pm–2am, aim to prove them wrong. The Barefoot Boogie, in Highgate, north west London is another venue (2) _____ hosts regular mixed-generation nights. Elizabeth Payne, (3) _____ runs the twice-monthly club, says it's a unique evening for everyone. 'It is one of the only places (4) _____ I can go to with my three children, (5) _____ ages range from two to fourteen, confident that we'll all have a good time,' she says. Places (6) _____ parents can take their children and know they'll be safe are useful for those days (7) _____ you have trouble getting a babysitter. But do not mistake it for a crèche. Payne had to circulate a memo (8) _____ explained to parents that they should only go if their children also wanted a night out.

P 61 FB

Vocabulary 3: Describing people

A Personality

1 The following adjectives can all be used to describe a person's character. Which of them are positive and which are negative? Make two groups in your notebook.

sociable	mean	tolerant	patient	sensitive
polite	sincere	selfish	decisive	lazy
reliable	cheerful	practical	mature	
bad-tempered	adventurous	moody	sensible	

2 Arrange the adjectives in exercise 1 into the columns below according to the prefix which is used to form the negative. If none of the prefixes is used for a particular word, write a new word which expresses the opposite idea.

un-	in-	im-	different word
unsociable	_____	_____	*mean – generous*
_____	_____	_____	_____
_____	_____	_____	_____
_____	_____	_____	_____
_____	_____	_____	_____

3 Think of two people you know, for example a relative and a friend, and describe what these people are like, using the adjectives you have just studied to help you.

B Appearance

1 One adjective in each group is not normally used before the noun in capital letters. Underline the adjective which does not fit.

1 flowing   untidy   bald   shoulder-length   straight   spiky   HAIR
2 dark   hazel   sparkling   almond-shaped   piercing   pierced   EYES
3 wrinkled   freckled   thinning   round   tanned   expressive   FACE
4 smooth   pale   dark   healthy   well-built   spotty   COMPLEXION

Which of these features can you see in the photographs above?

2 What is the difference between the words in each of the following groups?

a fat   plump   overweight
b thin   slim   skinny

3 Work in pairs. Take it in turns to compare and contrast two people in the photographs above and say which of the two people you would prefer to meet and why. As well as describing physical appearance and clothes, you should also talk about personality.

Writing:
FCE Part 2

Descriptions

1 Read the following Writing Part 2 instructions.

Your teacher has asked you to write about someone you met for the first time in unusual circumstances. Explain what happened and describe the person. Write your **story** in **120–180** words.

2 Listening 2: FCE Part 4

You will hear three teenagers discussing the Writing Part 2 question above and deciding what they are going to write about. For questions **1–7**, decide whether the idea was stated or not and mark **Y** for Yes, or **N** for No.

Marion had nearly reached her destination. | **1** |
Eilean didn't know how to mend the car. | **2** |
Steven and Marcia met in the theatre. | **3** |
Steven didn't do what he was supposed to. | **4** |
Marion and Eilean still write to each other. | **5** |
Karen invented her story. | **6** |
Karen was comfortable during the rescue. | **7** |

3 Read the following model answer to the Writing Part 2 question in exercise 1. Who wrote it: Marion, Steven or Karen? The person who wrote it decided to make some changes to the original story. What factual differences do you notice between the story in the recording and the one in the model?

Last summer while my parents and I were driving to the coast to spend our holiday with some relatives our car broke down. After we had been on the road for nearly three hours steam began to pour from the engine and we had to stop. My parents, who know nothing about mecanics, were extremly relieved when another driver pulled over and offered to help.

When his daughter Eilean stepped out of the passenger seat to stretch her legs I couldn't help noticeing how incredibly tall she was. I wondered how she had managed to fit into the car. But perhaps her most striking feature was her spiky green hair, wich seemed to grow out of her head like grass. That and her colourfull 'hippy' clothes were as bright and cheerfull as she was and we spent the whole time chating and laughing as if we had known each other for years.

We've kept in touch and she always says, rather misteriously, that Destiny brought us together. I must admit, I never thought I'd make a friend on the hard shoulder of a moterway.

4 The model answer contains ten spelling mistakes. Read the story again and try to find and correct the ten mistakes.

5 Organization
- The story in the model contains three paragraphs. What is the purpose of each of the paragraphs?
- What proportion of the answer
  a explains what happened?
  b describes the person?

Narrative elements
- As we saw in Unit 4, in addition to well organized paragraphs a good narrative should contain the following elements:
  a a variety of past tenses
  b a wide range of vocabulary
  c appropriate linking words (including relative clauses)
  Find examples of each of these in the model story.

Descriptive elements
- When we describe someone we can talk about their physical appearance, personality, clothes, actions (what they do or say) and their interests. Which of these appear in the model?

Now you are ready to write your story.

Don't forget!
- Plan your answer first.
- Check you have answered both parts of the question.
- Check your work for spelling and grammatical mistakes when you have finished writing.

⑥ Review

Error correction: Relative clauses

1 Read the text below about strange wedding ceremonies, ignoring any mistakes you find for the moment. Which ceremony do you find the strangest?

Ceremonies with a difference

0	Saying 'I do' at the bottom of a large fish tank which may seem an odd	*which*
00	way to get married but since 1994, when the Marriage Act changed the	✓
1	rules for civil weddings, strange ceremonies can have become increasingly	_____
2	popular and couples can now marry almost anywhere they choose them.	_____
3	Before 1994 couples followed rules written in 1837, which said they had to	_____
4	marry in the parish where they lived there. These rules did not exist in	_____
5	Scotland, and Gretna Green, which it is just across the border, was the place	_____
6	for English couples to go if they needed a secret wedding. Although there is	_____
7	no longer any reason for to go to Gretna Green, the 4,500 couples that still	_____
8	get married there each year are looking for a little romance, which they do	_____
9	not think they can find it in English registry offices. Couples who want to	_____
10	get married in more exclusive surroundings only can choose from as many	_____
11	as 4000 different venues which ranging from an opera house to a castle. In	_____
12	Tampa Bay, Florida in 1997, 24 couples got married hanging upside down	_____
13	on a rollercoaster. In Britain one couple wed while were running the London	_____
14	Marathon, and another, whose ceremony took its place at their local football	_____
15	stadium, watched to their team win 3–0 before going off on their honeymoon.	_____

2 In the text above some of the lines are correct and some have a word which should not be there. If a line is correct, put a tick (✓) in the space at the end of the line. If a line has an extra word which should not be there, write the word in the space. There are two examples at the beginning (**0** and **00**).

Vocabulary

A Phrasal verbs

Complete the spaces in sentences **1–8** below with the correct form of an appropriate phrasal verb. Use the verbs and particles from the boxes.

fall	bring	get	look
let	tell	fall	get

out	over	for	off
on	up	down	up

1 When I kept getting into trouble at school, my parents understandably felt I had _____ them _____ .

2 He was _____ _____ for hitting his sister and made to apologize to her.

3 I was _____ _____ by my parents to believe that honesty is the best policy.

4 I was extremely disappointed when I found out that my uncle had spent three years in prison: I had always _____ _____ to him and considered him a role model.

5 I don't _____ _____ very well with my mother-in-law. I don't think she's forgiven me for taking her son away from her.

6 It was love at first sight. I _____ _____ him immediately.

7 They're always _____ _____ over the silliest of things. They'll be talking to each other again tomorrow, you'll see.

8 He wasn't ready for a new relationship as he still hadn't _____ _____ his divorce.

B Describing people

Complete the crossword using the following clues.

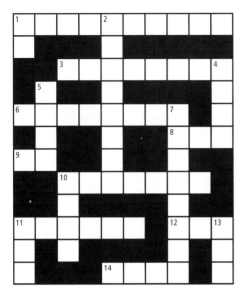

Across

1 Someone who doesn't like meeting and spending time with other people is _____ .
3 Hazel eyes are _____ brown in colour.
6 'Thank you for your donation to our charity. It was extremely _____ of you.'
8 'He's going to have his left _____ pierced.'
9 negative prefix for *decisive*
10 'She's so _____: she only ever thinks about herself.'
11 unattractively thin
12 'Unfortunately, he's in a _____ mood today.'
14 Unlike Mediterraneans, people in northern Europe tend to have a rather _____ complexion.

Down

1 negative prefix for *adventurous*
2 'She's such a _____ child: always so happy and positive.'
4 'She looks much nicer with shoulder-length _____ .'
5 opposite of 6 across
7 'Please try to be _____ about this. Think with your head rather than with your heart.'
10 attractively thin
11 'He was too _____ to ask her to go out with him, so he got his friend to do it for him.'
13 negative prefix for *honest*

Use of English:
FCE Part 3

Transformations

For questions **1–7** complete the second sentence so that it has a similar meaning to the first sentence, using the word given. **Do not change the word given.** You must use between two and five words, including the word given.

1 He doesn't find it hard to make new friends.
 difficulty
 He has _____ new friends.

2 My relationship with Jerry is none of your business.
 nothing
 My relationship with Jerry _____ you.

3 His guitar playing style was strongly influenced by Eric Clapton.
 a
 Eric Clapton had _____ his guitar playing style.

4 I don't think I'm strong enough to lift it.
 the
 I don't think I _____ to lift it.

5 We're getting a friend to repair the roof.
 having
 We _____ by a friend.

6 They took his tonsils out when he was 11.
 taken
 He _____ when he was 11.

7 We don't want a complete stranger to do it.
 have
 We don't want _____ a complete stranger.

Use of English

Introduction

In Paper 3, the Use of English Paper, you are given 1 hour 15 minutes to complete five different tasks. In this unit we will look specifically at three of the parts:

Part 1   Multiple choice cloze
Part 2   Open cloze
Part 4   Error correction

Information on the content of the other two parts, Part 3 (Transformations) and Part 5 (Word formation), appears at frequent intervals throughout this book.

What do you know about the Use of English Paper?

Look at the following statements and decide which are true and which are false. If you think a statement is false, give reasons for your answer.

1 All five parts of the Use of English paper are in the form of a text. _____
2 You should read texts through at least once before you attempt the task. _____
3 All five parts of the paper contain one example. _____
4 You should not write the answer for the examples on your answer sheet in the exam. _____
5 One mark is given for each correct answer in the Use of English paper. _____
6 In Part 1 (Multiple choice cloze) if you are not sure of the answer it is better to leave a blank. _____
7 In Part 2 (Open cloze) you sometimes have to write two words. _____
8 In Part 3 (Transformations) the key word must not be changed in any way. _____
9 If a line is correct in Part 4 (Error correction) you should leave a blank on the answer sheet. _____
10 In Part 5 (Word formation) an answer is given no marks at all if the word is misspelt. _____

Part 1: Multiple choice cloze

What to expect in the exam

● Part 1 of the Use of English Paper focuses mainly on vocabulary. The following examples show some of the different features of language which are tested in the Multiple choice cloze.

Look carefully at the words in *italics* and underline the answer **A**, **B**, **C** or **D** which best fits each space.

1 **Knowing the meaning of a word**
If you need anything *during the exam*, you should ask one of the _____ .
A invigilators   **B** surveyors
C observers   **D** spectators

2 **Knowing the grammar of a word**
His doctor _____ *him to eat* less and do more exercise.
A said   **B** suggested
C advised   **D** insisted

3 **Knowing which words go together**
a The match was postponed because of the _____ *rain*.
A strong   **B** hard
C forceful   **D** heavy

b Could you *get* _____ *touch with* John and arrange a time to meet?
A the   **B** a
C in   **D** to

4 **Phrasal verbs**
He was offered the job, but he *turned* it _____ because of the low salary.
A up   **B** down
C off   **D** on

5 **Linking words**
We'll let you buy a motorbike _____ you ride it carefully.
A as if   **B** whenever
C although   **D** as long as

Look at the title of the text below. What do you think you will read about?
Now read the text through quickly, ignoring the gaps, and check your predictions.
Read the text again and for questions **1–15**, decide which answer **A, B, C** or **D** best fits each space and underline it. There is an example at the beginning **(0)**.

Too old to rock'n'roll?

The world's biggest and oldest rock stars are still **(0)** _____ with performing in front of **(1)** _____ . This irresistible urge to **(2)** _____ concerts means they are constantly **(3)** _____ their retirement until a later date. **(4)** _____ , the question remains: is rock music an art form that can really be performed by middle-aged people?

Most of these rockers do have to keep in **(5)** _____ . Mick Jagger, who remains astonishingly athletic in **(6)** _____ performances, takes a personal trainer **(7)** _____ tour. And with an act that **(8)** _____ enough dancing on **(9)** _____ to tire out a 20-year-old, Tina Turner proves that age has had **(10)** _____ effect on her ability to put on a good show. Yet she has never seen the inside of a gym. She seems to have a natural energy, which means she doesn't worry about dieting or exercising.

Paul McCartney **(11)** _____ his vegetarianism for enabling him to keep fit enough to rock'n'roll. McCartney also believes that he and bands **(12)** _____ the Stones and the Who still perform because they can. What these bands have **(13)** _____ is that they perfected the craft of performing in clubs before they became famous, something only a tiny minority of chart bands do now.

For the Rolling Stones it's also a matter of pride, a way of answering **(14)** _____ who say they are too old. Nothing gives them **(15)** _____ pleasure than the knowledge that theirs have been the highest money-earning tours of all time.

	A	B	C	D
0	capable	interested	get on	in love
1	spectators	audiences	public	observers
2	make	represent	give	show
3	putting off	giving up	keeping on	cutting down
4	Despite	In spite	However	Whereas
5	conditions	fitness	health	shape
6	direct	live	vivid	open
7	for	on	in	at
8	involves	composes	implies	consists
9	screen	scene	step	stage
10	little	few	small	slight
11	admits	attributes	thanks	reasons
12	like	as	how	such
13	in all	at all	in common	on the whole
14	those	anyone	ones	they
15	further	bigger	better	greater

Preparing for Paper 3

It is important when recording vocabulary to note down and learn whole phrases, and not only individual words. Write down two expressions, collocations or phrasal verbs from the text above for each of the following verbs. Include any dependent prepositions and/or adjectives which are used in the expression. The first two have been done for you.

1 give   _give concerts_   _give someone great pleasure_
2 have   _____   _____
3 put   _____   _____
4 keep   _____   _____

79

Part 2: Open cloze

1 What type of person do you think lives behind each of these doors?

2 Read the following text, which is about a door which was used in a film. Which of the doors in the photos is most similar to the one mentioned in the text?

Selling a door

It looks like **(1) an** ordinary, battered front door, but **(2) it** came to symbolize the negative side **(3) of** celebrity for its owner.

The door is, in fact, famous **(4) for** its starring role in the British film, *Notting Hill*. But **(5) the** owner of the house, Caroline Freud, got so tired **(6) of** crowds of tourists having **(7) their** photo taken in front of it that she sold it – the door, that is.

Usually it is the actors **(8) who** are remembered for their roles in a hit film, but the door was **(9) so** important that it was actually written into the script. **(10) At** the beginning of the film, William Thacker, played by Hugh Grant, says: 'So this is where I spend my days and years… in a house with a blue door **(11) that** my wife and I bought together before she left me for a man who looked like Harrison Ford… .'

The house previously belonged to Richard Curtis, who wrote the film, and **(12) his** wife, Emma Freud. Shortly after the film came out they sold it **(13) for** £1.2 million and moved to a quieter location. It **(14) was** bought by Caroline Freud, who quickly discovered that living behind **(15) such** a famous door brought problems.

What to expect in the exam

● In Part 2 of the Use of English paper there is a text with 15 gaps to be filled. This task focuses mainly on grammar. The following are some of the typical types of words which are omitted. Look at the words in **bold** in the text above and write each one with its number next to the corresponding type. The first two have been done for you.

Type of word	Number and example
Articles	*(1) an*
Prepositions	
Auxiliary verbs	
Personal pronouns	*(2) it*
Possessive adjectives	
Relative pronouns	
Intensifiers	

3 Read the continuation of the text below and think of the word which best fits each space. Use only **one** word in each space. There is an example at the beginning **(0)**.

More famous doors

Jenny Cooper, a locations adviser for **(0)** ___the___ London Film Commission, said many people **(1)** _____ allowed their homes to **(2)** _____ used as film sets found tourists turning up on the doorstep **(3)** _____ months afterwards. Public attention, it seems, is an inevitable consequence of owning a house that has featured in a film.

A celebrity sale, however, **(4)** _____ not always add to **(5)** _____ value of a house. Freddie Mercury's old house in London is very private, but **(6)** _____ became a place of pilgrimage to **(7)** _____ fans. **(8)** _____ whole of his garden wall was covered in graffiti and this detracted from its value. The wall has **(9)** _____ cleaned, but messages from adoring fans are still written **(10)** _____ the pavement.

The front door of the Apple Studios was covered in graffiti by the Beatles; when it **(11)** _____ sold it made £20,700, almost five times its estimate. And the plain white door from John Lennon's mansion in Surrey was sold by Christie's **(12)** _____ £2,300 in 1994. There is **(13)** _____ a passionate market for memorabilia that if you have something that immediately brings a film to mind, then it will sell well.

Indeed, the *Notting Hill* door fetched £6,000 at auction. As **(14)** _____ the film fans, they will now have to use their detective skills to find the wooden star of the film. **(15)** _____ famous blue door has been replaced by a plain black one.

Part 4: Error correction

Part 4 contains a text with a number of errors. As in Part 2 (Open cloze) the emphasis in this part is on grammar.

There are usually between three and five correct lines in the text, while the other lines contain an unnecessary word which should not be there.

1 Look carefully at **1–7** below and underline two words in each sentence which should not be there. The first one has been done for you.

1 When I'm at <u>the</u> work, I usually have <u>a</u> lunch at half past one.
2 You really must to try to persuade your parents to let you to see the film.
3 I have a niece who she never says 'thank you' for anything that you give it her.
4 When you reach to the traffic lights, you'll see a bus stop opposite of a bank.
5 When he was finished work, he has phoned his friend and they arranged to meet.
6 Because of we live in a village we have to spend a lot of time while travelling.
7 There were several of people from South America on the course, but the most of the participants were from European countries.

2 Both errors in each of the sentences **1–7** above are of the same type. Explain why the two words in each sentence are unnecessary. Use the words in the box below.

Example:
1 *These two articles are not necessary for different reasons. We say 'at work', 'at school' and 'at home', and 'have a meal' is correct, but you don't need an article in 'have lunch', 'have breakfast' or 'have dinner'.*

pronouns	infinitives	prepositions	articles
linking words	auxiliary verbs	expressions of quantity	

3 Look at the title of the paragraph below. What do you think the text will say?
Read through the text quite quickly and check your predictions.
Who do you think wrote it? Give reasons for your answer.

4 Some of the lines in the text are correct, and some have a word which should not be there. If a line is correct, put a tick (✓) in the space at the end of the line. If a line has a word which should not be there, write the word in the space. There are two examples at the beginning (**0** and **00**).

A dog is for life

0	Before that you decide to keep a dog you should learn all	*that*
00	you can about them first. You could perhaps ask a friend who	✓
1	owns one, or else go to your local library, which it probably	_____
2	has books about the dog care. If you get a dog, it's unfair	_____
3	to leave it at home on its own all day, as they are get lonely	_____
4	in the same way that much people do. Try to make sure that	_____
5	somebody is with it for at least some of the time. All dogs	_____
6	need exercise themselves, so if you aren't lucky enough to	_____
7	have a garden, it's better if you live near of a park or some	_____
8	other type of open space where your dog can run around freely.	_____
9	Keep it on a lead at other times, though, especially in areas	_____
10	with plenty traffic or on farmland. In the home you should	_____
11	teach at your dog how you want it to behave and to do what	_____
12	it's told. If you will find this difficult, take it along to a training	_____
13	centre, where it will also learn to behave around other dogs as well.	_____
14	Finally, don't forget that all pets which need to be fed. Dog food	_____
15	can be particularly expensive, so be sure you can afford the extra cost before buying your new friend.	_____

Vocabulary 1: Shopping

1 Complete each of the spaces below with a word from the box.

foodstuffs	own-brand	cashier	value	brands
trolley	out-of-town	receipt	convenience	checkout
corner	range	till	aisles	

I prefer a trip to a large **(1)** _____ supermarket to shopping in the local **(2)** _____ shop because there's so much more variety. You can choose between all the usual well-known **(3)** _____ , or if you prefer, there are the store's cheaper **(4)** _____ products. As well as tinned and frozen **(5)** _____ food, there's a wide **(6)** _____ of fresh fruit and vegetables, meat, fish and other **(7)** _____ . The household goods are particularly good **(8)** _____ for money, compared to other shops.

Once I've walked down all the **(9)** _____ , filling my **(10)** _____ with enough food to last a month, I head for the **(11)** _____ . I try not to look when the amount I've spent is displayed on the **(12)** _____ and I try not to listen as the **(13)** _____ reads it out. I hand over my credit card and hurriedly put the **(14)** _____ in my purse, preferring not to look at it until I get home.

2 What are the advantages of shopping in smaller local shops?
Do you plan carefully what you are going to buy? Do you ever buy things on impulse?
What shops have you been in during the last fortnight? What did you buy?

Speaking: Supermarket psychology

Did you know that supermarket chains tend to design their stores in the same way? For example, supermarkets sell a lot of milk, so they usually put it at the back of the store, leading customers to walk past, and hopefully buy, lots of other products.

In which area of the supermarket do you think they put the following products? Give reasons for your answers.

Products
confectionery
(chocolates and sweets)
bread
alcoholic drinks
fruit and vegetables
fresh meat

Areas of the supermarket
at the back of the shop
in the middle of the shop
at the checkouts
near the entrance
near the exit

Listening 1:
FCE Part 2

Note taking

You will hear part of a radio programme in which the head of a supermarket chain explains how supermarkets are planned. For questions **1–10** below, write the names of the supermarket sections for each number and complete the notes.

How to go about it

- As you listen to the recording the first time, try not to spend too long writing the words or phrases in the space, as you may miss the answer to the next question.
- You could write abbreviations the first time you hear the answer.
  Example: *fr + veg* for *fruit and vegetables*
  The second time you hear the recording you can finish writing the word or phrase, or change your answer if you think it's wrong.

- Here are the names of the sections you will need to write in the left hand column below. Think of possible abbreviations for each one.
  confectionery
  alcoholic drinks
  pre-packed meat
  fresh meat
  bakery
- At the end of the Listening test you will have five minutes to transfer all of your answers onto a separate answer sheet.

1   *entrance*   at side so that customers visit _____ as possible
2   *fruit and vegetables*   customers feel they are entering _____
3   _____   situated here to keep _____ interested
4   _____   at the back of the store in order not to _____ customers
5   _____   prevents customers relating the product to _____
6   *freezer goods*   usually only _____ are sold here
7   *end of aisle areas* sales here are often _____ than for a mid-aisle position
8   _____   the smell creates a _____ atmosphere
9   _____   by now, customers will be used to _____
10 *checkouts*   products which encourage customers to _____

How do your ideas in the speaking task compare with those of Matthew Brereton?

Think of a supermarket you know. Is it designed the way he describes?

Reading:
FCE Part 3

Gapped text

You are going to read a newspaper article about shopaholics. Seven paragraphs have been removed from the article. Choose from the paragraphs **A–H** the one which fits each space **(1–6)**. There is one extra paragraph which you do not need to use. There is an example at the beginning **(0)**.

Before you do the task, read the text and the paragraphs on page 84 through quickly and answer the following questions.

What type of people are shopaholics?
What do they buy?
What effect does it have on them?

I JUST HAD TO HAVE THEM!

shopping: a curable disease?

An American psychiatrist has launched trials of a drug to help people who cannot stop spending. Professor Lorrin Koran of Stanford University in California believes he has found a cure for shopaholics.

0	*H*

Until now, few psychiatrists have regarded the problem as worthy of serious medical attention. Koran, however, describes it as a 'hidden epidemic' comparable to compulsive gambling, kleptomania and pyromania.

1	

The considerable interest in the supposed cure comes as no surprise to Koran, who has been aware of the extent of the problem for many years. But just what type of people suffer from it?

2	

However, an increasing number of men are also becoming addicted to shopping. They usually collect power tools and car accessories. One man could not stop buying spanners, even though he already had 4,000, while another had bought over 200 different seat covers for his car.

3	

Whereas the former get pleasure from shopping and only occasionally splash out on something expensive, typical shopaholics go on a binge at least once a week. They experience urges to buy items that are not needed and then feel sadness and remorse.

4	

For Laura, 44, who has a liking for designer clothes, Koran's trial is a lifeline. As she made her way through an expensive shopping centre in Stratford last week, she confessed that she recently spent $35,000 on fashion accessories, getting herself $22,000 into debt.

5	

She has tried giving up her own cards and leaving her handbag at home, but has never managed to stop shopping. Her addiction was the main cause of her split with a boyfriend of nine years. 'It is ruining my life,' she said.

6	

However, not everyone agrees that compulsive shopping is a disease which needs treating. Lee Smith, a retail consultant, claims that people have always used shopping as a way of cheering themselves up.

A With good reason: they often get into financial difficulties. 'The thrill they have is in the *purchase* and not in the possession,' said Koran, who identifies low self-esteem as a common factor. 'They are filling their life with things because they feel empty inside.'

B Since the announcement of his test programme, Koran's office has been inundated with hundreds of calls from shopping addicts keen to become his guinea-pigs.

C In the 12-week trial, Laura and 23 others will be treated with a drug which restores levels of serotonin. Serotonin carries messages between nerve cells in the brain and deficiencies are thought to lead to compulsive behaviour.

D Koran's clinic is ideally located in Silicon Valley, the high-tech region near San Francisco that has seen some of the fastest wealth creation in America's history. He believes that a clear distinction must be made between recreational shoppers and those who cross the line to addiction.

E One man has managed to accumulate an impressive 3,000 steering wheel covers. What makes this all the more surprising is that he doesn't even own a car.

F Saleswomen at her favourite boutiques assume she is a rich businesswoman rather than a design assistant at a furniture store. 'I've been doing it since I was 12 when my father would give me his credit card,' she said.

G According to Koran's research, the majority of shopaholics are women. Most buy items that improve their appearance such as clothes, shoes, make-up and jewellery.

H The news will come as a great relief to millions of people suffering from compulsive shopping disorder, a condition which is thought to afflict up to one in 30 million American women.

Reacting to the text ◯

Do you ever buy things to cheer yourself up? If so, give some examples.
If you were a shopaholic, what would you buy?

Language focus 1: The present perfect

A The present perfect simple

The present perfect links past events and situations with the present. The present perfect simple is used:

1 to give news of recent past events with some relevance to the present.
*An American psychiatrist **has launched** trials of a drug to help people who cannot stop spending.* (The trials are taking place now.)

2 to describe something that started in the past and continues until the present.
*Koran **has been** aware of the extent of the problem for many years.* (He is still aware now.)

3 to describe events which occurred at some time between the past and the present (exactly when they happened is not important).
*She **has tried** giving up her own cards and leaving her handbag at home, but she **has never managed** to stop shopping.* (She is still a shopaholic now.)

4 to talk about something which occurred in the past, but in an unfinished time period (ie which includes the present).
*His office **has received** 180 calls from shopaholics so far this week.* (And there may be more in the rest of the week.)

Practice

1 Which of the four descriptions above can be used to explain the use of the present perfect in these sentences?

  a I've known Keith since we started school together.
  b I've had several jobs but never liked any of them.
  c Fishing is so frustrating. I haven't caught anything all day!
  d I've been shopping this afternoon.
  e I've lost my pen. Can you help me look for it?
  f I've already seen that film twice.

2 Look back at the reading text and underline more examples of the present perfect simple. In each case, say why the present perfect is used.

3 a Decide which of the time expressions in the box you would use with the present perfect and which with the past simple. Make two groups of expressions in your notebook.

yet	last summer	in September
so far today	in the last few days	since I got up
two weeks ago	before I came here	for the last two years
over the last week	on my 10th birthday	when I was younger
already	this month	

  b Choose four expressions from each group in exercise **3a** and write sentences about yourself, using the appropriate tense.

  Example: *So far today I've eaten two bars of chocolate.*

B The present perfect continuous

The present perfect continuous can be used:

1 to emphasize the duration of a situation or activity.
*I've **been waiting** here for ages.*

2 to suggest that a situation or activity is temporary.
*I'm decorating my room so **I've been sleeping** on the sofa.*

3 to suggest that a situation or activity is incomplete.
*I've **been painting** the kitchen. I hope to finish it soon.*

4 to focus on the repetition of a situation or activity.
*I've **been** trying to phone Tim all day, but there's no reply.*

Like the present perfect simple, the continuous form can be used to talk about the effects in the present of a past event.
Continuous: *I think she's been crying. Her eyes are very red.* (activity)

Simple: *You've cut yourself. There's blood on your shirt.* (single action)

However, it is not normally used to talk about the number of things that have been completed.
Continuous: *I've been writing letters this morning.* (focus on the activity)

Simple: *I've written five letters this morning.* (focus on the finished result)

Practice

1 For questions **1–4** explain the difference in meaning between sentences **a** and **b** and why the present perfect simple or continuous is used in each case.
  1 a I've been reading a new novel. I can't put it down.
    b I've read a new novel. I really enjoyed it.
  2 a He's been staying with his aunt, but he's hoping to buy a place of his own.
    b She's lived in the same house since she was born.
  3 a We've been going to the local shop to do our shopping.
    b I'm afraid they're not here. They've gone shopping.
  4 a I've been baking all day. I'm exhausted.
    b I've baked a couple of cakes. Would you like to try one?

2 Complete the spaces in this telephone conversation with the past simple, the present perfect simple or the present perfect continuous form of the verbs in brackets.
  Dave: Hi Andy, it's Dave. I **(1)** ＿＿＿＿＿＿ (just/hear) that you and Sandra are getting married next May. How long **(2)** ＿＿＿＿＿＿ (you/be) engaged?
  Andy: About six months. I **(3)** ＿＿＿＿＿＿ (propose) to her when we were in Fiji. We **(4)** ＿＿＿＿＿ (keep) it secret for a month or so after that, just until we **(5)** ＿＿＿＿ (be) sure of the date for the wedding.
  Dave: So **(6)** ＿＿＿＿ you ＿＿＿＿ (make) all the arrangements yet?
  Andy: Yes, more or less. Of course, since we got engaged we **(7)** ＿＿＿＿＿ (save) up for a flat as well. We **(8)** ＿＿＿＿＿＿ (both/work) overtime to earn a bit extra. We **(9)** ＿＿＿＿＿＿ (already/save) enough to pay a deposit. Anyway, how about you? What **(10)** ＿＿＿＿ you ＿＿＿＿ (do)?

Vocabulary 2: *Come*

A *to come as*

Look at the following two sentences from the reading text.
*The considerable interest in the supposed cure **comes as no surprise to** Koran.*
*The news will **come as a great relief to** millions of people.*

Notice the adjective + noun collocation *great relief*. Other possible adjectives which collocate with *relief* are *tremendous* and *enormous*. In the following sentences, three of the alternatives **A**, **B**, **C** and **D** fit each space. Which one does not?

1 The news of their engagement *came as a* _____ *surprise*.

   A big   **B** great   **C** complete   **D** pleased

2 It *came as a* _____ *shock* to discover that our house had been broken into.

   A great   **B** terrible   **C** permanent   **D** dreadful

B *to come to*

1 Complete each of the spaces **1–6** with one of the words from the box. The first one has been done for you.

harm	~~power~~	nothing	end	decision	conclusion

1 It was a sad day for this country when they *came to* _*power*_ .
2 If you do exactly as we ask, your son won't *come to any* _____ .
3 We'll go on strike unless you *come to a/an* _____ soon.
4 We hid under the seats just as the film was *coming to a/an* _____ .
5 When he told me he wasn't going, I *came to the* _____ that he wasn't interested in me.
6 I spent ages planning it and then, because of one silly mistake, it all *came to* _____ .

2 For each of the sentences in exercise 1, discuss with your partner who you think is speaking and why they are saying it.
Example: 1 It might be someone complaining about the government. He or she probably voted for a different party in the elections.

C Phrasal verbs with *come*

1 Work out the meaning of the phrasal verbs in **bold** in the following sentences. Use the context of the sentence to help you.

1 We were walking in the woods when we **came across** an old abandoned cottage.
2 My parents are out tonight. Would you like to **come round** and watch TV with me?
3 Do you remember the meaning of 'binge'? It **came up** in the last lesson.
4 I don't feel very well. I think I'm **coming down with** flu.
5 That's *my* suggestion. If you **come up with** a better idea, let me know.

2 Which of the phrasal verbs in exercise 1 can be used with each of the following?

a mysterious illness   *my old school reports*   *in the exam*
to my flat   *a solution to the problem*

3 Write five sentences of your own. Each sentence should include a phrasal verb from exercise 1 and one of the phrases from exercise 2.

Language focus 2: Contrasting ideas

Rewrite the following sentence in three different ways using *although, however* and *despite* instead of *but*. In each case the grammar of the sentence will be different and for one of the words you will need two sentences.

*The weather was bad **but** she enjoyed the trip.*

 Check your answers on pages 211 and 212 of the Grammar reference.

Practice

For **1–6**, complete each of the spaces with one of the words in the box.

although	but	whereas
however	in spite	despite

1 _____ it's quite expensive, we tend to go to the supermarket for fresh fish.
2 He didn't get the job, _____ of the fact that he was the most highly qualified candidate.
3 He went to work this morning _____ not feeling very well.
4 They said that they'd sent the parcel on February 1st. _____ , I didn't receive it until the 28th.
5 Esme left the house at ten this morning _____ she didn't say where she was going.
6 In Italy people often live in flats, _____ in Britain people tend to live in houses.

Writing:
FCE Part 1

Letters: A complaint

1 Read the following Writing Part 1 instructions.

You recently bought a portable CD player via the Internet. Unfortunately, you found the service from the company very disappointing.

Read the printed web page below, together with the receipt which came with the CD player. Then, using the information and the notes you have made, write a letter to Elektra Online, complaining about the service and asking once again for your refund.

Write a **letter** of between **120 and 180** words in an appropriate style.
Do not write any addresses.

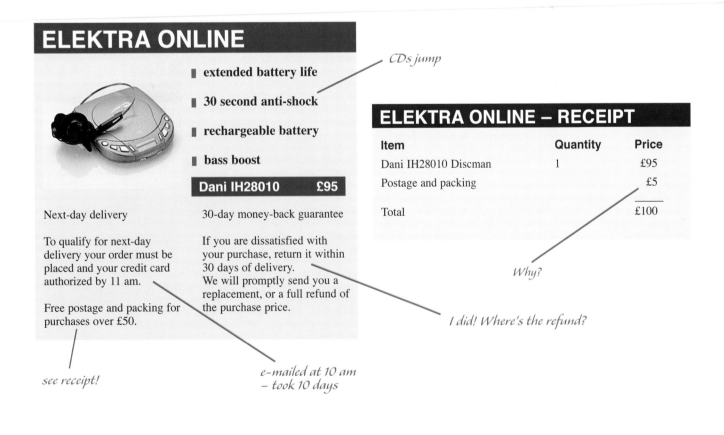

2   Read the model letter below, which a student has written in answer to the Writing Part 1 instructions on page 87, and answer the following questions.

1   What is the purpose of each paragraph in the letter?
2   Find examples of verbs in the passive. Why is the passive used in this letter?
3   Which linking words are used to contrast ideas?
4   Find alternative words and expressions which are used in the letter to mean:

to complain about   *to buy*   *to say or write something formally*
not working properly   *to ask for*   *to hope*

5   Underline any more words and expressions which could be used in other letters of complaint.

Web mail: Message

Dear Sir or Madam,
I am writing to express my dissatisfaction with the service I have received from your company since purchasing a portable CD player from you via the Internet.

Firstly, although I placed my order before 11am, the Discman was delivered ten days later and not, as you advertise, on the following day. Furthermore, I was charged an extra £5 for postage and packing, despite the fact that your conditions clearly state that this is free on orders over £50.

To make matters worse, when the Discman eventually arrived, I discovered that it was faulty, as it caused my CDs to jump. I therefore returned it to you requesting a refund. According to the terms of your money-back guarantee, I was supposed to receive this money immediately. However, I have been waiting for over a month and it has still not been repaid.

As you can imagine, I am rather disappointed with the service offered by your company. I trust you will now give the matter your immediate attention and credit my account with £100.

Yours faithfully

K. Budgen

---

3   Read the following Writing Part 1 instructions. You recently went on a shopping excursion to France with Brighton Marina Coaches. You were disappointed with the trip and did not enjoy it.

Read the advertisement on page 89, together with the notes you have made. Then, using the information, write a letter to the coach company complaining about the excursion and asking for some money back. Write a **letter** of between **120 and 180** words in an appropriate style. Do not write any addresses.

BRIGHTON MARINA COACHES

*Shopping trip to Boulogne
and nearby hypermarket*

**Wednesday 22nd March
via Folkestone and Eurotunnel**

After two hours in the popular 'Eco' hypermarket we move on to the delightful town of Boulogne. Spend the afternoon in the pleasant shopping streets near the harbour, or visit the Haute Ville, the old walled town with its charming restaurants and antique shops.

Travel in comfort on our air-conditioned coach (toilet, video, refreshments).

**Pool Valley Bus Station
Coach departs at 7.30 am
Returns 9.00 pm
Cost: £19 return**

Hypermarket and Boulogne
- *crowded, long queues at checkouts*
- *only 1 hour in Boulogne*
- *restaurants closed when we got there*

Coach
- *air-conditioning not working – very hot!*
- *no cold drinks*

Got home at 11.30pm!

Ask for some money back

Don't forget!

- Organize your letter into paragraphs.
  First paragraph: give your reason for writing
  Body of letter: explain what happened
  Final paragraph: say what you now want
- You can add relevant points of your own, eg consider the consequences of the restaurants in Boulogne being closed.
- Linking words such as *therefore, consequently, as a result* will be useful here.
- Refer to the advert as well as your notes. Contrast linkers will be useful here, eg *despite, although, however, whereas* etc.
- Use formal language throughout your letter.
- Write between 120 and 180 words.

Vocabulary 3: Towns and villages

1 Match the words **1–8** with the words **a–f** to form places you might find in a town. You may use some of the words more than once.

1 shopping	a area	***Example:***	
2 pedestrian	b block	*shopping centre* and *shopping precinct*	
3 housing	c site		
4 industrial	d estate		
5 residential	e precinct		
6 office	f centre		
7 building			
8 apartment			

Can you think of an example for each of these in the area where you live?
Are they *on the outskirts* of your town or village or *in the centre*?

2 The following adjectives can all be used to describe a town or a village. Which of them are positive and which are negative? Make two groups in your notebooks.

lively	pleasant	run-down	picturesque	shabby
dull	quaint	depressing	prosperous	bustling

Which adjectives would you use to describe the area where you live?

3 In Part 1 of the Speaking Test, you may be asked to talk about where you live. Ask and answer the following questions with your partner.

- Whereabouts in (*name of town or area*) do you live?
- How long have you lived there?
- What are the amenities like? (eg shops, sports facilities, cinemas, libraries)
- Is everything within easy walking distance?
- What are the good points about living there?
- Is there anything you don't like about it?
- What changes have there been in your local area in recent years?
- Have they been changes for the better or for the worse?

Listening 2:
FCE Part 4

Matching

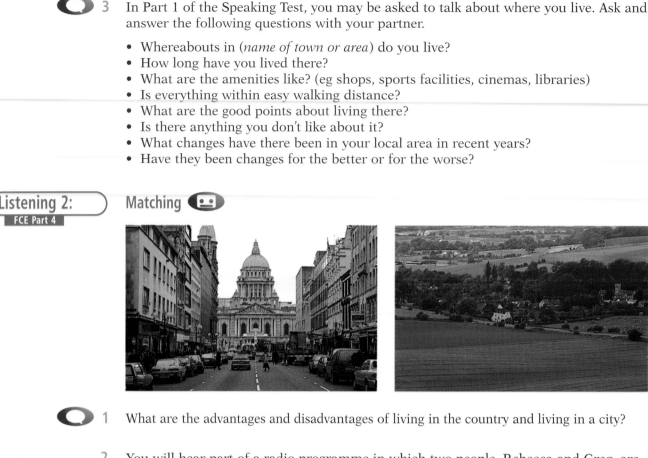

1 What are the advantages and disadvantages of living in the country and living in a city?

2 You will hear part of a radio programme in which two people, Rebecca and Greg, are interviewed about their life in the countryside. Answer questions **1–7**, by writing **R** for Rebecca, **G** for Greg, or **N** for Neither in the boxes provided.

Who prefers the noise of the city?	**1**
Who mentions the dangers of life in the country?	**2**
Who objects to the neighbours?	**3**
Who lives close to the local amenities?	**4**
Who says there is no public transport?	**5**
Who finds country life boring?	**6**
Who would not go back to living in the city?	**7**

Language focus 3: Expressing preferences

The following sentences from the listening show three different ways of expressing preferences.

a *prefer* + gerund + *to* + gerund

*Now **we prefer** living with less noise (to living in a noisy city).*

b *would prefer* + infinitive with *to* + *rather than* + infinitive without *to*

***I'd prefer to stay** in the village and work at home **rather than do a** nine-to-five job in an office.*

c *would rather* + infinitive without *to* + *than* + infinitive without *to*

***I'd rather drive** to work everyday **than give up** my life in the country.*

Practice

For questions **1–4**, complete the second sentence so that it has a similar meaning to the first sentence. Use up to five words including the word in **bold**.

1 I think we'd prefer to watch rather than take part. **rather**
I think we'd _____ part.

2 My sister thinks it's better to buy books than borrow them. **to**
My sister prefers _____ them.

3 I'd rather phone him than send an e-mail. **rather**
I'd prefer _____ send an e-mail.

4 I'd prefer to stay in tonight. **not**
I'd rather _____ tonight.

Speaking:
FCE Part 2

Talking about photos

Look at these two photos. They show different places where people live.

Student A: Compare and contrast the photographs and say what you think it would be like to live in these places.

Student B: When your partner has finished, say which of the two places you think would be safer.

How to go about it

When you are comparing and contrasting life in the two types of places, you could consider the following aspects:

contact with other people
comfort   noise   space
surroundings   leisure time
convenience   expense

Now change roles.

Student A: Compare and contrast the photographs on page 90 and say which area you think would be more expensive to live in.

Student B: When your partner has finished, say which of the two places you would prefer to live in.

Vocabulary: Shopping

1 Complete each of the phrases with an appropriate word from the box. The first one has been done for you.

meat	range	convenience	~~walking~~	brand
out-of-town	own-brand	goods	value	corner

1 easy _____*walking*_____ distance
2 wide _____ of products
3 good _____ for money
4 local _____ shop
5 fresh _____ counter
6 large _____ supermarket
7 frozen _____ food
8 cheap _____ goods
9 well-known _____ of washing powder
10 household _____ section

2 Write five sentences, each including one of the phrases in exercise 1.

Example:
There is a very good shopping centre within easy walking distance of our house.

Use of English:
FCE Part 4

Error correction

Read the text below and look carefully at each line. Some of the lines are correct and some have a word which should not be there.

If a line is correct, put a tick (✓) in the space at the end of the line. If a line has a word which should not be there, write the word in the space. There are two examples at the beginning (**0** and **00**).

Dear Audrey,

0	I just had to write and tell you about the new flat which George and	✓
00	I have just bought and where we are intend to live after I retire next	*are*
1	year. As you may know, I have spent most of my childhood living	_____
2	in Scotland, and I have always been dreamed of moving back there	_____
3	one day. Although George loves the place where we live now,	_____
4	however he is very fond of Edinburgh and he agreed to go and look	_____
5	at some properties on the outskirts of the city. Unfortunately,	_____
6	despite of the fact that houses are usually cheaper in Scotland,	_____
7	everything we liked was too much expensive for us, and after a week	_____
8	of looking, we came up to the conclusion that we would have to think	_____
9	about living somewhere else. But then, on our last day in Edinburgh,	_____
10	while we were walking along Prince's Street, we came across to an	_____
11	old school friend of mine, who told me that the school we were used	_____
12	to go to had just been converted into flats. Naturally, I was very	_____
13	curious about to see the old building, so George and I went to	_____
14	have a look at. As soon as the salesman showed us the first flat, we	_____
15	knew where we had to buy it – so that's what we did. Now we are	_____
	the proud owners of the old gymnasium.	

Use of English:
Transformations

A The present perfect

1 Match each sentence **1–3** with two of the sentences **a–f** which both express a similar idea.

1 I haven't done this before.

2 I haven't done this for five years.

3 I've been doing this for five years.

a It's five years since I started doing this.
b It's five years since I last did this.
c I've never done this.
d The last time I did this was five years ago.
e It's the first time I've done this.
f I began doing this five years ago.

2 Complete the second sentence so that it has a similar meaning to the first sentence, using the word given. **Do not change the word given.** You must use between two and five words, including the word given.

1 I haven't spoken to her since she had her baby.
last
The _____ her was before she had her baby.

2 I haven't eaten Greek food before.
time
This is the _____ Greek food.

3 My nephew began to play tennis in 1999.
since
My nephew _____ 1999.

4 He hasn't seen his sister for many years.
ages
It's _____ his sister.

5 The last time I went swimming was three months ago.
for
I _____ three months.

6 I've never seen a supermarket as big as this before.
supermarket
This is the _____ seen.

B Language of contrast

Complete the second sentence so that it has a similar meaning to the first sentence, using the word given. **Do not change the word given.** You must use between two and five words, including the word given.

1 Although he can speak Russian fluently, he still has problems with listening.
able
Despite _____ Russian, he still has problems with listening.

2 Although there has been an improvement in his behaviour, his teacher is still concerned.
the
Despite _____ has improved, his teacher is still concerned.

3 In spite of a good performance, she didn't win the match.
lost
Although _____ the match.

4 Although the price of the car had increased, we decided to buy it.
increase
We decided to buy the car, _____ in the cost.

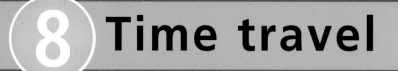
1 Space hotels such as the one in the picture may soon become a reality.

What do you think it would be like to stay in one of these?
How would you spend your time? What might be some of the drawbacks of being a guest? Would there be any dangers?

2 Now read this text about holidays in space. How many of the things you spoke about are mentioned in the text?

Wish you were here?

*B*een to Benidorm, Bali and the Greek Isles? Tired of all the typical tourist resorts? Why not treat yourself to a holiday in space?

In just a few years from now your local travel agent may well try to tempt you in this way into taking a short break in a futuristic space hotel, with the chance to look down on all the sights of our planet from over 60 miles up.

| 0 | *I* | Now, at the start of the new millennium, it is beginning to become a reality. With the first short commercial passenger flights into space already fully booked, private companies are now turning their attention to holidaymakers wanting to spend longer periods of time outside the Earth's atmosphere. | 1 |

The hotel will rotate as it orbits the Earth every 90 minutes, resulting in weightlessness at its centre and 20 per cent of normal gravity in all other areas. | 2 |

Mark Levy of Gerard and Burns says: 'We are currently working out what experiences we can provide for the 200 guests which the hotel will accommodate – a 30-minute space walk, for example, or maybe one day an optional trip orbiting the Moon.' | 3 |

Before that can happen engineers have to develop safe and low-cost spacecraft to transport us there. NASA has already invested a billion dollars in a project to build a reusable space vehicle. | 4 | One such company, Dream Ships of California, is about to start building its Cosmos Freeway hypersonic aircraft, which will be capable of travelling at Mach 10 at a height of 65 miles and able to fly from New York to London in 20 minutes.

Don't forget!

- To help you, look for and underline lexical, grammatical and sequence links (see the How to go about it box on page 55). In the example **(0:I)**, there are two clear links:
  Not so long ago... with *Now, at the start of the new millennium...*
  and... *the idea of space travel for all was just a dream.* with... *it is beginning to become a reality.*
- Make sure you look at the sentences both before *and* after the space in the text.

3 Read the following instructions for this Part 3 Reading task.

Eight sentences have been removed from the article. Choose from sentences **A–I** the one which fits each gap (**1–7**). There is one extra sentence which you do not need to use. There is an example at the beginning **(0)**.

A He also foresees games played in weightless conditions including 'zero-gravity basketball' and 'air tennis'.

B And everyone will notice the effects of space adaptation syndrome, which affects one's sense of direction and causes bodily fluids to move towards the head.

C Tourists will soon be preparing to stay for several days in an orbiting space hotel, such as the one designed by American construction company, Gerard and Burns.

D So book your tickets now.

E This lack of space is not the only discomfort the first guests will have to put up with.

F And more than a dozen small private companies in the US and Europe are racing to do the same.

G It will probably take some two years to assemble and fit out the hotel, which is expected to travel about 200 miles above the planet.

H But there are one or two potential problems which might make people think twice before heading for space.

I Not so long ago the idea of space travel for all was just a dream.

Reacting to the text

Would you like to spend a few nights in a space hotel, or have the potential problems put you off?
What other unusual types of holiday do you think will exist in the future?

Noticing language: Phrasal verbs

Each of the following sentences from the reading text contains a phrasal verb. Match each phrasal verb in **bold** to a word or expression in the box with a similar meaning.

go towards	compensate for
tolerate	think about and plan
provide with everything that will be needed	

1 We are currently **working out** what experiences we can provide for the 200 guests.
2 The view will definitely **make up for** the drawbacks.
3 This lack of space is not the only discomfort the first guests will have to **put up with**.
4 It will probably take some two years to assemble and **fit out** the hotel.
5 But there are one or two potential problems which might make people think twice before **heading for** space.

5 [ ] Thousands of small objects orbiting the Earth – parts of old satellites and other space debris travelling at several thousand miles per hour – could do serious damage to spacecraft.

Even if they do manage to get there safely, many of the passengers are likely to suffer space sickness: feel dizzy, sweat and maybe vomit. **6** [ ]

But for those who are prepared to put up with the lack of comfort in space, the view will definitely make up for the drawbacks. 'From nowhere else can you appreciate the full size and wonder of the Earth,' says Mark Levy. 'It's a chance not to be missed.' **7** [ ] The holiday of a lifetime awaits you.

Language focus: The future

A Making predictions

The following sentences from the reading text all represent opinions, predictions or expectations about the future. Decide which of the words and expressions in **bold** express:

a certainty   **b** probability   **c** possibility

1 The view **will definitely** make up for the drawbacks.
2 Many of the passengers **are likely to** suffer space sickness.
3 It **will probably** take some two years to assemble and fit out the hotel.
4 Your local travel agent **may well** try to tempt you in this way.
5 But there are one or two potential problems which **might** make people think twice before heading for space.
6 Small objects orbiting the Earth... **could do serious damage to spacecraft.**

What is the negative form of each of the phrases in bold?
Example: *will definitely – definitely won't/will not*

Practice

Look at the following predictions for the year 2015. Make your own predictions by completing each space below with either the positive or the negative form of one of the words or expressions in section A.

1 Robot pets _____ take over from animals in the home.
2 The car _____ cease to be the main means of transport.
3 Children _____ receive most of their education at home.
4 Human cloning _____ be legal in most countries.
5 Scientists _____ have found a cure for cancer and AIDS.

B Other futures

Match each of the future forms **1–9** with an explanation **a–i**.

1 Dream Ships of California <u>is about to start</u> building a hyper-sonic aircraft.
2 This time tomorrow <u>I'll be flying</u> over France on my way to Italy.
3 When you come to visit us, I <u>will have finished</u> all my exams.
4 The train <u>leaves</u> at seven o'clock tomorrow evening.
5 That suitcase looks very heavy. Here, <u>I'll carry</u> it for you.
6 <u>I'm meeting</u> Susana at eight o'clock.
7 <u>I'm going to try</u> and book a flight to the Moon.
8 Considering his lack of effort, I'd say he<u>'s going to fail</u>.
9 The hotel <u>will rotate</u> as it orbits the Earth every 90 minutes.

a something which is on the point of happening
b a prediction based on present evidence
c timetabled or scheduled events
d actions or events in progress at a certain time in the future
e actions or events which will be completed by a certain time in the future
f an intention or plan
g future fact
h an arrangement
i an offer to help; a decision made at the moment of speaking

ⓖ Check your ideas in Parts A and B of the Grammar reference on page 212.

C Time linkers

Complete each of the following spaces with a word or expression from the box. There may be more than one possible answer.

> as soon as   by the time   when   before   until

1 I'd like you to make a brief plan of your composition _____ you start writing it.
2 What an awful traffic jam! _____ we get to the airport, the plane will have left.
3 Don't open your Christmas presents yet. Let's wait _____ your father gets up.
4 I'll phone you _____ I know the date of our wedding.

Which tense is used after these time linkers to talk about the future?

Practice

1 In sections A and B below choose the most likely alternative. For sections C and D complete the spaces with an appropriate future form of the verbs in brackets.

A
I've just heard on the radio weather forecast that it **(1)** *is raining/is going to rain* tomorrow. That's a real shame because **(2)** *we're going/we'll go* to the countryside for a picnic and **(3)** *we'll have to/we're having to* eat in the car if the weather's bad.

B
Lola's plane **(4)** *is about to take off/takes off* at six tomorrow morning, so **(5)** *I'll get up/I get up* at four and give her a lift to the airport. While you're still in bed, **(6)** *we'll be driving/we're driving* along the motorway!

C
I should be able to leave work a little early tomorrow. I **(7)** _____ (see) a client at four, but I don't think our meeting **(8)** _____ (last) very long. We **(9)** _____ (only/sign) a few papers so I expect we **(10)** _____ (finish) by half past four.

D
Kath: What time **(11)** _____ (we/meet) tomorrow to go to the cinema?
Pascal: Well, the doors **(12)** _____ (not/open) until four, but we could have a coffee beforehand.
Kath: That's a really good idea. In that case, I **(13)** _____ (get) the three o'clock bus and I **(14)** _____ (probably/see) you there at about 3.30. OK?

2 **◐** Discuss these questions with your partner.

What will you be doing this time tomorrow?
What plans have you made for next weekend?
Are you planning to buy anything special in the near future?
How will your life have changed in ten years' time?

Vocabulary: Travel

1 Complete each of the spaces **1–6** with a word from the box.

| journey | travel | flight | voyage | cruise | trip |

1 Our _____ was delayed because of bad weather, so we had to spend the night at the airport.
2 The _____ from London to Brighton takes under an hour by train.
3 I'm afraid Ms Curtis is away on a business _____ . She'll be back on Tuesday.
4 My interests include music, _____ and good food.
5 About 1,500 people died when the Titanic sank on its first _____ in 1912.
6 I wouldn't recommend going on a Caribbean _____ . You're on the ship for most of the holiday, so you don't see much of the different islands.

2 If you go sightseeing in a city, what types of places do you visit?
Where would you go to get the best view of your town or city?
Which are the most popular tourist resorts in your country?

3 For questions **1–8**, decide which is the correct alternative. Pay close attention to the words before and after each pair of words before making your decision.

Last year we went on **(1)** *holiday/ holidays* to Scotland and booked two weeks on a **(2)** *camping/campsite*, where we **(3)** *stayed/lived* in a caravan. Unfortunately, we couldn't really **(4)** *enjoy/relax* because it was very noisy and it rained nearly every day. We all laughed, though, when my dad fell over in a puddle, but he didn't think it was very **(5)** *funny/fun*. One day we went on a half-day **(6)** *excursion/tour* to a castle, but it was **(7)** *full/crowded* with noisy tourists so we were almost glad to get back to the caravan. Dad's promised that this year he'll take us all on a **(8)** *pack/package* holiday in the Mediterranean to make up for last year's disaster.

Speaking 1:
FCE Part 1

Interview

In Part 1 of the Speaking Test the examiner might ask you about your holidays.

Student A: Imagine you are the examiner. Ask your partner the following questions.
Student B: You are the exam candidate. Answer the questions as fully as possible.

- Where do you usually spend your holidays?
- What types of things do you like doing on your holiday?
- Do you know where you're going next summer?
- What's the best holiday you've ever had? And the worst?
- Would you prefer to go on holiday with your family or your friends? Why?
- Is there anywhere you would particularly like to visit? Why?
- Would you like to go on a cruise? Why/Why not?
- When you go on holiday do you usually buy souvenirs for yourself?

Now change roles and follow the same instructions again.

Speaking 2:
FCE Part 2

Talking about photos

Before you do the following Speaking Part 2 task study the Useful language section below.

The two photographs on this page show people enjoying their holiday in different places.

Student A: Compare and contrast these photographs and say what type of people go on these holidays and what they do there.

Student B: When your partner has finished, say in which of the places you would prefer to spend a holiday.

Now change roles and repeat the instructions for the photos on pages 100 and 101.

Useful language

Student A

Try to use a variety of expressions to impress the examiners. Here are some alternatives to *perhaps, maybe* and *I think*.

Speculating about the places and the people

looks + adjective	*This place looks popular/ crowded/isolated/exotic.*
looks like + noun	*It looks like the type of place where wealthy/adventurous/ young/independent people go.*
looks as if + verb phrase	*This resort looks as if it's very popular with tourists/ couples/families/walkers.*

Speculating about what people do there

I suppose...   I imagine...   I expect...

*They **could** be looking for something different.*
*They **might** want to breathe fresh air.*
*They **may** go there to relax.*

Student B

*I'd **prefer to** spend a holiday here **rather than** in this place.*
*I'd **rather** go to a campsite **than** stay in a hotel.*

Remember to give your reasons.

Listening:
FCE Part 1

Multiple choice

You will hear people talking in eight different situations. For questions **1–8**, choose the best answer, **A**, **B** or **C**.

Before you do the task…

How to go about it

- In questions 1, 2 and 3 you will hear the type of distractors which you encountered in the Part 1 listening exercise in Unit 4.
- In question 4 you are asked to identify the place which the man is describing: *a cathedral, an art museum* or *a castle*. What are the similarities and differences between the three alternatives?

- In question 5 you have to identify the man who is talking: *the boy's father, a chemist* or *a doctor*. Think about how each of the three people might speak to the teenage boy.
- Remember to listen carefully the second time to check your answers.

Now you are ready to do the task.

1 You overhear this man talking about his hotel.
How does he feel about his room?
A impressed
B disappointed
C angry

2 Listen to this woman in an interview.
What job has she applied for?
A a tour operator
B a travel agent
C a restaurant manager

3 You hear a woman talking to a tour guide.
What is the woman's problem?
A She doesn't have her passport.
B She has left her money in the hotel.
C She thinks she has been robbed.

4 You overhear a man talking about a place he tried to visit on holiday.
What place is he describing?
A a cathedral
B an art museum
C a castle

5 Listen to this conversation between a man and a teenage boy.
Who is the man?
A the boy's father
B a chemist
C a doctor

6 You hear a local resident talking about tourists in her town.
What is she complaining about?
A They have no money to spend.
B There are too many of them.
C They make too much noise.

7 You hear this boy talking to his mother.
Why is he disappointed?
A He thinks his parents' idea is boring.
B His parents had promised to do something else.
C He's tired of doing the same things.

8 You hear a man telephoning a railway station.
What does he want to do?
A cancel his ticket
B change the date of his ticket
C change the destination of his ticket

Reading 2:
FCE Part 2

Multiple choice

1 Look at this photograph together with the photograph on the opposite page.

What effects, both positive and negative, do you think tourism might have on places like these and the people who live there? What are the benefits to tourists of going to places like these? Are there any negative effects?

2 You are going to read a newspaper article about the effects of tourism. For questions **1–5**, choose the correct answer **A**, **B**, **C** or **D**.

How to go about it

- Before you begin to answer the multiple choice questions in Part 2 of the Reading Paper, read the text through fairly quickly to form a general impression.
- Read the following text in no more than three minutes and compare the writer's views with your ideas in exercise 1. Does he give any arguments which you did not mention?

TRAVEL NARROWS THE MIND

Is your journey really necessary?
John Rentoul makes the case against travel and tourism.

I do not understand the modern fashion for long-distance travel. Of course, there was once an evolutionary advantage to it all; people moved around in the search for food and better living conditions. But now we do so without a purpose.
5   We travel thousands of miles to get to the other side of the world, and then two weeks later we come back again. What for? To see the sights… and make a mess of them? To get to know other cultures? You must be joking.

The instinct to explore has been exhausted. Humans have
10 been everywhere, done everything. They have climbed to the top of Everest so often the summit resembles a rubbish dump. Driven by their genes to invent ever more absurd frontiers to cross, the sort of people who might once have trekked across the Rocky Mountains are now chartering jets
15 so they can freefall parachute over Antarctica.

This restlessness and our ever increasing desire to travel long distances is disastrous for the environment. Air travel burns up unimaginable quantities of fuel and is the most energy-hungry thing that people can do. It is a scandal that aviation fuel for
20 international flights is not taxed. If the governments of the world could agree to do something about it, they would have a permanent source of income – and put the brakes on the fastest-growing source of global warming gases.

As for the idea that travel broadens the mind, widens people's
25 horizons and promotes international understanding, this is just nonsense. You can only really learn anything about foreign countries by living and working in them and I applaud those who do it. It is tourism I object to, and especially the desire to go to the remotest, wildest and often poorest places in the
30 world and build four-star hotels in them. It does not do the local people much good: the hotels are all owned by foreign companies and only 30 percent of the profits stay in the country. Instead, it encourages the demand for Coca-Cola and McDonalds and accelerates the homogenization of world

1 What does the author say about the fashion for long-distance travel?

   A It enables us to understand other cultures.

   B There is no longer any point to it.

   C It helps us to relax.

   D It takes up a lot of time.

2 Why do people do things such as freefall parachuting in Antarctica, according to the author?

   A They are trying to solve personal problems.

   B They feel the need for greater challenges.

   C It is safer than climbing mountains.

   D They want to go trekking in isolated places.

3 Why, according to the author, should aviation fuel be taxed?

   A It would ultimately help reduce pollution.

   B It would enable governments to buy more fuel.

   C It would help governments stay in power.

   D Other types of fuel are taxed.

4 What does the author mean when he says that tourism 'accelerates the homogenization of world culture' (line 34)?

   A Everyone is eating fast food.

   B People are rapidly becoming the same wherever you go.

   C People in remote places are becoming poorer.

   D The pace of life is speeding up.

5 What does the author feel about road travel?

   A Distances are too long.

   B Motorways are safe.

   C Other countries are safer than the United Kingdom.

   D Driving can be dangerous.

Don't forget!

- Apart from the general understanding questions, which usually come last, the multiple choice questions follow the same order as the text.
- If you have problems choosing the best answer, eliminate those answers which are obviously wrong, then check the answer or answers which you have not eliminated. If you're still not sure, make an intelligent guess. Do not leave a question unanswered.

Reacting to the text

Do you agree with the writer's opinions?
Give reasons for your answer.
What effect does tourism have on your own country?

35 culture. Go abroad and do exactly what you do at home.

But it is not just travel to remote places which is unwise. Even in the United Kingdom, there is no way I would travel
40 long distances by car. As with air travel, statistics may tell us that motorways are not dangerous, but no one can tell me that it is safe for people to be hurtling along within feet of each other at more than 70
45 miles per hour. If you have to travel long distances, the only civilized way is by train.

Next summer, as you hold on to your seat nervously during take-off, and prepare yourself for a week or two of jet lag and
50 sunburn, think of me, enjoying uninterrupted sleep on the overnight train to Glasgow.

Word formation: -en suffix

*...travel **broadens** the mind, **widens** people's horizons...*

1 Some verbs, such as *broaden* and *widen*, are formed by adding the suffix -*en* to the adjective (*broad*, *wide*). To form the verb you may need to add the suffix to the noun. Complete the table with the corresponding nouns and verbs.

Adjective	Noun	Verb
broad	*breadth*	*broaden*
wide	*width*	*widen*
deep		
high		
long		
short		
strong		
weak		
deaf		

2 Complete the spaces with one of the words from the table in exercise 1. You may need to change the form of the word.

1 It fits you very well, sir. The sleeves on the jacket are a little short, but we can certainly _____ them.
2 His life is not in danger now, but naturally the illness has _____ him considerably.
3 I'm pleased to see they're finally _____ the road. The extra lane will make a lot of difference.
4 Can you help me move the sofa? It's not very heavy, so it won't take much _____ to lift it.
5 She lives next to the airport and the noise of the planes is _____ .
6 On a recent expedition to Everest, Burns reached a _____ of 7,900 metres before turning back because of worsening weather conditions.

Writing:
FCE Part 2

Compositions

1 Read the following Writing Part 2 instructions.

You have been doing a project on travel and tourism. Your teacher has asked you to write a composition giving your opinions on the following statement.

Travel broadens the mind and widens our horizons.

Write your **composition**. You should write between **120 and 180** words.

2 The writer of the article 'Travel narrows the mind' did not agree with this statement. However, there are two sides to any argument. Read this example composition. How does the writer feel about travel?

Travel abroad is no longer a luxury and nowadays most people in my country have had at least one foreign holiday. Personally, I think this has benefited our society in a number of ways.

Firstly, it enables us to observe and value other cultures and to understand that ours is not the only way of life. Consequently, this helps combat ignorance and narrow-mindedness, which so often lead to racial prejudice and even violence. Secondly, foreign tourists can learn from and 'borrow' those aspects of other cultures which are better than in their own country. It seems to me that the improvement in my country's eating habits owes a great deal to foreign travel.

Another benefit is that more people can now see the world's most spectacular natural sights and visit its most important historic monuments. As a result, we discover our planet and become more knowledgeable in a way which is simply not possible with the Internet or television.

To conclude, I strongly believe that if we travel with an open mind, our horizons will be widened even further.

3   In Unit 3 you saw a composition which looked at both sides of the argument. You can also answer this type of question by considering only one point of view, giving reasons to support your opinion. How many reasons does the writer give to support his/her opinion in the model above? What is the purpose of the first and last paragraphs?

4   Underline any linking devices which the writer uses. The first one has been done for you. Under each of the following headings write down those linkers which are used to:

1 Introduce the writer's opinion *Personally, I think*	3 Show the result or consequence of something
2 Indicate the order of points	4 Bring the composition to an end

Can you add any more linking devices to each of these categories?

5   Look at the following Writing Part 2 instructions.

Your class has been doing a project on travel and transport. Your teacher has asked you to write a composition with the following title.
The best way to travel in a town or city you know well.
Write your **composition**. You should write between **120 and 180** words.

6   Decide which town or city you would like to write about and which means of transport. Note down all the positive features of this type of transport in the town or city you have chosen, together with examples of the benefits to travellers.

Example:	Positive feature		Benefits
(underground)	*comfortable*	→	*can read or sleep; arrive at destination free of stress*
(car)	*good car parks*	→	*no time wasted looking for parking spaces*

7   You now need to organize your ideas into paragraphs.

Paragraph 1:   Your introductory paragraph should contain one or two sentences introducing your choice and making a general statement saying why you think it is the most suitable.

Paragraphs 2 and 3: Select three or four of the best arguments from exercise 6 and decide on the order you will write them in your composition.

Paragraph 4:   You will only need to write one or two concluding sentences in your final paragraph. Restate your opinion and leave the reader in no doubt that yours is the best choice.

Don't forget!
- Write in a formal or semi-formal style.
- Use appropriate linking devices (see exercise 4 above and page 35 of Unit 3).
- Write between 120 and 180 words.
- Check your work when you have finished.

Now you are ready to write your composition.

8 Review

Transformations: Future forms

1 In the box below match each sentence **1–6** with a sentence **a–f** which expresses a similar idea. The first one has been done for you.

1 She isn't going to go out.
2 She's likely to go out.
3 She's about to go out.
4 She might not go out.
5 She's unlikely to go out.
6 She'll have gone out.

a She'll probably go out.
b She may not go out.
c She isn't planning to go out.
d She won't be at home.
e She probably won't go out.
f She's on the point of going out.

2 Complete the second sentence so that it has a similar meaning to the first sentence, using the word given. **Do not change the word given.** You must use between two and five words, including the word given.

1 Where are you going to spend your holidays this year?
planning
Where _____ your holidays this year?

2 He was about to say something when the phone rang.
point
He was _____ something when the phone rang.

3 Unemployment will probably rise in the next few months.
likely
Unemployment _____ in the next few months.

4 She's unlikely to change her mind about the job.
probably
She _____ change her mind about the job.

5 The plants will probably all be dead by the time we get home.
have
The plants _____ by the time we get home.

Word formation

Use the word given in capitals at the end of each line to form a word that fits the space in the same line. There is an example at the beginning **(0)**.

A disastrous holiday

Last year I won a **(0)** _competition_ in a newspaper and the prize was a holiday for two in a   **COMPETE**
well-known Mediterranean resort. It turned out to be an extremely **(1)** _____ experience   **PLEASE**
and one which my husband and I would not like to repeat.
Our room overlooked the road, which was unfortunately being **(2)** _____ at that time,   **WIDE**
and the noise from the machinery was **(3)** _____ . For some strange reason the road   **DEAF**
works went on twenty-four hours a day and as a result we suffered several **(4)** _____ nights. **SLEEP**
(5) _____ to put up with the constant noise, we decided to complain to the manager.   **ABLE**
We **(6)** _____ expressed our dissatisfaction with the room and asked if we could possibly   **POLITE**
change. However, our request was not **(7)** _____ as the hotel was fully booked and   **SUCCEED**
there were no spare rooms.
The situation **(8)** _____ when my husband suffered food poisoning as a result of   **WORSE**
eating some local seafood. By that stage we'd had enough and decided to **(9)** _____ our   **SHORT**
stay and catch the first available flight home. They say that travel **(10)** _____ the mind   **BROAD**
but we shall happily narrow our horizons this year and enjoy a week in our own back garden.

Use of English:
FCE Part 1

Multiple choice cloze

For questions **1–15**, read the article below and decide which answer **A**, **B**, **C** or **D** best fits each space. There is an example at the beginning **(0)**.

Marrakech

Where can you go in January for almost guaranteed **(0)** _____ – without travelling for most of the day to get there? The answer is Marrakech in Morocco, a four-hour **(1)** _____ from Britain, where the **(2)** _____ temperature is a pleasant 66°F.

Marrakech is a city of **(3)** _____ beauty, with its pink buildings and green palm trees contrasting with the snow-covered **(4)** _____ of the Atlas Mountains in the distance. For tourists, there's the added attraction of excellent food at reasonable prices and high quality accommodation, such as Hotel La Momounia, **(5)** _____ as one of the top hotels in the world.

(6) _____ Marrakech is one of Morocco's busiest and most modern cities, the influence of the Middle Ages is still very evident. **(7)** _____ can admire the battlements, towers and mosques, which were built **(8)** _____ centuries ago. And forget about shopping malls – for perfumes, fabrics, antiques, spices and crafts, **(9)** _____ the 'souks', open-air market-places where you'll almost **(10)** _____ find something to take back home.

For those who want to **(11)** _____ sport Marrakech has plenty to offer. **(12)** _____ golf and tennis, there is also skiing on the slopes of the High Atlas Mountains, where the **(13)** _____ of the surrounding area are quite spectacular. Alternatively, you could just relax **(14)** _____ a heated swimming pool and dream **(15)** _____ your next visit.

0	A sunset	B suntan	C <u>sunshine</u>	D sunny
1	A travel	B trip	C flight	D voyage
2	A middle	B medium	C ordinary	D average
3	A big	B great	C extremely	D high
4	A peaks	B hills	C heads	D surfaces
5	A thought	B regarded	C believed	D judged
6	A Because	B However	C Despite	D Although
7	A Spectators	B Viewers	C Sightseers	D Onlookers
8	A several	B plenty	C often	D all
9	A work out	B put up with	C head for	D make up for
10	A likely	B certainly	C probably	D possibly
11	A do	B practise	C practice	D go in
12	A As well	B More than	C In addition to	D Moreover
13	A sights	B views	C visions	D overlooks
14	A by	B next	C yourself	D you
15	A with	B on	C of	D at

Writing:
FCE Part 2

Articles

You see this announcement in an international magazine.

HOLIDAY COMPETITION

Write an article about a holiday destination you know well, giving details of what tourists can see and do there. The top ten articles will be included in the next edition of our magazine.

How to go about it

Use the Multiple choice cloze text on Marrakech above as a model.
How many paragraphs are there?
What type of information does each one contain?
What tense is used throughout the article?
Are there any expressions which you could use in your own article?

Write your **article** for the competition. You should write **120–180** words.

9 Fact or fiction?

Reading 1:
FCE Part 2

Multiple choice

1 Do you believe that alien life forms exist? If so, what appearance might they have? What scientific explanations are often given for UFOs?

2 You are going to read an article about UFOs. Read through the text quickly and for question 1 choose the best answer **A**, **B**, **C** or **D**.

1 Which of the following sentences best sums up the writer's views?

A Aliens have visited our planet.

B All UFO sightings can be explained scientifically.

C Alien life forms may exist.

D Most UFOs are practical jokes.

UFOs – have we been visited?

Is there a scientific explanation for UFOs or do alien life forms really exist? Kevin McCullough investigates two cases of UFO sightings.

On a cold, dark winter's evening in 1988, Jon Hickes and Richard Williams were driving to a friend's house near Canterbury when they saw a bright red object glowing
5 above the fields about 500 metres in front of them. As they drove nearer to investigate they were amazed to find a large area of molten metal, bubbling on the ground like a pool of volcanic lava. When firemen arrived
10 shortly after, it took them over an hour to cool down the boiling mass and make it safe.

Samples of the solidified metal were taken to the nearby University of Kent where they
15 were found to contain iron and small amounts of tin and chromium. James Radcliffe, a specialist at the university, concluded that material such as this could not have come from a meteor, and military
20 experts, for their part, were quick to point out that **it** could not have fallen from any aeroplane or spacecraft; space debris does not hit the earth's surface in a liquid state.

Of course, there were suggestions that the
25 whole thing might have been a hoax, but a practical joke on this scale would have been very difficult to set up. The only factory in
60 the area capable of producing molten metal
30 had recently closed down, and besides, arranging for large quantities of the metal to be dropped from the sky would not be very easy. Clearly, this was not a simple
65 open-and-shut matter.

Unexplained aerial phenomena of this nature have been observed and noted down for centuries, but the modern preoccupation with UFOs began in 1947, when there was
70 an unusually large number of reported sightings. In the last 50 years there have been over 10,000 such reports in Britain alone. Most of these can be attributed to man-made objects such as aircraft and satellites, or astronomical phenomena such
75 as shooting stars. Just over five per cent of
45 cases, however, remain unexplained, leading many UFO experts to the conclusion that aliens have indeed visited our planet.

In another case in the 1980s Les and Linda Burnham were cycling together along a
50 country road near Rye in Sussex when a sudden, blinding light almost caused them to fall off their bicycles. As the couple stopped to cover their eyes, they felt
85 intense heat and heard a deafening roar like
55 the sound of high-speed train. A minute or so later they were able to look up again, and were greeted with the sight of a huge, diamond-shaped metal object floating above the treetops, spitting flames and
60 emitting a loud, high-pitched noise.

They watched in shocked silence as the gigantic structure climbed high into the air and disappeared at great speed out to sea. Then, they claimed, five or six jet aircraft
65 appeared from nowhere and raced off after the mysterious object.

As they cycled the short distance home, Les and Linda suffered headaches and sickness, and during the next few days experienced
70 diarrhoea and minor skin burns. As a result of illness and depression Linda was unable to go to work for nearly six weeks.

Underneath where the object had been floating, an area of woodland had burnt
75 down, electricity cables had snapped and the road surface had melted. Whatever caused it, the heat must have been incredibly intense to do all that. As for the jet aircraft, military bases denied all
80 knowledge of them and to this day their origin, like that of the diamond-shaped object, remains a mystery.

Secret military activities or rare atmospheric phenomena may account for some of the
85 unexplained sightings but the origins of others could lie elsewhere. And until the opposite is proved, that 'elsewhere' might include visits from extraterrestrial beings.

3   Now read the text again and for questions **2–8**, choose the correct answer.

2 What are we told about the object which Jon Hickes and Richard Williams witnessed?

   A It was very hot.

   B It came up through the ground.

   C They watched it change from solid to liquid.

   D It was 500 metres wide.

3 'it' in line 21 refers to

   A a meteor.

   B a spacecraft.

   C the metal.

   D the university.

4 What does the writer mean when he says, 'this was not a simple open-and-shut matter' (line 32)?

   A It was a complicated hoax.

   B The factory was no longer open.

   C The sighting is still being investigated.

   D There was no obvious explanation for the incident.

5 Records of mysterious happenings in the sky were first made

   A 50 years ago.

   B in 1947.

   C hundreds of years ago.

   D in the nineteen eighties.

6 The object which Les and Linda saw

   A was travelling at the same speed as a train.

   B made two different sounds.

   C was made of metal and diamonds.

   D was on fire.

7 As a result of their experience Les and Linda

   A began to feel unwell soon afterwards.

   B were ill for several weeks.

   C were badly burnt.

   D started feeling sick when they got home.

8 According to Les and Linda, the jet aircraft they saw

   A were involved in secret military activity.

   B followed the strange object.

   C probably came from a nearby military base.

   D were the same shape as the unidentified object.

Reacting to the text ⬤

Do you know any other stories of mysteries which have never been solved? What theories have been put forward to explain what happened?

Language focus 1: Modal verbs of speculation

Look at these extracts from the text and answer the questions.

a *James Radcliffe...concluded that material such as this* **could not have come** *from a meteor.*

b *Of course, there were suggestions that the whole thing* **might have been** *a hoax.*

c *Whatever caused it, the heat* **must have been** *incredibly intense to do all that.*

1 Which of the forms in **bold** express
   a certainty about what did or didn't happen?
   b a possible explanation for what happened?

2 Which verb form is used after each of the modal verbs?

3 Which of the following modal verbs can be used in place of *might* in sentence **b** without changing the meaning?
   could   should   may   can

4 Is it possible to use *must* in place of *could* in sentence **a**?

 Check your ideas on page 213 of the Grammar reference and read more about modal verbs of speculation.

Practice

1 Can you explain what happened in the following situations?
Write two or three sentences for each using modal verbs.

Example: 1
He might have been working in the garden.
He could have fallen over while playing football.
He may not have had a wash for several days.

1 His face and hands are very dirty.
2 Angela's crying.
3 The kitchen window is broken.
4 There's a red mark on Derek's shirt collar.
5 Jonathan was late for school.
6 Nobody in the class did their homework last night.

2 Match each of the sentences **1–6** with a suitable continuation **a–f**.

1 Don't make too much noise.   *b*
2 What do you mean, you don't know what to do?   ____
3 Would you lend me yours?   ____
4 I've tried calling several times but there's never
   any answer.   ____
5 You should ask her.   ____
6 I want everyone to search the area.   ____

a She might not be living there any more.
b He might still be asleep.
c He can't have got very far.
d You can't have been paying attention.
e I must have left mine at home.
f You never know; she might be interested.

3 Look at sentences **a–f** in exercise 2 again and for each one decide whether the speaker is talking about the past or present. What form of the verb is used after the modal verb in each case?

4  Use modal verbs to speculate about possible contexts for each of the sentence combinations in exercise 2.

Example: 1 'This could be a mother speaking to her children. They might be playing in the house and their father may be ill in bed.'

Listening:
FCE Part 4

True/False

1 Do ghosts really look like this?
What are the typical characteristics of ghosts?
Where are they normally seen? What do they do?
Have you or anyone you know ever seen a ghost?

2 You will hear a radio interview with the Chairman of the Ghost Club, Alastair Agnew. For questions **1–7**, decide which of the statements are true and which are false according to the listening. Write **T** for True or **F** for False in the boxes provided.

You can see through ghosts.   1 ____

Ghosts may be only partially visible.   2 ____

Footsteps are heard in over half of the reported sightings of ghosts.   3 ____

One explanation for the sounds is that they are cassette recordings.   4 ____

Ghosts sometimes touch people.   5 ____

Ghosts often haunt buildings near former execution sites.   6 ____

The presence of ghosts can be detected by all domestic animals.   7 ____

Language focus 2: Question tags

1 The following two sentences from the listening both end with a question tag. Look at the words in **bold**. How are questions tags formed?

*That's a fair enough description of a ghost, **isn't it**?*

*And as Chairman of the Ghost Club **you would not** agree with that explanation, **would you**?*

2 Listen to the two examples from the recording again. In which of the sentences in 1 is the interviewer:

a asking a real question because she is *unsure* if her statement is true or not?

b expecting agreement to her statement, which she feels *sure* is true?

How can you tell the difference?

Read more about question tags on page 213 of the Grammar reference.

3 Add an appropriate question tag to each of the following statements.

1 You don't believe him, _____ ?
2 You won't let me down, _____ ?
3 You went away for the weekend, _____ ?
4 He's not playing very well, _____ ?
5 He's already passed First Certificate, _____ ?
6 I'm right about that, _____ ?
7 You can play chess, _____ ?
8 Let's phone Paul, _____ ?

 Now listen to the recording to check your answers.

4 Listen to the sentences in exercise 3 again and next to each question tag draw an arrow to show if the intonation is rising ⤴ or falling ⤵ at the end.

5 Practise saying the sentences with the same intonation as the speakers in the recording.

Use of English:
FCE Part 2

Open cloze

For questions **1–15**, read the text below and think of a word which best fits each space. Use only **one** word in each space. There is an example at the beginning **(0)**.

How to go about it

- Look at the title and try to predict what you are going to read about. The title of this text is 'How to tell a ghost story'. What do you think are the essential ingredients of a good ghost story?
- Read the text through first, ignoring the spaces, for a general understanding. Compare what it says with your own ideas.
- Now start completing the spaces. Look at the whole sentence and not just the words before and after the space. You may also need to look at the previous or next sentence to make your decision.

- What are some of the typical types of words which are omitted in the Open cloze? See page 80.
- Make sure there is only *one* word in each of the spaces.
- Don't leave any spaces unfilled. If you're not sure, work out the part of speech required and make an 'intelligent guess'.
- The answers are never contractions (eg *can't, she's*) or hyphenated words (eg *three-hour, open-air*).
- Remember that you may need a word with a negative meaning (eg *not, without, unless*).

How to tell a ghost story

A classic ghost story must contain **(0)** ___*the*___ figure of somebody who is known to have **(1)** _____ alive, who is known to have died and **(2)** _____ form is seen after their death. You could have a ghostly animal, a ghostly dog for example, **(3)** _____ you can't have vampires or monsters **(4)** _____ they belong in horror. In a ghost story you're trying to chill people, to make them look **(5)** _____ their shoulder and frighten them, whereas in horror you're aiming to terrify people and **(6)** _____ them scream.

Atmosphere is the key. **(7)** _____ it you won't chill anyone. You need a sense of a haunted place, often a house, preferably isolated or **(8)** _____ some way unnerving, although not always; there have been a **(9)** _____ of good stories set in London in broad daylight and the unexpected appearance of a ghost there can work well.

Stories of knights in armour walking down stairs or ladies in white floating **(10)** _____ walls are fine, but your ghost needs to have some **(11)** _____ of reason or moral purpose for them to return and for you to see them.

The closer your ghost resembles a person, **(12)** _____ more chilling it becomes. Come back to the ordinary now and again in your story, otherwise it ceases to **(13)** _____ frightening. You need a balance between the everyday and the abnormal; something happens and then everything is normal for a while. In the back of **(14)** _____ minds people will **(15)** _____ wondering when it will happen again.

Vocabulary: *Give*

A Phrasal verbs with *give*

1 Look at these sentences from the listening. Match each of the phrasal verbs in **bold** with its definition **a–c**.

1 ...ghosts look solid, just like real people. The only thing that **gives** them **away** is the fact that, as you rightly say, they can walk through walls.

2 So a building that was once used as a church for example may **give off** the smell of incense.

3 We'll be **giving out** their address at the end of the programme.

a to produce and send into the air
b to show someone's true nature or identity
c to announce or broadcast information

2 Work out the meaning of the phrasal verbs in **bold** in the following sentences. Use the context of the sentence to help you.

1 She's such a gossip – you can't tell her anything! She loves **giving away** other people's secrets.

2 I'm so unfit! I really ought to **give up** smoking.

3 I'm going to **give out** the test papers now but you mustn't begin until I tell you.

4 I'd like you to **give in** your homework at the end of the lesson. I'll mark it tonight and **give** it **back** to you tomorrow.

5 Although my parents were against the idea at first, I went on about the all-night party so much that eventually they **gave in** and agreed to let me go.

B Expressions with *give*

1 In sections **A** and **B** below match a sentence beginning on the left with a suitable ending on the right.

A

1 Convinced it was a ghost, she **gave a piercing**...

2 When he heard the good news he **gave a broad**...

3 She said goodbye, **gave** him **a tender**...

4 Hearing his ex-girlfriend's name, he **gave a deep**...

5 As she spoke, her son **gave** her **a blank**...

a **sigh** and dreamt of getting back together with her.

b **look** as if he hadn't understood a word.

c **smile**, showing all his teeth.

d **scream** and ran out of the building.

e **kiss** on the cheek and walked out of his life for ever.

B

1 It's been great to see you again. **Give my best**...

2 After the accident I had to **give full**...

3 Your gifts of toys will **give great**...

4 She was **given a nasty**...

5 Sharon Stone **gives an impressive**...

6 The President **gave a lengthy**...

a **shock** when she discovered her purse was missing.

b **performance** in this, her latest film.

c **speech** on the challenges facing the country.

d **details** of what had happened to the police.

e **regards** to your family.

f **pleasure** to the many children in the orphanage.

2 The expressions in exercise 1A all refer to *physical actions* of some kind. Match each of the following general meanings to each expression in 1B.

a to cause someone to experience an emotional feeling
b to perform or present something in public
c to communicate information, opinions or greetings

3 Here are three more expressions with *give*. Match each expression to one of the general meanings in exercise 2.

to give an open-air concert   to give someone a pleasant surprise
to give someone expert advice

4 The *verb + adjective + noun* combinations in sections 1A and B are fairly *strong* collocations. When you hear the first two words of the combination, you can predict quite accurately what the next word will be. For example, if someone begins, *he gave a broad...* there is a very strong chance that the next word will be *smile*.

Cover up the sentence endings in the right hand column of exercises 1A and B and see how many of the *nouns* you can remember for the corresponding *verb + adjective* combinations on the left.

5 **a** Describe situations in which you might:

- give a broad smile
- give a piercing scream
- give a deep sigh
- give a nervous laugh
- give someone a blank look

b Think of a time when someone or something:

- gave you a nasty shock
- gave you a pleasant surprise
- gave you great pleasure
- gave an impressive performance
- gave a lengthy (and boring!) speech

Example:
You might give a broad smile when you find out you've passed an exam, or you ask someone to go out with you and they say 'yes'.

Writing 1:
FCE Part 2

Short stories

Your teacher has asked you to write a short story for the school's English language magazine. It must begin with the following words:

I heard a noise and went downstairs to investigate.

Write your **story** in **120–180** words.

Don't forget!

- Plan your story before you start writing. Think of a general outline of what is going to happen.
- You may choose to write a ghost story. To help you with ideas, use the information from the listening activity on ghosts and the Open cloze text on how to tell ghost stories.
- Look at page 204 of the Wordlist.
- Look again at pages 50 and 51 to remind yourself of the ingredients of a good narrative.
- Consider using one or two expressions with *give*.

Gapped text

1 These photos of children were taken on the night of Hallowe'en.

What do you know about this festival?
Can you answer the following questions?
When is Hallowe'en?
What does the word 'Hallowe'en' mean?
Why is Hallowe'en celebrated?
Why do people dress up as witches and ghosts?
What is 'trick or treat'?
Why are pumpkins made into lanterns?
Look on page 201 to find the answers.

2 You are going to read an article about Hallowe'en. Seven paragraphs have been removed from the article. Choose the most suitable paragraph from the list **A–H** for each part **(1–6)** of the article. There is one extra paragraph which you do not need to use. There is an example at the beginning **(0)**.

How to go about it

- In this text, the grammatical links are particularly important. To help you key reference words – *this, them, he, it* and *they* – are shown in **bold italics**, together with other relevant words. In the example **(0)**, '***This sensation***' refers back to 'the excitement' in paragraph **H**.

- Check your answers by looking for further grammatical and lexical links in the paragraphs both before and after the spaces. In paragraph **H** in the example, *the books* is related to *my library* in the first paragraph. Underline any words which help you make your choice.

THE TROUBLE WITH HALLOWE'EN

One of my greatest disappointments as a child was not having been born in America. I knew from <u>my library</u> that they had a great deal of fun over there. They had Disneyland on their doorstep and perhaps more importantly, they celebrated Hallowe'en.

| 0 | *H* |

This sensation was aroused by tales of ghosts, skeletons, dressing up, doing clever things with exotic vegetables (I had never seen a pumpkin) and annoying grumpy old neighbours. It just had to be fun.

| 1 | |

Considering my love of America and its traditions as a child, I suppose I should see ***this development*** as a cause for rejoicing. However, I have recently had cause to wonder whether Hallowe'en is such a good thing after all and I now view the whole thing with deep suspicion.

| 2 | |

Indeed, I ***enjoyed it*** so much I didn't want to stop. This led to a disagreement between James and myself as to how much of the pumpkin each of us should be allowed to carve. The disagreement turned into a heated argument and James left the scene in a raging temper.

| 3 | |

Feeling a bit of a killjoy after the pumpkin incident, I decided to act as mediator. Yes, ***he could go***, I decreed, provided he went with a group of friends.

| 4 | |

This problem was resolved when a neighbouring parent agreed to escort the trick-or-treat party on their rounds. But by then, there had been another row. 'No way!' I shouted. 'No way am I going to let you cut holes in a perfectly good sheet just to make a ghost costume which will only be used for ten minutes!' Only after being assured that it was partly made of polyester did I give in.

| 5 | |

James had other ideas. He intended to ***eat them*** all immediately. And so began another argument which might have gone on until bedtime if we had not been rescued by the arrival of numerous other trick-or-treaters.

| 6 | |

They have of course ***dried up*** now, but they left their mark and a feeling that Hallowe'en may be more trouble than it is worth. Guy Fawkes Night seems a safer, less controversial alternative.

A However, our supply of tangerines had run out. There was only one thing for it: we would have to dip into James's sweet collection. Needless to say, it ended in tears.

B Worse was to follow. While I made pumpkin soup in the kitchen I heard shrieks of protest from the sitting-room. James wanted to go trick-or-treating. His mother thought he was too young.

C Dressing up was great fun. James decided we should all be ghosts and his mother and I spent the best part of the afternoon working on the costumes.

D This change of attitude occurred last October, when I spent my first Hallowe'en with my girlfriend's son, James. At first it all seemed quite enjoyable. The pumpkin was overpriced, but I had never made a death's head mask before and I found it very satisfying cutting out the teeth shapes in its mouth.

E Now it was his mother's turn to get upset. It just wasn't safe for the boy to go knocking on strange people's doors on a dark, foggy October night.

F Twenty years on we now have EuroDisney on our own doorstep and Hallowe'en is almost as important in Britain as New Year's Eve or Christmas Day.

G It all seemed worthwhile when James returned from his expedition clutching an impressive quantity of sweets and fruit. At least he would spend his pocket money on something other than chocolate for the next few weekends.

H Exactly what Hallowe'en meant, <u>the books</u> never really explained: I knew its origins were Irish, but little more. However, this element of mystery added to *the excitement*.

Reacting to the text 🔵

Do you sympathize with the writer that 'Hallowe'en may be more trouble than it's worth'? Why/Why not?
Many people in Britain, including the police, do not like Hallowe'en. What reasons do you think they give? What do *you* think?

Word formation: Adjectives

1 The following adjectives in **bold** are all taken from the text on Hallowe'en. For each adjective write the form which is indicated in brackets at the end of the line. The first one has been done for you.

1 a dark, **foggy** October night	*fog*	(noun)
2 the arrival of **numerous** other trick-or-treaters	_____	(noun)
3 a safer, less **controversial** alternative	_____	(noun)
4 an **impressive** quantity of sweets and fruit	_____	(verb)

2 All four words in each of the groups below require the same suffix to form adjectives. Choose the correct suffix -*y*, -*ous*, -*al* or -*ive* and then decide what, if any, further changes are necessary.

Example:

anger *(angry)*   hunger *(hungry)*   thirst *(thirsty)*   guilt *(guilty)*

suffix: -y   changes: ang~~e~~ry, hung~~e~~ry

1 ambition	religion	infection	caution
2 occupation	profession	emotion	sensation
3 cloud	wind	rain	ice
4 decide	include	explode	offend
5 biology	geography	economy	history
6 danger	disaster	humour	poison
7 compare	imagine	compete	sense
8 anxiety	variety	curiosity	generosity
9 benefit	influence	residence	finance
10 health	wealth	fun	luck

Collaborative task

Imagine that you have been asked to organize an event in your neighbourhood to celebrate an important festival or occasion in your country. Talk to your partner about each of the suggestions below and say how they might appeal to different people and then choose two that you think would be most popular.

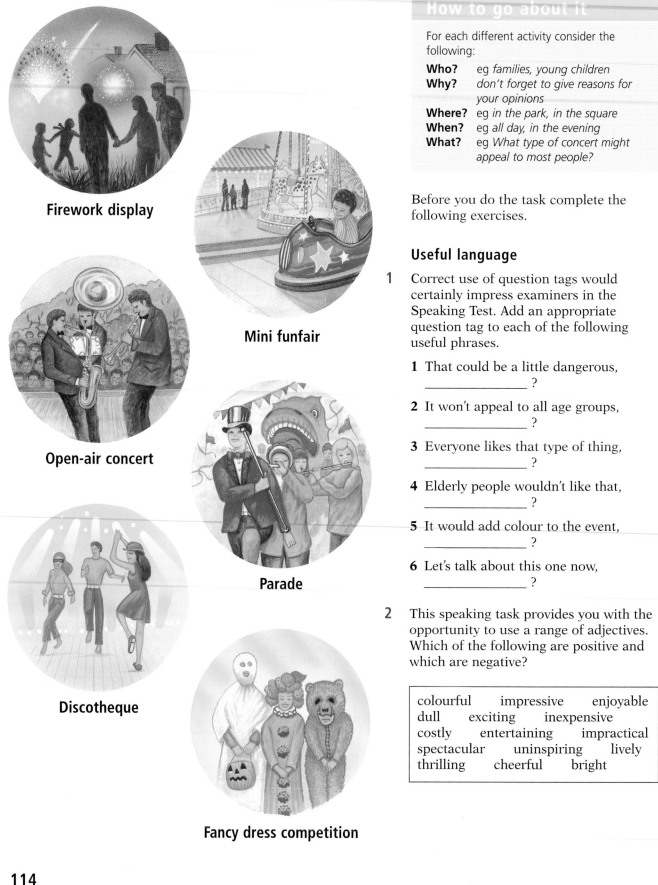

Firework display

Mini funfair

Open-air concert

Parade

Discotheque

Fancy dress competition

How to go about it

For each different activity consider the following:

Who? eg *families, young children*
Why? *don't forget to give reasons for your opinions*
Where? eg *in the park, in the square*
When? eg *all day, in the evening*
What? eg *What type of concert might appeal to most people?*

Before you do the task complete the following exercises.

Useful language

1 Correct use of question tags would certainly impress examiners in the Speaking Test. Add an appropriate question tag to each of the following useful phrases.

 1 That could be a little dangerous, _____ ?

 2 It won't appeal to all age groups, _____ ?

 3 Everyone likes that type of thing, _____ ?

 4 Elderly people wouldn't like that, _____ ?

 5 It would add colour to the event, _____ ?

 6 Let's talk about this one now, _____ ?

2 This speaking task provides you with the opportunity to use a range of adjectives. Which of the following are positive and which are negative?

colourful	impressive	enjoyable
dull	exciting	inexpensive
costly	entertaining	impractical
spectacular	uninspiring	lively
thrilling	cheerful	bright

Speaking 2:
FCE Part 4

Further discussion

Thinking about the Part 3 task on page 114, discuss these Speaking Part 4 questions.

- What other activities do you think might be popular in a celebration like this?
- How important are festivals in your country?
- What problems might there be during public events like these?
- What is the best organized event you have ever been to?
- How do you normally celebrate special occasions?

Writing 2:
FCE Part 2

Informal letters

1 Read the following Writing Part 2 instructions.

You attended an event last weekend to celebrate a traditional festival in your country. Write a letter to your English-speaking penfriend, describing the event. Briefly explain the origins of the festival to your penfriend, then describe what happened and say whether you enjoyed yourself.

Write your **letter** in **120–180** words. Do not write any addresses.

2 Underline key words in the question and say why you think the words you have underlined are important.

Example: *'last weekend' is important. It would clearly be wrong to write in your letter that the event occurred last Tuesday.*

3 Now read the following model letter and answer the questions below.

Dear Maria Luisa,
Sorry it's taken me so long to write, but as you know I've been decorating the house. In fact, I finished last Saturday, so I celebrated by going to a Bonfire Night party here in the village. Every November 5th we commemorate the Gunpowder Plot of 1605, when Guy Fawkes and a group of Catholic conspirators tried unsuccessfully to blow up Parliament with gunpowder.
There's always a bonfire and the one they had built on the village green was enormous. It gave off an impressive amount of heat, which is very welcome on these chilly November nights. As you can imagine, the effigy of Guy Fawkes, which is burnt on top of the fire, disappeared in a matter of minutes.
Unfortunately, the firework display was disappointing, but I imagine it must be very costly to put one on. Anyway, the organizers made up for it by providing some excellent food. The baked potatoes and sausage rolls were delicious and the mulled wine certainly kept everyone smiling!
Well, that's all from me. Let me know what you've been doing recently.
All the best
Andy

4 Has the writer answered all the parts of the question? In which paragraphs does Andy:
a explain the origins of the festival?
b describe what happened?
c say whether he enjoyed himself?

5 Find examples in the model of the following features. Explain the meaning of the phrasal verbs and the adjectives.

Phrasal verbs: eg *blow up* – to destroy with an explosion
Adjectives: eg *enormous* – very big
Linking words: eg *but, in fact*
Relative clauses: eg *It gave off an impressive amount of heat, which is very welcome...*
Useful expressions for informal letters: *Sorry it's taken me so long to write*

Now you are ready to write your own letter.

⑨ Review

Word formation

1 The adjective *healthy* is formed by adding *-y* to the noun *health*. Which of the following words are formed in the same way?

thirsty	guilty	lively	happy	mystery	stormy	sleepy
silly	hilly	party	nasty	cloudy	lengthy	injury

2 Write the adjective formed from the following nouns.

Noun	**Adjective**
1 finance	*financial*
2 commerce	
3 psychology	
4 politics	
5 anxiety	
6 variety	
7 influence	
8 residence	
9 mystery	
10 advantage	

3 Write five sentences using five of the adjectives you formed in exercise 2.

   Example: Since my brother lost his job he's been having serious financial problems.

4 To form the adjectives for the following verbs, the suffix *-ive* is used. What other spelling changes are required?

compare	defend	compete	describe
receive	represent	produce	

Vocabulary: Collocations with *give*

In the following expressions with *give*, write an appropriate noun for each of the adjectives. Choose from the words in the box. The first one has been done for you.

pleasure	smile	surprise	look	performance	scream
kiss	details	speech	shock	sigh	~~concert~~

1 give an open-air ___ *concert* ___
2 give someone a tender ___
3 give a broad ___
4 give someone a blank ___
5 give a piercing ___
6 give someone a nasty ___
7 give a deep ___
8 give someone great ___
9 give an impressive ___
10 give someone full ___
11 give a lengthy ___
12 give someone a pleasant ___

116

Use of English: FCE Part 3

Transformations

For questions **1–8**, complete the second sentence so that it has a similar meaning to the first sentence, using the word given. **Do not change the word given.** You must use between two and five words, including the word given.

1 The goalkeeper was injured, so maybe he isn't playing today.
might
The goalkeeper was injured, so he _____ today.

2 I expect you were pleased to get home after such a terrible holiday.
must
You _____ get home after such a terrible holiday.

3 I'm sure he didn't phone, because I was at home all day.
have
He _____ , because I was at home all day.

4 It's possible that someone stole your purse when we were in the restaurant.
might
Someone _____ when we were in the restaurant.

5 Tim hasn't had a single cigarette today so perhaps he has stopped smoking completely.
may
Tim hasn't had a single cigarette today so he _____ up smoking completely.

6 You can keep a secret, can't you?
give
You wouldn't _____ you?

7 If you don't let me have your essay tomorrow, there'll be trouble!
better
You _____ in your essay tomorrow or there'll be trouble!

8 When she spoke to him, he laughed nervously.
a
He _____ when she spoke to him.

Use of English: FCE Part 5

Word formation

Read the following story of an unsolved mystery. Use the word given in capitals at the end of each line to form a word that fits the space in the same line. There is an example at the beginning **(0)**.

A strange journey

It was a warm, **(0)** <u>sunny</u> October morning in 1593 and in front of the palace in Mexico City	SUN
there were the usual bustling crowds of people moving **(1)** _____ across the plaza.	NOISE
One soldier stood out from the rest. Unlike the **(2)** _____ grey uniform of the other	TRADITION
palace guards his was a bright **(3)** _____ one and he carried a different kind of gun.	COLOUR
(4) _____ , the strange soldier said his orders that day were to guard the governor's	SURPRISE
palace in Manila, in the Philippines. '**(5)** _____ I am not in Manila,' he said, 'but	EVIDENCE
this is a palace so I am doing my duty.' By now, officers were **(6)** _____ of the	SUSPICION
man and his **(7)** _____ tale of overnight transportation thousands of miles	AMAZE
from Manila to Mexico City. And when he told them that the governor of Manila had	
been killed the night before he was **(8)** _____ .	PRISON
(9) _____ afterwards a ship arrived from the Philippines. It brought news that the	SHORT
governor had been murdered – on the night before the soldier had appeared. The soldier	
was released and sent back to Manila. Over 400 years later his **(10)** _____ journey	MYSTERY
through space and time remains unexplained.	

Writing

Introduction

In Paper 2 you have to complete two different writing tasks in 1 hour 30 minutes; the compulsory Part 1 task and then another from a choice of four in Part 2.

Part 1

You will either have to write   **a** a formal transactional letter
         or   **b** an informal transactional letter
Guidance is given in the form of input material, such as a letter, notes or adverts.

A transactional letter is one which is written in order to achieve a specific result or in response to someone else's request for action. Examples include:
• making a complaint
• requesting information
• giving information in reply to a letter you have received

Part 2

You will have a choice of four questions. Expect to find the following task types:

c an article
d a discursive composition
e a report
f a short story
g a description (often as part of another task type such as a short story or a letter)
h an informal non-transactional letter*
i a letter of application
j background reading text: there are always two options for this question

*The purpose of a non-transactional letter is usually to interest and/or inform the reader by talking about an experience you have had, communicating your opinion about something or giving advice.

Extracts

Decide which writing task type **a–j** each writing extract **(1–10)** is taken from.

1 Anyway, I hope that answers all your questions. Remember we can always put you up for the night if you want – just let us know when you're thinking of coming.
2 Some people feel that the practice of cloning animals is unethical and should therefore be banned. However, others argue that it has many important advantages.
3 Have you ever wondered what it would be like to be an animal in a cage? I have, and it's made me realize just how cruel zoos are.
4 Moreover, when I informed your assistant of this, he was extremely rude to me and refused to discuss the matter further.
5 As soon as the class had finished, Molly rushed out of the school and headed straight for the park. She desperately hoped it wasn't too late.
6 I have gained a considerable amount of relevant experience in this field, and consequently feel I would be a great asset to your company.
7 I've just got back from Krakow – have you ever been? I had such a brilliant time I just had to write and tell you about it!
8 To sum up, although the food in both restaurants is of the highest quality, Cagney's offers a greater selection of dishes and provides its customers with better service.
9 The person I most look up to is my uncle. Despite the difficulties he's faced, he is always very cheerful and his piercing blue eyes seem to light up when he smiles.
10 The two short stories from *Crime Never Pays* which I enjoyed most have many similarities. To begin with, 'Ricochet' and 'Three is a Lucky Number' are both about unsuccessful attempts to murder someone.

Formal or informal?

The following comments were made about extracts similar to those on page 118. Circle the appropriate alternative and match each sentence to the feature of language which is being commented on.

1 The use of 'can't' and 'isn't' show that the letter is *formal/informal*.

    a phrasal verbs

2 'Furthermore' is a very *formal/informal* word.

    b question forms

3 'Make up for' is a more *formal/informal* word for 'compensate'.

    c punctuation

4 An exclamation mark would not be used in *formal/informal* writing.

    d contractions

5 'Would you mind telling me when it starts?' sounds quite *formal/informal* to me.

    e linking words

Now look at the extracts again and decide whether each one is formal, informal or neutral. Give reasons for your decisions, commenting on the language used.

Example: *Extract 1 is informal. There is a contraction and a phrasal verb is used: 'put you up'. Starting a sentence with 'anyway' is informal, as is the use of the dash.*

Answering questions

Part 1: Transactional letters

1 Read the following Part 1 question and the two sample answers on page 120. Which answer do you think is better?

You have seen the advertisement below in an international newspaper and you are considering applying for the job. You know your friend worked in the same place last year and you have decided to write and ask him/her all about it. Read the advertisement and the notes you have made. Then write a letter to your friend telling him/her about your plans and asking for information and advice.

WORKING HOLIDAYS
in the South of England

Jobs available picking fruit in the county of Kent from June to September.

Strawberries, apples, pears, plums or cherries – depending on the month

• *Cooking facilities available*
• *Bring a tent*

Ask about:
Go July – which fruit?
Work 1 month/travel the next
*   – earn enough?*

Good camping facilities?
Days off?
Any more advice?

Write a **letter** of between **120 and 180** words in an appropriate style. Do not write any addresses.

A

Dear friend:

Thanks for your letter. I was really upset to hear about the argument you had with Marco last week. Even though you have fallen out with him I would recommend you to make it up with him. He's really easy-going and you were made for each other.

Anyway, this summer I am thinking in going fruit picking in the south of England. I know you have worked in the same place last year and I have decided to write and ask you all about it. I would be grateful if you could to tell me which fruit it is picked in July and how many days a week I would have to work. I'm going to work one month, then travel. Did you earn enough money? Furthermore, I would be grateful if you could to tell me wether the camping facilities are good? I'm going to buy a tent.

Anyway, I must to go now. If you can think in anything else that is worth knowing, please do not hesitate to contact me.

Kisses
Lola

B

Dear Bea,

I'm pleased to hear your university course is going well. I hope to start mine in September, but in summer I want to go fruit picking in England for a month, like you did last year. Before I apply for the job there are a few things I'd like to ask you first. I'm planning on going in July when my exams have finished, but I'd rather not pick strawberries as I know it's back-breaking work. Can you tell me which fruit is picked in that month? When I'm not working, I really want to go sightseeing in London so if you can remember how much free time you had, I'd like to know that, too. Then, after the job has finished, I'm thinking of setting off on a month's tour of England. It really depends on how much money I can earn – do you think I'd have enough to do that? Anyway, I'd better close now. Let me know if you have any other advice, such as suggestions on how to get there and what clothes to take.

Hope to hear from you soon.

All the best
Tania

2   Now read the two letters again and answer the questions in the categories below. First Certificate examiners use these categories when marking Writing Part 1 answers.

Content:	**a** Has the writer included all the main points in the notes? **b** Is the content of the letter relevant?
Organization and cohesion:	**a** Is the letter organized into suitable paragraphs? **b** Are ideas connected with appropriate linking words and presented in a logical order? **c** Does the letter have an appropriate opening and ending?
Range and accuracy:	**a** Is there a good variety of vocabulary and structures? **b** Has the writer managed to avoid repetition of language? **c** Has he/she copied whole phrases from the question?
Style and format:	**a** Is the style appropriate to the task/reader? Is it consistent? **b** Is the answer clearly set out as a letter?
Target reader:	Would the reader understand the writer's plans and be clear about what he/she wants to know?

3   Answer the following Part 1 question.

You and your family have decided to go on a family activity holiday in the UK. You have found the following advertisement and you would like to have more information. Write to Trident Adventure Holidays, covering all the points in your notes.

Don't forget!

Answer these questions about the writing task before you begin.

- Who is the target reader?
- Will you use a formal or an informal style?
- Will your questions be direct or indirect?

would arrive Fri. July 26th – OK?

all the time?

anywhere else?

sailing?

FAMILY ADVENTURE HOLIDAYS
in the picturesque Lake District

Activities include:
- canoeing
- mountain biking
- climbing
- initiative exercises

Parents are encouraged to participate with their children in the activities.

Holidays run from Saturday to Saturday throughout July and August.

£230 – includes all activities, accommodation and meals

cost of extra night?

For more details write to:
Trident Adventure Holidays
1 Lake Street
Oxford OX1 9EP

what's that?

Write a letter of between **120 and 180** words in an appropriate style. Do not write any addresses.

4   When you have written your letter, check it using the questions in exercise 2.

Part 2

The following questions are typical of those you might be asked in Part 2 of the Writing paper. There is one example of each type: articles, short stories, compositions, reports and letters. Read each of the questions and put a tick (✓) next to those you feel you would be most able to answer. Give reasons for each of your ticks.

1   Your college magazine has invited you to write an **article** about a member of your family who helped you in some way. Describe the person and explain what they did that was helpful to you.

2   You have decided to enter a short **story** competition. The competition rules say that the story must begin or end with the following words:
They were sad to leave, but they had no choice.

3   You have had a class discussion on the following statement:
It should be illegal for parents to smack their children.
Your teacher has asked you to write a **composition** giving your views on the statement.

4   You have a part-time job in a games centre, where people can go to play computer games. The owner would like to buy some new software and he has asked you to write a **report**, suggesting two games for the centre. You should briefly describe each game and explain why you think the customers would enjoy both games.

5   You recently visited a place which you had not been to for a long time. Your cousin, who now lives abroad, also knew this place very well. Write a **letter** to your cousin, describing the changes and your feelings about them. Do not write any addresses.

Answering the question

1   To ensure your answer is relevant, underline the key words in the question. Find the answers to the following questions for number 1 above, underlining the relevant words.

    1   What do you have to write ?   4   What is special about this person?
    2   Who for?   5   What two things do you have to include in
    3   Who do you have to write about?   your answer?

2   It is important to write your answer in an appropriate style. Look at question 1 again. Think about the target reader. Will you write in a formal, neutral or informal style?

3   Now underline the key words in each of the other questions and decide which style would be most appropriate.

4   Write an answer to one or more of the questions above. Write your answer in **120–180** words in an appropriate style.

10 Nothing but the truth

Vocabulary 1: Crime and punishment

A Crimes and criminals

1 Match each of the following definitions with the word for a criminal from the box. There is one extra word which you do not need to use.

vandal	kidnapper	arsonist	blackmailer	shoplifter	smuggler
mugger	drug trafficker	hijacker	pickpocket	murderer	

A person who...
1 kills someone. _____
2 takes goods into or out of a country illegally. _____
3 deliberately sets fire to a building. _____
4 steals things from people's pockets or bags in public places. _____
5 threatens to give away secrets unless he/she is given money. _____
6 takes things from shops without paying for them. _____
7 holds someone prisoner until he/she is given money. _____
8 takes control of an aeroplane by force. _____
9 deliberately damages other people's property. _____
10 attacks people in the street and steals their money. _____

2 Write the name of the crime committed by each of the criminals in exercise 1. Which of the crimes involve theft of some kind?

Example: mugger – *mugging*

3 Match each verb from the box with an appropriate pair of nouns.

burgle rob steal	**a** _____ an office/a house
	b _____ money/jewellery
	c _____ a bank/a person

B Punishment

1 Look at the following types of punishment which can be given by courts. Put them in order from the least to the most severe.

a to sentence someone to life imprisonment
b to order someone to do 200 hours of community service
c to sentence someone to death
d to order someone to pay a £200 fine
e to give someone a two-year prison sentence

 2 Decide what punishment, if any, should be given to the person or people below. Discuss your ideas using some of the language of agreement and opinion in the box.

- a 73-year-old woman who stole a scarf from a department store
- three 16-year-old vandals who set fire to litter bins and sprayed paint on parked cars
- a gang of armed men who hijacked a plane with 135 passengers on board and threatened to blow it up
- two men who mugged another, robbing him of £10 and breaking several of his teeth
- a businessman who has earned millions from drug trafficking

Giving opinions	**Agreeing and disagreeing**
In my opinion...	*I totally agree.*
To my mind...	*I think so, too.*
From my point of view...	*I agree up to a point.*
Personally, I think...	*I really don't think so.*
I strongly believe...	*I completely disagree.*

Listening 1:
FCE Part 2

Note taking

 1 What are the best ways to protect your house from burglary?
How well is your house protected?

2 Read the following Listening Part 2 instructions. Try to predict the type of information you will hear for each question before you listen.

You will hear part of a radio programme, in which a police officer talks about burglary. For questions **1–10**, complete the missing information.

BURGLARY

- almost half of burglaries occur [_____ **1**]
- most burglaries take [_____ **2**] minutes

OPERATION BUMBLEBEE

- targets criminals who [_____ **3**]
- led to a [_____ **4**] decrease in burglary in first year

HOUSEHOLDERS

- don't hide keys [_____ **5**]
- deter burglars with a [_____ **6**]
- ask for advice about choosing [_____ **7**]
- fit locks to the [_____ **8**]

NEIGHBOURHOOD WATCH SCHEMES

- particularly helps protect people like the [_____ *and* _____ **9**]
- over [_____ **10**] people benefit from the schemes

Speaking 1: FCE Part 3

Collaborative task

Here are some different methods of tackling crime. Talk to your partner about the advantages and disadvantages of each approach and then choose which you think is the least and most effective.

Speaking 2: FCE Part 4

Further discussion

Discuss these Speaking Part 4 questions with your partner. Try to develop your answers and give reasons and examples to support your opinions.

- What do you think are the main causes of crime in your country?
- Do you have any other suggestions for reducing crime in your local area?
- Do you think the police should carry guns?
- Do you think the death penalty is a valid form of punishment?

When she saw the broken chair the teacher said she wouldn't let us go home until the person who was responsible for the damage (**1**) <u>owned up</u>. In the end Brian Ogilvie said he'd done it, but that it had been an accident. He (**2**) <u>made up</u> a story about falling over backwards onto it and the chair just falling apart under his weight. Our teacher will believe anything and she was completely (**3**) <u>taken in</u> by his words, totally unaware that the chair had been broken in an act of pure vandalism. She (**4**) <u>let him off</u> with nothing more than an unconvincing warning.

But he didn't (**5**) <u>get away with</u> it. The next day the teacher (**6**) <u>found out</u> the truth when she overheard Ogilvie (**7**) <u>showing off</u> to his friends in another class about how he'd managed to deceive the teacher. The headteacher was informed, and after (**8**) <u>looking into</u> the incident, decided to suspend him for a month.

Vocabulary 2: Phrasal verbs

1 Read the story and decide whether you feel the punishment was suitable.

2 Read the story again. Work out the meaning of each of the underlined phrasal verbs using the context of the sentence and of the story as a whole.

3 Write four sentences, each one including one of the phrasal verbs from the story. Then rewrite the sentences, leaving a space where the verb should be. Ask your partner to complete the spaces with an appropriate phrasal verb.

Writing 1:
FCE Part 2

Choose **one** of the following questions and write **120–180** words.

1   You have been doing a class project on crime. Your teacher has asked you to write a contribution for the school's English language magazine with the following title:

What can ordinary people do to help in the fight against crime?

Write your **article**, giving other students practical suggestions for beating crime.

How to go about it

Style
- Who is the target reader?
- Should the style be formal, neutral or informal?

Organization and ideas
- Introductory paragraph:
  Why is it important for ordinary people to help in the fight against crime? Can they do very much to help?

- Paragraphs two and three:
  Think of your discussion in the speaking activity.
- To finish your article you could:
  encourage readers to take action.
  and/or *give them advice on the first thing they should do.*
  and/or *ask them to consider the consequences of not doing anything.*

2   Your teacher has asked you to write a story for the school's English language magazine. It must begin with the following words:

He quickly put the tin of soup into his pocket and moved towards the checkout.

Write your **story**.

How to go about it

- Plan your story before you start writing
- Look again at pages 50 and 51 in Unit 4 for the ingredients of a good narrative.
- Use a range of past tenses:
  Past perfect to describe what had happened before the main events of the story.

- Past continuous and past simple to describe the main events of the story.
- Use some of the vocabulary you have learnt in this unit.
- Begin with the words in the question.

Reading:
FCE Part 1

Multiple matching

1   In this introduction to an article from a teenage magazine called *Sugar* you are going to read about a 14-year-old boy whose mother hired a private detective to spy on him.

   Why do you think she did this?

How do you think the boy reacted when he found out?
How would a private investigator spy on a teenage boy?

Now read the introduction and check your predictions.

Is someone being paid to spy on you?

Sounds unlikely, doesn't it? But private detectives all over Britain are spying on teenagers. They aren't working for the government or the police; they've been hired by ordinary parents. Incredibly, each week around 500 parents are thought to hire investigators to spy on their own children. But what does it feel like to discover that your mum or dad has paid someone to investigate your life? A few weeks ago, 14-year-old Liam found out that his Mum had done just that.

The boy who was spied on
'When mum told me that she'd hired someone to spy on me, I was totally stunned. She said she'd only done it because she was worried I was hanging out with the wrong type of lads. She says it shows she

cares about me, but it'll take a while before I get over the shock and I'm ready to trust her again.'

The mum who spied on him
Liam's mum explained her side of the story. 'I wanted to be sure that Liam wasn't hanging out with the wrong crowd, so I hired someone to investigate. I only did it because I want the best for him. The detective bugged our telephone for four days, followed Liam to the local youth club and took a few photos. I did feel a bit guilty, but I don't regret doing it at all. It was such a relief to know he wasn't part of the local gang. Now I can sleep at night without worrying about him.'

0 | *H*

At around £250 a day, hiring a private investigator can be pricey but that doesn't put many parents off. Spying on teenagers is a growing trend and there are hundreds of investigation agencies around the country. So what is it that parents are so intrigued to find out? It seems that the main reasons for parents hiring an investigator are to find out who their child is hanging out with, whether he or she is up to no good and what their boyfriend or girlfriend is really like.

1 |

One investigator, Mark Cox, told us, 'I'm often hired by parents who want me to watch their children and I generally find that parents are much more worried about their daughters than their sons.' But why don't these parents just talk to their kids about their worries? 'Parents aren't always aware of what teenagers are up to; they don't talk to them and don't know what's going on in their lives,' says Mark. 'That's where I come in.'

2 |

Rather worryingly, a legal advisor told us, 'There is no general right to privacy in England. As long as he or she doesn't trespass on your property, it is perfectly legal for an investigator to take pictures of you or record what you say. And if your mum or dad owns the phone they can let an investigator tap it. Investigators are not allowed to interfere with personal property such as your letters but they may read them if they're left in view.'

3 |

Understandably, human rights groups see this as a worrying trend. A spokesperson from human rights group Liberty spoke to us. 'Although we wouldn't argue that it should be against the law for parents to spy like this, we do believe these private detective agencies ought to be properly regulated to ensure they act responsibly. This is a sensitive issue and certain limits should be imposed on what can and cannot be done.'

4 |

Sugar's agony aunt Wendy Granditer gave us her views. 'Parents spying on children is a terrible invasion of privacy. It's like reading someone else's diary. Even if they do find out their children have been misbehaving, they're going to have to reveal where they got their information from. Children are unlikely to want to discuss a problem with their parents once they discover they've been spied on. It will only make the relationship between them worse. I can see why parents worry, but they shouldn't go behind their children's backs.'

5 |

Will we ever be free from the risk of being investigated or will we always be looking over our shoulders? In a society where security cameras film our every move and all our private details are recorded on computers, will our privacy vanish completely? According to Mark Cox, we can all help stop the number of teen investigators growing. 'It's all down to families communicating with each other,' he says. 'If everyone started speaking to each other honestly, secrets and suspicion could become a thing of the past.' Let's just hope he's right.

6 |

So, do you think hiring private investigators to track teenagers is a good idea or is it a blow to your personal freedom? Phone in and register your vote.

- If you think teen investigators are a good idea phone 0660 191 952

- If you think they're a bad idea call 0660 191 953

We'll reveal the results in a future issue of *Sugar*. You can also send your opinions for publication on our 'Readers' Articles' page to the usual *Sugar* address.

2 You are now going to read the rest of the article. Choose the most suitable heading from the list **A–H** for each part (**1–6**) of the article. There is one extra heading you do not need to use. There is an example at the beginning (**0**).

A Creating more problems
B Are they breaking the law?
C Out of touch
D Legal support for children
E What lies ahead?
F For or against?
G A need for control
H What's the worry?

Reacting to the text 🔵

Do you agree with Wendy Granditer that phone tapping and parents spying on children is 'an invasion of privacy'?
Does *everyone* have 'a right to privacy'? Even royalty and other famous people?

Noticing language

Complete the spaces with a word or words from the text, using the guidelines on meaning to help you. The numbers in brackets refer to the numbers of the paragraphs where the words can be found.

a a noun meaning 'freedom from interference by other people'

(2) *a right to* _____
(4) *an invasion of*

b a noun meaning 'a general tendency or direction'

(0) *a growing* _____
(3) *a worrying*

c (a part of the body) this fixed phrase means 'to do something without someone's knowledge or consent'

(4) *to go behind someone's* _____

d (a part of the body) this fixed phrase means 'to be concerned about what people might be doing or saying about you'

(5) *to look over one's* _____

e an informal phrasal verb meaning 'spend one's time with friends, doing nothing in particular'

(0) *to* _____ _____ *with friends*

f informal fixed phrase meaning 'to be doing something naughty'

(0) *to be* _____ _____ *no good*

Language focus 1: Passives

1 In the next column there is a summary of the main points in the article on spying. Complete each space in the text with one of the verbs in the box. You may use some verbs more than once. There is an example at the beginning **(0)**.

be	to be	being	is	are
was	will	have	had	

2 Many of the numbered verbs in exercise 1 are passive constructions. Put these passive verbs in the appropriate part of the table below depending on the tense.

How is the passive formed?

Tense	Example
Present simple	
Present continuous	*Is someone being paid...?*
Present perfect	
Past simple	
Past continuous	
Past perfect	
Future simple	
Infinitive	
Gerund	

Read more about passives in **A** and **B** on pages 213 and 214 of the Grammar reference.

Is someone (0) _being_ **paid to spy on you?**

The use of private investigators to spy on children is a growing trend in Britain today. These spies **(1)** _____ not working for the government or the police; they **(2)** _____ been hired by ordinary parents who **(3)** _____ worried about what their children might be up to. One 14-year-old boy spoke of his feelings a few weeks ago when he **(4)** _____ told by his mother that he **(5)** _____ been spied on. He said that he **(6)** _____ still very shocked at what she **(7)** _____ done.

A lack of communication between parents and teenagers is blamed for the trend and the whole question of an individual's right to privacy **(8)** _____ raised. Whilst there is nothing illegal in this type of investigation, there is a feeling that the detective agencies ought **(9)** _____ properly regulated in order to protect teenagers' rights.

In an age when security cameras **(10)** _____ constantly filming us in the high street and our personal details **(11)** _____ recorded on computers, the question is asked as to whether we **(12)** _____ ever be free from the risk of **(13)** _____ investigated or will teenagers **(14)** _____ spied on for years to come. We might never know the answer to these questions since, after all, would you know if your phone **(15)** _____ being bugged?

Passive constructions with the infinitive

*...each week around 500 parents **are thought to hire** investigators...*

This phrase has the same meaning as:

*...**it is thought that** each week around 500 parents hire investigators...*

Change the following sentence in the same way:

They are believed to have stolen £3 million.

It _____ .

The infinitive (*to do*) or the perfect infinitive (*to have done*) can be used after the passive of these verbs:

believe   consider   expect   know   say   think

Transformations

For questions **1–6**, complete the second sentence so that it has a similar meaning to the first sentence, using the word given. **Do not change the word given.** You must use between two and five words, including the word given.

1 It is forbidden to take cameras into the courtroom.
   must
   Cameras _____ into the courtroom.

2 It is known that Smith broke into several houses.
   known
   Smith _____ into several houses.

3 They do not think he is dangerous.
   be
   He _____ dangerous.

4 They'll make you pay a fine if they catch you smoking.
   made
   You _____ pay a fine if they catch you smoking.

5 I told nobody about our conversation so I'm sure someone tapped my phone.
   must
   I told nobody about our conversation so my phone _____ by someone.

6 The lawyer is still waiting for his client to contact him.
   contacted
   The lawyer _____ his client yet.

Read more about this type of passive construction in **C** on page 214 of the Grammar reference.

Further practice: Passives

Complete each of the spaces in the following text with an appropriate active or passive form of the verb in brackets. You may need to use more than one word in each space.

Man fined £800 for not clearing his dog's mess

A dog owner **(0)** *has been ordered* (order) to pay a record £800 after **(1)** _____ (let) his pet foul a grass verge within yards of a waste bin. Paul Humphris, 52, who got his black Labrador, Billy, from a rescue centre 13 years ago, **(2)** _____ (find) guilty of failing to clean up after him.

Sue Bell, the association's president, said: 'I hope this case **(3)** _____ (send) out a strong message against dog fouling, but I do feel sorry for the man concerned.'

Mr Humphris, a purchaser from Banbury, said: 'This is the first time I **(4)** _____ (fine). I cannot believe what has happened. Usually I **(5)** _____ (put) my dog's mess in one of the council bins. On this particular evening it was freezing cold, wet and raining and I was lazy, I have to admit that. But normally people **(6)** _____ (fine) about £50 for dog fouling.'

Cathy Wainwright, the warden who **(7)** _____ (catch) Mr Humphris in December, said she was pleased with the result. 'The high fine imposed reflects the severity of the offence and will hopefully serve as a warning to other irresponsible people who **(8)** _____ (not/clean) up after their pets.'

Yesterday the court **(9)** _____ (tell) how Ms Wainwright followed Mr Humphris on foot to his home after seeing him let his dog foul the verge. Soon afterwards Mr Humphris **(10)** _____ (invite) to meet Ms Wainwright to discuss the matter, but he declined, claiming he was unhappy about **(11)** _____ (follow). The case then went to court three times, with Mr Humphris eventually **(12)** _____ (order) to pay £400 costs as well as a £400 fine.

Writing 2:
FCE Part 2

Articles

1 Look at these sentences from the article, 'Is someone being paid to spy on you?'

Incredibly, each week around 500 parents are thought to hire investigators.
Rather worryingly, there is no general right to privacy in England.
Understandably, human rights groups see this as a worrying trend.

Each one begins with an adverb which expresses the writer's attitude to or opinion of what follows. In **1–8** below replace the underlined phrase with an adverb from the box.

Astonishingly	Interestingly	Curiously	Personally
Happily	Sadly	Not surprisingly	Unfortunately

1 <u>In my opinion</u>, I think that any form of physical punishment is unacceptable.
2 <u>I'm absolutely amazed that</u> some private investigators are teenagers themselves.
3 <u>It is sad that</u> there is a growing trend towards violence in our schools.
4 <u>It is regrettable that</u> many parents just don't communicate with their children.
5 <u>It's strange that</u> some kidnap victims end up sympathizing with their captors.
6 <u>As you would expect</u>, most parents worry about their children's safety.
7 <u>It's worth noting that</u> most children don't leave home until they get married.
8 <u>I'm pleased to be able to say that</u> this is an exception rather than the rule.

2 The article is written for a teenage magazine and the style is quite informal. Look at these different techniques which are used in the article to achieve the informal style.

Technique	Examples
• Informal language	*kids, pricey, to hang out, to be up to no good*
• The use of contractions	*they aren't working, they've been hired*
• More informal linking words	*And, But, So* (to start a sentence)
• Questions involving the reader	*Sounds unlikely, doesn't it?*
• Giving an example	*A few weeks ago, 14-year-old Liam found out that his mum had done just that.*
• Leaving the reader to think	*Let's just hope he's right.*

Notice that articles are also usually given a heading, in this case a question:
Is someone being paid to spy on you?

3 At the end of the article readers were invited to send their opinions to *Sugar* for their 'Readers' Articles' page. Here is one reader's reply to the question:

Do you think hiring private investigators to track teenagers is a good idea or is it a blow to your personal freedom?

Which of the techniques you saw in exercise 2 are used?

How would they feel?
   Would parents like it if their kids hired private detectives to spy on them? I don't think so, do you?
   Clearly, parents need to know what their children are up to. After all, they're responsible for bringing them up and they can only do this if they know where their teenage sons and daughters go and who they hang out with. But there are other ways of finding out.
   Fortunately for me, my parents wouldn't dream of spying on me. They talk to me if they think something's wrong and I know I can discuss my problems without being told off or shouted at. Naturally, they get upset if I do something I shouldn't, but they're aware it's all part of growing up and they don't get too angry.
   Everyone has a right to privacy and grown-ups ought to think twice before going behind their children's backs. Let's face it, they were all young once and I bet most of them got up to things they weren't supposed to. I know *mine* did – they talk to me about it!

4 How are the writer's ideas organized in the model answer? What information is contained in each paragraph?

Paragraph 1: _____
Paragraph 2: _____
Paragraph 3: _____
Paragraph 4: _____

5 The teenage magazine *Sugar* has asked its readers to write an article for the 'Readers' Articles' page giving their opinions on the following question.

Should parents be punished if their children commit crimes?

To help you think about what you are going to write, discuss the following questions.

Situation:	How serious is teenage crime in your country? What types of crimes are committed by teenagers?
Causes of teenage crime:	What are the main reasons for crime amongst youngsters? To what extent can parents be held responsible for their children's crimes? What circumstances are out of the control of parents? Consider: • their children's upbringing • the parents' relationship with their children • the parents' social background/economic situation • the people that their children hang out with What can parents do to prevent their children from committing crime?
Effects of punishing parents:	What might be the positive and negative effects if parents were ordered to pay fines or sent to prison for their children's crimes?

6 You should give your article a heading to attract the readers' attention and open with a statement or question which will interest the target readers. Ideally, this first sentence should link with the heading.

Match the following headings **1–4** with an appropriate opening sentence **a–d**.

1 A growing trend, but what are the causes?
2 It's their fault
3 Victims of society
4 Grow up!

a Why should parents be punished for the evils of society?
b Growing up is all about becoming more mature and taking responsibility for your own actions.
c Have you ever wondered why there is an increasing number of teenagers who commit crimes?
d Clearly, parents have to take at least some of the blame for what their children get up to.

Don't forget!

● Use a style appropriate to the target reader.
● Use the techniques and language you have just studied.
● Organize your ideas into logical paragraphs.
● Close in an interesting way by giving an opinion or asking a question.

Now write your **article** in **120–180** words.

Listening 2:
FCE Part 3
Multiple matching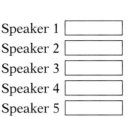

1 Have you ever failed to tell the whole truth to your parents?
Did they find out? What were the consequences?

2 You will hear five people talking about how they were 'economical with the truth' to
their parents. Match the speaker to the correct description in the list **A–F**. Use the
letters only once. There is one extra letter which you do not need to use.

A property was stolen   Speaker 1 [   ]

B some money was stolen   Speaker 2 [   ]

C the lie was unnecessary   Speaker 3 [   ]

D helping the father brought results   Speaker 4 [   ]

E the mother found the evidence Speaker 5 [   ]

F a telephone call spoiled the fun

3 Now listen to the recording again and choose the best answer **A**, **B** or **C**.

1 Who found out first that Speaker 1
was lying?
   A her mother
   B the school
   C the police

2 Why didn't Speaker 2 go back to check
the windows?
   A It was a long way from the car to
   the house.
   B He knew he would be back soon.
   C He thought they were closed.

3 Why didn't Speaker 3's parents like
parties in the house?
   A The house was new.
   B They didn't like their children's
   friends.
   C They wanted to celebrate somewhere
   else.

4 What did Speaker 4 do with the
practice letters?
   A He threw them away.
   B He burned them.
   C He tore them up.

5 In what way did Speaker 5 misbehave
at school?
   A She smoked cigarettes.
   B She was rude to teachers.
   C She organized parties.

Which situation would you least
like to have been in?

Language focus 2: Past necessity

Compare the use of *need* by speakers 1 and 5 in these
extracts from the listening.

Speaker 1:
*I **needn't have lied** after all – I found the money in the
bottom of my jacket pocket.*

Speaker 5:
*I **didn't need to tell lies**. I knew how to get round my dad.*

Which of the following sentences applies to which speaker?

a She didn't lie because she knew it wasn't necessary.
b She lied but she only realized it wasn't necessary
afterwards.

 Read more on page 214 of the Grammar reference.

Practice
Complete each of the following spaces using the verb in
brackets and the correct form of *need*.

1 I wrote 250 words in my composition but noticed later that
the word limit was only 180. I _____ (write)
so much.

2 Today's a public holiday so last night I _____
(set) my alarm clock. This morning I got up at 11.30!

3 Last summer I had my head shaved. It was great – I
_____ (go) to the hairdresser's for ages
after that.

4 I stayed up until midnight last night to get my homework
finished. I _____ (bother) – the teacher
is off sick today.

5 I was a bit concerned that my mum wouldn't like the
earrings I bought her , but I _____ (worry) –
she wears them every day.

10 Review

The passive

Complete each of the following spaces with the correct passive form of the verb in brackets.

1 This bank _____ (rob) twice since it opened in January this year.
2 Two men _____ (arrest) yesterday in connection with the theft.
3 I think people who commit acts of vandalism should _____ (make) to pay for the damage they cause.
4 We're getting used to _____ (burgle): that's the third time it's happened to us this year.
5 Millions of pounds' worth of drugs _____ (smuggle) into the country each year.
6 I don't think he _____ (give) a prison sentence; he'll probably just have to pay a fine.
7 The causes of the fire _____ (currently/look) into by the police.
8 I was shocked when the teacher shouted at Sue. She _____ (never/tell) off before that in her life.

Use of English:
FCE Part 4

Error correction

Read the text below and look carefully at each line. Some of the lines are correct and some have a word which should not be there.

If a line is correct, put a tick (✓) in the space at the end of the line. If a line has a word which should not be there, write the word in the space. There are two examples at the beginning (**0** and **00**).

Shoplifting

0	People have been shoplifting for as long as there have been shops, but	✓
00	the problem has increased in the 1960s with the growth of self-service.	*has*
1	It has now been become one of the most costly crimes in Britain and	_____
2	each year shops lose more than £750 million in stolen by goods. Only	_____
3	about 20 per cent of all shoplifters are being organized or professional, but	_____
4	nearly they represent a major headache for shopowners. Their crimes,	_____
5	along with theft by shop staff, result in more greater losses than everything	_____
6	is stolen by amateurs. They are rarely caught and even when they are, many	_____
7	shops decide not to report the thief. The police often consider turning up to	_____
8	arrest for a shoplifter as a low priority and court cases require a great deal	_____
9	of time and effort. Incredibly, of the few thieves who are caught, only one	_____
10	per cent are prosecuted and most of these are let them off with a small fine.	_____
11	Shopowners, however, they are fighting back. Technology is the main	_____
12	weapon and the installation of any CCTV cameras is now commonplace in	_____
13	both small and large businesses. One London camera shop uses the shame	_____
14	as an effective deterrent; a sign in its window warns that shoplifters will be	_____
15	photographed taken and their picture placed in the shop window.	_____

Vocabulary

A **Phrasal verbs**

The following phrasal verbs have appeared either in this unit or in previous units.

1 In A and B complete each sentence beginning **1–6** with an appropriate ending **a–f**. The first one has been done for you.

A Phrasal verbs with *off* and *out*

1	The judge let him off	a	for being rude.
2	He told her off	b	the truth about him.
3	He was showing off	c	with a fine.
4	I found out	d	over something stupid.
5	He gave out	e	to his classmates.
6	They fell out	f	the books.

B Phrasal verbs with *up* and *away*

1	He made up	a	in the south of England.
2	She owned up	b	with that noise any more.
3	I grew up	c	the whole story.
4	I can't put up	d	with it again, hasn't he?
5	He's got away	e	by the gun in his car.
6	He was given away	f	to doing it.

2 Choose four phrasal verbs from the box below and write an example sentence for each verb you have chosen.

split up with	set up	turn up	give up
take up	bring up	come up	make up for

B **Crimes**

Read this short news article and for questions **1–3** choose the correct alternative. In each of the spaces write an appropriate preposition.

The home of Lady Agatha Carruthers was **(1)** *burgled/stolen* by two teenage boys in the early hours of this morning. The boys, who were seen leaving the house, **(2)** *stole/robbed* jewellery worth £300,000 _____ the former Government Minister, before making their getaway on bicycles. This incident comes just a week after a similar break-in, in which Lady Carruthers was **(3)** *stolen/robbed* _____ her entire collection of antique watches.

Writing:
FCE Part 2

Short stories

You have decided to enter a short-story competition organized by an international young people's magazine. The competition rules say that the story must end with the following words:

I swore then that I would never tell another lie as long as I lived.

Write your **story** in **120–180** words.

Don't forget!

- Look again at the 'ingredients' of a good narrative on pages 50 and 51 in Unit 4.
- Try to include two or three phrasal verbs.

11 What on Earth's going on?

Vocabulary 1: Weather

1   All the words in each of the groups **1–7** below can be used with one of the nouns in the box to form strong collocations. For each group of words write the noun which can be used in the appropriate space. There is an example at the beginning **(0)**.

sunshine
showers
~~sky~~
sea
storm
clouds
rain
wind

0 overcast
clear   *sky*
stormy

1 violent
severe   _____
electric

2 fine
heavy   _____
torrential

3 strong
gale-force   _____
light

4 warm
brilliant   _____
glorious

5 rough
calm   _____
choppy

6 thick
storm   _____
angry-looking

7 light
scattered   _____
snow

2   Study the words in exercise 1 for two minutes. Then cover up the adjectives and see how many you can remember for each noun.

3   Describe the photos above using as many of the adjective + noun collocations as possible. What types of weather do you prefer? What weather conditions do you least like?

Reading:
FCE Part 4

Multiple matching

1   Which of the following occur in your country?

droughts	floods	avalanches	hurricanes	earthquakes	tornadoes

Have you experienced any of these? What was it like?
What are the worst weather conditions you have had to endure?

2   You are going to read a magazine article in which people describe their experiences with natural disasters. For questions **1–13**, choose from the people **(A–D)**. The people may be chosen more than once. When more than one answer is required, these may be given in any order. There is an example at the beginning **(0)**.

Which of the people suggest the following?

I was impressed with how people reacted.	**0**	C
Preparations were made for the disaster.	**1**	
I didn't think it could happen here.	**2**	
We didn't think we would be in any danger.	**3**	**4**
The experience had a long-lasting effect on me.	**5**	
Disaster had struck in the same place before.	**6**	
I tried unsuccessfully to see it happening.	**7**	
We were without electricity.	**8**	**9**
We had a very narrow escape.	**10**	
It has not affected my feelings for the place.	**11**	
We had to hide our real feelings.	**12**	
I slowly became aware of how serious it had been.	**13**	

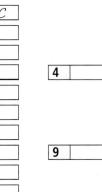

LUCKY TO BE ALIVE

A

David Crossland, 50, was on holiday with his wife, Louise, in the Bahamas when the giant Hurricane Floyd hit New Providence Island.

'We were on holiday on Providence Island last year when Hurricane George was due to hit, but it changed direction. So this year, when Hurricane Floyd was heading towards us, Louise and I were convinced it would change course. But a week into our holiday the island was in the direct path of the hurricane and the hotel staff feared the worst. All of the ground-floor windows and balcony doors in the hotel were boarded up. At one point I tried to open the balcony door in our bedroom to catch a glimpse of the hurricane but the winds were so strong I couldn't move it. All we could do was lie in our bed in the candlelight and wait.

When the all clear was given at 2 pm we were able to go out and see the devastation. It was shocking. There were parts of houses, trees and debris everywhere and a tidal wave had destroyed many homes on the island. Such a shame for the island, but hurricanes could never put us off going back there.'

B

When Pat Beddows reached 40, she set herself a mountainous challenge in the Himalayas. During the trek disaster struck.

'I set off in a group of 20 from Gangotri, a village at 4,000 metres in the foothills of the Himalayas. As we sat having lunch, we watched huge chunks of ice break away from a glacier, then fall into the water. Unaware of the risk we were taking we climbed down into the glacier to take a closer look. Suddenly, I heard a thundering noise and our guide started screaming: "Run! Run! Climb up!"

A tidal wave of water and ice was heading straight for us and we scrambled up the rocky slopes to safety. Chunks of ice the size of cars were being thrown into the air barely five metres away. If the guide hadn't shouted at us to get out of the way, the consequences would have been tragic. When we got back to

camp we were told that, three years earlier, 16 people had died there in a similar incident. I realized how lucky we all were and I burst into tears.'

C

Teacher Caroline Casterton, 25, was visiting friends in Istanbul when an earthquake struck.

'I was fast asleep in my friends' apartment when the tremor shook. At first it was total confusion. There was a power cut so it was pitch black and everything inside the building was shaking and moving. It lasted only 45 seconds but it felt like an eternity. It was absolutely terrifying. For the next four days and nights I slept on the streets with thousands of others and the scale of the devastation gradually began to sink in.

Yet out of the chaos there was the most incredible sense of camaraderie. Everyone seemed so united and I witnessed so much courage and kindness. Since that day I have taken far less for granted and I really do feel life is for living in the present. Now I'm teaching the pupils at my school to be far more aware of the misfortunes of other people.'

D

Doug Glenwright, 33, was sitting in his front room in Birmingham, England, when he had the shock of his life.

'Last week we were watching on the television how tornadoes wrecked Oklahoma, where you'd expect to see them. Then suddenly last night one of them came down our street. The first I became aware of it was when I saw a dustbin bag come up from the street and fly past the window like a kite. Then branches of trees and all sorts of other debris were pulled up into the air. Telephone lines were knocked down by the hurricane-force winds and the heavy rain caused four feet of flood water in some people's kitchens.

Naturally my wife and I were both nervous, but we couldn't let the children see so we laughed and joked our way through it. We didn't think it was very funny, though, when we saw the massive hole it had made in our roof.'

Reacting to the text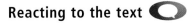

How do you think you would have felt in each of the situations in the text?
Can you remember a time when you were frightened or concerned for your safety?

Language focus 1: Conditionals

A Real or imaginary?

Look at the following statement from text B of the reading.
If the guide hadn't shouted at us to get out of the way, the consequences would have been tragic.

Read the following explanation and underline the correct alternatives.

In this sentence the speaker is referring to a situation in the *present/past/future*. The situation she describes is imaginary because we know that the guide *shouted/didn't shout* at them to get out of the way and that the consequences *were/were not* tragic.

B Context

1 In which of the four situations described in the reading do you think each of the following were said?

Zero conditional: *This **occurs** if the 'plates' underneath the earth's surface **rub** together or **pull** apart.*

First conditional: *You **will be** much safer if you **stay** in the hotel.*

Second conditional: *If we **lived** in Oklahoma, we **would see** a lot more of these.*

Third conditional: *If we **had known** it was going to happen, we **would have got** out of the building earlier.*

Mixed conditional: *If we **had ignored** his warnings, we **wouldn't be** alive today.*

2 Identify the verb forms in **bold** in each of the conditional sentences in exercise 1.

C Meaning

1 Match each of the explanations **a–e** to a conditional sentence in exercise B1.
   a an imaginary situation in the past
   b an imaginary situation in the present
   c a possible future situation and its likely result
   d the likely present result of an imaginary situation in the past
   e a scientific fact, or something that is always true (*if* means *whenever*)

2 Do the following two sentences refer to past, present or future situations?
   a *If we have another tornado here, we'll sell the house and move to a different area.*
   b *If we had another tornado here, we'd sell the house and move to a different area.*

   Why are different tenses used in each sentence?
   What does each sentence tell us about how the speaker views the possibility of the event occurring?

3 Explain the difference in meaning between the following pairs of sentences.
   1 a If it doesn't rain tomorrow, we'll go for a picnic.
     b If it doesn't rain tomorrow, we may go for a picnic.
   2 a If it didn't rain so much, we would all be a lot healthier.
     b If it didn't rain so much, we might all be a lot healthier.

4 a Which of these words and expressions can be used in place of *if* in the following sentence without changing the meaning?

   as long as   as far as   provided   providing   promising   on condition

   *You can watch the film on TV **if** you help me do the washing up first.*

   b Which word meaning *if not* can be used in the following sentence?
   We'll probably go to the beach tomorrow _____ it rains.

   Read more about conditional sentences on page 214 of the Grammar reference.

Practice

1 Each of the following sentences contains a mistake. Find the five mistakes and correct them.
   1 If you'd have asked me, I would have lent you some money.
   2 I'll give you a ring if I'll find out what time he's arriving.
   3 What would you do if she doesn't come to your party?
   4 If I would drink coffee after six in the evening, I can never sleep.
   5 If they lose another match, I'd never go to see them play again.

2 **Student A:** On page 202 you will find the second half of four conditional sentences. For each one, write three possible beginnings.

   Example:
   a *If I could speak English fluently,*
   b *If I went to live in the capital,*   I'd get a good job.
   c *If my dad asked the right people,*

   Student B: On page 200 you will find the first half of four conditional sentences. For each one, write three possible continuations.

   Example:
                                          a *I'd probably be married.*
   If I were 10 years older,   b *I wouldn't have to go to school.*
                                          c *I'd be able to vote.*

   Read out the sentence halves you have written and your partner will try to guess the sentence half you were given.

Conditionals: Expressing regret

The third conditional can be used to express regrets. For each of the following situations imagine what the person might be thinking. Write a third conditional sentence for each picture.

0 *If I'd brought my umbrella,*
    I wouldn't have got so wet.

1 _____

2 _____

3 _____

4 _____

5 _____

Listening 1:
FCE Part 2

Note taking

1 Which parts of the world suffer hurricanes and earthquakes?
How do rescue teams find and save earthquake victims?

2 You will hear part of a radio interview with Paul Murphy, a member of IRC, the International Rescue Corps. For questions **1–10** answer the questions.

1 What is Paul Murphy's normal job?   _____
2 What work does the IRC sometimes do in the United Kingdom?   _____
3 Who does a disaster-struck country usually ask for help?   _____
4 What does the IRC have which other rescue agencies do not?   _____
5 What do all the members of the organization have in common?   _____
6 Apart from the heat, what were the main problems for Paul
   in Nicaragua?   _____
7 How long did the rescue of the woman in Japan take?   _____
8 What had helped her to survive?   _____
9 How did she feel?   _____
10 What can governments do to prevent loss of life in earthquakes?   _____

What qualities do you think you need to become a member of a rescue team?

Vocabulary 2: *Put*

A Phrasal verbs with *put*

1 Look at this sentence from section A of the reading text 'Lucky to be alive'.

*Such a shame for the island, but hurricanes could never **put** us **off** going back there.*

What is the meaning of *put off* in this sentence? Choose from the following:

A postpone   **B** distract   **C** discourage   **D** cause to dislike

Now match the remaining three meanings to each different use of *put off* in the following sentences.

1 Because of the rain they had to **put** the cup final **off** until the following week.
2 Turn the TV down. I'm trying to read and the noise is **putting** me **off**.
3 I soon realized that all he ever talked about was football. It **put** me right **off** him.

2 In A and B below, the particle required for the spaces in each of the three sentences is the same. Decide what the missing word is and then choose the appropriate meaning **A**, **B** or **C** for each of the three phrasal verbs.

A
1 It's too quiet for me. Why don't we **put** the radio _____ ?
2 All the clothes which fitted me last summer are too tight for me now. I must have **put** _____ weight.
3 If you're cold, you should **put** your coat _____ .

    A place on your body   **B** increase   **C** start something working

B
1 Don't shout out the answer. If you want to say something, **put** your hand _____ .
2 If they keep **putting** _____ the price of cigarettes, I'll have to stop smoking, I just can't afford it.
3 If you want people to come to the concert, you should **put** posters _____ around the school to advertise it.

    A increase   **B** fix to a wall or board   **C** lift into the air

B Expressions with *put*

1 Complete the spaces **1–12** in the following short texts (**A–D**), using the words in the box. The first one has been done for you.

effort	~~night~~	cigarette	touch
position	blame	money	feet
risk	book	smoking	pressure

A
When Anne first came to London she had nowhere to live so I offered to put her up for the **(1)** _night_ at my house and then help her to find a flat of her own. The next morning I put her in **(2)** _____ with my friend Richard, who was looking for a flatmate, and she went to see him. Unfortunately, Anne gets through 30 cigarettes a day and I'd forgotten that Richard won't put up with anyone **(3)** _____ in his flat. He doesn't see why other people should put his health at **(4)** _____ as well as their own, he always says. When he opened the door and saw Anne there smoking, he told her she'd have to put out her **(5)** _____ before she went in. Needless to say, Anne decided to look elsewhere for accommodation.

B
My parents used to put **(6)** _____ on me to study harder. They said I wouldn't get into university if I didn't put more time and **(7)** _____ into my school work.

C

After a hard day at work I like nothing more than to put my **(8)** _____ up as soon as I get in and read a good novel. This particular story is so well written I just can't put the **(9)** _____ down.

D

Naturally I was upset. I'd been putting some **(10)** _____ aside each week in order to pay for our holiday and during the night someone broke in and stole it. And then the policeman who came had the cheek to put the **(11)** _____ on me; he said it was my fault for leaving such a large amount of cash in the house. I know it was wrong to shout at him, but put yourself in my **(12)** _____ ; I'm sure you'd have done the same.

2 Underline the phrases with *put* in exercise 1 and try to work out the meaning using the context.

Speaking ⬤

What do you think the picture shows?
Who are these people and why are they there?

Use modal verbs of speculation and the Useful language on page 98 to say what you think:
- may have happened
- might be happening now
- could happen next

Reading

Read the following text about Christiana Tugwell and answer the following questions.
What is she protesting against? How is she doing this?
How does her mother feel about her protest?

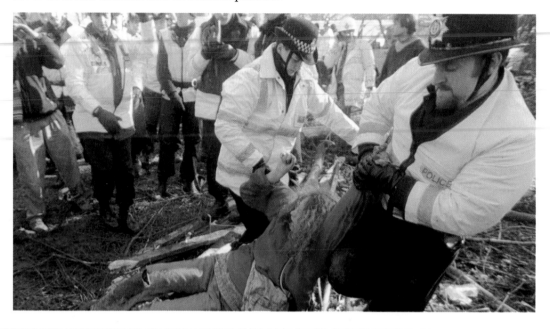

Teenager Christiana Tugwell and a small band of fellow school-age environmentalists have spent the past five months fighting proposals being put forward by the property developer, Countryside Residentials, to build 66 luxury detached houses in an area of woodland. They have received support at their protest camp from other residents who want to save the wood and the wildlife it contains. They have built a network of underground tunnels, which they will occupy to prevent the developers from starting work. Countryside Residential said it had been careful to preserve wildlife on the site, employing ecologists to do surveys and spending tens of thousands of pounds protecting animal and plant life.

'I began organizing the local campaign when I realized just how many local residents were against the developments. They were writing letters of protest to the council but this was simply not enough. So in order to put more pressure on the council and to raise national awareness, I started camping on the proposed development site. I was the ring-leader and had to bully some friends to join me. They weren't keen on sleeping rough and neither was I, but something had to be done.

My mum's initial reaction was "you're going to get cold" and "are you sure you want to do this?" After the first week she sent some friends to try to make me come home. They said I'd get into trouble, but I was determined to stay. I even spent three nights at the camp on my own. Even though she wanted me home, mum was always supportive and even brought us vegetarian sausages.

'Mum and I don't always see eye to eye on everything. But we agree that as long as what I want to do is not completely stupid, she lets me do it. I'm very stubborn and if I think I can do it, normally I can. I'd never done anything like this before, apart from a few anti-McDonald's demonstrations. Although we both support the campaign, our methods are very different: I believe in direct confrontation but she doesn't. She can't climb trees, dig tunnels or camp out, whereas I can. Her way is to raise awareness by writing letters and distributing leaflets, which also has its place.

'She worries about possible violence from the people trying to evict us and so do I, but there won't be any violence on our part: we are pacifists. I don't want to worry her, but stopping the development is more important.'

Reacting to the text ⬤

What is more important: defending woodland for wildlife or building houses?
Christiana says she is a pacifist. Do you think violence can ever be justified as a way of protesting?
She says she has taken part in anti-McDonald's demonstrations. What do you think were her reasons?

Language focus 2: *So, neither* and *nor*

1 Look at the ways in which Christiana expresses how people's feelings, behaviour or abilities are the same or different.

a The same
They weren't keen on sleeping rough and *neither was I.*
She worries about possible violence from the people trying to evict us and *so do I.*

b Different
I believe in direct confrontation but *she doesn't.*
She can't climb trees, dig tunnels or camp out, whereas *I can.*

When is *neither* or *so* used?
How do you decide which auxiliary verb to use?

Ⓖ Check the formation of *so, neither* and *nor* phrases on pages 214 and 215 of the Grammar reference.

2

a Match each statement **1–8** with a reply **a–h**.

1 I'm not very interested in <u>politics</u>.	**a** So would I.
2 I don't know how to <u>play chess</u>.	**b** I don't.
3 Last night I didn't <u>sleep very well</u>.	**c** Neither are we.
4 Next week I'm going to <u>start revising for the exams</u>.	**d** So is mine.
5 I'd like to <u>go for a drink</u> now.	**e** Mark does.
6 I've never <u>been windsurfing</u>.	**f** Nor did I.
7 I really enjoy <u>going for long walks</u>.	**g** So are we.
8 My favourite TV programme is '<u>Friends</u>'.	**h** Neither have I.

b Change the underlined part of each statement **1–8** to make sentences that are true for you.

c ◯ Read out the sentences you wrote in **b**. Respond to your partner using *so, neither* and *nor*.

Use of English:
FCE Part 4

Error correction

1 Look at the title of the text below. What do you think you will read about? Now read the text through quickly and check your predictions.

Choose life: get on your bike

0	As Mrs Spencer set off for to work yesterday morning, she was joining	*to*
00	hundreds of other regular motorists around Britain giving up their cars for	✓
1	National No Car Day. On any one normal day, Mrs Spencer would have	_____
2	got into her yellow Fiat Punto and driven to the school where does she	_____
3	works as a dinner lady. 'When my husband said he was going to cycle to	_____
4	the work, I decided I would give it a try as well,' said Mrs Spencer,	_____
5	41, from Stevenage, Hertfordshire. 'I suppose I haven't really been cycled	_____
6	for a year, but when we were first get married we used to have a tandem.'	_____
7	It was not just Mrs Spencer and her husband, Mike, who were making the	_____
8	sacrifice of giving up their cars yesterday. The couple's children, Rachel,	_____
9	12, and Hannah, 14, they usually take the school bus, but Rachel also took	_____
10	the public bus to home from an after-school class. The organizers of National	_____
11	No Car Day wish there were more than people like the Spencers. The	_____
12	Environmental Transport Association, a 'green' motoring organization, does	_____
13	not want the people to give up their cars altogether, just to be more selective	_____
14	about their use. Seventy-five per cent of those journeys are less than five miles,	_____
15	which can be cycled in less than half of an hour. People often do not realize	_____
	that they could save a great deal of time if they cycled in urban areas.	

2 Read the text again and look carefully at each line. Some of the lines are correct and some have a word which should not be there. If a line is correct, put a tick (✓) in the space at the end of the line. If a line has a word which should not be there, write the word in the space. There are two examples at the beginning (**0** and **00**).

What to expect in the exam

- The unnecessary words are mainly grammatical (eg auxiliary verbs, pronouns, articles and prepositions).
- There are usually between three and five correct lines in the text.

Speaking:
FCE Part 3

Collaborative task

1 One vocabulary item has been given for each of the six categories below. Add two more items from the box to each category.

dropping litter
dumping waste
nature reserve
endangered
    species
unleaded petrol
global warming
exhaust fumes
cigarette butts
oil slick
greenhouse effect
plastic containers
bottle bank

Recycling
recycled paper

Keeping cities clean
dog mess

River and sea pollution
toxic effluent

Traffic pollution
carbon monoxide

Climate change
rising sea levels

Animal welfare
facing extinction

How to go about it

● Appropriate use of some of the vocabulary from exercise 1 would impress the examiners.
● When commenting on your partner's opinions you can use *so*, *neither* or *nor* and the language you saw on page 123 of Unit 10 for agreeing and disagreeing.

2 Read the following Speaking Part 3 instructions.

Imagine that you belong to an environmental group and you want to inform people of current environmental problems. Talk with your partner and decide which three categories are the most important for your local area. Then discuss what ordinary people can do to help.

Writing:
FCE Part 2

Compositions

Your class has been doing a project on the environment. Your teacher has asked you to write a composition about the following statement:

Nothing can be done to save the environment.

You should state whether you agree or disagree with this statement, explaining your reasons clearly.

How to go about it

● Decide whether you agree or disagree with the statement.
● Use the categories in the speaking activity and make notes under some of them.
● Remember that the maximum number of

words is 180, so you will only be able to write about two or three of the issues.
● Look at the information on pages 102 and 103 of Unit 8 and write a plan.
● Use appropriate linking devices.

Now write your **composition**. You should write between **120 and 180** words.

Listening 2:
FCE Part 1

Multiple choice 😀

You will hear people talking in eight different situations. For questions **1–8**, choose the best answer, **A**, **B** or **C**.

What to expect in the exam

- In Unit 4 you saw how contrast linkers such as *although*, *whereas* and *but*, as well as other words and expressions, can be used to create distractors in listening exercises.

- Look at question 1, together with the tapescript and choose the best answer. Which structure is used to create distractors? Which words help you to choose the answer?

1 You hear a man talking about a new fire station that has just been built. Where was it built?

    A in the city centre

    B in the countryside

    C on the outskirts of the city

Tapescript

I really can't understand why they put it all the way out there. They maintained that if they'd built it in the heart of the city there would have been problems getting out to fires in the rural areas. Too far and too much traffic, they said. But that's exactly why it would have made more sense to build it in the centre instead of on the edge. You know, it takes a fire engine nearly 20 minutes to get from that suburb to the other side of the city.

Now do questions **2–8** below. In questions 2, 3 and 4 you will hear conditional sentences. These are used to create distractors as in question 1 above.

2 Listen to this man speaking. Who is he?

    A a shopkeeper

    B a town councillor

    C a local resident

3 You hear an environmentalist speaking on the radio about a recent project. How does she feel?

    A pessimistic

    B disappointed

    C pleased

4 You overhear this woman talking to her friend about her holiday. Why did she enjoy it?

    A She liked the beaches.

    B There wasn't much traffic.

    C There weren't many people.

5 You hear a conversation between two people. What is the relationship between them?

    A They are married.

    B They are teachers in the same school.

    C They are neighbours.

6 You are listening to the radio when you hear the following being read. What is it?

    A a story

    B a news report

    C a weather forecast

7 You overhear this conversation between a man and his neighbour. What is he doing?

    A asking for help

    B apologizing

    C complaining

8 You hear Brian talking about a recent environmental disaster. What is he going to do?

    A help clean up

    B take part in a protest demonstration

    C write to his Member of Parliament

11 Review

Vocabulary

A Weather

1 Match the adjectives **1–3** with the nouns **a–d** to make appropriate adjective + noun collocations. Each adjective may be used with more than one noun.

1 light   **a** storm
2 heavy   **b** wind
3 strong   **c** showers
            d rain

2 Add an appropriate noun from the box to each of the adjectives **1–10** below. The first one has been done for you.

sea	sky	wave	showers	storm
rain	clouds	~~breeze~~	sunshine	wind

1 gentle _breeze_
2 angry-looking _____
3 rough _____
4 torrential _____
5 scattered _____
6 brilliant _____
7 overcast _____
8 tidal _____
9 violent _____
10 gale-force _____

B _Put_

Complete each of the spaces in sentences **1–6** with one of the words from the box.

in	down	off	out	up	on

1 This is a great book. I just can't put it _____
2 I'm afraid you'll have to put _____ your cigarette. This is a non-smoking area.
3 When I'm next in London, could you put me _____ for the night?
4 Could you put the radio _____ ? I want to listen to the news.
5 My bank manager put me _____ touch with a very good accountant.
6 Never put _____ until tomorrow what you can do today.

Conditional sentences

Complete the spaces in the following sentences with the appropriate form of the verb in brackets.

1 If the weather _____ (stay) good next weekend, we _____ (probably/go) away somewhere.
2 Why didn't you phone us? If I _____ (know) you were coming, I _____ (could/prepare) something special to eat.
3 Absolutely no way! I _____ (not/do) a bungee jump even if you _____ (pay) me.
4 I thought this might happen. If you _____ (take) my advice, you _____ (not/be) in this mess now.
5 If you ever _____ (do) that again, I _____ (make) you pay for it!
6 That was very kind of you. I don't know what I _____ (do) if you _____ (not/help) me.
7 If I _____ (be) at home on Sunday afternoon, I _____ (always/watch) the film on telly.
8 I _____ (go) to the cinema more often if I _____ (have) the time, but unfortunately it's just not possible.

144

Use of English:
FCE Part 3

Transformations

Complete the second sentence so that it has a similar meaning to the first sentence, using the word given. **Do not change the word given.** You must use between two and five words, including the word given.

1 It's too wet to play tennis today.
if
We could play tennis _____ wet today.

2 It's a good thing I spoke to you or I would have forgotten her birthday.
if
I would have forgotten her birthday _____ to you.

3 I only wrote the letter because my mother made me do it.
not
If my mother hadn't made me do it, _____ the letter.

4 I will help you only if you tidy your room.
not
I will _____ tidy your room.

5 I got soaking wet because I forgot to take my umbrella with me.
remembered
If _____ my umbrella with me, I wouldn't have got soaking wet.

6 Some people say that giving up smoking causes your weight to increase.
you
Some people say that if you _____ on weight.

7 I've had enough of the neighbours' noise.
put
I refuse _____ the neighbours' noise any more.

8 The factory fumes are endangering the health of local residents.
put
The health of local residents _____ risk by the factory fumes.

9 I eat meat, but it has to be well cooked.
provided
I eat meat _____ well cooked.

10 You can borrow it, but you must give it back next week.
long
You can borrow it _____ it back next week.

Writing:
FCE Part 1

Formal transactional letters

You are a member of an environmental group. Last weekend you attended a demonstration against a proposed by-pass for the town of Oldbury. You have just seen a newspaper report about the event, which is incorrect.

Read the newspaper report below, together with your own comments. Then write to the editor, correcting the errors and asking the newspaper to send a reporter to interview you. Write your letter in **120–180** words.

DEMONSTRATION LEADS TO ARRESTS

Last weekend police arrested six demonstrators who were protesting against the building of a by-pass for Oldbury. The protesters claim that the construction of the road will lead to the extinction of a rare species of snail.

An estimated 200 people gathered on the outskirts of the town to express their disapproval and prevent the construction company from starting work. A small group of protesters sat in the road and chanted slogans at workers and police, blocking access to the site. A spokesman for the council said that the 'troublemakers' were all unemployed youngsters from other parts of the country, 'who had nothing better to do with their time'.

and the destruction of woodland!

over 2,000!

no – a silent demonstration

not true – many were local residents

12 Looking after yourself

Speaking ⊙

Compare and contrast what each of these two people eats.
Who do you think eats more healthily?
Does their diet tell you anything about their lifestyle?
What does 'a balanced diet' consist of?
How well does this term describe what *you* eat?
What are the advantages and disadvantages of fast food?

Language focus 1: Countable and uncountable nouns A

1 The word *plate* is usually countable: we can say 'a plate', 'two plates', 'three plates' and so on.

The word *bread* is usually uncountable: we say 'bread' or 'some bread', rather than 'a bread' or 'two breads'.

Decide which of the following words are countable, and which are uncountable. Some of them can be both countable and uncountable. How does this affect the meaning?

milk	diet	chicken	health	chip
chocolate	meal	pepper	spaghetti	cake

2 The word *bread* can be made countable by saying 'a loaf of bread' or 'two slices of bread'. Write the following uncountable nouns next to an appropriate expression to make them countable. Some of the nouns can be used with more than one expression.

sugar	cheese	jam	milk	toast
cake	spaghetti	salt	chocolate	

1 a piece of _____
2 a slice of _____
3 a plate of _____
4 a teaspoonful of _____
5 a pinch of _____
6 a bar of _____
7 a jar of _____
8 a carton of _____

Ⓖ See page 216 of the Grammar reference.

Listening:
FCE Part 3

Multiple matching

○ 1 Have you ever been on a diet?
What type of diet was it? How effective was it?

2 You will hear five people talking about food and dieting. For questions 1–5, choose from the list **A–F** what each speaker says about the subject. Use the letters only once. There is one extra letter which you do not need to use.

A I follow the advice given in books.   Speaker 1 ☐
B One form of dieting was too expensive.   Speaker 2 ☐
C I used to feel under pressure to lose weight. Speaker 3 ☐
D I have never been on a diet.   Speaker 4 ☐
E I had to change my eating habits.   Speaker 5 ☐
F I don't follow all the advice I am given.

Don't forget!

● Underline the key words in each of the six different statements. This helps you to focus on what to listen for. Are any of the statements similar to each other?

● Listen carefully both times to everything each speaker says. Then make your final decision.

○ 3 The last woman said: *We are constantly under attack from advertising and the media, who tell us that 'thin is beautiful'.*

To what extent is this the case in your country?
What are the dangers of dieting?

Language focus 2: Countable and uncountable nouns B

Why does the woman say 'Just a few' and not 'Just a little'?

The following sentences are all from the listening activity. Complete each of the spaces with one of the words from the box. Some words will be used more than once and more than one answer may be possible for each space.

little	few	much	many	some	any	no
deal	number	piece	lot	plenty	several	

Speaker 1
You drink nothing but lemonade with **a)** _____ salt and pepper for about seven days without **b)** _____ food.

I wasn't earning a great **c)** _____ of money and I simply couldn't afford to keep it up.

Speaker 2
I used to eat a **d)** _____ of junk food.
I ate very **e)** _____ fresh food and this had a serious effect on my health.

And now if I get hungry between meals, I have a **f)** _____ cheese or **g)** _____ nuts, just to fill the hole.

Speaker 3
When I want to treat myself I have a **h)** _____ of cake or a **i)** _____ biscuits.
As long as you eat sweet things after a meal, then there's **j)** _____ problem.
I only ever eat chocolates after lunch or dinner. And never too **k)** _____ of course – just one or two.

Speaker 4
A sensible, balanced diet: **l)** _____ of fresh fruit and vegetables… **m)** _____ glasses of water a day – and **n)** _____ snacks between meals.

Speaker 5
A large **o)** _____ of people follow diets, but very **p)** _____ of them are happier as a result.
I don't pay **q)** _____ attention to what others think or say.

It's just not natural

Genetic modification can give us easy-peel oranges, cancer-fighting strawberries and blue potatoes. But if you don't want your food fiddled about with, can you avoid it?

| 0 | *H* |

When you bite into an apple, do you ever wish it was a pineapple instead? Well, now you can have the best of both worlds. Australian scientists have created a fruit with the convenience of an apple and the taste of a pineapple. The aim of the Snack Apple is to persuade children to eat more fresh fruit and vegetables and it's just one illustration of how far science is prepared to go in pursuit of this worthy ideal.

| 1 | |

First on the scene was frozen-food company Iceland which came up with chocolate-flavoured carrots, made by freezing the vegetables with granules of chocolate sauce. And plant breeders have a range of mini-vegetables such as carrots, broccoli and cauliflower, which they hope will make them popular snack foods with youngsters and a healthier alternative to crisps.

| 2 | |

But science can now do much more than this and create new types of foods by means of genetic manipulation. A gene may be transferred from a different species in order to increase the nutritional value of the plant, or to make it more resistant to pests and disease. Incredibly, scientists have used a gene from a fish to give antifreeze properties to tomatoes and so increase their growing season.

| 3 | |

Despite the benefits, however, not everyone is in favour of genetically modified (GM) foods or 'Frankenfoods', as the media calls them. Because there are no long-term studies to prove the safety of GM foods, their long-term effect on human health is unknown. There is also a great deal of concern for the environment, with fears that GM crops might spread their genes by pollination to other plants growing nearby. This kind of genetic pollution would be very difficult to clean up.

| 4 | |

There is particular controversy surrounding soya, a common ingredient in processed foodstuffs. One of the problems is that imports of soya from the US contain both GM and non-GM beans because it's not thought practical to separate them at their source. It is therefore difficult to avoid GM soya because we don't know which products contain it and which don't. A large number of consumers object to this and have called for clearer labelling of GM products.

| 5 | |

As a result, a spokesperson for Iceland recently announced that the company would buy soya for its own-brand products only from Brazil, where the GM crop isn't grown. Iceland's Michelle Gray explained that this was for reasons of both safety and consumer choice. 'We realize that scientific opinion is divided on the safety of GM soya, so we thought it best to be on the cautious side and ensure our customers can have products without GM soya if they want them.'

| 6 | |

But should we reject all GM foods? There are plans to introduce more appealing products: peas which contain more vitamin C and broccoli, strawberries and tomatoes with more of the anti-cancer compound, sulphophane. We could also have blue potatoes. The genes that make one natural blue dye have recently been transferred from bacteria to flowers, so why not to food plants? Scientists are already working on blue roses using this technology. And if your main objection to fruit is the unpeelable orange, there are also plans for an orange that will practically peel itself.

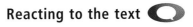

Reading:
FCE Part 1

Multiple matching

1 How many fruits and vegetables can you name? Which of them do you like most and least? How often do you eat them? What things were you made to eat when you were younger? Did you ever try to avoid eating them? If so, how? Would you eat chocolate-flavoured vegetables?

2 You are going to read a magazine article about genetically modified foods. Choose the most suitable summary sentence from the list **A–H** for each part **(1–6)** of the article. There is one extra summary sentence which you do not need to use. There is an example at the beginning **(0)**.

A We may see a range of new products in the future.
B New techniques can improve the nature of crops.
C Many consumers want to be able to choose.
D There is a variety of products aimed at children.
E One company has responded to consumer demand.
F Scientists are convinced of the advantages of genetic manipulation.
G Some people are worried about the consequences of genetic manipulation.
H Science is using extreme methods for a good cause.

Reacting to the text

How appealing would you find blue potatoes?
Should scientists be allowed to 'fiddle with' the genetic structure of plants?
Are the potential advantages more important than the risks?

Language focus 3: Reported speech

1 Look at the following sentence from the text together with the original direct speech. What change is made to the verb tense when it is reported?

Reported speech: *Michelle Gray explained that this **was** for reasons of both safety and consumer choice.*

Direct speech: 'This **is** for reasons of both safety and consumer choice,' explained Michelle Gray.

2 Complete the columns below, to show how verb tenses and other words and expressions change in reported speech.

Direct speech		Reported speech
a 'We're meeting her tomorrow.'	→	They said they _were meeting_ her _the next_ day.
b 'I've seen him twice today.'	→	She said she _____ him twice _____ day.
c 'She's been living here for years.'	→	He told me she _____ living _____ for years.

d 'I spoke to her last week.' → He said he _____ to her _____ week.

e 'I was working yesterday.' → He told me he _____ working _____ before.

f 'We'd asked her several times.' → They said they _____ her several times.

3 Name the tense in each sentence in exercise 2.
Example: a *present continuous → past continuous*

4 What happens to the modal verbs *will, may, can* and *must* in reported speech?
What happens to *would, might, could, should* and *ought to*?

5 What happens to these time expressions in reported speech?
*two days ago   next month   tonight
this morning   now*

Check your ideas on page 215 of the Grammar reference.

6 Write down at least five things that different people have said recently. Then report the different statements to the class using reported speech.

Speaking:
FCE Part 2

Talking about photos ◯

Student A: Here are two photographs which show people eating in different places. Compare and contrast the photographs and say how you think the people are feeling in each of them.

Student B: When your partner has finished, say what you think the people are celebrating.

Now change roles.

Student A: Compare and contrast the photos again and say whether you prefer eating in formal or informal situations and why.

Student B: When your partner has finished, say which of the two situations you would prefer to eat in.

Language focus 4: Reporting verbs

1 Look at these different ways of reporting what people say:

  a 'I'll get you a drink,' said Jan to Tom.
  Jan told Tom she would get him a drink.
  Jan **offered to get** *Tom a drink.*

  b 'You should go and see a doctor,' said Tim.
  Tim said I should go and see a doctor.
  Tim **advised me to go** *and see a doctor.*

2 Which of the following verbs follow the same pattern as *advise* (verb + object + infinitive) and which are like *offer* (verb + infinitive)?

order	*urge*	*refuse*	*threaten*
persuade	*warn*	*tell*	*remind*
ask	*promise*	*encourage*	*recommend*

3 Report the following sentences using an appropriate verb from exercise 2. There is an example (**0**) at the beginning.

  0 'I'll give you the £5 back next week,' he told her.
  He *promised to give her the £5 back the following week.*

  1 'I'm not going to clean my room!' she said.
  She _____ .

  2 'Don't forget to take your sandwiches, John,' said his father.
  John's father _____ .

3 'If you don't turn your music down, I'll call the police,' said my neighbour.
  My neighbour _____ .

4 'Don't take the car out. The roads are very icy,' said her friend.
  Her friend _____ .

5 'Get out of my office immediately!' shouted his boss.
  His boss _____ .

6 'You really ought to report the theft to the police,' my friend told me.
  My friend _____ .

4 Look at the following structures which can follow the verb *recommend*.

  The doctor recommended me to do exercise.
  The doctor recommended (that) I (should) do exercise.
  The doctor recommended doing exercise.

  Which structure is not possible with the verb *suggest*?

5 ◯ Work with a partner. You each have various problems and you would like your partner's suggestions and advice. Student A should turn to page 200 and Student B should turn to page 202 to find out what your problems are.

Use of English 1:
FCE Part 1
Multiple choice cloze

1 Apart from dieting, what other ways do you know of controlling weight?

2 Read through the following text, ignoring the spaces for the moment, and answer the following questions.

What does the 'alternative diet' consist of?
How effective is it?

3 For questions **1–15**, read the text again and decide which answer **A**, **B**, **C** or **D** best fits each space. There is an example at the beginning **(0)**.

An alternative diet

Karaoke enthusiasts can now enjoy their sometimes nervous **(0)** _____ safe in the knowledge that they are at **(1)** _____ losing some weight. Thanks to Tokyo-based Daiichikosho, which sells and **(2)** _____ out karaoke equipment, karaoke machines can now **(3)** _____ how many calories the singer has burnt while singing the song. **(4)** _____ 40,000 users of its karaoke song-broadcasting service **(5)** _____ Japan have now **(6)** _____ up for the company's 'Karaoke diet'.

Such factors as the volume and pitch of the singer's voice and the tempo and length of the song were **(7)** _____ into consideration before assigning calorie burning values to more than 1,000 favourite tunes. '**(8)** _____ , the longer and livelier one sings, the **(9)** _____ calories are burned,' said a company spokesman.

(10) _____ to Daiichikosho, the Beatles 'Let It Be' burns up 11.4 kcal; but for those **(11)** _____ in shedding a little more weight, a rendition of Frank Sinatra's classic 'My Way' will **(12)** _____ in the loss of 15.6 kcal. An average man will burn up approximately 81 kcal **(13)** _____ a ten-minute walk, suggesting that karaoke may not be the ideal weight loss programme.

In fact, indulging in karaoke (literally 'empty orchestra') can be counter-productive to any diet as the singing of such songs usually **(14)** _____ a drink – causing the singer to **(15)** _____ back on the same calories they may have just lost.

	A	B	C	D
0	performances	representations	productions	realizations
1	same	least	time	all
2	borrows	hires	hands	spends
3	turn up	come across	put down	work out
4	Over	Several	Many	Various
5	for	through	by	throughout
6	gone	taken	signed	registered
7	taken	brought	held	put
8	Increasingly	Intentionally	Naturally	Deliberately
9	fast	harder	many	more
10	Regarding	Concerning	Believing	According
11	enthusiastic	interested	keen	concerned
12	lead	cause	provide	result
13	during	while	meanwhile	until
14	requires	requests	asks for	wants
15	bring	place	put	get

Writing 1:
FCE Part 2

Reports

1 Read the following Writing Part 2 instructions.

What would *you* recommend the manager should do?

You have a part-time job in a restaurant. The manager wants to make the restaurant more popular with families and has asked you to carry out a survey among people of various ages and write a report.

Write your **report** in **120–180** words summarizing the findings of your survey and making one or two recommendations of your own.

2 Read the model answer and give each section a heading. There is one extra heading which you do not need to use.

A What their children want to eat
B Further recommendations
C Introduction

D Most popular dishes
E Parents' views on food
F Facilities

3 Who is the target reader and what style has the writer used?

1 _____
The aim of this report is to show what different family members expect from a restaurant. The report is based on a survey of 50 people aged between 8 and 45.

2 _____
Several younger parents agreed that a family restaurant should have nappy-changing facilities. Many of those under 16, on the other hand, felt that a non-smoking area was an important feature.

3 _____
Most parents expected to see a wide range of dishes on the menu, catering for all ages and tastes. Understandably, price is a significant factor and 80 per cent of those interviewed said they preferred restaurants which offered cheaper children's portions.

4 _____
Not surprisingly, over 90 per cent of those under 12 wanted chips with everything, whereas a large number of teenagers thought that a visit to a restaurant was an ideal opportunity to try new dishes.

5 _____
As a result of the survey, I would recommend that the restaurant should offer reduced prices for large families. I also suggest extending the menu to include meals which are suitable for young children.

4 Find examples of:

  a words and expressions used with countable and uncountable nouns
  eg *Several younger parents*

  b reported speech
  Which verbs are used to introduce the reported speech? eg *agreed*

  c making recommendations
  Which two verbs are used?

5 Find words or phrases which are used to:

  a introduce the report   eg *I was asked to write a report on…*
  b contrast ideas   eg *However,*
  c comment on the findings   eg *Interestingly,*

6 Read the following Writing Part 2 instructions.

As part of your town's cultural exchange programme, a group of foreign students will be visiting your area for two weeks. You have been asked to write a report for the group leader about regional and/or national dishes. You should give information about what the students can expect to eat in your area and comment on the popularity of the different dishes with young people.

7 Before you do the task consider this possible plan.

Introduction: Explain the purpose of your report and how you obtained the information contained in it.

Most popular dishes: Briefly describe at least two dishes and mention how popular they are with young people. Give reasons if appropriate.

Least popular dishes: Give examples and say why they are not popular.

Recommendation: Recommend your favourite regional and/or national food.

Look at the Wordlist on page 205 for useful vocabulary.

8 Who is the target reader? What style will you use for the report?
Look at page 202 to see how an English person answered the question.

Now you are ready to write your report in **120–180** words.

Language focus 5: Reported questions

1 Look at these examples of reported questions from the person who wrote the report on the opposite page. Write down the original direct questions that were asked.

  1 I asked everyone what facilities a family restaurant should have.
  'What _____?'

  2 I asked them whether they thought it was important to have a non-smoking area.
  '_____?'

2 What changes are made to direct questions when we report them? Consider the following:

• word order   • verb tenses
• auxiliary verbs *do, does, did*   • yes/no questions

 (G) Check your answers on pages 215 and 216 of the Grammar reference.

3 Report the following questions which the interviewer asked.

  1 'What type of food do you expect to see on the menu?'
  I asked everyone _____
  _____

  2 'How important is the price of the food?'
  I asked parents _____
  _____

  3 'Do you always eat the same things when you go to a restaurant?'
  I asked teenagers _____
  _____

  4 'What other things would you like a restaurant to offer?'
  I asked everyone _____
  _____

Vocabulary: Health matters

1   In parts **A** and **B** below complete the spaces with one of the words from the box.

A | ear   stomach   ~~nose~~   heart   blood |

0   If you get a...   <u>_nose_</u>   **bleed,**   pinch it with two fingers until it stops.
1   She'll have a...   _____   **attack**   when she sees what you've done!
2   Of course he has a...   _____   **ache.**   He ate far too many cream cakes.
3   With such high...   _____   **pressure**   you should eat less salt.
4   She's got a bad...   _____   **infection**   so she can't come swimming.

B | ankle   nose   eye   throat |

1   That's a nasty...   **black**   _____ .   Did somebody hit you?
2   She's got a very...   **sore**   _____ .   She can hardly speak.
3   You've got a...   **runny**   _____ .   Would you like a handkerchief?
4   It's just a badly...   **sprained**   _____ .   You haven't broken anything.

2   Cover up the words on the right in exercises 1A and B. How many can you remember? Now cover up the words on the left. Can you remember more the second time?

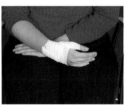

3   Choose the correct alternative in each sentence.

1   My father wrapped a *bandage/band* round my sprained wrist.
2   You've cut your finger. You should put *a plaster/plaster* on it.
3   The doctor gave me a *receipt/prescription* for a course of antibiotics.
4   When I broke my arm, I had it in *a plaster/plaster* for about five weeks.
5   The nurse gave him an *infusion/injection* in his arm to help him sleep.

4   When was the last time you were ill?
    Do you often have accidents? What about when you were younger?
    Which of the conditions in exercise 1 have you suffered?

Word formation: Noun suffixes

1   Use the examples in **A** to help you complete the appropriate noun forms in **B**.

A Verb	Noun	Adjective	Noun
improve	*improvement*	sore	*soreness*
infect	*infection*	sensitive	*sensitivity*

B treat	_____	weak	_____
prescribe	_____	severe	_____

2   Write the noun form of the following verbs and adjectives. Use the suffixes *-ion, -ity, -ment, -ness, -ance* and *-ence*

Verbs	Nouns
amuse	_____
decide	_____
appear	_____
entertain	_____
explain	_____
perform	_____
imagine	_____
develop	_____

Adjectives	Nouns
important	_____
fit	_____
sincere	_____
happy	_____
secure	_____
evident	_____
careless	_____
original	_____

3   Mark the stress on the verbs, adjectives and nouns in exercise 2.

Use of English 2:
FCE Part 5

Word formation

For questions **1–10**, read the text below. Use the word given in capitals at the end of each line to form a word that fits in the space in the same line.

A knee injury

My brother hurt his knee in a skiing **(1)** _____ recently. He didn't | **COMPETE**
think it was serious at the time but it soon began to affect his **(2)** _____ | **ABLE**
to walk properly and he complained of **(3)** _____ in his leg. It slowly got | **STIFF**
worse and he eventually had to go into hospital for an **(4)** _____ . He's | **OPERATE**
resting at home now and the doctors say that in the **(5)** _____ of cases | **MAJOR**
like this, as long as there are no **(6)** _____ , people are able to resume | **COMPLICATE**
their normal **(7)** _____ within a few weeks. They gave him a few gentle | **ACTIVE**
exercises to do and he's already beginning to notice an **(8)** _____ . | **IMPROVE**
Sudden **(9)** _____ obviously have to be avoided and he often complains | **MOVE**
of **(10)** _____ , but he'll be as right as rain soon. | **TIRE**

Writing 2:
FCE Part 1

Transactional letters: Giving information

1 Read the following Writing Part 1 instructions.

You have received a letter from a friend, asking for information about a health spa you went to last year. Read his letter and an advertisement for the health spa, on which you have written some notes. Then write a reply to your friend, answering his questions and saying whether you would recommend the spa to him.

Write a **letter** of between **120–180** words in an appropriate style. Do not write any addresses.

These exams have left me feeling run-down and exhausted. In fact, I'm seriously thinking of spending some time in a health spa to recover. I know I laughed last year when you decided to go to one but it doesn't seem such a bad idea now. What were the facilities and food like in the place you went to?

My main worry is that I might get bored. Could you let me know what there is to do there and whether you think I'd enjoy it?

Hope to hear from you soon.

All the best,
Trevor

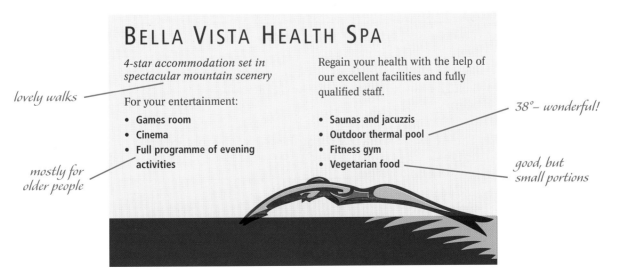

BELLA VISTA HEALTH SPA

4-star accommodation set in spectacular mountain scenery

Regain your health with the help of our excellent facilities and fully qualified staff.

lovely walks

For your entertainment:

- **Games room**
- **Cinema**
- **Full programme of evening activities**

- **Saunas and jacuzzis**
- **Outdoor thermal pool**
- **Fitness gym**
- **Vegetarian food**

mostly for older people

38° – wonderful!

good, but small portions

Review

Open cloze

For questions **1–15**, read the text below and think of the word which best fits each space. Use only **one** word in each space. There is an example at the beginning **(0)**.

Roast ghost

New Zealander Kay Martin got the fright of **(0)** _her_ life a **(1)** _____ weeks ago. According to the *Auckland Sunday Star*, she and a friend were chatting over a drink **(2)** _____ they heard a chicken squawking. They came **(3)** _____ the conclusion that it **(4)** _____ escaped from a neighbour's garden and they went outside in **(5)** _____ to catch it. But there were **(6)** _____ chickens anywhere. Then Kay realized with horror that the sound was coming from **(7)** _____ own kitchen – coming, in fact, from the oven, **(8)** _____ she had put a chicken to roast half an hour earlier. 'It was **(9)** _____ if it was calling to me from its grave,' she said. 'I was **(10)** _____ amazed I couldn't speak.'

As they approached, the squawking noise reached a crescendo. They removed the tray **(11)** _____ the oven and as the chicken began to cool, the squawking died away. Ms Martin chopped the neck **(12)** _____ and threw it in the sink. She noticed that the vocal chords were **(13)** _____ perfect condition. 'A **(14)** _____ of steam was coming up the neck from the stuffing inside the chicken,' she said, 'and this had caused the dead bird to squawk.' She has **(15)** _____ eaten any chicken since.

Transformations

For questions **1–8** complete the second sentence so that it has a similar meaning to the first sentence, using the word given. **Do not change the word given.** You must use between two and five words, including the word given.

1 'Did you buy a bandage, Roy?' asked Graham.
   he
   Graham asked _____ a bandage.

2 His condition improved so rapidly he went home four days after the operation.
   such
   There _____ in his condition he went home four days after the operation.

3 'I wouldn't go to that restaurant if I were you, Matt,' I said.
   advised
   I _____ to that restaurant.

4 I'm amazed by how much English he knows.
   of
   His _____ me.

5 'Can you swim, Sarah?' asked her teacher.
   her
   Sarah's teacher asked _____ to swim.

6 'I'll drive you to the station, Dawn,' he said.
   offered
   He _____ a lift to the station.

7 'There'll be very few people at the party,' she told Roger.
   not
   She told Roger there _____ people at the party.

8 'Let's eat out tomorrow,' said Chris.
   suggested
   Chris _____ day.

Vocabulary: Health matters

Complete each of the following collocations by writing an appropriate part of the body in each of the spaces.

1 a black _____
2 a sore _____
3 a sprained _____
4 a runny _____

5 an _____ infection
6 a _____ bleed
7 a _____ attack
8 a _____ ache

Use of English:
FCE Part 5

Word formation

For questions **1–7** use the word given in capitals at the end of each line to form a noun that fits in the space in the sentence. In each case a different suffix from the box is required to form the noun. There is an example at the beginning **(0)**.

-ment	-ity	-ion	-ness	-ship	-ence	-ance	~~-or~~

0 Alexander Graham Bell, the _inventor_ of the telephone, was born in Edinburgh in 1847.   **INVENT**

1 It is our _____ to speak which makes us so different from other mammals.   **ABLE**

2 Juliet had not been getting on well with her boyfriend, so she decided to end their _____ .   **RELATE**

3 I wouldn't have the _____ to go fishing; I'd hate the idea of sitting there all day waiting for something to happen.   **PATIENT**

4 The couple next door had another _____ last night; we could hear them shouting at each other.   **ARGUE**

5 Russell Crowe gave an impressive _____ as a gladiator in the film of the same name.   **PERFORM**

6 He could not hide his feeling of great _____ at the death of his dog, Georgia.   **SAD**

7 She told the teacher that someone had stolen her book, but he didn't believe her _____ .   **EXPLAIN**

Collocation revision: Units 1–12

1 In each of the spaces below write one word which collocates with *all* three of the other words. The question numbers also refer to the relevant unit of the book where the collocations appeared. If you can't think of a word, look at the contents map on pages ii and iii. The topic areas will give you a clue.

1 second-hand
shabby
trendy
_____

2 talented
session
rock
_____

3 handy
labour-saving
useful
_____

4 horror
action
science-fiction
_____

5 challenging
monotonous
badly-paid
_____

6 flowing
shoulder-length
spiky
_____

7 prosperous
bustling
run-down
_____

8 business
day
weekend
_____

9 a piercing scream
_____ a nervous laugh
a broad smile

10 death
life
two-year prison
_____

11 strong
gale-force
light
_____

12 fast
convenience
takeaway
_____

2 Use other collocations from the first 12 units of the book to help you create your own exercise. Write three words or expressions which can all be used with the same verb or noun, in the same way as the exercise in 1 above. Write four examples like this for another student to complete.

Part 1: Multiple choice

Part 1 contains eight short unrelated extracts with multiple choice questions. In each extract you will hear either one person speaking (monologue) or a conversation between two people (dialogue). There are several different types of questions which test your ability to understand, for example, the general idea or main points of the extract, *what* people's opinions are, *how* they feel, *where* they are or *who* they are speaking to.

Predicting

In all parts of the listening paper it is important to use the questions to help you predict what you will hear. This will then help you in your understanding of what you actually do hear. Look at this question from Part 1:

1 You are on a bus and you overhear a conversation between two women.
   What has one of the women just bought?
   A a blouse
   B a skirt
   C a dress

Discuss the similarities and differences between each of the three options.

Example: 1
Both a skirt and a dress are worn over the lower part of the body, whereas a blouse is not.

Distractors

Simply hearing the same word or phrase which is in one of the alternatives will not guarantee that you have found the right answer. These words could be distractors.

Read the following tapescript for question 1 above. What is the answer?

Woman 1: That's lovely. Celebrating something, are you?
Woman 2: Yes, well, my nephew's getting married next week, so I needed something a bit special. It's pure silk, you know.
Woman 1: Yes, I can see that. Must have cost a fortune!
Woman 2: Not really. Cheaper than getting a dress, that's for sure, and I'll probably wear it a lot more, too. It'll go really well with a skirt I bought last week. The sleeves are a bit short, but if I wear a jacket over it, no one'll notice.

Which key words and expressions helped you decide on the answer?
Which are used to create distractors?

Listening

You will hear people talking in seven more situations. For questions **2–8**, choose the best answer, **A**, **B** or **C**.

What to expect in the exam

- In Part 1, you will hear the questions being read out before each extract. As you listen to the question consider the similarities and differences between each alternative and try to predict what you might hear.

2 You hear part of a sports commentary on the radio. What sport is it?

   A tennis

   B basketball

   C football

3 Listen to this man on the telephone. Who is he phoning?

   A a friend

   B his doctor

   C his boss

4 Listen to this man and woman speaking. Where are they?

   A in a cinema

   B in a restaurant

   C at home

5 You hear this woman telling her friend about a restaurant.

   What does she say about it?

   A The waiters were rude.

   B The food was badly cooked.

   C It was too formal.

6 You hear a woman talking to her husband in a supermarket.

   How does she feel?

   A confused

   B annoyed

   C disappointed

7 You hear this man talking to his friend on the phone about a day trip to London. What is he going to do at the end of the day?

   A stay in a hotel

   B stay at his friend's house

   C travel back home

8 You hear this man talking. Who is he?

   A a policeman

   B a social worker

   C a teacher

Part 2: Note taking

1 Look at the statements **1–8** about Part 2 of the listening paper and decide which are True and which are False. If a statement is false, give reasons for your answer.

   1 You only hear the Part 2 recording once.   _____

   2 You usually have 30 or 45 seconds to read through the questions.   _____

   3 You should use this time to predict the missing information from each space.   _____

   4 You have to write between three and five words in each space.   _____

   5 You have to rephrase the words you hear so that they fit into the sentence.   _____

   6 You do not usually hear the answers in the same order as the questions.   _____

   7 For difficult questions, keep listening – you'll hear the answer sooner or later.   _____

   8 You should check the spelling of your answers.   _____

2 Now read the following Listening Part 2 question.

   Listen to this tourist guide talking about the programme of events for a two-day visit to Cardiff. For questions **1–10** on page 160, fill in the missing information.

   Before you listen, predict the type of information you might hear for questions **1–10**.

   Example: 1 *This might be a place, like 'in the park' or 'in the street' or it could be a period of time; 'meet in half an hour'.*

What to expect in the exam

- The words in the question may not be the same as the words you hear. In questions 1 and 8, for example, the word 'meet' is not spoken in the recording.
  For question 1, you will hear the following: '…so we'd like you to be in … at 9 o'clock'.

What other ways might the tourist guide say this for number 8?

- The word order you hear may also be different. In question 2 you will hear these words: 'and as part of the exhibition there's a tour which actually takes you…'.

Trip to Cardiff

Friday morning: Visit to Rhondda Heritage Park: meet in [_____ **1**] at 9.00 am

Coal mining exhibition including [_____ **2**] tour

Friday afternoon: Cardiff Bay Visitor Centre: walk around [_____ **3**]

Remember to take [____ **4**]

Friday evening: Welsh male voice choir

Tickets: £4.50   £2.50 for children [_____ **5**]

Saturday morning: Free for shopping

St Mary Street for good [_____ **6**]

Souvenirs on [_____ **7**] of David Morgan's store

Saturday lunch

Picnic in Bute Park: meet at [_____ **8**] at 13.00

Saturday afternoon: Visit to Vale of Glamorgan to try [_____ **9**]

Saturday evening: Cultural events

Either: Cardiff International Arena for [_____ **10**]

or: New Theatre for opera ('Carmen')

Part 3: Multiple matching

1 In Part 3 you will hear five short extracts which are all related in some way. You have 30 seconds to read the questions and see what makes each question similar to or different from the others. Read the Part 3 task below and study this example:

Example: **A** I will need a specific qualification to do this job.
You often get qualifications by taking exams, for which you have to study. **B** *and* **F** *also mention aspects of studying.* **E** *is different from* **A** *because…*

2 Complete the example sentence in 1 and then discuss questions **B–F** in the same way. Underlining key words may help, but be careful of distractors when you listen.

Can you predict any of the language you might hear for each of the sentences?

Example: **A** What words do you know which are related to *qualification*?

> **What to expect in the exam**
>
> ● You may hear the language which guides you to the correct answer:
>   **a** at the beginning of the extract
>   **b** in the middle of the extract
>
> **c** at the end of the extract.
> **d** in more than one part of the extract
> ● Listen *both times* to *all* of what the speaker says before making your final decision.

---

3 You will hear five young people talking about the job they would like to do. For questions **1–5**, choose from the list **A–F** what each speaker says. Use the letters only once. There is one extra letter which you do not need to use.

A I will need a specific qualification to do this job.   Speaker 1 [____]

B I combine work with studying.   Speaker 2 [____]

C I disagree with the careers advice I have been given.   Speaker 3 [____]

D I heard about this job from someone in my family.   Speaker 4 [____]

E I think I have the necessary personal qualities.   Speaker 5 [____]

F I am studying a relevant subject.

Part 4

In Part 4 there are four possible task types: true/false, yes/no, multiple choice or matching. Each of these tasks is represented in the following questions. Read the interviewer's introduction from the recording for the Part 4 listening task below, and then answer questions **1–4**.

Tapescript

On 'Youth Matters' today we look at what it's like to have a famous dad. Jenny Hadley's here to tell us about life with her pop star father, Tony Hadley, from the top 1980s band, Spandau Ballet. Ask your mum if you've never heard of them!

1 Tony Hadley does not have any children.   *Is this statement True or False?*

2 The interviewer's mother likes going to the ballet.   *Is this stated: Yes or No?*

3 Jenny Hadley is on 'Youth Matters' to talk about   *Choose **A**, **B** or **C**.*
   A her relationship with her mother.
   B what it is like to be famous.
   C life as a pop star's daughter.

4 Who used to sing with Spandau Ballet?   *Write **I** for Interviewer, **J** for Jenny or **N** for Neither.*

Multiple choice

1 Only one of the task types mentioned above will appear in Part 4. In this section we will focus on the multiple choice question task.

What to expect in the exam

● For multiple choice question tasks you are given one minute to read the questions before you hear the recording. However, for each of the other Part 4 task types you only have 30 seconds.

● Although a particular option might be true, it may not be the correct answer to the question you are asked. In question **4** below, for example, **A**, **B** and **C** are all true, but only one answers the question: 'What does she particularly admire about her father?'

2 You will hear an interview with the daughter of a famous pop star. For questions **1–7**, choose the best answer **A**, **B** or **C**.

1 Jenny realized her father was famous when
   A she sang on stage with him.
   B she travelled round the world with him on tour.
   C she saw the audience's reaction to him.

2 When Jenny sees her father on television
   A she gets excited.
   B she does not pay much attention.
   C she thinks it's strange.

3 When she hears other people talk about her father
   A she feels proud.
   B she gets embarrassed.
   C she is indifferent.

4 What does she particularly admire about her father?
   A He likes talking.
   B He is very patient.
   C He is always cheerful.

5 What aspect of her father's fame does she feel uncomfortable about?
   A His fans wait outside their house.
   B The family receives a lot of presents.
   C He is not at home very often.

6 What does Jenny say about acting?
   A She has some acting experience.
   B She is currently having drama lessons.
   C She is thinking of becoming an actress.

7 At Geri Halliwell's birthday party, Jenny
   A asked her for her autograph.
   B had a long conversation with her.
   C arranged to meet her again.

Vocabulary 1: Money

1 Name the items shown in the photographs above.
Which of them are used most in your country?
What are the advantages and disadvantages of each method of payment?

2 For **1–5**, complete each of the spaces with one of the items from the box.

| rate of interest | rate of exchange | stock market | account | currency |

1 He made all his money on the Wall Street _____ .
2 I can't afford to borrow any money from the bank; the _____ on a personal loan is 15 per cent!
3 You get a free mobile phone if you open a savings _____ with the Western Bank.
4 She tried to buy something in a Dublin shop with British pounds, but of course, Ireland has a different _____ .
5 I never change my money at the airport. I usually find that town centre banks offer a better _____ .

3 Complete each of the spaces with an appropriate preposition from the box. In each section **1–4** the preposition required for both spaces is the same.

| on | in | for | to |

1 Are you saving up _____ anything at the moment?
How much will you have to pay _____ it?
2 What do you like spending your money _____ ?
How common is it for people to buy things _____ credit
a in your country? **b** in your family?
3 Imagine you were seriously _____ debt. How many possible ways are there of solving your problem?
Do you know anyone who has invested _____ shares on the stock market?
4 If a friend of yours asked to borrow £50 from you, would you lend it _____ them?
Does anyone owe any money _____ you at the modment?

4 Work with a partner and discuss each of the questions in exercise 3.
Don't forget to ask each other further questions and develop your answers.

Multiple matching

1 You are going to read a text about a 14-year-old boy who set up his own business importing motorized skateboards and scooters.

What difficulties do you think he had to overcome?

2 Now read the following Reading Part 1 instructions.

Read the text on page 164 about a teenager who set up his own business. Choose the most suitable heading from the list **A–I** for each part (**1–7**) of the article. There is one extra heading which you do not need to use. There is an example at the beginning (**0**).

How to go about it

- Before you read the article, look at the headings to get an idea of the main points in the text.

- Use the questions and clues next to each heading below in order to help you predict what you might read in each paragraph.

A Coming up with the idea	*This phrasal verb first appeared in Unit 7. What does it mean?*
B The price of speed	*How is speed normally measured?*
C Going on to achieve greater things	*In Unit 2 you saw two uses of 'go on'. What does it mean when it is followed by the infinitive?*
D Getting the customers	*What do you think 'get' means here?*
E A dream come true	*This is short for 'A dream which _____ come true'.*
F Raising the finance	*What do you do when you 'raise' money?*
G A transatlantic deal	*Which countries or continents might be mentioned in this paragraph?*
H No laughing matter	*If it's no laughing matter, then it's a very _____ one.*
I Schoolboy success	*Don't forget – the last heading is always the example!*

Don't forget!

- The headings summarize the *main ideas* in each part of the text, so you should read the text for a general understanding and not

worry if you do not understand every single word in it.
- In the exam you have to write your answers on a separate answer sheet.

Reacting to the text

Would the motorized scooters and skateboards be popular in your country?
What qualities do you think you need to be a successful entrepreneur at 14?
If you could have your own business, what type of business would it be?
What would be the advantages and disadvantages of being your own boss?

Life in the fast lane

Henrietta Lake talks to a remarkable 14-year-old entrepreneur who is certainly going places.

| 0 | *I* |

Between studying for nine GCSEs, including business studies, 14-year-old Dominic McVey has set up his own company, Scooters UK. The business, which imports motorized scooters and skateboards from the United States, has already made a profit of over £5,000 on sales of the equipment.

| 1 | |

Dominic needed £3,000 to set up his business and pay for the initial stock. He used savings from birthday and Christmas money and cashed in some investments that his father had made when Dominic was born. The young entrepreneur had also invested in shares on the stock market. 'I had to do the deals in my dad's name because I was too young,' he says, 'but he doesn't know anything about the market, so I told him what to buy and sell.'

| 2 | |

'I realized the potential for the business when I noticed that a lot of inner-city streets were being closed to cars or they were chock-a-block with traffic,' he explains. 'I thought there would be a great market for these scooters and skateboards, particularly now that more restrictions on cars in town centres have been introduced.'

| 3 | |

'You can take a smaller one with you on a train in a backpack and then unfold it and use it when you get into town. Men in suits are riding them up and down Wall Street in the US and it is my aim to get them to do the same in this country. I approached the American manufacturer and, after doing some research into their company and the scooters, I was allowed to become their UK distributor.'

| 4 | |

The motorized scooters, which sell for £499 and can travel at up to 22 mph, are not classified as motor vehicles and do not need a licence or tax. He also sells unmotorized skateboards for £129. They have special high-speed wheels and are capable of reaching 10 mph.

| 5 | |

'I ride them around town in busy areas and usually end up with a crowd of people running down the street wanting to know where to buy them, or winding down their car windows at traffic lights,' he says. Recently he went with his mother on a sales trip to Paris. 'The scooters are really popular there because the centre of the city is pedestrianized at the weekend. I went out with 500 leaflets and came back with none.'

| 6 | |

In the early stages Dominic had to overcome one or two obstacles. When he tried to open a business account at his bank, he made an appointment to see the manager. However, the bank thought it was a joke and when he arrived there they had not set up any time for the meeting. 'This really upset me,' says Dominic, 'but I managed to get a good rate of interest on the account because they were so embarrassed. I think people should take children more seriously.'

| 7 | |

Now that he has succeeded in setting up the business Dominic wants to expand it. He plans to open a showroom for his scooters in the City of London, 'right by some traffic lights so people stop and look'. His idea would then be to sell the business and look for further opportunities to make money. 'I'd like to be able to retire before I'm 40,' he tells me.

3 For questions **1–4**, choose the answer (**A**, **B**, **C** or **D**) which you think best fits according to the text.

1 How did Dominic raise the necessary money to set up his company?

  A He invested all his savings on the stock market.

  B He borrowed it from his father.

  C He used money from a variety of sources.

  D It was a birthday present.

2 What type of people does he want to buy his scooters?

  A fashionable people

  B Americans

  C businessmen

  D people who do not own a car

3 Why did Dominic go to Paris?

  A He went shopping with his mother.

  B He wanted to see the new pedestrian precinct.

  C He took some scooters to sell there.

  D He wanted to distribute information about his scooters.

4 What upset Dominic about his visit to the bank?

  A The manager laughed at him.

  B The manager refused to see him.

  C The meeting with the manager was very short.

  D The manager did not expect him to turn up.

Language focus 1: Ability

1 In the following sentences from the text, complete each of the spaces with the correct form of the verb in brackets.

  a The motorized scooters… *can* _____ (travel) at up to 22 mph.

  b They have special high-speed wheels and *are capable of* _____ (reach) 10 mph.

  c I'd like to *be able* _____ (retire) before I'm 40.

  d I *managed* _____ (get) a good rate of interest on the account because they were so embarrassed.

  e Now that he has *succeeded in* _____ (set) up the business Dominic wants to expand it.

2 Appropriate forms of *be able to* can be used in all five sentences in exercise 1. For example:

  a The motorized scooters *are able to* travel at up to 22 mph.

  e Now that he *has been able to* set up the business Dominic wants to expand it.

Can you explain the following in relation to *can* and *could*?

- *Can* is possible in **a** and **b** but not in **c**.

- *Could* is possible in the following sentence, but it is not possible in sentences **d** and **e**.
  Dominic could read and understand financial newspapers when he was only eight.

- However, four forms are possible in this sentence:
  They *couldn't find/didn't manage to find/didn't succeed in finding/weren't able to find* the missing climbers, so they abandoned the search.

  G Check your ideas on page 216 of the Grammar reference.

3 Rewrite the underlined parts of the sentences in **1–6** using the verb given in **bold**.

  1 When he was younger he <u>was able to swim</u> a length of the pool underwater.
    capable _____

  2 After trying for several years he <u>finally succeeded in giving up</u> smoking.
    managed _____

  3 I ran out of time so I <u>didn't manage to finish</u> both parts of the Writing Paper.
    unable _____

  4 We <u>managed to find out</u> what was wrong with the computer.
    succeeded _____

  5 One day you'll <u>manage to find</u> a job you like.
    able _____

  6 I'm afraid I <u>wasn't able to buy</u> the brand of dog food you asked for.
    manage _____

4 In which sentences in exercise 3 is it possible to rewrite the underlined part using *can/can't* or *could/couldn't*?

5   Tell your partner about something:
- you could do when you were younger but can't do now.
- you couldn't do when you were younger but can do now.
- you managed to do last weekend.
- you would like to be able to do.
- you don't think you'll ever succeed in doing.

Vocabulary 2: *Make* and *do*

A *Make* or *do*?

1 Complete each of the spaces with the correct form of either *make* or *do*. When you have finished, check your answers in the article about Dominic McVey. The numbers in brackets refer to the paragraphs in which the answers appear.

1 The business has already _____ a profit of over £5,000. **(0)**
2 He cashed in some investments that his father had _____ . **(1)**
3 I had to _____ the deals in my dad's name because I was too young. **(1)**
4 After _____ some research into their company and the scooters, I was allowed to become their UK distributor. **(3)**
5 When he tried to open a business account at his bank, he _____ an appointment to see the manager. **(6)**
6 His idea would then be to sell the business and look for further opportunities to _____ money. **(7)**

2 For each of the following groups of words and phrases decide which one is not usually used with the verb in capital letters. What do the other three have in common?

Example: 0
'Make a profit', 'make money', 'make a loss' are to do with increasing or decreasing the amount of money you have. This is also true of business, but we say 'do business with someone'.

0 MAKE
a profit
money
<u>business</u>
a loss

1 MAKE
a plan
damage
an appointment
an arrangement

2 DO
homework
a course
an effort
a degree

3 MAKE
up your mind
someone a favour
a decision
a choice

4 DO
the housework
the washing-up
the ironing
the beds

5 MAKE
a speech
a phone call
an experiment
a complaint

6 MAKE
an exercise
a film
a cake
a cup of tea

7 DO
badly in an exam
well at school
your best
progress

8 MAKE
a mistake
a mess
a job
a lot of noise

B Phrasal verbs with *make* and *do*

1 In each of the sentences **1–8** work out the meaning of each underlined phrasal verb. Use the context of the sentence to help you.

1 Put your coat on and <u>do it up</u>, Sofia. Otherwise you'll catch a cold.
2 They had a row, but the next day they <u>made it up</u> and they're closer than ever now.
3 Is that story true, or did you <u>make it up</u>?
4 They bought an old run-down cottage and <u>did it up</u>. Now it looks as good as the day it was built.
5 The quality of the recording was so bad we couldn't <u>make out</u> what the speakers were saying.
6 When the guard asked to see her train ticket my American friend Mary <u>made out</u> she couldn't understand English.
7 I'm really hungry. I <u>could do with</u> something to eat.
8 A mobile phone is essential for my job. I really <u>couldn't do without</u> it.

2 Write a short story of about 80 words including a total of six phrasal verbs and expressions with *do* and *make*.

Formal letters: An application

1 Read the advert and the letter of application and answer the following questions.

Who is the target reader?
What effect do you think the letter would have on that person?

STUDY GRANTS in the UK

St George's House is offering grants to students wishing to study English in one of their three UK centres this summer. Grants cover:

- **two months' tuition fees**
- **full board and accommodation**
- **help towards travel costs**

Write to the address below, stating why you are applying and how you would expect to benefit from the grant.

The Director
St George's House
13 Southdown Road
York, YO12 4XJ

Dear Sir or Madam,

I saw your advertisement in Monday's issue of the 'Guardian' and I would like to apply for a grant to study English in one of your schools this summer.

It would be better for me if it was in your Manchester school as I have a cousin living there, who I have never met. Furthermore, the night life in Manchester is said to be excellent and I would be able to go clubbing every night after class. Manchester would also be a good base for travelling and I could visit Wales, the Lake District and the birthplace of the Beatles, Liverpool.

I would be grateful if you could put me in a class of no more than six students as it is difficult to learn if the class size is larger. I would particularly like to have help with idiomatic expressions in order to sound more like a native English speaker.

I know you offer free unlimited access to the Internet and that would be very useful to me, too. I hope you will consider my application.

Yours faithfully
Ausra Zeronys

---

2 You are going to write your own application for one of the advertised grants at St George's House. Here is a possible paragraph plan.

Paragraph 1:	A short opening paragraph stating your reasons for writing.
Paragraphs 2 and 3:	Give relevant information about yourself, explaining why the grant would be useful and how you would benefit from studying English in the UK.
Paragraph 4:	A suitable, brief closing paragraph, re-stating your interest in obtaining the grant.

3 Here are four reasons to support your application. Can you add at least four more?

- *You could not afford to study in the UK without the grant.*
- *A period of study in the UK would help you to get a job in your own country.*
- *A recent illness has caused you to fall behind in your studies.*
- *You are interested in learning about British culture and the British way of life.*

What further details could you add to each of the reasons?

Example: You could not afford to study in the UK without a grant.
Although you have saved up enough money to pay the travel costs, both of your parents are unemployed and would be unable to pay for tuition or accommodation.

4 Now you are ready to write your letter of application. Write **120–180** words.

Don't forget!

- Use formal language throughout the letter.
- Provide relevant personal information together with an explanation of the different ways in which you will benefit from the grant.
- The information you give does not need to be true.

Listening 1:
FCE Part 4

Yes/No

1 Which of the following jobs could you *not* do if you were blind? Give reasons for your answers.

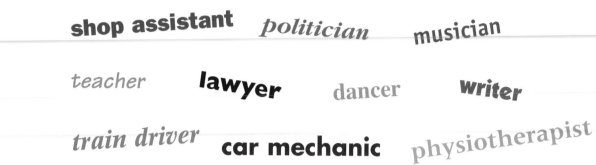

shop assistant   *politician*   **musician**

teacher   **lawyer**   *dancer*   **writer**

train driver   **car mechanic**   physiotherapist

What difficulties would you face in those jobs you *could* do?

2 Read the following Listening Part 4 instructions.

You will hear part of a radio interview with Grace, a singer who suffers from an eye disease. For questions **1–7** decide whether the idea is stated or not and mark **Y** for Yes, or **N** for No.

She has been partially sighted since birth.	1
She went to the doctor after playing with her mother.	2
She can only see things which are straight in front of her.	3
She left one school because of bullying.	4
Her father tried to discourage her from being a singer.	5
She does not find touring stressful.	6
She is no longer shy about her eyes.	7

Do you know of anybody else who has managed to overcome their disability and achieve success?

Word formation: Miscellaneous nouns

1 In the listening exercise Grace says:

My **sight** *didn't develop until I was about a year old.*

The noun *sight* comes from the verb *see*.
What is the noun form of the following verbs?

choose   *lose*   *complain*   *speak*

Check your answers in exercise 2 of *make* and *do* on page 166 in this unit.

2 Use the verb given in capitals at the end of each line to form a noun that fits in the space in the sentence. You may need to use a plural form.

1 _____ of mobile phones have fallen recently.   **SELL**
2 Don't forget to print your name below your _____ .   **SIGN**
3 I roared with _____ the first time I heard that joke.   **LAUGH**
4 You'll find yourself in trouble if your _____ doesn't improve.   **BEHAVE**
5 Communications were revolutionized with the _____ of the Internet.   **ARRIVE**
6 The capacity of human _____ to overcome illness is remarkable.   **BE**
7 Many foreign students are asked to show _____ of their age in pubs.   **PROVE**
8 I'm not sure I agree with the _____ that 'Money is the root of all evil'.   **SAY**

FCE Part 3

Gapped text

1 Discuss how you might react in the following situations:

- You see someone drowning in a freezing cold river.
- You hear some people shouting that they are trapped in a building.
- You see an old man being attacked in the street late at night.
- You are in the mountains when your friend falls and breaks his leg.

2 You are going to read a magazine article about a rescue. Seven sentences have been removed from the article. Choose from the sentences **A–H** the one which fits each space **(1–6)**. There is one extra sentence which you do not need to use. There is an example at the beginning **(0)**.

My river hero

It was just after 9.30 on a cold, wet February morning that I got a call from my 17-year-old son Matthew. **0** **H** Terrible thoughts started going through my head but before I really had a chance to worry, he added very matter-of-factly, 'I've just saved a baby girl from drowning.' **1**

Matthew loves fishing and you'll find him by the River Medway in Maidstone in his spare time. That day the water was high and dangerous because there'd been a lot of rain. Matthew was sitting by the river when he heard a woman scream, 'My baby, my baby, she's dying!' **2**

He ran up to them to see if there was anything he could do to help. In the water he saw an upside down pushchair. **3**

At the local hospital, the doctors praised Matthew for reacting so quickly. **4** But it wasn't only Emily that was lucky to be alive. A few days later I was reading the local paper when I saw a danger warning for the river. It was only then that I realized I could have lost my son, too.

Soon afterwards, Matthew, myself and my two younger daughters went along to Emily's second birthday party. There, her grandmother drank a toast to Matthew. **5** It sent a shiver down my spine and it still makes me go all funny thinking about it now.

6 He made the front page of the local paper and even appeared on television. I'm proud of my son. He's a caring lad who puts other people before himself. And he has obviously got a level head – I think I'd have panicked. He'll always be my river hero.

A Without thinking, Matthew dived in and went underwater to push the chair up towards the little girl's mum.

B He was hailed as a hero and received a lot of attention from the media.

C She thanked him for saving Emily's life and said they'd think of him on every one of her birthdays.

D He was warned against going fishing again until the river water had gone down to its normal level.

E What I didn't know at that stage was that he had put his own life at risk in order to save her.

F They said that if little Emily had been in the freezing water for just another three seconds, the outcome could have been horribly different.

G He looked over to see a woman and a young girl by the water's edge.

H 'Mum, I'm at the hospital,' he said.

Reacting to the text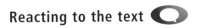

Have you ever been in a life-threatening situation?
Have you ever rescued someone or had to be rescued yourself?

Language focus 2: Verbs followed by prepositions

1 Write an appropriate preposition in each of the following sentences.

1 The doctors praised Matthew _____ reacting so quickly.

2 She thanked him _____ saving Emily's life.

3 He was warned _____ going fishing again.

Check your answers in the reading text.

2 Match each sentence beginning **1–7** with a suitable ending **a–g**. Complete each of the spaces with an appropriate preposition.

1 The other driver blamed me *for*   ☐ *d*

2 I really must apologize ____   ☐

3 She'll never be able to forgive him ____   ☐

4 My parents tried to prevent me ____   ☐

5 In order to discourage children ____   ☐

6 I'm just phoning to congratulate you ____   ☐

7 My aunt in London insisted ____   ☐

a ...being late. It won't happen again, I promise.

b ...seeing him again, but we met secretly after school every day.

c ...smoking, parents should set a good example and give it up themselves.

d ...causing the accident, but it really wasn't my fault.

e ...putting me up for the night, though I'd have preferred to stay in a hotel.

f ...leaving her to bring up the children on her own.

g ...passing all your exams. You deserved to do well.

What form of the verb is used after prepositions?

3 ⬤ Talk to your partner about the last time you:

• apologized

• thanked someone

• were congratulated

• were prevented from doing something

Vocabulary 3: Ways of looking

1 Read the following sentences. What is the difference in meaning between the three underlined verbs?

a In the water he <u>saw</u> an upside down pushchair.

b <u>Look at</u> my new dress. Do you like it?

c He <u>watched</u> her open her bag and take out a gun.

2 Underline the most appropriate alternative in the following sentences.

1 I think I'll get the mechanic to *see/look at* the engine. It doesn't sound very healthy.

2 Could you turn the light on? I can't *see/look at* what I'm doing.

3 You spend far too much time *looking at/watching* television.

4 Isn't it beautiful? I've never *seen/looked at* a fox before.

5 *See/Watch* carefully how I do it first, then you can have a go.

3 Match each verb **1–5** with its definition **a–e**.

1 gaze   **a** look rapidly and then look away again immediately

2 stare   **b** see for a short moment and not very well

3 glimpse   **c** look very closely and carefully (often with difficulty)

4 glance   **d** look for a long time, especially with interest or admiration

5 peer   **e** look for a long time, eg because you are surprised or shocked

4 Complete the following sentences with a word from exercise 3. The words in **bold** are commonly used with the missing words.

1 He _____ **inquisitively** into the box to see if there was anything interesting in it.

2 Bored with the lesson, I _____ **quickly** at my watch to see how long was left.

3 He _____ **admiringly** at her as she spoke.

4 For several minutes the young child _____ **open-mouthed** in amazement at the enormous cake.

5 She **caught a brief** _____ of her idol as he drove past in his limousine.

Listening 2:
FCE Part 1

Multiple choice

You will hear people talking in eight different situations. For questions **1–8** choose the best answer, **A**, **B** or **C**.

What to expect in the exam

- Two very typical types of question in Part 1 of the Listening Paper focus on:
  a the feelings, attitude or opinion of the speakers (see questions 1–4 below).
  b the identity of the speakers or the relationship between them (see questions 5–8 below).
- Remember that the tone of voice of the speakers may be important, as well as the language they use.

- As you listen to the questions being read out, think about the similarities and differences between each of the three alternatives and how the speaker might sound in each case. Look at question 1 below, together with the comments, and then talk about questions 2–8 in the same way.
- You will hear each recording twice. Listen carefully both times.

1 You hear this woman talking to a friend about her husband's work situation.
   How does the speaker feel?
   A annoyed   *she'd probably talk in an angry tone about something negative that has happened*
   B worried   *she might sound concerned about possible future problems*
   C relieved   *the tone would be more positive, as something bad has come to an end*

2 You overhear this man talking to his wife about a friend.
   What does he say about their friend's success?
   A He was lucky.
   B He worked hard for it.
   C He didn't deserve it.

3 You hear this woman talking to her friend about going rock climbing.
   How does she feel about it?
   A She thinks she'll enjoy it.
   B She does not want to do it.
   C She is nervous about it.

4 Listen to this woman talking to her son on the phone.
   What is she doing?
   A giving him advice
   B criticizing him
   C congratulating him

5 You overhear this young man talking on the phone.
   Who is he talking to?
   A his girlfriend
   B his mother
   C his sister

6 You hear a woman talking to a young man.
   What is the woman's relationship to the man?
   A his neighbour
   B his boss
   C his mother

7 You hear this man giving part of a speech.
   Who is he?
   A a politician
   B a sportsman
   C the manager of a sports centre

8 You hear someone being interviewed on the radio.
   Who is the speaker?
   A an explorer
   B a lorry driver
   C an inventor

Use of English:
FCE Part 4

Error correction

For questions **1–15** read the text below and look carefully at each line. Some of the lines are correct and some have a word which should not be there.

If a line is correct, put a tick (✓) in the space at the end of the line. If a line has a word which should not be there, write the word in the space. There are two examples at the beginning (**0** and **00**).

Pocket money

0	I try to make my children earn for their pocket money	*for*
00	by doing the housework. I encourage them to save up	✓
1	for buy any big things they want, but inevitably I end	_____
2	up paying for treats like meals out and their trips to the	_____
3	cinema. My daughter, Lucy, she is passionately interested	_____
4	in designer clothes, which they are expensive but seem to	_____
5	last. Last week I spent about £100 on her a couple of dresses.	_____
6	I don't make her to pay for any of her own clothes but I do	_____
7	say what she can and can't have. Alex is also much younger	_____
8	than his sister so he doesn't get quite as much pocket money	_____
9	as she does. What interests in him is football and every other	_____
10	week his father takes him to watch his favourite team,	_____
11	Chelsea, play. That must costs a fortune so we insist on	_____
12	him paying a little towards the price of the ticket himself.	_____
13	I try to teach my children the value of its money and help them	_____
14	to understand that it doesn't grow on trees. I know they will	_____
15	be thank me for doing so when they are older.	_____

Use of English:
FCE Part 3

Transformations

In **1–6** below complete the second sentence so that it has a similar meaning to the first sentence, using the word given. **Do not change the word given.** You must use between two and five words, including the word given.

1 Mr Yates said it was Helen who had started the fight.
blamed
Mr Yates _____ the fight.

2 The rescue team was unable to find the missing climbers.
succeed
The rescue team _____ the missing climbers.

3 'I'm sorry I'm late,' said Adrian.
apologized
Adrian _____ late.

4 She warned us not to go out alone after dark.
warned
She _____ going out alone after dark.

5 The immigration officials did not let him come into the country.
prevented
The immigration officials _____ into the country.

6 We demanded to see the manager.
seeing
We _____ the manager.

Vocabulary

A *Make* and *do*

1 Complete each of the following spaces with the correct form of either *make* or *do*.

1 Do/Did you always _____ your best at school?
2 When and where do you usually _____ your homework?
3 Do you learn from the mistakes you _____ in your homework?
4 Have you _____ any plans for next weekend?
5 Are you good at _____ decisions?
6 Think of three things that you would find it difficult to _____ without.
7 How often do you _____ phone calls? How long do you spend on the phone?
8 What would you like to _____ for a living?

2 Write answers for each of the questions in exercise 1.

B Ways of looking

Match a sentence beginning **1–5** with an appropriate ending **a–e**.

1 For several minutes she sat gazing...

2 Once in the street she could only stare...

3 Every couple of minutes she glanced...

4 She put on her glasses and peered...

5 She only caught a very brief glimpse...

a with difficulty at the tiny writing on the poster.

b of her attacker, so she couldn't describe him very well.

c in wonder at the beautiful mountain scenery.

d in disbelief as the fire destroyed her house.

e anxiously up at the clock, wondering when he would phone.

Word formation: Miscellaneous nouns

Make the noun form of the following words and put them into pairs, according to their noun endings.

relieve	say	arrive	sign	advertise
honest	approve	believe	depart	poor

Example:
relieve – relief
believe – belief

Transactional letters

Writing: FCE Part 1

You are studying English in Hastings and your cousin is coming to live and work in England. She wants to open a savings account and has asked you to send her information from two banks.

Using your notes below, write a letter to your cousin giving her the information. You should also suggest which account you think is better and explain why.

Write a **letter** of between **120 and 180** words in an appropriate style. Do not write any addresses.

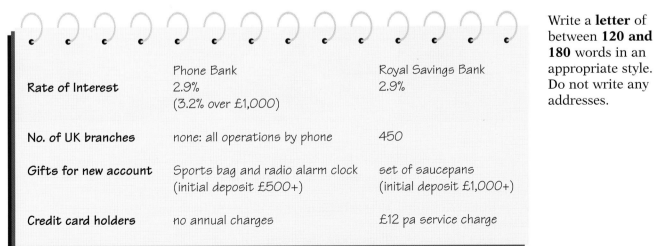

	Phone Bank	Royal Savings Bank
Rate of Interest	2.9% (3.2% over £1,000)	2.9%
No. of UK branches	none: all operations by phone	450
Gifts for new account	Sports bag and radio alarm clock (initial deposit £500+)	set of saucepans (initial deposit £1,000+)
Credit card holders	no annual charges	£12 pa service charge

14 As pretty as a picture

Vocabulary 1: The Arts

1 Both words in each of the pairs below can be used in combination with one of the words in the box. Write an appropriate word from the box in each of the spaces. There is an example at the beginning **(0)**.

novel	opera	~~concert~~	painting	stone	classical	gallery

0 open-air _concert_
jazz

1 _____ ballet
music

2 _____ singer
house

3 _____ sculpture
statue

4 portrait _____
art

5 abstract _____
priceless

6 detective _____
historical

2 Which people do you associate with each of the following areas of the arts?

music	literature	art	opera	ballet	sculpture

Example: Theatre: _actor, actress, director, cast, playwright, audience_
Check your answers in the Wordlist on page 205.

Multiple matching

1 Look at these photographs and discuss the following questions.
What do you think these animals are painting?
Would you like to buy one of their paintings? Why/Why not?

2 You are going to read an article about two gorillas, Koko and Michael, who both paint. Read the summary sentences and the text quite quickly. As you read answer the following questions.
What makes Koko and Michael's pictures so different from those painted by other animals?
What does their work tell us about the origins of art?

3 Choose the most suitable summary sentence from the list **A–H** for each part (**1–6**) of the article. There is one extra summary sentence which you do not need to use. There is an example at the beginning (**0**).

A Sign language has enabled them to name their creations.
B Apes can be as expressive as humans when communicating.
C Their choice of colours reveals certain similarities with humans.
D Only humans had previously been thought capable of depicting concrete objects.
E Their work gives us new insights into the origins of art.
F Their ability to paint might have been influenced by sign language.
G It cannot be considered art in the true sense of the word.
H We have known for some time that animals can paint.

Palette of the apes

Have you ever thought, 'I wish I could paint'? Well don't give up hope. As Emma Bayley discovers, even a monkey can do it.

0 *H*

There's nothing new about art galleries organizing exhibitions of pictures painted by animals. There was a brief craze for ape art in the late 1950s when chimps were encouraged to paint by biologists investigating the origins of art. Later it was elephants, whose work, like that of the chimps, was seen as a form of absract expressionism and fetched prices close to that of human artists. Recently, however, a new dimension has been added by two remarkable gorillas called Michael and Koko.

1

What is different is the representational quality of their pictures. They appear able to paint things from the world around them. 'I noticed when they were quite young they were doing pencil drawings that were realistic,' says Dr Francine Patterson of the Gorilla Foundation in California. 'Koko, for instance, drew a glass, a banana and a bus.' This was a first. Never before had animals been recorded producing pictures with form.

2

These great apes have been raised and taught to speak using American sign language by Dr Patterson. Michael knows around 400 signs whereas Koko has managed to learn more than 1000 and has even chatted to fans on the Internet. Through sign language, the gorillas joke, lie and get embarrassed, but perhaps the most incredible indication of their awareness is that they give their artwork titles. One of Michael's pictures was inspired by a bouquet of flowers. When asked afterwards what he'd call the painting, he signed 'Stink Gorilla More' – 'stink' being gorilla-speak for 'flowers'.

3

Perhaps we should not be so surprised by their ability to express themselves through the medium of art. It may well be that language acquisition has shaped the apes' ability to create form in their paintings. 'It's possible,' says Patterson. 'Language and art are both examples of symbolic representation so the two may be linked.'

4

Most extraordinary are the pictures they have made to illustrate emotions. Koko uses red and pink to depict love, green and brown for hate and a mixture of darker tones for anger. At a young age, in tests devised for humans, 80 to 90 per cent of the colours Koko used to represent emotional states were the same as a human would select. As Patterson says, this shows that the way the brains of apes and humans process information is not entirely different. But whether Koko and Michael are in the same league as Picasso or Jackson Pollock is a matter for some debate.

5

Traditionally, art is defined as something which is created to have a lasting aesthetic presence after it has been produced. Studies show that apes do have an aesthetic sense and Patterson herself is convinced Koko has a judgement of beauty and ugliness that's virtually the same as ours. But it's clear that Michael and Koko do not create their paintings to have a lasting presence. The fact is that acrylic paints have proved to be a great gorilla delicacy and after laying their paintbrushes down, they like to eat their artworks.

6

Perhaps it doesn't matter that these apes eat their paintings. It's remarkable enough that they create them in the first place, bearing in mind that their giant hands place a physical limit on their work. Their ability to paint meaningful pictures suggests that art may have existed a long time before the human cave paintings of 45,000 years ago. 'I would say art goes back at least a million years to our common ancestor,' says Patterson. 'It is much deeper in our species than we thought.

Reacting to the text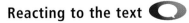

Do you think pictures painted by animals can be considered art? Why/Why not?
Why do some people pay vast sums of money for artworks? Would you?

Language focus: Hypothetical situations

A Wishes

1 The reading text began with this sentence:

Have you ever thought, 'I wish I could paint'?

We use *wish* (or for more emphasis *if only*) to express how we would like things to be different if we had the power to change them. The *I wish* sentence above means that you can't paint, but would like to be able to.

2 Look at the following sentences and then complete each of the three rules below with words from the box.

1 I wish it wasn't/weren't so cold here in winter.
2 If only I had more time to study.
3 I wish you would stop interrupting me!
4 I wish he wouldn't drive so fast.
5 I wish I hadn't gone to see that boring play last night.
6 If only you'd told me earlier.

> *would*   the past perfect   the past simple

a We use *wish/if only* + _____
to express wishes about present states.

b We use *wish/if only* + _____
to express irritation at other people's actions or behaviour.

c We use *wish/if only* + _____
to express wishes and regrets about the past.

3 a Reword the following sentence so that it sounds more natural.
I wish I would give up smoking.

b What is the difference in meaning between these sentences?
I wish she could come to my party on Saturday.
I hope she can come to my party on Saturday.

🄖 Check your ideas on page 217 of the Grammar reference and read more about expressing wishes.

Practice

1 In **1–5** below underline the correct alternative in each sentence.

1 I wish I *could/would/did* remember where I put my reading glasses.

---

2 I wish I *don't/didn't/won't* have to do so much homework. I never have any time to myself.
3 The car has broken down again! I'm beginning to wish we *wouldn't buy/didn't buy/hadn't bought* it.
4 I wish they *didn't/would/had* turn their music down next door. I can't hear myself think!
5 If only *you'll listen/you'd have listened/you'd listened* to me! None of this would have happened.

2 In **1–5** below complete each space with the correct form of the verb in brackets.

1 What glorious sunshine! I bet you wish you _____ (be) on the beach right now, don't you?
2 I wish you two _____ (stop) shouting! You're driving me mad!
3 It has rained every day of this holiday. If only we _____ (go) to Greece instead!
4 I can't afford to buy any new clothes. If only I _____ (have) a job!
5 One minute you want to come, the next minute you don't. I wish you _____ (make) up your mind!

B *It's time* and *would rather*

Choose the correct alternative in the following sentences.

1 I'd rather you *didn't/wouldn't/don't* bring a mobile phone to school.
2 It's time you *went/will go/go* to bed now.

🄖 Check your ideas in sections B and C of the Grammar reference on page 217 and read more about *it's time* and *would rather*.

Practice

You have decided to spend the day complaining, telling different people how you would like them to change! The people you are going to speak to are:

- your mother or father
- your brother, sister or cousin
- your best friend
- a neighbour
- the leader of your country
- another person of your choice

Write one sentence for each person beginning with one of the following phrases:

I wish you...
It's time you...
I'd rather you...

Then compare your sentences with those that your partner has written. Are you unhappy about any of the same things?

Word formation: Adjective suffixes *-ible* and *-able*

The suffixes *-ible* and *-able* are used to form a number of adjectives, as in the following two examples from the text.

*two **remarkable** gorillas*
*the most **incredible** indication of their awareness*

1   Add an appropriate prefix and/or suffix to the part of the word in bold in the sentences below. The completed word may be an adjective, an adverb or a noun. Nouns may be singular or plural. There is an example at the beginning **(0)**.

0   This chair is a little <u>un</u> **comfort** <u>able</u>. I'm going to sit somewhere else.
1   The weather in Britain is so _____**predict**_____ : you should always take an umbrella with you, just in case.
2   We know it will be a difficult match, but we are **reason**_____ confident of success.
3   No one can touch their right elbow with their right hand. It's a physical _____**poss**_____ .
4   I wouldn't say I was **incred**_____ rich, but I'm certainly **comfort**_____ well-off.
5   Please do not leave any **valu**_____ in your room. The management will not accept **respons**_____ for theft.
6   We usually get away to the coast or the mountains in summer. It can get _____**bear**_____ hot in the city.
7   We'll have to walk to the village. It's _____**access**_____ to cars.
8   The accuracy of her written work has improved **consider**_____ since she started the course.

2   What for you would be the most *enjoyable* way to spend a weekend?
What would be the worst *imaginable* way to spend a Sunday?
Do any of the following describe your last weekend? What did you do?

forgettable   *unbelievably boring*   *reasonably enjoyable*
remarkably good   *memorable*

Speaking:
FCE Part 3

Collaborative task

Imagine that some friends are coming to visit you for the weekend. Your friends have two young children and you would like to take the whole family out for the day. Discuss with your partner the potentially good and bad points about each of the options below and then agree on three of the places or events that you might take your visitors to.

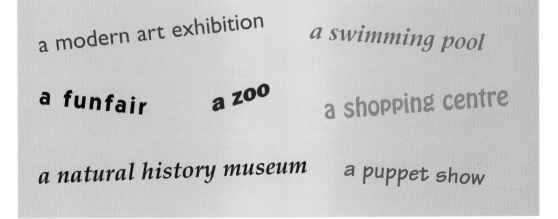

a modern art exhibition   a swimming pool

a funfair   a zoo   a shopping centre

a natural history museum   a puppet show

Vocabulary 2: Animals

1 Complete each of the spaces with the names of animals from the box to complete these well-known similes.

| a fox | a mule | a bat | an owl | a mouse | a peacock | a bee |

1 as blind as _____
2 as busy as _____
3 as quiet as _____
4 as cunning as _____
5 as stubborn as _____
6 as wise as _____
7 as proud as _____

2 Complete these expressions using the names of the animals from the box.

| bear | fish | cat | fly | dog | frog | horse |

1 She's so kind and gentle. She wouldn't hurt a _____ .
2 I'm so hungry I could eat a _____ .
3 She's upset about splitting up with Gary, but I told her there were plenty more _____ in the sea.
4 My two kids don't give me a moment's peace. They fight like _____ and _____ all the time.
5 I was so pleased to see him again. I rushed up and gave him a really big _____ hug.
6 I'm sorry I can't speak any louder. I've got a bit of a _____ in my throat.

3 Match each of these groups of nouns to an animal from the box.

| horse | bird | cat | fish |

a _____
  feathers
  beak
  wings

b _____
  gills
  scales
  fin

c _____
  whiskers
  paws
  fur

d _____
  hooves
  tail
  mane

 4 Discuss the following with your partner, giving reasons for your answers. Which of the animals in exercises 1 and 2:
• makes the best pet?
• is the most useful to humans?
• makes the most noise?
• is the ugliest?
• is the most attractive?

Listening:
FCE Part 4

Multiple choice 🔲

Which of the following would you definitely *not* want to do?
How would you feel in each of the situations?

- ride an elephant
- hold a tarantula in your hand
- collect honey from a bee hive
- spend an hour in a room full of snakes
- pick up a rat
- spend an evening working as an assistant to a lion tamer
- swim in a tank with sharks

2   You will hear an interview with a woman who went scuba diving in a tank which had sharks in it. For questions **1–7**, choose the best answer **A**, **B** or **C**.

1   Visitors to Deep-Sea World can

    A touch the sharks.

    B get very close to the sharks.

    C see the sharks in their natural habitat.

2   How did Sue's friends feel about her dive?

    A They were worried about her.

    B They reacted in different ways.

    C They all thought she was very lucky.

3   Why was Sue not allowed to wear all her diving equipment?

    A in order to protect the animals and plants

    B in order not to frighten the sharks

    C in order to prevent damage to the glass tank

4   How many other people did she dive with?

    A three

    B four

    C five

5   The divers were warned that the sharks could

    A bite them.

    B damage their breathing equipment.

    C break an arm or a leg.

6   According to Sue, sharks may attack people when

    A they do not have enough food.

    B they feel threatened.

    C they are in the breeding season.

7   Sue and her friends had to make sure

    A they didn't step on any fish.

    B they didn't stay in the tank too long.

    C they kept swimming all the time.

Sue says that the aim of the aquarium is 'to increase awareness of the marine environment'. Do you think aquariums and zoos serve a useful purpose or should all animals be allowed to live in their natural habitat?

Writing 1:
FCE Part 2

Set books

If you have read one of the set books you may decide to answer either question 5a or 5b in Part 2 of the Writing Paper (Paper 2). You may be asked to write a composition, a report, a letter or an article.

1 Look at the following example questions **1–7** and for each one decide which of the following (**A–F**) you are being asked to write about.

A the book in general   **C** individual events in the story   **E** a character
B the overall story   **D** the setting   **F** a relationship

1 Write an **article** for your school's English magazine about a book you have read. Tell readers what you did and did not enjoy about the book and say whether you would recommend it.

2 Write a **composition** explaining how the beginning of the book you have read is important to the development of the rest of the story.

3 Your local English language bookshop wants your help in designing a poster to advertise the book you have just read. They have asked you to write a **report** suggesting two pictures showing different scenes from the book and explaining why they should be included on the poster.

4 Which character in the book you have read did you like the least? Write a **composition** saying who the character is and giving reasons for your choice.

5 A friend has written to you asking about the book you have read. Write a **letter** to your friend explaining what you learnt from your reading about the time and/or place in which the story is set.

6 Did you like the ending of the book you read? Write a **composition** explaining why or why not.

7 Write a **composition** briefly describing a place or building which appears in the book you have read and explaining its importance to the story.

2 Look at the following example answer. Which of the above questions is it answering?

Animal Farm

    After overthrowing Jones at the beginning of 'Animal Farm' the animals enter the farmhouse quietly and carefully. They are amazed at 'the unbelievable luxury' of the rooms and the furniture, such as the horsehair sofa and the soft feather beds. They decide never to live there and it is turned into a museum as a symbol of the terror and oppression of Jones's reign.

    However, the pigs eventually move into the farmhouse and it soon symbolizes the inequality between themselves and the other animals. They grow fat there, drink whisky and even sleep in the beds, while the others do all the work. As in Jones's time, the leaders live comfortably whereas the workers suffer.

    Furthermore, Napoleon spends most of his time in the house, waited on by dogs in his own private apartments. In this way, the new dictator separates himself from the other animals, including the pigs.

    At the end we see him talking to the humans as equals in the dining room. It is in the farmhouse, then, that we see best how Napoleon occupies Jones's position.

3 Has the writer answered both parts of the question satisfactorily?
What is the purpose of each of the four paragraphs?
Which words are used to link ideas?
Has the writer quoted directly from the text?

4   Choose one of the example questions and write your answer in **120–180** words, with reference to one of the set books.

How to go about it

- Underline the key words in the question.
- Write down as many ideas as you can which will be relevant to the question.
- Check in the book that your information is correct and add any further ideas which might be useful. If you notice any short, relevant quotations, make a note of them.
- Decide which of your ideas you will include in your answer. The word limit is 180 words, so be selective.

- Organize your ideas into a paragraph plan which is relevant to the task type. Four paragraphs should be enough if you are writing a **composition**.
- If you are writing a **letter**, decide how you will begin and end it.
- If you are writing a **report**, consider what headings, if any, you will use.
- If you are writing an **article**, interest the reader from the very beginning.

Vocabulary 3: Television

1   Can you give an example of each of the following types of TV programme?

sitcom	sports programme	quiz show	soap opera
music programme	chat show	documentary	comedy programme
game show	news broadcast	current affairs programme	detective series

2   What are your three favourite types of programme?
Which three types do you like the least? Why?

Reading 2:
FCE Part 4

Multiple matching

1   Look at the following challenge from the 'Kill Your TV' Web site.
Would you accept the challenge?
Do you think you would be successful?

2   You are going to read various e-mails sent to the Web site by people who took up the challenge. For questions **1–15** on page 182, choose from the people **(A–F)**. The people may be chosen more than once. When more than one answer is required, these may be given in any order. There is an example at the beginning **(0)**.

The kill your TV challenge

If you want to experiment with a TV-free life and prove that TV is not addictive, take up this challenge:

Go entirely without TV for a month. No news, no sports, no cartoons – absolutely nothing. If you decide to take up the challenge, e-mail me at the end of the month and let me know how it went. I'll post your comments on this page. Good luck!

Don't forget!

- Read the e-mails through quite quickly to get a general idea.
- Underline the key words in the questions. The example and the first two have been done for you.
- Read the text again and underline the parts of the text which give you the answers, as in the example.

- Do not leave any questions unanswered. **Be careful!** Just because a word in the text is the same as a word in the question, this does *not* necessarily mean that this is the correct answer.
  eg The word 'education' or 'educational' appears in texts **D**, **E** and **F**, but only one answer is correct for question 11.

We <u>found out</u> about your challenge <u>after</u> we had <u>given up</u> television. `0` | `D`

I <u>nearly didn't succeed</u> in the challenge. `1` `2`

Television was <u>dominating</u> our lives. `3`

I feel healthier as a result. `4`

I managed to do some home improvements. `5`

Some alternatives are no better than television. `6` `7`

I'll probably continue to watch too much television. `8`

We speak to each other more now. `9` `10`

Television has educational benefits. `11`

I wasn't entirely successful in the challenge. `12`

You need to achieve a balance. `13` `14`

The rest of my family like watching television. `15`

Comments

A Nikki Bowen

After one month without the TV I've become fitter, having spent less time in front of the box and more time outside. Of course, I've also spent more time in front of the computer, which can sometimes be as bad as passively watching television. And now that I'm 'allowed' to watch television, I have no real desire to, apart from the occasional episode of 'The Simpsons'. Not all television is bad, of course. The problem only arises when these activities take up too much of your time and you start to get your priorities wrong. I gave up television, not because it is bad in itself, but because it was eating up time that I could spend doing other, more productive activities.

B Steve Tyler

I really thought I'd have no difficulty in getting by without a telly, so when I took up your challenge I was honestly surprised at how much I missed the ability to watch those shows I truly enjoy. In some respects I failed, as I had some episodes of 'The X-Files' recorded for me so I could watch them when the 30 days were up. In general, though, I discovered that listening to the radio is a better alternative to the television. For one thing it enabled me to get on with the job of doing up the kids' bedroom.

C Pete Simpson

When I scored 18 on your questionnaire I realized I should give up watching TV for a while and try to cure my addiction. Although there were several times when I was on the point of reaching for the 'on' button, I surprised myself by managing to get through the month. I certainly watch less television now than I used to, but I'm sure it's just a matter of time before I'm back to my bad old ways. The only permanent cure would be to throw away the telly – and I don't think my wife and kids would thank me for that.

D Leanne Watson

<u>My husband and I got rid of the TV about a month before we came across your Web site.</u> We did it to protect our kids from the effects of television and because we felt it was taking over our lives. As a result our daughters are calmer and more relaxed and we're all a lot more communicative. One thing that has been most surprising is other people's reactions to our decision to no longer watch TV. They find it hard to understand why we would want to do such a thing. Most speak of the educational benefits, though few watch anything but soaps and sitcoms.

E Jane Kennedy

I would have given up after a week if my mum and dad hadn't been there to stop me. I'm glad they did, though, as it's had a tremendous effect on my education and my general quality of life. I do my homework better and more quickly without the television on and whereas before there were times when I barely exchanged a word with my family, we've all now become great conversationalists.

F Dave Hamilton

Having successfully completed your challenge, I've now gone back to watching eight or so hours of television a week – which, you have to agree, is not excessive. Like all things, it needs to be taken in moderation. For me, television is as entertaining and educational as reading and is only harmful when you are unable to separate that which entertains and educates from that which simply passes the time. The same is true of the computer. Giving up the television just to spend three hours a day surfing on the Internet cannot be considered an improvement.

Reacting to the text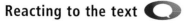

Do you agree with Dave Hamilton that 'television is as entertaining and educational as reading'? Give examples of programmes to support your opinion.

Do you think there is too much violence on television? Should there be more censorship?

Vocabulary 4: Phrasal verbs

1 What is the meaning of the following underlined phrasal verbs?

I realized I should <u>give up</u> watching television for a while.
If you decide to <u>take up</u> the challenge, e-mail me at the end of the month and let me know how it went.

2 The following sentences all come from the e-mails about television. Match each of the underlined phrasal verbs with its meaning below, using the context in the sentences to help you make your decisions. The phrasal verbs in **bold** appeared in earlier units of the book.

1 The problem only arises when these activities **take up** too much of your time.
2 I gave up television… because it was <u>eating up</u> time that I could spend doing other, more productive activities.
3 I really thought I'd have no difficulty in **getting by** without a telly.
4 (Listening to the radio) enabled me to <u>get on with</u> the job of **doing up** the kids' bedroom.
5 I surprised myself by managing to <u>get through</u> the month.
6 The only permanent cure would be to <u>throw away</u> the telly.
7 My husband and I got rid of the TV about a month before we **came across** your Web site.
8 We felt (television) was <u>taking over</u> our lives.

a find by chance
b start or continue doing something
c get rid of
d use or occupy
e use or consume in great quantities
f repair or redecorate
g take control of
h manage to live or survive (intransitive verb)
i manage to survive a difficult period of time (transitive verb)

Writing 2:
FCE Part 2

Compositions

Your class has been discussing the quality of television programmes. Your teacher has asked you to write a composition giving your opinions on the following statement.

Most of what is shown on television is not worth watching.

Write your **composition**. You should write between **120 and 180** words.

How to go about it

- Write down some ideas for your composition. Consider: entertainment value, educational benefits, violence, cultural relevance, news programmes, advertisements and satellite and cable TV.
- Decide whether you are going to consider both sides of the argument (Unit 3) in your composition or only one (Unit 8). Look again at the relevant unit of the book.

- Select those ideas which you intend to use. The word limit is 180, so be selective. Some examples should be included in your composition to support your ideas.
- Decide which linking devices you will use.
- Remember to check your composition when you have finished writing. Can you make any improvements?

Now you are ready to write your composition.

Word formation

For questions **1–10** read the text below. Use the word given in capitals at the end of each line to form a word that fits in the space in the same line. There is an example at the beginning **(0)**.

A record-breaking fish

The world's **(0)** _oldest_ known captive goldfish, named Tish, has	OLD
died **(1)** _____ at home in his tank. Tish, who had reached the	PEACE
(2) _____ age of 43, was won by seven-year-old Peter Hand at a fair.	REMARK
He **(3)** _____ shared his bowl with Tosh, who died in 1975; he also	ORIGIN
outlived the family's other pets, **(4)** _____ dogs, rabbits and hamsters.	INCLUDE
When Peter left home his parents took **(5)** _____ for Tish, who moved	RESPONSIBLE
with them to Yorkshire, where they now live in **(6)** _____ . His	RETIRE
(7) _____ in the *Guinness Book of Records* came when he turned 41.	APPEAR
The normal procedure of counting the microscopic growth rings on a fish's	
scales could not be used to establish **(8)** _____ of his age. Because	PROVE
he had been kept indoors and was unaffected by **(9)** _____ changes,	SEASON
this method was **(10)** _____ and friends of the family had to sign	RELY
affidavits, written statements supporting the owner's claim.	

Vocabulary

A The Arts

Complete the spaces in the following sentences with an appropriate word. The beginning of each missing word has been given to help you.

1 He had a full-length **po**_____ painted of himself.
2 The museum contains several bronze **sc**_____ of animals.
3 I am reading a great **no**_____ at the moment. It's by a contemporary author.
4 There'll be 16 groups playing live the weekend after next at the Bletchley
   op_____-_____ jazz festival.
5 You really can't put a value on this Chinese vase. It's **pr**_____ .
6 Shakespeare is England's best-known **pl**_____ .
7 This piece of music is by a famous 18th century German **co**_____ .
8 We went to a marvellous **ex**_____ of contemporary art at the weekend.

B Animals

1 Which animal is being described below?

> This animal lives in small groups. Its sharp claws and teeth are used for killing and eating other animals, both small and large. It has light brown fur, whiskers on its face and the male can be identified by the beautiful golden mane on its head and neck.

2 Now write descriptions of three other animals. Use the Wordlist on page 205 to help you. When you have finished, give your descriptions to your partner, who will try to guess which animals you have described.

C **Phrasal verbs**

Complete the spaces in the following sentences with an appropriate phrasal verb.
1 Please _____ _____ your rubbish when you have finished your lunch.
2 Some people worry that aliens will come and _____ _____ the world.
3 His new car has a huge engine and is very powerful, but, of course, it _____ _____ petrol.
4 I really must _____ _____ _____ my homework or I'll never finish it!
5 The temperature was -10°C but the climbers _____ _____ the night by keeping a fire burning.

Transformations: Hypothetical situations

In **1–8** below complete the second sentence so that it has a similar meaning to the first sentence, using the word given. **Do not change the word given.** You must use between two and five words, including the word given.

1 It's a pity I don't live nearer the school.
   wish
   I _____ nearer the school.
2 I regret telling her about my new boyfriend.
   wish
   I _____ her about my new boyfriend.
3 I'd prefer you not to wear those jeans to the wedding.
   rather
   I'd _____ those jeans to the wedding.
4 We really ought to go home now.
   went
   It's _____ home.
5 I'd really like to go with them, but there's no room in their car.
   wish
   I _____ with them, but there's no room in their car.
6 You should have brought your umbrella!
   brought
   If _____ your umbrella!
7 I don't like you speaking to me like that!
   wish
   I _____ to me like that!
8 It would be nice to know what my dog was thinking.
   wish
   I _____ what my dog was thinking.

Compositions

Your class has been discussing the role of zoos in the modern world. Your teacher has asked you to write a composition giving your views on the following statement.

Zoos no longer serve a useful purpose.

Write your **composition**. You should write between **120 and 180** words.

afedersiniz

permisi

disculpe

ursäkta mig

entschuldigen Sie

elnézést

mi scusi

excusez-moi

Multiple matching

1 Can you identify any of the languages above? Would you like to learn any of them?
How important is it to learn a foreign language?
In what ways might English be useful to you in the future?
What problems can occur if you don't know the language of the country you go to visit?

2 You will hear five different people talking about how learning another language was useful for them. For questions **1–5**, choose from the list **A–F** what each speaker says about his or her experience. There is one extra letter which you do not need to use.

A Studying abroad brought success.

B Not everyone understands me when I speak.

C Doing things twice worked for me.

D Going to the cinema helped me learn.

E I made more progress the second time.

F Progress was very slow at first.

Speaker 1 ☐
Speaker 2 ☐
Speaker 3 ☐
Speaker 4 ☐
Speaker 5 ☐

Vocabulary 1

A Phrasal verbs with *turn*

1 Speaker 5 in the listening says: *all three French-owned companies that I applied to turned me down at the interview stage*. What is the meaning of *to turn someone down*?

2 Match each sentence beginning **1–7** with an appropriate ending **a–g**.

1 Why are you two still awake? **Turn**
2 They left port at sunrise but were forced to **turn**
3 It's amazing that this small seed will gradually **turn**
4 According to this map we have to **turn**
5 The party starts at 8pm but people won't **turn**
6 We had no reason to be suspicious of him, but it **turned**
7 I can't hear what they're saying. **Turn**

a **off** the motorway at the next exit.
b **out** that he was wanted by the police for burglary.
c **back** by rough seas and strong winds.
d **up** the sound a bit, will you?
e **into** a beautiful rose.
f **up** until much later.
g **off** the light and go to sleep.

3 Now write the infinitive of each of the seven phrasal verbs with *turn* from exercise 2 next to its meaning below.

a become _____
b increase the volume _____
c become known _____
d arrive _____
e leave a road _____
f return _____
g disconnect _____

B Compound adjectives

Two common types of compound adjectives are formed using either adjectives referring to countries and languages:

Examples: *French-owned companies, Spanish-speaking teachers*

or numbers:

Examples: *a two-month course in Paris, a four-hour flight*

Note that a hyphen is used between the two words in the adjective and that a noun used with a number to form an adjective is singular.

1 For questions **1–8**, complete each of the below with one of the compound adjectives from the box.

Irish-made	one-hour
American-educated	five-minute
English-speaking	11-year-old
Italian-born	1,000-word

1 When I've finished my studies I hope to work in an _____ country, like the States or Australia.
2 The language school is just a _____ walk from the beach.
3 My _____ grandmother used to tell me stories of her childhood in Rome.
4 As part of my language project I have to write a _____ report on the growth of English on the Internet.
5 Our firm has just taken on an _____ accountant: he studied in Boston, I believe.
6 We have four _____ lessons before lunch at my school.
7 I bought this tablecloth in London but it's _____ .
8 This remarkable _____ boy can already speak five languages fluently.

2 What compound adjectives could you use to describe the following? There is an example at the beginning **(0)**.

0 a journey which takes three hours → a ___*three-hour*___ journey
1 a bank note which is worth five pounds → a _____ note
2 a shift which lasts from 8pm to 8am → a _____ shift
3 a team with ten men → a _____ team
4 a meal with a starter, main course and dessert → a _____ meal
5 a holiday which lasts a fortnight → a _____ holiday

3 Use compound adjectives to tell your partner about:

- the age of your brothers and sisters, eg *I've got a seven-year-old sister.*
- the number and duration of lessons each day at your school
- the duration of your last holiday and the length of the journey
- the time taken to get from your house to your school/place of work/town centre
- the length of this book

Reading 1:
FCE Part 2 Multiple choice

1 How important has English become in your country? Give examples to illustrate your views.
Could English one day become the only language in the world? Why/Why not?

2 You are going to read an article on the influence of English today. For questions **1–7**, choose the correct answer **A**, **B**, **C** or **D**.

Don't forget!

- Read the text through quite quickly first to get a general idea of the context. As you read this text try to answer question 1 only. This type of question tests your global understanding of the text.

1 Faced with the dominance of English, what does the writer think will happen to the world's other languages?

A Most of them will die out.

B They will only be spoken at home.

C Many will exist alongside English.

D They will consist mainly of English words.

Speaking in one tongue

As American English threatens to dominate the world, could the Internet offer the best hope of saving dying languages?

English is spreading fast and it has been predicted that one in ten of the world's 6000 languages will become extinct over the next century. Up to half of the world's languages are no longer being taught to children, threatening them with eventual
5 extinction. Even countries with millions of native language speakers are so worried by the growth of English that they have devised policies to fight back.

The French have brought in regulations to combat what they see as an American cultural invasion. Corporations and
10 government bodies are not allowed to use English terms where there are French equivalents. And to ensure there are as many of these as possible, a Terminology Commission has been set up with the task of creating them. There is widespread concern that the American influence could mean local films, TV, music
15 and books get pushed into the background. In order to protect local languages and culture, the European Union introduced new legislation, which states that half of the TV programmes shown in member states must be European.

New technology does not make things easy for other languages.
20 It is especially difficult to hold back the tide of English words in high-tech industries because many of the innovations are American. The Germans have their own words for 'computer', 'smart-card', 'DVD', 'modem' and 'handheld PC', but hardly anyone uses them. Until recently all university subjects in
25 Malaysia were taught in Malay. Now, however, universities have had to make exceptions for Information Technology, as the majority of IT textbooks are in English and they simply do not have the time or resources to translate them.

Today there is another medium to worry about: the Internet.
30 English accounts for about 90 per cent of traffic and the World Wide Web will only accelerate its spread around the world. Unlike broadcasting, however, most communication on the Net is written, so it needn't pose the same threat to regional

accents and dialects. It is also decentralized and more
35 interactive than broadcasting, which may help to prevent the disappearance of minority languages.

Even if English were universally adopted, this would not mean the end of diversity. Languages are constantly adapting and English is not exactly the same the world over: you only have
40 to compare American and British English to realize that. The Net, too, is an instrument of change. Because Net communication is mainly written, many people use abbreviations to speed things up and this trend means the language is evolving with Internet use. In 10 to 20 years from
45 now the English on the Net may well be unrecognizable compared with the English we know now.

English will continue to spread and evolve with the Net but people will still speak their own languages. In most cases they'll use English for electronic communication, but native
50 languages at home. Languages are more than just a means of communication: they are also an important part of regional cultures and identities and they do not disappear easily. For centuries the trading world spoke Latin but it didn't do away with French or German. Instead, Latin became the dead
55 language.

Languages have their own dynamics and there is little governments can do to change their course. In 18th-century Germany, Frederick II set up a commission to get rid of French words from German. It failed because the dynamics of a
60 language come from the bottom up rather than the top down.

English may dominate but it won't wipe every other language off the face of the Earth and it won't be the same English spoken everywhere. This may not be enough to prevent the disappearance of some of the world's languages, but it does
65 mean that there will not be a boring worldwide uniformity.

2 According to the writer, one reason why some languages will become extinct is that
  A English has become the first language in some countries.
  B there are not enough language teachers.
  C young people are not learning them.
  D they are not spoken all the time.

3 The French government introduced regulations in order to
  A restrict the number of English films on television.
  B increase the number of native language speakers.
  C control the amount of American English spoken.
  D limit the use of English words.

4 What does 'they' refer to in line 27?
  A university subjects
  B Malaysian universities
  C exceptions
  D IT textbooks

5 The writer says that as a result of the Internet some languages might
  A become more widespread.
  B be saved from extinction.
  C only be used in written form.
  D no longer be used on radio and television.

6 According to the writer, what effect will the Internet have on English?
  A English on the Internet could soon be difficult to understand.
  B English will be quicker to read.
  C British English words will not be used on the Internet.
  D The appearance of English could change considerably on the Internet.

7 What does the writer mean when he says 'the dynamics of a language come from the bottom up rather than the top down' (line 59)?
  A People, not governments, determine what happens to a language.
  B Changes in language are not determined by how powerful a country is.
  C The least frequent words of a language are the first to change.
  D Unwanted foreign words disappear naturally.

Reacting to the text ◯

Do you agree with the writer that 'there is little governments can do' to influence the way a language does and does not change?
To what extent has English influenced your own language?

Vocabulary 2: Abbreviations

1 What do the following abbreviations from the text stand for?

TV _____   PC _____

IT _____   DVD _____

2 The following abbreviations, written in **bold**, are often used in written English. Some may appear in the notes in Part 1 of the Writing Paper. What does each one mean?

1 There are several ways to learn a language, **eg** private classes, books, **etc**.
2 It gets very crowded during the peak holiday season, **ie** from June to September.
3 **NB** Examination fees can be paid via our website at **www**.collegefees.com.
4 **PS** Let me know **ASAP**.
5 He wrote '**PTO**' at the bottom of the letter, but there was nothing on the other side.

Check your answers in the Vocabulary section of the review at the end of this unit.

3 The following abbreviations are also used in spoken English. What do they stand for?

BBC _____   MP _____

UN _____   FBI _____

CD _____   EU _____

Language focus: Expressing purpose

A *In order to*, *so as to* and *so that*

1 The full infinitive or *in order to* + infinitive can be used to show the purpose of an action, as in these two sentences from the text:

> The French have brought in regulations **to combat** what they see as an American cultural invasion.

> **In order to protect** local languages and culture, the European Union introduced new legislation.

In order to can also be used in the negative.
*I set two alarm clocks **in order not to** oversleep.*

So as (not) to + infinitive is another possibility.
*He left work early **so as not to** miss his daughter's birthday.*

So (that) + a clause is yet another way of expressing purpose.

2 Look at the following examples and decide which verb forms are used after *so (that)* to refer to the future and which verb forms are used to refer to the past.

1 I turned the light on so I could see what I was doing.
2 Put your bag by the door so that you don't forget it when you leave.
3 I'm going to buy a phrase book so I can at least order a coffee in Polish.
4 I wore my raincoat so that I wouldn't get wet.
5 I've put an extra blanket on your bed so that you won't get cold again tonight.

G Check your answers in the Grammar reference on page 217 and read more about expressing purpose.

Practice

1 Complete the following sentences in an appropriate way.

1 We've decided to get my grandmother a mobile phone so that…
2 We're going to get to the football match two hours before the start in order…
3 I'm taking the First Certificate exam so…
4 I pretended to be ill so…
5 She logged on to the Internet in order…
6 He went up the stairs very quietly so as…
7 I'm going to do my homework as soon as I get home so…

2 Think of three reasons for each of the following. Use clauses of purpose in your answers.

Why do people:
- go to nightclubs?
- do dangerous sports?
- learn languages?
- go on diets?
- get married?
- take exams?

Example:
People go to nightclubs… *so as to* meet new people.
in order to have a good time.
so that they can dance.

B *In case*

*I'll take my credit card **in case** I run out of cash.*

The first action (taking the credit card) prepares for a possible situation or problem in the future (running out of cash). When *in case* is followed by the present simple it has a future meaning.

To refer to past situations we use *in case* + the past simple. *I wore my raincoat **in case** it rained.*

Practice

Complete the following sentences in an appropriate way.

1 Take a spare pen into the exam in case…
2 We decided not to take the car in case…
3 You should insure the contents of your house in case…
4 I'm taking a sandwich to work in case…
5 My mum gave me some extra money in case…
6 We've left a key with the neighbours in case…

Role-play: Expressing purpose

1 Work in pairs. Decide who is Student A and who is Student B and follow the relevant instructions.

Student A:
You are a rather fussy, over-protective parent whose teenage son/daughter is going away on a one-week camping trip with some friends. It is the first time he/she has been away on holiday without you, and you are going to give advice on what items he/she should take. Write down eight things which you consider to be essential for the trip, together with your reasons. Use the expressions above (*so that*, *in case*, etc). Use the prompts in the box below to help you.

Student B:
You are a teenager who is about to go on a one-week camping trip with a group of friends. Your parents always worry too much and one of them is going to give you lots of advice about what to take. You just want to have a good time, so you're not interested in boring details. Write down at least eight items you want to take on the trip, together with your reasons. Use the expressions above (*so that*, *in case*, etc). Use the prompts in the box below to help you.

food	drink	cooking equipment
emergency provisions		medicines
clothing	entertainment	

2 When you have each prepared your lists, take it in turns to talk about each of the items giving your reasons. Try to agree on at least five items which will be taken on the trip.

Who was the most persuasive?

Writing:
FCE Part 2

Articles

Your college magazine has asked you to write an article giving advice to next year's First Certificate students about how to prepare for the examination throughout the course.

Write your **article** for the magazine, based on your own experience. You should write between **120 and 180** words.

How to go about it

When planning your article, consider the following:
- organizing and learning new vocabulary
- studying grammar
- improving reading, listening, writing and speaking skills
- where and when to do homework
- organizing your time
- watching videos, reading books etc

Clauses of purpose might be useful when giving the reasons for your advice.
Examples:
*I've read several short stories this year **in order to prepare** for the Reading Paper.*
*I'd recommend buying a separate notebook **so that you can organize** new vocabulary.*
*Try to learn as many collocations as possible **in case they come up** in Paper 3.*

Reading 2:
FCE Part 3

Gapped text

1 What aspects of American school life have you seen depicted in films and on television? What impression do you have of American high schools?

2 You are going to read an article on page 192 about an American high school. Eight sentences have been removed from the article. Choose from the sentences **A–I** the one which fits each space **(1–7)**. There is one extra sentence which you do not need to use. There is an example at the beginning **(0)**.

Don't forget!

- Read the whole text through quickly before you begin to do the task. Are any of the aspects that you discussed in exercise 1 mentioned in the article?
- In the exam, you have to write your answers on a separate sheet.

American high

Grades, jocks, security, cheerleaders... just what is life really like at a US high school? Luke Norris visits the States to find out.

Arriving at the start of day at Montclair High School, New Jersey, is like walking on to the set of teen movie *American Pie*. The Blue Crew (as they call the jocks in the school's navy sports shirts) are hanging out by the gym and students are parking cars and meeting friends. [0] [*I*]

School starts with a buzzer at 8am and ends, after six periods and the all-important lunch, at 2.30pm. Then there's a diary of non-stop club meetings. You're not considered a nerd if you belong to four or five clubs (at Montclair there are more than 50); it all adds weight to your college application. [1]

Years run from 13/14-year-old freshmen (9th grade) to 17/18-year-old seniors (12th grade). Every student has to complete four years of school; they gain credits for taking classes and need 119 to graduate. There's not a big emphasis on exams, which means there's a less disciplined atmosphere. [2]

The teachers also have a lot to do with this. 'They're really approachable people and they're always willing to help,' explains Mona, an 11th grade student. [3]

Freedom is a buzz word, but that doesn't mean 'no rules'. At Montclair there are plenty, like no hats in school or no mobile phones. [4] Frisking for guns and metal detectors at school gates is still rare, though, even after the recent high school shootings.

One word that comes up again and again is cliques. But pupils do not stick to the same one all the time, as movies like *American Pie* would have us believe. 'Most people drift in and out of cliques and rarely have a single set of friends,' says Mona.

Another myth about American high schools is locker culture. Those who cherish their lockers and put pictures inside are a rare breed. [5] When class is out, the cafeteria, which serves amazingly typical burgers and fries, or a clubroom are the places to hang out.

The formal end-of-year dance or prom, on the other hand, is a big thing, with student councils raising money all year to put it on. So is the year book, which comes out at the end of the school year and is full of pictures of pupils taking part in extra-curricular activities. [6] 'Biggest gossip,' 'Best-looking' or 'Most likely to succeed' are just a few of the titles.

The impression I am left with is that students in the US get a lot more freedom than their UK peers. But what do they think British schools are like? [7] Classmate Dani nods: 'Yeah, proper discipline and a lot more serious.'

A Even seniors describe school as 'fun' and 'relaxed'.

B And if they don't manage to get their photo in it, students can always compete for an entry as one of The Superlatives.

C But senior prom is perhaps the most important event of high school.

D There are also security guards in every corridor who check for hall passes.

E 'Strict teachers, smart uniforms,' says Noah, 17.

F Most say they are just a place to leave books and things.

G 'We can e-mail them at home for advice on most things,' she adds.

H Many happily stay until after 6pm doing sport, choir and drama.

I Inside, seniors, dressed in the 'uniform' of khakis and T-shirts, slam locker doors as they head to class.

Reacting to the text ⬤

How does Montclair High School compare to your own school? Would you prefer to study there?

Vocabulary 3

A American English

1 Look at the following differences between American and British English. The American words appeared in the reading text.

1 The equivalent of **high school** in British English is secondary school.
2 In American English you **graduate** from high school or university, whereas in British English you only graduate from university.
3 Americans talk about seeing a **movie**; British people tend to use the word film.
4 **Jock** is an American word used to describe someone who is very keen on sport.

2 Match the British English words **1–7** with the American English equivalents **a–f**. One has been done for you.

British English	American English
①flat	**a** elevator
2 lift	ⓑapartment
3 wardrobe	**c** pants
4 curtains	**d** drapes
5 garden	**e** trashcan or garbage can
6 dustbin	**f** yard
7 trousers	**g** closet

3 Write the equivalent British English word for the American English word on the right. There is an example at the beginning **(0)**.

British English	American English
0 _lorry_	truck
1 _____	subway
2 _____	gas station
3 _____	freeway
4 _____	vacation
5 _____	railroad
6 _____	parking lot
7 _____	round trip ticket

4 Write the following in British English. As well as vocabulary, you may need to change the spelling of certain words.

1 She took the garbage out to the trashcan in the yard.
2 The truck driver slowed down and pulled into the gas station on the freeway.
3 'I can't find my pants anywhere, mom!'
   'Try looking in the closet, honey.'
4 No cookies and candies for me, thanks, I'm dieting.
5 It was early fall. The sidewalks in the neighborhood were covered with leaves of different shapes and colors and the summer vacation was just a distant memory.

B Education

1 Explain the difference between each of the following pairs of words.

1 nursery school / primary school
2 a state school / a public school
3 grammar school / a comprehensive school
4 a degree / a career
5 a teacher / a professor
6 a qualification / a title

2 Write down one subject for each of the following. Use the Wordlist on page 205 to help you. If you are no longer at school, think back to when you were.

1 the subject you most enjoy _____
2 your least favourite subject _____
3 a subject which you would like to be better at _____
4 the subject that you think is the most useful for your future _____
5 the least practical subject _____

15 Review

Use of English:
FCE Part 1

Multiple choice cloze

For questions **1–15**, read the text below and decide which answer **A**, **B**, **C** or **D** best fits each space. There is an example at the beginning **(0)**.

Studying English abroad

(0) _____ as more English is being taught in **(1)** _____ schools worldwide, so there are a **(2)** _____ number of language schools in English-speaking countries that are **(3)** _____ courses for younger learners. In Britain, most young learners' courses are **(4)** _____ to 11-year-olds and upwards, with a few that cater for children as young as seven. But what is a **(5)** _____ age to start sending children abroad to study? **(6)** _____ , even adult learners find the experience of travelling to a strange country and encountering people who speak a barely **(7)** _____ language challenging.

A **(8)** _____ deal depends on how a child has been **(9)** _____ up . For example, **(10)** _____ they have been exposed to new things and have already started to learn independence, then they are **(11)** _____ to enjoy the experience. **(12)** _____ , children who have previously travelled abroad with their parents will be well prepared to undertake a study **(13)** _____ in an English-speaking country on their **(14)** _____ . Getting **(15)** _____ to the idea that other countries have different customs and cultures is an important stage in the process of learning a foreign language.

0 **A** <u>Just</u>	**B** Same	**C** Even	**D** Only
1 **A** initial	**B** early	**C** primary	**D** young
2 **A** rising	**B** raising	**C** growing	**D** increasing
3 **A** granting	**B** offering	**C** setting	**D** studying
4 **A** open	**B** fit	**C** suit	**D** access
5 **A** beginning	**B** first	**C** usual	**D** sensible
6 **A** At last	**B** At the end	**C** Finally	**D** After all
7 **A** comprehensible	**B** comprehensive	**C** understanding	**D** misunderstood
8 **A** big	**B** great	**C** wide	**D** large
9 **A** turned	**B** brought	**C** put	**D** grown
10 **A** so that	**B** in case	**C** if	**D** because
11 **A** about	**B** easily	**C** possibly	**D** likely
12 **A** More of	**B** On the other hand	**C** In addition	**D** Further on
13 **A** travel	**B** trip	**C** journey	**D** voyage
14 **A** own	**B** self	**C** alone	**D** lonely
15 **A** to know	**B** on well	**C** aware	**D** used

Vocabulary

A Abbreviations

What are the abbreviations for the following?

1 for example   _____
2 and so on   _____
3 that is to say   _____
4 please note   _____
5 World Wide Web   _____
6 postscript   _____
7 as soon as possible _____
8 please turn over   _____

B Compound adjectives

Complete each of the spaces with a suitable noun. Choose from the words in the box.

lesson shift meal holiday composition clock note baby girl

1 the 24-hour _____
2 an eight-hour _____
3 a two-month-old _____
4 a three-course _____
5 a 180-word _____
6 a 45-minute _____
7 a three-week _____
8 a ten-pound _____

C American English

What are the American English equivalents of the following British English nouns?

1 trousers _____
2 dustbin _____
3 wardrobe _____
4 garden _____
5 motorway _____
6 lorry _____
7 car park _____
8 pavement _____

Use of English:
FCE Part 3

Transformations

For questions **1–6**, complete the second sentence so that it has a similar meaning to the first sentence, using the word given. **Do not change the word given.** You must use between two and five words, including the word given.

1 You should put an extra jumper on so that you don't get cold.
   order
   You should put an extra jumper on _____ cold.

2 He left early because he didn't want to miss the last bus.
   as
   He left early _____ the last bus.

3 I've kept the receipt for the shirt because it may not fit you.
   in
   I've kept the receipt for the shirt _____ fit you.

4 She took something to read to avoid getting bored.
   would
   She took something to read _____ get bored.

5 The workers were offered a three per cent pay increase but they didn't accept it.
   turned
   The workers _____ of a three per cent pay increase.

6 What time did Mike eventually get to the party?
   turn
   What time _____ at the party?

Ready for Speaking

Introduction

Paper 5, the Speaking Test, consists of four separate parts and lasts about 14 minutes. You will probably take the test with another candidate, though it is possible to be part of a group of three. There are two examiners: the Interlocutor, who conducts the test and asks the questions, and the Assessor, who listens to the test and assesses your performance. The Interlocutor also assesses and contributes to your final mark.

1 Read the descriptions of the four parts of the Speaking Test below and match each one to a diagram **a–d**. The arrows (→) show who is speaking to whom.

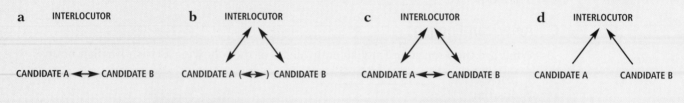

Part 1: Interview   Total time: 3 minutes

The Interlocutor asks you questions which require you to give basic personal information about yourself. You may speak with your partner in this part if you want to, though you do not have to.

Part 2: Talking about photographs   Total time: 4 minutes

You have one minute to compare and contrast two photographs and add some further comment about them. You also have up to 20 seconds to comment on your partner's pictures. You do not talk to your partner in this part.

Part 3: Collaborative task   Total time: 3 minutes

The Interlocutor listens while you and your partner perform a speaking task together. You may be asked to try to agree or reach a decision by the end of the task.

Part 4: Further discussion   Total time: 4 minutes

The Interlocutor asks further questions related to the topic introduced in Part 3. As well as responding to these questions you should also interact with your partner and comment on what he or she says.

2 The following comments were all made by students who had just taken the Speaking Test of the First Certificate exam. Look at each one and answer these questions:

Does the student set a good example to follow in the Speaking Test? Why/Why not? If not, how would you avoid making the same mistake?

Part 1   **a** 'The examiner asked us some really simple questions at the beginning of the exam. So I just gave some short, simple answers, as I would in my own language.'

  b 'Before the exam, my partner and I learnt and rehearsed some nice long answers to all the typical questions they ask you about yourself in the exam. We knew exactly what we were going to say to each other.'

  c 'I was a bit nervous in this part, but the questions were not difficult so I tried to answer them as fully and as naturally as I could, as if I was talking to someone I knew. It helped me to relax for the rest of the test.'

Part 2   **a** 'I used some really good vocabulary to describe in detail what everyone in the pictures was wearing, what they were doing and so on.'

b 'The examiner stopped me after about a minute and I hadn't finished what I wanted to say!'

c 'I was concentrating so much on the pictures when the examiner gave them to me that I forgot to listen to the instructions! I had to ask her to repeat them.'

Part 3 **a** 'I did really well in this part of the exam. I had lots of ideas and I seemed to be speaking for most of the three minutes. My partner was a bit quiet, though.'

b 'We had to agree on the three most important qualities of a good language learner. It was easy – we did it in about two minutes.'

c 'We had to choose two designs for a new set of postage stamps. We found one we both liked but when the examiner stopped us after three minutes we were still trying to agree on the second.'

Part 4 **a** 'The examiner didn't really say very much in this part. We did most of the talking.'

b 'My partner said that computers would eventually replace books. "Nonsense," I said, "you must be mad." I thought that was really good – an expression of disagreement and a modal verb of deduction in one sentence!'

c 'We had to talk about the environment, which I don't know much about, so I changed the topic of conversation to pets; I've got two dogs and a hamster, you see.'

Part 1: Interview

1 Choose three of the following categories and for each one write three questions you could ask another student.

work/study	sport/keeping fit	family	travel/holidays
future plans	English	animals	music
fashion	going out	friends	

Begin your questions with the following words:

What... ?	Where... ?	Who... ?	Why... ?
When... ?	How... ?	How long/often/much... ? etc	

If you write a question which only requires a short answer, write another which will encourage the other student to say more.

Example: *Where do you live? What do you like about living there?*

2 Work with another student. Interview each other using the questions you have prepared. Develop your answers, making sure they are relevant to the question.

3 Listen to two students, Christina and Paolo, doing Part 1 of the Speaking Test and answer the following questions.
1 Does the interlocutor ask any of the same questions you prepared?
2 Why does the interlocutor interrupt Christina at the beginning?
3 What advice would you give to Paolo to help him improve his performance?

Don't forget!

- Do not learn long pre-prepared answers for this part of the exam. They may not be entirely appropriate to the question you are asked and they will probably not sound very natural.
- Do, however, make sure you know individual items of vocabulary which are relevant to yourself. For example:

Your hobbies and interests.
'I'm really keen on rock climbing and walking.'
The course you have decided to study.
'I would like to study for a degree in aeronautical engineering.'
What your parents do.
'My mother's a systems analyst.'

197

Part 2: Talking about photographs

Useful language

'Fillers' are words or phrases which enable you to think while you are speaking. Look at the following examples and think about the equivalent expressions you would use in your own language.

Buying time	**Gathering your thoughts**
Well…	*I'm not quite sure, but I think…*
Let me see…	*I haven't thought about it before, but*
What else (can I say)?	*perhaps…*
Is there anything I can add to that?	*I don't really know, but I imagine…*

Don't forget!

● Do not describe the photos in detail.
● Make sure you address both parts of the instructions.

Student A: Look at these two photographs. They show grandfathers with their grandchildren. Compare and contrast these photographs and say how important grandparents can be in situations like these. You only have a minute for this, so don't worry if your teacher interrupts you.

Student B: When your partner has finished, say if an older relative has taught you to do something. (20 seconds)

For Student B's photographs, turn to page 201.

Listen to Christina and Paolo doing the Part 2 task. Paolo's two photographs are on page 201. How well does each person compare and contrast the photographs?

Part 3: Collaborative task

The History Museum in your town would like to attract more visitors and various ideas have been put forward. First, talk with your partner about the proposals shown below saying how they might appeal to different people. Then choose two which you think would be the most successful in attracting new visitors. You have only three minutes for this, so don't worry if your teacher interrupts you.

How to go about it

- When talking about the different people each activity might appeal to think about: people of different ages, people with different interests and people with different personalities.
- For each activity you could also mention what type of people the activity would not appeal to.
- You will gain marks for using a range of

vocabulary. What other words do you know with a similar meaning to these adjectives? *interesting   boring   good*
- Use some of the useful language and expressions of agreeing and disagreeing from page 123 in Unit 10.
- Involve your partner in the interaction, asking questions if necessary.

Listen to Christina and Paolo doing Part 3 and answer questions 1–3.

1 Which activities do Paolo and Christina choose?
2 At what point in their conversation do they make their decision?
3 How does Christina encourage Paolo to talk?

Part 4: Further discussion

Now discuss the following questions with your partner.

Don't forget!

- Develop your answers, justifying your opinions and giving examples if necessary.
- Interact with your partner, listening and responding to each other's comments.

- What do you think makes a good history museum?
- How could the teaching of history in schools be improved?
- Do you agree that learning about the past is important for our future?
- What was the most important moment in the history of the twentieth century?
- What has been the most important moment in your life so far?
- What items from our lives today will be in the history museums of the future?

Listen to Part 4 and answer the following questions.

1 How well do Christina and Paolo interact with each other:
  a in the first half of Part 4?
  b in the second half of Part 4?
2 Who helps the interaction more, Christina or Paolo?

Additional material

Unit 11
Language focus: Conditionals, page 136
Student B
1 If I lived in Britain, …
2 If I wanted to make new friends, …
3 If you help me with my homework, …
4 If it rains this weekend, …

Unit 12
Language focus: Reported speech, page 150
Student A
1 Tell each other your problems (see below) and give each other suggestions and advice. Use the following phrases:
You should…   Why don't you… ?   If I were you, I'd…

- I'm finding it difficult to sleep at night.
- I'm addicted to the Internet. I spend six hours a day on it.
- I think my best friend is stealing things.
- I get very nervous when I take exams.

2 Change partners and report your conversations using the verbs *suggest*, *recommend* and *advise*.

Unit 2
Writing: FCE Part 2, Articles, page 23
1 Read this model answer to the writing question on page 23 and answer the questions below.

A strange way to enjoy yourself

(1) *Have you ever seen a smile on the face of a long-distance runner? Running 10 kilometres or more certainly doesn't sound much fun, but this sport is a powerful addiction and once you've started, you'll find it difficult to give it up.*

(2) *So what is the attraction of running? For me, whether I'm working or studying, there is no better way of getting rid of stress. I can think my problems through and at the end of the race I have the answers. And simply completing a half or full marathon increases my confidence and makes me feel on top of the world.*

(3) *If you're thinking of taking it up yourself, don't try to do too much at the beginning. You should set yourself realistic targets and always do warm-up exercises before you run. Also, make sure you buy a good pair of running shoes to protect your knees and back from injury.*

(4) *And don't be put off by the expressions on the faces of the runners - they're enjoying every minute, and so will you!*

---

2 Match each of these summaries to a paragraph in the article.
   a Benefits of the sport and reasons for liking it.
   b Closing comment.
   c What the sport is and what is special about it.
   d Advice to people who want to do this sport.

3 Who is the article written for (the target reader)?

4 Is it written in a more formal or informal style? Find examples of the following:
   a Contractions: eg *she's, won't*
   b Informal linking words: eg *But*
   c Direct questions
   d Phrasal verbs

5 Match each of the features **1–3** with its purpose **a–c**.

1 The title	**a** to involve the reader
2 Direct questions	**b** to encourage the reader to take up the sport
3 The final sentence	**c** to attract the reader's attention

6 Now write your own answer to the question on page 23. Read the How to go about it box on the same page before you begin to write.

Ready for Reading
FCE Part 3, page 40
Removed sentences

A Mrs Stevens said: 'I was becoming increasingly desperate because he is 82, and I am 78; I was beginning to think I would never see him again.

B Mr Rider immediately flew back with his wife to England to meet his long-lost sister.

C A search of New York addresses was unsuccessful.

D The Riders had just returned from a six-week break in London, which explained the unanswered calls.

E Mrs Stevens, 78, tried repeatedly to make contact again, but each time her efforts were in vain.

F Mrs Stevens phoned every day for six weeks, but her calls all went unanswered.

G Eileen Stevens lost touch with Percival Rider, a former army bandsman, in 1962.

Unit 5
Writing: FCE Part 2, Application letters, page 62
1 Read this student's answer to the letter of application question on page 63. Would it have a positive effect on the target reader? Give reasons for your answer.

Dear Sir or Madam,

I really liked the sound of the job I saw advertised in the publication 'Summer jobs in the UK'. I'm still quite young and I recently completed a short course on garden design. My level of English is intermediate and I know quite a bit about plants and flowers. I am particularly interested in the cultivation of roses and the use of trees in landscape design. If you have a look at my CV you'll see I've had lots of different jobs. One of them was working for a couple of months on a campsite similar to those mentioned in your advertisement. I've put in a little note from my last boss with this letter. I like being part of a team and I'd love to have a go at working in a foreign country. By the way, how many hours do I have to work? And how long's the contract for? If you want I can start at the beginning of June. Let me know what you think.

Yours faithfully
Pascal Sylvestre

---

2 Rewrite the letter substituting the expressions below for those parts which are too informal. You should also make the questions less direct and organize the letter into appropriate paragraphs.

a As you will see from my curriculum vitae
b I look forward to receiving your reply
c I am writing to express an interest in
d I have a great deal of experience
e I will be available to work from
f I have a good knowledge of gardening
g I enclose a reference from my previous employer
h I am 25 years old
i I would enjoy the experience of working abroad
j This includes a temporary position

Unit 9
Reading: FCE Part 3, page 112

Answers to Hallowe'en questions

When is Hallowe'en?
The night of the 31st of October.

What does the word 'Hallowe'en' mean?
All Hallows' Eve. The evening before All Hallows Day or All Saint's Day (1st November).

Why is Hallowe'en celebrated?
Hallowe'en was originally a pagan festival of the dead. Celts in Ireland had a festival called 'Samhain' (pronounced 'sow-in'), which marked the official end of summer and the beginning of the Celtic New Year. On this night the souls of the dead were said to come out and move freely in the land of the living. The tradition of Hallowe'en was taken to the United States by Irish emigrants, and it is now spreading in Britain and other European countries.

Why do people dress up as witches and ghosts?
In addition to the souls of the dead, the Devil, witches and numerous spirits are believed to be out, and at the peak of their supernatural powers.

What is 'Trick or treat'?
According to an old Irish peasant practice, villagers would go from house to house to ask for soul cakes (bread with currants) in return for promises of prosperity or protection against bad luck. Now children and teenagers go from house to house asking for small gifts of money, fruit or sweets in return for not playing tricks on the people inside.

Why are pumpkins made into lanterns?
According to Irish legend, when a notorious drunkard called Jack died, he was refused entry to Heaven because of his meanness, and he was banned from Hell because he had tricked the Devil on several occasions. However, the Devil gave him a piece of coal to help him find his way in the dark of purgatory, which Jack put into a turnip to make a lantern. The Irish made similar lanterns to represent the souls of the dead on Hallowe'en, but when they emigrated to America they could not find many turnips so they used pumpkins instead.

Ready for Speaking: Part 2, page 198

Student B: Look at the two photographs below. They show people in an emergency situation. Compare and contrast these photographs and say how serious you think each of the situations looks. Remember, you have only about a minute for this, so don't worry if your teacher interrupts you.

Student A: When your partner has finished, say if you think you could be a policeman/woman. (20 seconds)

Unit 11
Language focus: Conditionals, page 136
Student A
1 ...I'd probably be extremely popular.
2 ...the world would be a happier place.
3 ...I'll never speak to you again.
4 ...he starts to cry.

Unit 12
Language focus: Reported speech, page 150
Student B
1 Tell each other your problems (see below) and give each other suggestions and advice. Use the following phrases:
You should...   Why don't you... ?   If I were you, I'd...

- I'd like to go on holiday, but I haven't got much money.
- I want to lose weight, but I don't know the best way.
- No one phones me on my mobile phone.
- I want to go to a concert, but I have to go to a wedding.

2 Change partners and report your conversations using the verbs *suggest*, *recommend* and *advise*.

Unit 12
Writing: FCE Part 2
Model report, page 152

Introduction
This report looks at some of my country's national dishes and their popularity among young people. It is based on a survey of 90 people aged between 14 and 19.

Most popular dishes
Fish and chips is perhaps the best-known food in my country. Interestingly, only half of those interviewed said that it was their favourite dish. However, almost everyone agreed that it was the tastiest fast food available. Nearly 40% felt the best traditional food was roast beef served with Yorkshire pudding, a mixture of flour, eggs and milk, which is baked in the oven. Not surprisingly, desserts are popular with most young people. Trifle was mentioned several times for its rich combination of cream, custard, jelly and fruit.

Least popular dishes
A large majority said that steak and kidney pudding was their least favourite food. Although they like steak, the kidney makes the overall flavour too strong. They said the same of liver, which is fried with onions and mushrooms.

Recommendations
I recommend your students try a full roast beef dinner. Pubs usually serve this, together with a range of other traditional dishes.

Wordlist

Unit 1
Items of clothing
belt
blazer
blouse
boots
bow tie
(baseball) cap
cardigan
dinner jacket
dress
dressing gown
dungarees
fancy dress
hat
helmet
high-heeled shoes
(sports) jacket
jeans
jumper/pullover/
   sweater
overcoat
raincoat
scarf
shirt
shoes
shorts
skirt
slippers
socks
suit
sweatshirt
swimming costume
swimming trunks
top
T-shirt
tie
tights
tracksuit
trainers
trousers
waistcoat

Jewellery
bracelet   necklace
brooch   pendant
earrings   ring

Adjectives: The pattern of clothes
checked   plain
flowery   spotted
patterned   striped

Other adjectives for clothes
baggy
casual
colourful
designer
formal
long-sleeved
loose-fitting
pleated
second-hand
shabby
short-sleeved
smart
tasteful
tight-fitting
trendy
(un)fashionable
waterproof
worn out

Materials for clothes
cotton   nylon
denim   silk
leather   suede
woollen

Verbs for clothing
dress up as sbdy/sthg
fit
get (un)dressed
go with
match
put on
suit
take off
wear

Unit 2
Musical instruments
accordion
cello
clarinet
double bass
drum(s)
flute
guitar
keyboards
organ
electric/grand piano
saxophone
tambourine
trombone
trumpet
violin
wind/stringed
   instrument

Music: People
backing vocalist
concert audience
DJ/disc jockey
lead singer/guitarist
rock/folk/rap, etc
   band/singer/star
session musician

Playing and performing
a live album/concert/
   gig/performance
a music/rock festival
have a record in the
   charts
be in tune
give a concert
on tour/on stage/on
   the radio
play a tune/a record/a
   track
sing/perform/mime a
   song

Sports

do…
aerobics
athletics
gymnastics

go…
cycling
diving
horse-riding
jogging
running
sailing
skiing
snowboarding
(wind)surfing
swimming

play…
badminton
baseball
basketball
football
golf
handball
hockey
rugby
tennis
volleyball

Sports: People

athlete
baseball/basketball etc
   player
cyclist
diver
golfer
gymnast
jogger
runner
skier
snowboarder
swimmer
(wind)surfer

competitor
opponent
participant
referee (basketball/
   football/rugby)
runner-up
spectator
supporter
team
umpire (badminton/
   tennis/volleyball)
winner

Sports: Places

athletics/cycling track
athletics/football/
   sports stadium
basketball/tennis/
   volleyball court
football/hockey/
   rugby pitch
golf course
gym

ice-skating rink
motor-racing circuit
ski slope
swimming pool

Sports: Events

play/take part/
   compete in…
a football match
a golf/tennis
   tournament
a sporting event
a surfing/swimming
   competition
an athletics meeting
the national/world
   championship

**Sports: Equipment
and special clothes**

badminton/tennis
   racket
baseball/table tennis
   bat
football/rugby boots
golf clubs
hockey stick
running/tennis shoes
safety helmet
shin/knee pads
shuttlecock
skateboard/surfboard/
   snowboard
skiing/swimming
   goggles
skis and ski poles
sweatband

Sports: Verbs

beat an opponent/
   opposing team
break/hold a record
do/play a sport
draw a match/game
go in for a sport
lose a game/match
practise a shot
take up a new sport
win a medal/match/
   competition/game

Unit 3

**Appliances, devices
and gadgets**

calculator (D)
coffee maker (A)
cooker (A)
dishwasher (A)
electric carving
   knife (G)
electric pencil
   sharpener (G)
electric
   toothbrush (G)
food mixer (A)
freezer (A)

fridge/
   refrigerator (A)
hairdryer (A)
juice squeezer (A)
liquidizer (A)
microwave
   oven (A)
remote
   control (D)
toaster (A)
vacuum
   cleaner (A)
washing
   machine (A)

**Other inventions and
equipment**

cable and satellite TV
clothes steamer
compass
computer
discman/walkman
DVD player
headphones
laptop (computer)
mobile phone
music centre/system
palm top
radar
space blanket
video recorder
word processor

Adjectives for devices

clever
disposable
essential
handy
ingenious
labour-saving
portable
simple
useful/useless
unusual

**Equipment and
machines: Verbs**

click on (an icon)
dial a number
log on to the Internet
plug in/unplug
print out
save on disc
surf the Net
switch on/off

Unit 4

Types of film

action film
animated film
cartoon
comedy
historical drama
horror film
remake
romance

science fiction film
thriller
western

**People and elements
of a film**

acting
action scenes
actor/actress
animation
cast
director
film/movie star
main character
make-up artist
photography
plot
producer
screenplay
script
soundtrack
special effects
stuntman/woman
supporting role

**Films: Other
vocabulary**

a box office hit
a dubbed/subtitled
   film
a film critic
a good/bad review
give a good/bad
   performance
go to an audition
have a part in a film

Unit 5

Jobs

accountant
architect
baker
butcher
chef
childminder
civil servant
company director
cook
dustman
electrician
engineer
firefighter
flight attendant
gardener
hairdresser
journalist
judge
lawyer
librarian
nanny
nurse
photographer
plumber
police officer
politician
receptionist

scientist
secretary
shop assistant
surgeon
teacher
vet
waiter/waitress

Career

apply for a job
get a job
go for an interview
look for a job

change career
devote yourself to a
   career
give up your career
start a career

be dismissed/sacked
be made redundant
be out of work/a job
resign from a job

Earn

earn a good living
earn a high/low salary
earn a lot of money
earn a weekly wage

Work

work as a nurse
work flexitime
work for yourself
work hard
work long hours
work one's way up to
   the top
work overtime
work part/full-time
work shifts

Work: Skills

artistic skills
computer skills
language skills
organizational skills
telephone skills

Adjectives for jobs

badly-paid
challenging
monotonous
responsible
satisfying
stressful
tiring
unpleasant
well-paid

**Work: Other
vocabulary**

form a new company
go into business
join a company
run a business
set up a company

a colleague

Wordlist

Unit 6

Adjectives for personality
a new recruit
a temporary job
be on/take sick leave
be one's own boss
be promoted
be/go on strike
be self-employed
get paid
retire
take time off (work)

Adjectives for personality
adventurous
affectionate
ambitious
bad-tempered
bossy
brave
caring
cheerful
clever
clumsy
confident
creative
decisive
dull
easy-going
energetic
enthusiastic
fair
fussy
generous
hard-working
honest
intelligent
kind
lazy
lively
loyal
mature
mean
moody
nervous
outgoing
patient
polite
practical
reliable
reserved
responsible
rude
selfish
sensible
sensitive
shy
sincere
sociable
stubborn
sympathetic
tolerant

Adjectives for hair
curly/dyed/flowing/

shoulder-length/
spiky/straight/
thinning/untidy/wavy

be bald/balding
have a beard/
    moustache

Adjectives for eyes
almond-shaped/
hazel/piercing/
sparkling

Adjectives for faces
expressive/freckled/
round/tanned/thin/
wrinkled

Adjectives for complexion
dark/healthy/pale/
smooth/spotty

Adjectives for build
fat/overweight/plump
skinny/slim/thin
stocky/well-built

Unit 7

Shops
baker's
bookshop
butcher's
chemist's
clothes shop
department store
florist's
gift shop
greengrocer's
grocer's
hardware shop
jeweller's
local corner shop
newsagent
super/hypermarket

In a supermarket
aisle
cashier
cash register/till
counter
checkout
end of aisle area
receipt
shelf/shelves
shopping basket
shopping trolley

Goods on sale
alcoholic drinks
bakery
confectionery
dairy products
foodstuffs
freezer goods
fresh fruit/vegetables/
    meat/fish
household goods

own-brand products
pre-packed meat
soft drinks
tinned/frozen
    convenience food
toiletries
well-known brands

Shopping: Other vocabulary
a bargain
a discount
a (money-back)
    guarantee
a special offer/be on
    offer
ask for a refund
be faulty
be good value for
    money
be nearing/past its
    sell-by date
be on order
buy sthg in the sales
buy sthg on impulse
charge sbdy £10
have sthg in stock
make a purchase
postage and packing
same-day/next-day
    delivery
splash out on sthg

Places
apartment block
building site
housing estate
industrial estate/area/
    site
in the city centre
office block
on the outskirts
pedestrian area/
    precinct
residential area/estate
shopping centre/
    precinct/mall

Adjectives for towns and villages
bustling
depressing
dull
lively
picturesque
pleasant
prosperous
quaint
run-down
shabby

Adjectives for buildings
ancient   huge
attractive   imposing
beautiful   impressive
derelict   magnificent
deserted   tall

historic   ugly

Unit 8

Travel
to go on a/an...
cruise
excursion
flight
journey
package holiday
(business) trip
tour
voyage

be good/great fun
enjoy oneself
go camping
go sightseeing
pack one's suitcase
relax
stay on a campsite

a good view
a holiday/ski resort
brochure
souvenir

Unit 9

Ghosts
a haunted house
a spirit
give a piercing scream
haunt a building
moaning sounds
vanish (into thin air)
walk through walls

Strange phenomena: Adjectives
afraid
bizarre
chilling
frightened/frightening
mysterious
peculiar
scared stiff of sthg
spooky/scary
strange/weird
terrified/terrifying
unnerving

Festivals and celebrations
a bonfire
a custom
a fancy dress party
a firework display
a legend
a parade
a tradition

commemorate sthg
dress up as sthg/sbdy
set off fireworks

Unit 10

Crimes and criminals
arson/arsonist
assassination/assassin
blackmail/blackmailer
burglary/burglar
drug trafficking/drug
    trafficker
espionage/spy
hijack(ing)/hijacker
kidnap(ping)/kidnapper
mugging/mugger
murder/murderer
pickpocketing/
    pickpocket
robbery/robber
shoplifting/shoplifter
smuggling/smuggler
theft/thief
vandalism/vandal

Crime: Verbs
accuse sbdy of a crime
acquit sbdy of a crime
arrest sbdy for a crime
burgle a house/office
deter sbdy from
    committing a crime
find sbdy (not) guilty
    of a crime
give sbdy a prison
    sentence
order sbdy to do
    community service
order sbdy to pay a fine
rob a person/bank (of
    £2,000)
sentence sbdy to two
    years in prison/life
    imprisonment/death
steal money/jewellery
    (from a person/shop)

Unit 11

Weather
fine/heavy/torrential
    rain
light/scattered/snow
    showers
overcast/clear/stormy
    sky
rough/calm/choppy
    sea
strong/gale-force/light
    wind
thick/storm/angry-
    looking clouds
violent/severe/electric
    storm
warm/glorious/
    brilliant sunshine

Weather: Other vocabulary
be struck by lightning

flash of lightning
gentle breeze
gust of wind
hailstones/raindrops/
   snowflakes
it's pouring with rain
weather forecast

Natural disasters
avalanche
drought
earthquake
earth tremor
flood
hurricane
tidal wave
tornado

The environment
air/river/sea pollution
bottle bank
carbon monoxide
cigarette butts
conservation area
dog mess
drop litter
dump waste
endangered species
exhaust fumes
face extinction
global warming
greenhouse effect
natural habitat
nature reserve
nuclear power station
oil slick
ozone layer
preserve wildlife
raise awareness
recycled paper
rising sea levels
toxic effluent
unleaded petrol

Unit 12

Ways of cooking food

bake	poach
boil	roast
fry	sauté
grill	stew
heat	toast

Adjectives for food

bitter	savoury
bland	sickly
creamy	sour
crunchy	spicy
greasy	stodgy
heavy	sweet
hot	tasteless
rich	tasty
salty	

Illnesses and injuries
black eye
bruise (n & v)
chest pain

cold
cough
earache
ear infection
flu
headache
heart attack
high/low blood pressure
nose bleed
runny nose
sore throat
sprained ankle/wrist
stomach ache
toothache

Treatment
cure sbdy of an illness
give sbdy a prescription
give sbdy an injection
have one's arm/leg in
   plaster
have an operation on
   part of body
put a plaster on sthg
put sbdy on antibiotics
take some medicine/a
   pill/painkillers
take sbdy's temperature
treat sbdy for an
   illness/injury
wrap a bandage round
   part of body

**Health: Other
vocabulary**
(un)fit
(un)healthy
(un)well

to bleed
to catch a cold
to feel sick
to heal
to hurt
to injure
to wound

Unit 13

Money
bank/current/savings
   account
cashpoint machine
cheque book
coins
credit card
currency
mortgage
overdraft
personal loan
pocket money
rate of exchange
rate of inflation
rate of interest
stock market

Money: Verbs
apply for/take
   out/repay a loan
be (seriously) in debt
be overdrawn
borrow sthg from
   sbdy
buy sthg on credit
cash in an investment
have change for £10
inherit money
invest (money) in sthg
lend sthg to sbdy
open/close a bank
   account
owe money to sbdy
pay a bill/a fine/tax/
   the rent
pay by credit card/
   by cheque/by direct
   debit/in cash
pay (sbdy) for sthg
put money into an
   account/deposit
   money
save up for sthg
sell sthg for £100
spend money on sthg
take money out of an
   account/withdraw
   money

Unit 14

Art
abstract painting
art collector
art/portrait gallery
artist
exhibition
landscape
painter
portrait
portrait gallery
priceless painting

Ballet
ballerina
ballet dancer
choreographer
classical/modern ballet

Literature
author
(auto)biography
detective/historical/
   romantic etc novel
novelist
publisher
short story
writer

Music
cellist/pianist/
   violinist
classical music
composer

conductor
concert hall
musician
open-air concert
orchestra

Opera
opera house
opera singer
soprano
tenor

Sculpture
sculptor
stone/bronze
   sculpture/statue

Theatre
Act I Scene II
actor/actress
audience
cast
director
performance
play
playwright
rehearsal
stage

Television
cartoons
chat show
comedy/current
   affairs/music/
   sports programme
detective series
documentary
game show
news broadcast
quiz show
sitcom
soap opera

Animals
Birds: owl/peacock/
   pigeon/sparrow
Farm animals: cow/
   goat/pig/sheep
Fish: cod/shark/trout
Pets: budgerigar/cat/
   dog/goldfish/
   hamster/parrot
Insects: ant/bee/
   beetle/fly/wasp
Other animals: bat/
   bear/fox/frog/
   mouse/rat/snake

Parts of animals
Fish: fin/gills/scales/
   tail
Bird: beak/feathers/
   tail/wings
Cat: claws/fur/paws/
   tail/whiskers
Horse: hooves/mane/tail

Unit 15

Education: Schools
boarding school
comprehensive school
grammar school
nursery school
primary school
public school
secondary school
state school

headteacher
pupil
teacher

Further education
agricultural/teacher
   training college
college of further
   education
(open) university

graduate
lecturer
postgraduate
professor
student
undergraduate

Education: Subjects
art
biology
business studies
chemistry
design technology
drama
economics
games
geography
geology
history
home economics
humanities
information technology
law
literature
maths
modern languages
music
philosophy
physical education
physics
religious education
science
sociology

Qualifications
GCSEs
'A' Levels
degree
BA/MA/BSc/MSc
PhD

Education: Verbs
revise for an exam
do/sit/resit/take an
   exam
pass/fail an exam

Grammar reference

Unit 1

Habitual behaviour in the present

A The present simple is used for habitual actions or permanent situations in the present.
*I **go** for a run twice a week. She **lives** near the station.*

B Frequency adverbs are used to indicate how often an action occurs. They are usually placed:
1 before the main verb.
*I **always** go to bed before midnight.*
2 after the verb *to be* or an auxiliary verb.
*She is very **often** late for work.*
*They have **rarely** been seen together.*
3 *Usually, normally, frequently, sometimes, (very/quite) often,* and *occasionally* can also be placed at the beginning of the sentence or clause.
Occasionally *we go out to the cinema, but **usually** we stay in and watch a video.*
NB *always, rarely, seldom, hardly ever,* and *never* cannot be used in the same way.

C Variations
1 The present continuous + *always* is used to talk about things which occur frequently and which the speaker finds annoying.
*He's **always** complaining about something!*
2 Adjectives can be used as an alternative to *rarely, normally* and *(not) usually.*
*It's **rare/normal/(un)usual** for him to eat meat.*
3 *Tend to* + infinitive is used to make general statements about the habitual actions and situations of groups of people or individuals.
*British people **tend to drink** tea rather than coffee.*
*I **tend not to get** up very early on Sundays.*
4 *Will* + infinitive is used to talk about habitual behaviour. Frequency adverbs can also be added.
*She**'ll sometimes spend** the whole day reading.*
5 *Keep (on)* + gerund is used to talk about repeated actions, often annoying ones.
*Peter **keeps on** hitting me.*

Habitual behaviour in the past

A The past simple is used for regular actions or habitual behaviour in the past, often with a frequency adverb.
*I **hardly ever went away** on holiday when I was young.*

B *Used to* + infinitive is used to refer to past habits and situations which no longer occur or exist now.
*We **used to have** a cat, but he died last year.*
*I always **used to walk** to work until I bought a car.*
Note the negative and question forms:
*I **didn't use to like** cheese. Where **did you use to live**?*
NB *use to* cannot express present habitual behaviour.
I usually (not use to) play tennis twice a week.

C *Would* + infinitive is used to refer to past habits, but not past situations.
Habit: *My dad **would** often read to me when I was a young boy.*
Situation: *I used to (not would) have a bicycle.*
Stative verbs such as *have* (possession), *be, live, like, believe, think* (= have an opinion), *understand* and *know*

are not used with *would* to refer to the past.

Be used to/Get used to + noun or gerund

Be used to + noun/gerund means 'be accustomed to'.
*She's a nurse so she's **used to seeing** sick people.*

Get used to + noun/gerund means 'become accustomed to'.
*I want to leave Athens; I can't **get used to the heat**.*

Unit 2

Indirect questions

When asking indirect questions the same word order is used as when we make statements. The auxiliary verbs, *do, does* and *did,* are omitted.
Could you tell me what *time it is?*
Would you mind telling me where *he works?*
We'd like to know when *you first started singing.*

If or *whether* is used if there is no question word such as *where, what, why, when, who* and *how.*
Could you tell us if/whether *you are married.*

Indirect questions can sound more polite than direct ones and are useful for requesting information in formal letters.

Gerunds and infinitives

A The gerund is used in the following cases:
1 as the subject/object/complement of a clause or sentence.
Subject: ***Reading*** *in the car makes me feel sick.*
Object: *I find **shopping** for clothes really boring.*
Complement: *My favourite sport is **swimming**.*
2 after prepositions.
*I'm not very **good at making** things.*
NB *to* is a preposition in the following verbs:
*I **look forward to hearing** from you soon.*
*I can't **get used to living** without her.*
3 after certain verbs.
*Peter **suggested going** for a picnic.*

B The infinitive with *to* is used:
1 to express purpose.
*I'm learning English **to help** me get a better job.*
2 after many adjectives, eg *surprised, delighted, disappointed, easy, happy, important, lucky, necessary, normal, possible, surprised.*
*I was **surprised to hear** she had failed the exam.*
3 after certain verbs.
*He **offered to give** her a lift, but she **decided to go** by train instead.*

C Gerunds and infinitives after verbs
1 Verb + gerund
*Have you **finished cleaning** your room?*
The following verbs, like *finish,* are normally followed by the gerund:
a Certain verbs expressing likes and dislikes: *adore, detest, dislike, enjoy, don't mind, can't stand*
b Other verbs: *admit, avoid, can't help, consider, delay, deny, feel like, forgive, give up, imagine, involve,*

keep, mind, miss, postpone, put off, practise, prevent, resist, risk, suggest

2 Verb + infinitive with *to*

*He **promised not to tell** anyone what she had said.*

a The following verbs, like *promise*, are normally followed by the infinitive with *to*: *(can't) afford, agree, appear, arrange, ask, attempt, choose, decide, deserve, expect, help, hesitate, hope, learn, manage, offer, prepare, pretend, refuse, seem.*

b The infinitive with *to* is also used after:

would like, would love, would hate, would prefer.

3 Verb + gerund or infinitive

a *Like, love, hate* and *prefer* are usually followed by the gerund. However, the infinitive is also possible with little, if any, difference in meaning.

*I **love going/to go** for long walks in the hills.*

The infinitive is common for specific situations:

*I **hate to interrupt**, but we really must be going.*

b *Begin, start, continue* and *intend* can be followed by the gerund or infinitive with no change in meaning.

*When I arrived it **started to rain/raining**.*

c *Forget, remember, go on, mean, need, regret, stop* and *try* can be followed by the gerund or the infinitive, but with a change in meaning.

- *remember/forget* + gerund = (not) to recall a previous action

  *I **remember coming** here when I was young.*

  *I'll never **forget seeing** U2 in concert.*

  remember/forget + infinitive = (not) to remember what you have to do

  *We must **remember to feed** the cat before we go.*

  *Don't **forget to phone** me if you need any help.*

- *go on* + gerund = to continue with the same activity

  *Some footballers **go on playing** professionally until they're nearly 40.*

  go on + infinitive = to change to a different activity

  *After a successful career as a football player, Johan Cruyff **went on to become** a respected manager.*

- *mean* + gerund = to involve

  *Dieting usually **means giving up** things you enjoy.*

  mean + infinitive = to intend

  *I **meant to phone** the electrician but I forgot.*

- *need* + gerund = (passive meaning)

  *This house **needs painting**. (= needs to be painted)*

  need + infinitive = (active meaning)

  *I **need to get** some new shoes.*

- *regret* + gerund = to be sorry for a previous action

  *I **regret going** to see that film: it was so boring.*

  regret + infinitive = to be sorry for what you are going to say (formal use)

  *We **regret to inform** you that we are unable to repair your washing machine.*

- *stop* + gerund = to stop an activity you are doing

  *I've **stopped smoking**: it's too expensive.*

  stop + infinitive = to stop doing one thing in order to do another

  *If you're driving long distances, you should **stop to have** a rest every two hours.*

- *try* + gerund = to experiment in order to see what will happen

  ***Try resting** for a while: you might feel better then.*

  try + infinitive = to make an effort; to attempt to do something

  *Alan **tried to stop** the thief as he ran away.*

Unit 3 Comparisons

Comparatives and superlatives

A Forms

1 Regular one-syllable adjectives

a add *-er* and *-est* to the adjective:

Adjective	Comparative	Superlative
cheap	cheap**er**	the cheap**est**

Other examples: *clean, dark, light, short, tall, slow*

b add *-r* and *-st* to adjectives ending in *-e*:

late	lat**er**	the lat**est**

Other examples: *large, loose, safe, strange, wise*

c double the consonant of adjectives ending in a short vowel and a consonant, and add *-er* and *-est*:

thin	thin**ner**	the thin**nest**

Other examples: *fat, sad, wet, red, big, hot, fit*

2 Regular adjectives with more than one syllable

a use *more* and *most* in front of the adjective:

sincere	**more** sincere	the **most** sincere

Other examples: *boring, careful, modern, comfortable*

b change *-y* to *-i* and add *-er* and *-est* to adjectives ending in *-y* after a consonant:

happy	happ**ier**	the happ**iest**

Other examples: *dirty, friendly, funny, noisy, tidy, silly*

c a limited number of two-syllable adjectives can form the comparative and superlative in two ways:

stupid	stupid**er**	the stupid**est**
	more stupid	the **most** stupid

Other examples: *clever, common, polite, quiet, gentle*

d most adverbs form their comparative and superlative with *more* and *most*:

quietly	**more** quietly	the **most** quietly

a limited number have comparative and superlative forms with *-er* (or *-r*) and *-est* (or *-st*)

fast	fast**er**	the fast**est**

Other examples: *early, hard, late, long, soon*

3 a Irregular forms: adjectives

good	better	the best
bad	worse	the worst
far	farther/further	the farthest/furthest
old	older/elder	the oldest/eldest

b Irregular forms: adverbs

well	better	the best
badly	worse	the worst
little	less	the least
much	more	the most

c Irregular forms: determiners

little	less	the least
few	fewer	the fewest
much/many	more	the most

B Use

1 To talk about people or things that are different in some way we use:

a Comparative forms of adjectives/adverbs + *than*.

*I think listening is **more difficult than** reading.*

For small differences use *a bit, a little, slightly*.

*You need to work **a little harder**.*

For big differences use *much, a lot, far, significantly*.
*My new car's **much faster than** my old one.*

b Superlative forms of adjectives/adverbs:

*That's the **nicest** thing you've said to me all day.*

To emphasize the difference between one person or thing from all the others we can use *by far*:

*This is **by far the best** book I've ever read.*

c *Less ... than* and *the least*

*Rugby is **less popular** than football here.*

*That's my **least favourite** track on the album.*

2 *As ... as*

a For people or things that are the same in some way we use *as* + adjective/adverb + *as*.

*She's **as intelligent as** her sister.*

Almost, nearly, just, twice, three times, etc can be used to qualify the comparisons.

*There were **nearly twice as many people** at the party **as** last year.*

b *So* can replace the first *as* in negative sentences.

*It's **not so difficult as** I thought it would be.*

Quite and *nearly* can be used to qualify negative sentences of this type.

*Her new film isn't **nearly as bad as** her last one.*

(= her new film is much better than her last one)

*He's **not quite so impatient as** his brother.*

(= he's a little more patient than his brother)

c *The same* + noun + *as*

*My mum's **the same age as** my dad.*

3 *The* + comparative, *the* + comparative

We use this structure for things which occur together.

The more money I have, *the faster* I spend it.

Articles

A The definite article (*the*) is most commonly used:

1 when there is only one of something, either in existence or in a particular context.

*I'd like to speak to **the manager**, please.*

2 when something is mentioned again.

'I've read three novels and two plays by Camus.'
*'What did you think of **the plays**?'*

3 when both listener and speaker know what is being referred to.

*Hurry up! **The film** starts in 10 minutes.*

4 when talking about a specific aspect of something, where the noun is followed by *of*.

*We're studying **the history of** architecture.*

5 to speak generally about certain groups of singular countable nouns.

a Inventions: **The mobile phone** *is thought to pose a serious threat to health.*

b Animal species: **The whale** *is still hunted by some countries such as Japan.*

6 with adjectives referring to general classes of people, eg *the homeless, the blind, the deaf, the rich, the poor, the old, the young, the French, the Spanish*

*Not enough is being done to help **the homeless**.*

7 with superlatives.

*Who is **the greatest footballer** in the world?*

8 with musical instruments.

*I'd love to learn to play **the piano**.*

9 with types of transport which have a fixed timetable.

*Shall we get **the bus** or take **a taxi**?*

10 with some countries, eg *the USA, the UK*

11 with oceans, mountain ranges, deserts, rivers, etc, eg *the Atlantic, the Pyrenees, the Sahara, the Thames*

12 with some geographical areas.

*We're going to **the mountains** rather than **the coast**.*

B The indefinite article (*a/an*) is most commonly used:

1 when a singular countable noun is mentioned for the first time.

A man went into *a bar* with *a fish*.

2 when referring to any one of several things.

*It's quiet in here. Shall I put **a record** on?*

3 when talking about a person's job.

*My father is **a nuclear scientist**.*

4 with some numbers, eg *a hundred* and one dalmatians, *a thousand* people, *a million* pounds

5 when it means 'per' in some expressions, eg *twice **a** day, 50 miles **an hour**, £80 **a week***

C No article is used:

1 when referring to nouns in a general sense.

a Plural countable nouns
*Do you think **computers** will replace **teachers**?*

b Abstract nouns
*We sang songs of **love** and **peace**.*

c Other uncountable nouns
*Alan won't eat **cheese** or **meat**.*

2 with most streets, towns, cities and countries.

*I went to **Bond Street** when I was in **London**.*

3 when a town's name is used with a building, eg **Luton Airport, Oxford University**

4 in many common expressions, eg *to go home, to go to work/school/university/prison/hospital/ church/bed, to go on holiday, to be at home/work/ school/university, to be in hospital/church/bed/prison, to go by car/bus/coach/train/plane, to have breakfast/ lunch/dinner (but have **a** meal), at night (but in **the** morning/afternoon/evening)*

Unit 4

Past tenses

A The past simple is used to refer to:

1 completed actions which happened at a specific time.

*I **went** to the cinema last night.*

2 completed actions and situations which happened over a specific period of time.

*I **lived** and **worked** in Germany for three years.*

3 habitual actions or behaviour in the past.

*We **played** football in the street when I was a child.*

4 a series of consecutive events in the past.

*He **kissed** her, **said** goodbye and **closed** the door.*

B The past continuous is used to refer to:

1 temporary activities or situations in progress at a particular moment in the past.

*This time last week **we were sitting** on the beach.*

2 a past activity or situation which was already in progress when another action occurred (the activity or situation in progress may or may not continue).

*I **was reading** to my son when the lights went out.*

3 activities or situations occurring at the same time.

*Ann **was cutting** the grass while **I was cooking**.*

4 the background events in a narrative.

*It **was snowing** heavily and a cold wind **was blowing**. My brother and **I were reading** in front of the fire. Suddenly, there was a knock at the door…*

C The past perfect is used to:

1 show that a past action or situation occurred before another past action or situation.

*When I saw Tim, **he had** just **passed** his driving test.*

2 We use the continuous form to emphasize the duration of the first past action or situation.

***She had been waiting** for over two hours when he phoned to say he couldn't come.*

D Time linkers

1 The past perfect is often used with time linkers, eg *after, before, by the time, as soon as, once, when, until*

*I couldn't go out **until** I had done my homework.*

2 The past simple can be used if the order of events is clear:

*He sold his house **before** he left the country.*

or if the second event occurred as a result of the first.

***When** I realized what time it was, I ran outside.*

3 *After/afterwards*

After is used to show the order of two or more events in the same sentence.

***After** he'd cleaned the house, he went shopping.*

Afterwards means *after that* and can go at the beginning or the end of a clause.

*We had lunch and **afterwards** we went for a walk.*

*They sent the result slip in September and I received the certificate two months **afterwards**.*

NB *after* would not be correct in these two sentences.

4 *At last/in the end/at the end*

At last suggests that something good happens after a long period of time or more than one attempt.

*I've passed the FCE **at last**! I failed twice before!*

In the end has a similar meaning and may also suggest there have been one or more changes or problems. The result may be good or bad.

*The car broke down several times on the way but we got there **in the end**.*

NB *eventually* can also be used in this sentence.

At the end means at the point when something finishes.

*Hand in your books **at the end** of the lesson.*

5 *When/as/while*

These can all be used with the past continuous to introduce an action which was already in progress when another action occurred.

***As/When/While** I was running, I saw a rabbit.*

6 *During/in/for*

These are all used as prepositions when referring to time, and are followed by a noun. *During* and *in* are used to say *when* something happened.

*It rained a lot **during/in** the night.*

For is used to say how long something took or lasted.

*We went to Spain **for** two weeks **during** the summer.*

So and *such*

These 'intensifiers' are used to give emphasis.

1 *So* is used before:

a adjectives and adverbs without nouns.

*I'm **so tired**. I'll have to go to bed.*

b *much, many, little, few*

*You shouldn't eat **so much**, Ian.*

2 *Such* is used with or without an adjective before:

a singular countable nouns (the indefinite article *a/an* is also needed).

*She's got **such a wonderful voice**.*

b uncountable nouns and plural countable nouns (the article is not needed).

*Our neighbours are **such friendly people**.*

3 *So* and *such* can both be used with a *that* clause to talk about the results or consequences

*It was **such a boring place that** we decided to leave.*

*It was raining **so hard** we had to stop the car.*

Unit 5

Obligation and necessity

A *Must/Mustn't* + infinitive without *to*

Must is used:

1 for strong obligations imposed by the speaker. The speaker uses *must* to express his/her authority.

*You **must be** here by 8 am. (manager to employee)*

2 to give strong advice.

*It's a great film. You really **must go** and see it.*

3 to tell oneself what is necessary.

*I **must remember** to phone Roger.*

Must not or *mustn't* is used:

4 to talk about something that is not permitted.

*Passengers **must not smoke** on the aircraft.*

*You **mustn't** drive without your seatbelt on in Britain.*

5 to give strong advice.

*You **mustn't work** too hard. You'll make yourself ill.*

Past form

Must does not have a past form. *Had to* is therefore used to refer to the past.

*We **had to write** a formal letter in the exam.*

Question form

Must is possible in question forms:

***Must you wear** that horrible dress?*

although *have to* is more common:

*What do we **have to do** for homework?*

B *Have to/Don't have to*

Have to is used to refer to strong obligations imposed by another person rather than by the speaker or writer.

*I **have to be** at work by 8 o'clock. The boss will get angry if I'm late. (employee to a friend)*

Don't have to expresses a lack of obligation.

*I'm glad I **don't have to wear** a suit. It's so hot today.*

C *Need to/Don't need to/Needn't*

Need to is used to express necessity.

*Can we go to the baker's next? **I need to get** some bread.*

Don't need to/needn't express a lack of necessity.

We **don't need to/needn't leave** yet. *It's only 2 o'clock.*

D *Should/Shouldn't* + infinitive without *to*

Should and *shouldn't* are used to express obligation or give advice. *Ought to* can also be used with the same meaning as *should*.

You **ought to/should see** *a doctor about your backache.*

If you're on a diet you **shouldn't drink** *beer.*

E *Be supposed to/Had better*

Be supposed to is used to talk about what you should do because of a rule or because it is expected.

*Come on, it's 10 o' clock. You***'re supposed to be** *in bed!*

Had better + infinitive without *to* is used to talk about what you should do because you think it's a good idea.

*You***'d better ask** *your dad before you borrow the car.*

Permission

To express permission it is possible to use *can*, *may* (more formal) or *be allowed to*. In the negative these express lack of permission, or prohibition.

You **can order** *another drink but you* **can't have** *any more chips.*

We **aren't allowed to wear** *trainers to school.*

May is not possible in the past. *Could* and *be allowed to* are possible for general permission.

In my last job we had flexitime so we **could arrive** *more or less when we wanted to.*

Could is not used when referring to a particular situation in the past. Only *be allowed to* is possible.

I **was allowed to** *stay up late last night.*

Let and *make*

Both these verbs are followed by the infinitive without *to*. *Let* is used to express permission.

My dad never **lets me watch** *that programme.*

Let is not normally used in the passive. *Be allowed to* is used instead.

I **wasn't allowed to go** *to the party alone.*

Make is used to express obligation.

The teacher **made her do** *some extra homework.*

In the passive, *make* is followed by the infinitive with *to*.

He was **made to pay** *for the window he had broken.*

Unit 6

Too and *enough*

A *Too* means 'more than is necessary or desirable'.

1 *Too* + adjective/adverb

This jumper's **too big**. *Can I try a smaller size?*

2 *Too much/Too many* (+ noun)

I can't eat this. There's **too much salt** *in it.*

There are **too many people** *here. Let's go outside.*

3 *Too* + adverb/adjective (+ *for* + object) + infinitive

It's **too cold to play** *tennis today.*

He spoke **too quickly for me to understand** *him.*

B *Enough* means 'as much as is necessary'

1 Adjective/Adverb + *enough*

Are you **warm enough** *or shall I turn the heating on?*

2 *Enough* + noun

We'll have to stand because there aren't **enough chairs**.

3 *Enough* (+ *for* + object) + infinitive with *to*

I haven't got **enough time to see** *you today.*

Causative *have*: 'to have something done'

1 The structure *have* + object + past participle shows that the action is done for the subject by someone else and not by the subject. The subject causes the action to be done. Compare the following:

I cut my hair. (= I did it myself)

I had my hair cut. (= someone did it for me)

All tenses of *have* are possible, eg:

We've just had our washing machine repaired.

I'm having my eyes tested tomorrow.

2 The same structure can also be used for events (usually unpleasant) which are outside of the speaker's control.

John had his car stolen last week.

3 *Get* can be used instead of *have* in this structure. It is slightly more informal.

Where did you get your photos developed?

Relative clauses

Relative clauses give extra information about something or someone in the main clause.

A Defining relative clauses

Defining relative clauses contain information which is essential for our understanding of the whole sentence.

The man who normally comes to clean our windows is on holiday this month.

He's got a computer program which translates texts from Spanish into English.

In each case, the relative clause identifies which person or thing is being talked about.

Features of defining relative clauses

• No commas are required either at the beginning or the end of the relative clause.

• *That* can be used instead of *who* for people and *which* for things, particularly in spoken English.

	For people	For things
Subject:	*who/that*	*which/that*
Object:	*who/that/whom**	*which/that*
Possessive:	*whose*	*whose*

* *whom* is more formal than *who*

• The relative pronoun can be omitted if it is the object of the verb in the relative clause.

*I'm enjoying the book (***which/that***) you lent me.*

• The relative pronoun cannot be omitted if it is the subject of the verb in the relative clause.

That's the shop assistant **who/that** *served me the last time I came here.*

B Non-defining relative clauses

Non-defining relative clauses contain information which is not essential for our understanding of the sentence. We can identify which person or thing is being talked about without the information in the relative clause.

Their new house, which has five bedrooms and a games room, is much larger than their previous one.

At the party she spoke to Mr Peterson, whose father owned the company she worked for.

Features of non-defining relative clauses

- Commas are required both at the beginning and the end of the relative clause (except when the end of the relative clause is also the end of the sentence).
- *That* cannot be used in place of *who* or *which*.

	For people	For things
Subject:	*who*	*which*
Object:	*who/whom*	*which*
Possessive:	*whose*	*whose*

- Relative pronouns cannot be omitted from non-defining relative clauses.

  *Her maths teacher, **who/whom** everyone in the class adored, announced that he was leaving the school.*

- Non-defining relative clauses are more common in written English.
- *Which* can be used in non-defining relative clauses to refer to a whole clause.

  *No one phoned him on his birthday, **which** made him feel rather depressed.*

C Relative clauses and prepositions

1 Prepositions usually come at the end of defining and non-defining relative clauses.

In defining relative clauses the relative pronoun is usually omitted.

*The town I grew up **in** has changed a lot since I left.*

In non-defining relative clauses the relative pronoun is never omitted.

*Keith Rolf, **who** I used to work with, lives in Paris now.*

2 In more formal English, prepositions often come before the relative pronouns *whom* for people and *which* for things (in which case the pronoun cannot be omitted).

*We shall be visiting the room **in which** Turner painted some of his greatest works.*

*The head waiter, **to whom** we addressed our complaint, was not particularly helpful.*

D Relative adverbs: *where*, *when* and *why*

Where, *when* and *why* can be used in relative clauses after nouns which refer to a place (*where*), a time (*when*) or a reason (*why*).

Where has the meaning 'in/at which'

Defining:	They've booked a week in that campsite **where** we stayed last year.
Non-defining:	She's in Southlands Hospital, **where** you were born.

When has the meaning 'on/in which' and can be omitted in defining relative clauses.

Defining:	Do you remember that day (**when**) we went to Rhyl and it snowed?
Non-defining:	I'm going on holiday in September, **when** most people are back at work.

Why has the meaning 'for which' and can be omitted in defining relative clauses.

Defining:	The reason (**why**) I'm phoning is to ask you for Tina's address.

Unit 7

The present perfect

The present perfect links past events and situations with the present.

1 The present perfect is used:

a to give news of recent past events which have some relevance to the present.

*Be careful! **I've just dropped** a glass on the floor.*

b to describe something that started in the past and continues to the present.

***My wife and I have lived** in the same house ever since we got married.*

c to describe events which occurred at some time between the past and the present. Exactly when they happened is not known or not important.

***I've been** to Poland three or four times.*

d to talk about something which occurred in the past, but in a time period which includes the present.

***Judy's boyfriend has phoned** her three times this morning – and it's not even 11 o'clock!*

e after the expression *it/this/that is the first/second/third, etc time*

*This is the first time **I've seen** this programme.*

2 Time expressions

a The present perfect is commonly used with *ever, never, just, recently, so far, still, yet* and *already* when referring to a time period up to now:

*They haven't booked their holiday **yet**.*

*I've had three cups of coffee **so far** this morning.*

b *For* is used with periods of time to show how long something has lasted.

*I've known Eric **for** twenty years.*

Since is used with points in time to show when something started.

*I've had this watch **since** 1984.*

3 The present perfect continuous can be used:

a to emphasize the duration of a situation or activity.

It's been snowing all day.

b to suggest that a situation or activity is temporary.

My mum's not well, so I've been looking after her.

c to suggest a situation or activity is incomplete.

I've been painting the house – that's why it's in a mess.

d to focus on the repetition of a situation or activity.

He's been getting into trouble at school a lot recently.

4 The present perfect simple and continuous

a Both simple and continuous forms of the present perfect can be used to talk about the effects in the present of a past event.

Your new shoes are ruined! You've been playing football in them, haven't you? (an activity)

I can't do any sport for a few weeks; I've broken my arm. (a single action)

b The continuous form is not used if we talk about the number of things that have been completed or the number of times a thing has been done.

She's eaten six chocolate biscuits.

She's been eating chocolate biscuits.

c Stative verbs such as *have* (to possess/own), *think* (to have an opinion), *be, like, believe, understand* and *know* are not normally used in the continuous form.

We've known each other for a long time. ✔

We've been knowing each other for a long time. ✘

Contrasting ideas

1 *But* contrasts two ideas in the same sentence.

*The weather was bad **but** she enjoyed the trip.*

2 *Although* and *though* (informal) are also used to contrast ideas in the same sentence. They can go at the beginning of a sentence or in the middle.

Although the weather was bad, she enjoyed the trip.

*She enjoyed the trip **although** the weather was bad.*

Even used before *though* emphasizes the contrast.

*They managed to communicate, **even though** they couldn't speak each other's language.*

3 *However* contrasts ideas in two different sentences. It often comes at the beginning of the second sentence and is followed by a comma.

*The weather was bad. **However**, she enjoyed the trip.*

4 *Nevertheless* is a more formal alternative to *however*.

*The English aren't normally very emotional people. **Nevertheless**, they get very excited at sporting events.*

5 *In spite of* and *despite* are both followed by a gerund or a noun. They can go at the beginning of the sentence or in the middle.

*She enjoyed the trip **in spite of** the bad weather.*

***Despite** the fact that the weather was bad, she enjoyed the trip.*

***Despite** the weather being bad, she enjoyed the trip.*

If the subject of the verbs in the two clauses is the same, the gerund can be used immediately after *despite* or *in spite of* without a preceding noun/pronoun.

She played tennis despite feeling ill.

***She** paid for the meal despite **me/my** telling her not to.*

6 *Whereas* and *while* are used to contrast two ideas in the same sentence.

*The first photo shows a child having fun **whereas/while** the second one shows a rather sad man on his own.*

Expressing preferences

A *Prefer*

1 *Prefer* + gerund + *to* + gerund

This is usually used to talk about general preferences.

I prefer playing basketball to watching it.

2 *Would prefer* + infinitive with *to* + *rather than* + infinitive without *to*

This is normally used to talk about preferences on a specific occasion.

I'd prefer to walk to school today rather than go by bus.

B *Would rather*

would rather + infinitive without *to* + *than* + infinitive without *to* (same meaning as *would prefer to*)

I'd rather not talk about it at the moment.

I'd rather do nothing all day than go to school.

Unit 8

The future

A Predictions and expectations

Will + infinitive without *to* can be used to make predictions or talk about expectations for the future. These can be introduced by verbs such as *believe, expect, hope* and *think*. Adverbs such as *definitely, (almost) certainly* and *probably* may also be used; they come after *will* and before *won't*.

*United **will probably win** the league again this year.*

*'Where's Anne?' 'I expect she**'ll be** here soon.'*

*She definitely **won't pass** her exams; she's too lazy.*

Alternatives to *will*

1 The following structures can be used to talk about the probability of something happening in the future.

be (un)likely + infinitive with *to*

may/might/could well + infinitive without *to*

*There **may/could/might well be** a cure for cancer in the future. (= there will probably be)*

*They've got a map with them so they**'re unlikely (not likely) to get** lost. (= they probably won't get lost)*

NB *may well* is not usual in the negative.

2 *May/might/could* + infinitive without *to* can be used to talk about the possibility of something happening in the future.

*We **may/might/could see** fewer cars in the future.*

*We **may not/might not have** time to see the exhibition.*

NB *could not* expresses impossibility; see Unit 9.

B Other future forms

1 In addition to making predictions about the future, *will* is also used to talk about:

a decisions made at the moment of speaking, including offers and requests.

***We'll babysit** for you if you want to go out.*

*The phone's ringing. **Will you answer** it?*

b future facts; events which the speaker knows or believes are certain to happen.

***Summer will be** here soon.*

2 *Going to* + infinitive is used to talk about:

a predictions based on present evidence.

*Look at those clouds – **it's going to rain** soon.*

b intentions or plans.

***I'm going to stay** in tonight and read my book.*

Modal verbs can be used to express possible intentions.

***I may/might go** walking in the mountains tomorrow.*

3 The present continuous is used to talk about future arrangements which have already been made.

***Sue and Alan are getting** married on June 21st.*

4 The present simple is used:

a to talk about timetabled or scheduled events.

*The film **starts** at 9.15, just after the news.*

b to refer to the future after time linkers such as *when, before, after, until, by the time, as soon as.*

*Give me a call **as soon as you arrive**.*

5 The future continuous, *will* + *be* + *-ing*, is used to talk about actions or events which will be in progress at a certain time in the future.

*This time next week **I'll be lying** on the beach.*

6 The future perfect simple, *will* + *have* + past participle, is used to talk about actions and events that will be completed by a certain time in the future.

*By the end of today **we'll have driven** over 250 kms.*

7 The future perfect continuous, *will* + *have* + *been* + *-ing*, is used to talk about actions and events which continue to a certain time in the future.

*On 21 May **I'll have been living** here for exactly 10 years.*

8 *Be about to* + infinitive/*be on the point of* + gerund can be used to talk about the immediate future.

*Can I phone you back? I'm just **about to have** lunch.*

*The police say **they are on the point of solving** the crime.*

Unit 9

Modal verbs of speculation

A Certainty

If we are fairly certain about something, *must, can't* and *couldn't* can be used to express this.

1 For present situations the modal verbs *must, can't* and *couldn't* are followed by the infinitive without *to*.

'I haven't slept for two days.' *'You **must be** exhausted!'*

*Everyone here is wearing a football scarf, so we **can't be** very far from the stadium.*

The continuous infinitive can also be used.

*Why is he wearing his uniform? He **couldn't be going** to school – it's Saturday today.*

2 For past situations we use the same modal verbs + *have* + past participle.

*I can't find my book. **I must have left** it at school.*

*This composition isn't very good. You **can't have spent** very long on it.*

The continuous form can also be used.

*'And then I lost control of the car.' 'You **must have been driving** too fast.'*

NB *mustn't* is not normally used when speculating about present or past situations.

B Possibility

If we are not certain about something but think it is possible, we use *may (not), might (not)* or *could*.

1 For present situations these modal verbs are followed by the infinitive without *to*. The continuous infinitive is also possible.

*'Ed's not answering my e-mails.' 'He **might be** on holiday.'*

*He **could be telling** the truth, but it's hard to believe.*

2 For past situations we use the same modal verbs + *have* + past participle (the continuous form is possible).

*I think we **may have taken** the wrong road. This doesn't look familiar.*

*'Sean looked a little sad.' 'He **might not have been feeling** very well.'*

NB It is not possible to use *can* when speculating about present or past situations.

Question tags

A Form

Question tags are formed using either a modal verb, an auxiliary verb or the verb *to be* + subject pronoun. A negative tag is normally used with a positive statement, and a positive tag with a negative statement.

1 If the verb *to be* appears in the statement, it is repeated in the question tag.

*He **isn't** married, **is he**?*

*I'm late again, **aren't I**? (not **amn't I**?)*

2 If an auxiliary verb or a modal verb appears in the statement, it is repeated in the question tag.

*You've been to Warsaw before, **haven't you**?*

3 If the verb in the statement is a full verb (ie there is no modal verb or auxiliary verb), an appropriate form of the auxiliary verb *do* is required in the question tag.

*You **bought** it last year, **didn't you**?*

4 'Will you?' and 'can you?' are used with imperatives. 'Would you?' and 'could you?' are more formal alternatives.

*Open the window, **will/can/would/could you**?*

'Will you?' is used after a negative imperative.

*Don't forget to write, **will you**?*

5 If *let's* appears in the statement, the question tag 'shall we?' is used.

*Let's go home, **shall we**?*

6 If the statement contains negative words such as *nothing* or *nobody*, the question tag is positive.

*Nothing frightens you, **does it**?*

NB the pronoun *they* is used with *nobody/no one, somebody/someone* and *everybody/everyone*.

B Use and intonation

We can use question tags to ask a real question if we are unsure if the statement is true or not. In this case we say the question tag with rising intonation.

I've met you before, haven't I?

We can also use question tags when we expect someone to agree with a statement. In this case we say the question tag with falling intonation.

She can't sing very well, can she?

Unit 10

The passive

A Form

The verb *to be* + past participle.

Present simple:	*Goods worth £750 million **are stolen** from shops each year.*
Present continuous:	*A man **is being questioned** in connection with the robbery.*
Present perfect:	*Photos of the suspects **have been put** up around the town.*
Past simple:	*He **was taken** away in a van.*
Past continuous:	*The burglar didn't realize he **was being filmed**.*
Past perfect:	*Two people **had been mugged** there on the previous day.*
Future simple:	*All football supporters **will be searched** at the airport.*
Infinitive:	*He is hoping **to be released** from prison next week.*
Gerund:	*I can't even remember **being hit** on the head.*
Modal verbs:	*He **should be sentenced** to life imprisonment.*

B Use

The passive is used to focus attention on the person or thing affected by the action, rather than on the agent (the 'doer' of the action). If we are interested in the agent, we use the preposition *by*:

*Sue and Mark were brought up **by their grandparents**.*

When we talk about the instrument used by the agent to do the action, we use the preposition *with*:

*He was hit on the head **with a vase**.*

The agent is not usually included when:

1 it is clear from the context who the agent is.

Colin was arrested for dangerous driving. (by the police)

2 we don't know who the agent is or was.

My car was stolen yesterday afternoon.

3 when the agent is not important.

Stamps are often sold in supermarkets in England.

4 The passive is also used in formal notices:

Food may not be consumed on the premises.

C Passive constructions with the infinitive

The infinitive can be used after the passive of verbs such as: *believe, consider, expect, know, say, think*
The President is expected to arrive at 9.30 am.

The perfect infinitive (*have* + past participle) is used to refer to the past.

15 people are known to have died in the accident.

Past necessity

A *Needn't have* + past participle

This structure is used to talk about an action which was unnecessary. It indicates that the subject performed the action.

I needn't have prepared so much food for the party; everyone had eaten before they came. (I prepared lots of food but I realized afterwards that it wasn't necessary.)

B *Didn't need to* + infinitive

This structure is used to talk about an action which was unnecessary. It usually indicates that the subject did not perform the action.

I didn't need to prepare very much food for the party; everyone said they would bring something to eat. (I didn't prepare lots of food as I knew it wasn't necessary.)

Unit 11

Conditionals

Conditional sentences contain a conditional clause (introduced by words such as *if*, *as long as* and *unless*) and a main clause.

If the conditional clause comes before the main clause, a comma is needed (as in this sentence).

A comma is not needed if the conditional clause comes after the main clause (as in this sentence).

A Zero conditional

if + present simple or imperative

We use the zero conditional to talk about situations which are always true. *If* has the same meaning as *when, whenever* or *every time* in such sentences.

Everyday situations:	*My eyes hurt if I spend too long on the computer.*
Scientific facts:	*If you mix blue and yellow, you get green.*
Instructions: (*if* + imperative)	*If you don't know the answer, make an intelligent guess.*

B First conditional

if + present simple, *will* + infinitive without *to*

We use the first conditional to talk about possible situations and their probable results in the future.

She'll be very happy if you phone her.

It can be used for warnings, promises and threats.

I'll send you to bed if you don't behave yourself.

If you pass your driving test, I'll take you out for a meal.

Modal verbs can be used in the main clause in place of *will*. *May, might* and *could*, for example, introduce possible results if a condition is met.

If I finish my homework early, I might call you.

C Second conditional

if + past simple, *would* + infinitive without *to*

We use the second conditional to talk about imaginary, unlikely or impossible situations in the present or future.

If I knew the answer to number six, I would tell you.

If I had wings, I'd fly south in winter.

First or second conditional? Notice the difference in meaning between these two sentences:

First Conditional:
If they give me a pay rise, I'll buy a new car. (I feel there is a real possibility that they will give me a pay rise.)

Second Conditional:
If they gave me a pay rise, I'd buy a new car. (I feel it is less likely that they will give me a pay rise.)

The second conditional can also be used to give advice.

If I were you, I'd complain to the manager.

Both *was* and *were* are possible in the conditional clause after the subject pronouns *I/he/she/it*. *Was* is more common in spoken English.

If he were a little taller, he'd be an excellent goalkeeper.

The modal verbs *might* and *could* can be used in the main clause to indicate possible results.

If you worked a bit harder you might have more success.

D Third conditional

if + past perfect, *would/might/could have* + past participle.

We use the third conditional to talk about imaginary situations in the past.

If we hadn't taken a map, we would have got lost. (We took a map, so we didn't get lost.)

E Mixed conditional

if + past perfect, *would* + infinitive without *to*

Mixed conditionals are a combination of a second and a third conditional. They can express an imaginary past event and a possible or probable present result.

If you'd listened to my advice, you would not be in this situation now.

F Alternative words for *if*

As long as, provided (that), providing (that) and *on condition (that)* can be used in place of *if* to emphasize the condition.

I'll lend you £10 as long as you give it back tomorrow.

We'll go out in the boat tomorrow afternoon provided the sea isn't too rough.

So, neither and *nor*

A Use

To indicate that we have the same feelings, behaviour or abilities as others, we can use *so* (positive statements), and *neither* or *nor* (negative statements).

B Form

so/neither/nor + (modal) auxiliary verb or the verb *to be* + subject noun or pronoun

The rules for deciding which verb is used after *so, neither* or *nor* are the same as those for question tags (Unit 9). The verb is always positive. The clause with *so, neither* or *nor* can appear in the same sentence as the main clause, or it can be said by a different speaker:

She can't play a musical instrument and nor can I.

'I'll phone him tonight.' 'So will I'

'My mum isn't working tomorrow.' *'Neither is mine.'*

C If our feelings, behaviour or abilities are different from those of others, we use the following structure:

subject + (modal) auxiliary or the verb *to be*

He doesn't eat meat but I do.

'We're allowed to wear jeans to school.' *'We aren't.'*

Unit 12

Direct and reported speech

When reporting what someone has said or written we can use either direct speech or reported speech.

When we use direct speech we report the exact words which someone has used.

'I'm staying here tomorrow,' said Heather.

When we use reported speech, changes may have to be made to verb tenses, pronouns and certain words indicating place and time.

Heather said **she was** *staying* **there the next day**.

A Reporting statements

1 The following changes are usually made to verbs. In each case the verb 'moves back' one tense.

Direct speech		Reported speech
Present simple	→	Past simple
'I work in an office,' he said.		*He said he worked in an office.*
Present continuous	→	Past continuous
'We are going away on holiday,' she said.		*She said they were going away on holiday.*
Present perfect	→	Past perfect
'I've known her for a long time,' he said.		*He said he'd known her for a long time.*
Present perfect cont.	→	Past perfect continuous
'He's been playing tennis,' she said.		*She said he'd been playing tennis.*
Past simple	→	Past perfect
'I saw Nigel in town,' he said.		*He said that he'd seen Nigel in town.*
Past continuous	→	Past perfect continuous
'We were trying to help him,' she said.		*She said they'd been trying to help him.*

NB the modal verbs *will*, *must*, *may* and *can* change to *would*, *had to*, *might* and *could*.

2 No changes are made in the verb tense:

a if the verb in the direct speech is in the past perfect.

'He had never spoken about it before,' she said.

She said he had never spoken about it before.

b if the direct speech contains one of the following modal verbs: *would, might, could, should, ought to*

'You should go to the doctor's,' he said.

He said I should go to the doctor's.

c if the statement being reported is still true.

'I like fish,' she said.   *She said she likes fish.*

d if the reporting verb is in the present.

'It's 40° in Athens at the moment.' (Jeremy to his mother on the phone)

Jeremy says it's 40° in Athens at the moment. (Jeremy's mother to her husband)

3 Pronouns in direct speech may have to change when we use reported speech.

'I'll see **you** *soon,' said Peter.*

Peter said **he** *would see* **me** *soon.*

4 The following changes may also need to be made to words indicating place and time.

Direct speech		Reported speech
now	→	*then*
today	→	*that day*
this morning	→	*that morning*
tomorrow	→	*the next/following day*
next week	→	*the next/following week*
yesterday	→	*the day before, the previous day*
two days ago	→	*two days before/earlier*
last week	→	*the week before, the previous week*
here	→	*there*
come	→	*go*

5 *This, that, these* and *those* may change to *the*.

*'***That** *book you lent me is really boring,' he said.*

He said **the** *book I had lent him was really boring.*

B Reporting verbs for statements

1 *tell* is used with a direct object

He told me (that) he was getting married.

2 *say* and *explain* are used without a direct object.

She said (that) she was ill. (not *She said me…*)

They can, however, be used with an indirect object.

I explained to them (that) I'd left my passport at home. (not *I explained them…*)

3 Some reporting verbs can be used with an infinitive.

a verb + object noun/pronoun + infinitive with *to*
advise, ask, encourage, invite, order, persuade, recommend, remind, tell, urge, warn

'Don't forget to phone Jim,' he told her.

He reminded her to phone Jim.

b verb + infinitive with *to*
offer, promise, refuse, threaten

'I'll help you mend the car if you like.'

He offered to help me mend the car.

4 The following patterns can be used after both *recommend* and *suggest*:

He recommended/suggested (that) I (should) eat less sugar.

She recommended/suggested joining a youth club.

The infinitive with *to* can only be used after *recommend*.

C Reporting questions

When we report questions we make the same changes to verb tenses, pronouns and words indicating place and time as we do when we report statements. The following changes are also made:

Auxiliary verbs:	auxiliary verbs *do, does* and *did* are omitted
Word order:	is the same as that of a statement
Punctuation:	question marks are not used
Yes/No questions:	if there is no question word (*what, where, who* etc) in the direct question, we use *if* or *whether*.

'Does she smoke?'

He asked if/whether she smoked.

Ask and *tell*

Each of these verbs can be used in two different ways in reported speech.

1 *Ask*

   a Requests (*ask* + object + infinitive with *to*)

   'Can you help me, please?'

   He asked me to help him.

   b Questions

   'Can you ride a horse?'

   She asked me if I could ride a horse.

2 *Tell*

   a Commands (*tell* + object + infinitive with *to*)

   'Put your coat on.'

   She told him to put his coat on.

   b Statement

   'I can't find my coat.'

   He told her (that) he couldn't find his coat.

Countable and uncountable nouns

A Countable nouns are nouns which can be counted.

one plate   *two cats*   *five chairs*

B Uncountable nouns cannot be counted. They are not used with the indefinite article (*a/an*), they do not have a plural and they are used with a singular verb form.

*Can you get **some bread**?*

***A lot of damage** was done to the building.*

The following nouns are usually uncountable: *news, accommodation, health, progress, advice, homework, research, damage, information, spaghetti, English, work, knowledge, travel, furniture, luggage, weather, graffiti.*

C Nouns which are both countable and uncountable

   1 Many words for food and drink can be used both countably and uncountably.

   I've made a chocolate cake. (C)

   Could I have some more cake? (U)

   Would you like another coffee? (C) (= cup of coffee)

   I don't like coffee. (U)

   2 A word used countably may have a very different meaning from its countable version.

   *I'd like a double **room** for one night.* (C) (= hotel room)

   *There's no more **room** on this bus.* (U) (= space)

D Making uncountable nouns countable

   1 Some uncountable nouns have countable equivalents with similar meanings.

   *There isn't much **work** in this town.* (U)

   *There aren't many **jobs** in this town.* (C)

   *My job involves a lot of business **travel**.* (U)

   *I have to make a lot of business **trips**.* (C)

   2 Some other uncountable nouns can be made countable by using *piece(s) of* or *item(s) of*.

   *Let me give you a piece of **advice**.*

   *Two items of **news** caught my attention.*

   3 Certain other expressions are used with words for food and drink: *a plate of spaghetti, a pinch of salt, a loaf of bread, a slice of cake/toast, a spoonful of sugar, a bar of chocolate, a carton of milk, a jar of jam.*

E **1** Words used with countable nouns: *a/an, few, a few, many, a large number of, each, every, several.*

   2 Words used with uncountable nouns: *little, a little, much, a great deal of, a large amount of.*

   3 Words used with countable *and* uncountable nouns: *some, any, no, a lot of, lots of, all, plenty of, most.*

   Little and *few*

   These two words have more negative meanings. They mean 'not much/many' or 'not as much/many desired or expected'.

   Sue has made little progress since the beginning of term.

   There were very few people at the concert.

   A little and *a few*

   These have more positive meanings. They mean 'some' or 'more than expected'.

   I've managed to save a little money to buy Al a present.

   I've still got a few eggs – enough to make an omelette.

   Plenty of

   This means 'a lot of' or 'more than enough'.

   Don't hurry – we've got plenty of time.

Unit 13

Expressing ability

A *Can* and *be able to*

   Can and *be able to* are both used to express ability. However, *can* only has present tense (*can*) and past tense (*could*) forms. If another form of the verb is required, *be able to* is used.

Present:	*She can/is able to speak three languages fluently.*
Past:	*She could/was able to read when she was two.*
Infinitive:	*I'd like to be able to ski.*
Present perfect:	*He's never been able to save money.*
Will future:	*She'll be able to drive to work when she passes her test.*

B Present ability

   We use *can* or *be able to* to talk about present ability. *Be able to* is more formal than *can*.

   I can run faster than you.

   He is able to speak without moving his lips.

   The negative form of *can* is *can't* or *cannot*. To form the negative of *be able to*, *not* is used before *able*. You can also use *be unable to*.

   I cannot understand why she married him.

   Many of my students aren't able/are unable to pronounce the word 'taught' correctly.

   Be capable of + gerund can also be used to express ability. It means to have the ability, capacity or potential to do something.

   The team has some excellent players and is capable of winning the championship.

   The negative form *be incapable of* + gerund can be used or *not* can be placed before *capable*.

   She is incapable/isn't capable of looking after herself.

C Past ability

   1 When we talk about general ability in the past, both *could* and *was/were able to* are possible.

   She could sing really well when she was a child.

   My grandfather could play the trumpet when he was 90.

   Be capable of can also be used in the past.

   Joe wasn't capable of making toast without burning it.

   2 When we talk about ability to do something on one occasion in the past, *could* is not possible. Instead, *was/were able to*, *managed to* + infinitive or *succeeded in* + gerund have to be used.

   I managed to/was able to speak to Frank last night.

   Firefighters succeeded in controlling the flames.

   However, *could* can be used for ability on one occasion when it is used with verbs of the senses: *see, smell, hear, feel, sense, taste.*

I knew my wife had arrived; I could smell her perfume.

When we talk about inability to do something on one occasion in the past, *couldn't, weren't/wasn't able to, didn't manage to* and *didn't succeed in* are all possible.

I couldn't do the homework; it was too difficult.

I didn't manage to/wasn't able to repair the washing machine.

Verbs followed by preposition + gerund

1 These verbs can be followed by *for* + gerund:
   apologize, arrest, blame, forgive, praise, punish, tell off, thank
   Have you apologized to Jean for breaking her pen?

2 These verbs can be followed by *from* + gerund:
   discourage, prevent, stop
   The police prevented him from leaving the country.

3 *Congratulate* and *insist* are followed by *on* + gerund.
   He insisted on paying for the meal.

4 *Warn* can be followed by *against* + gerund.
   We tried to warn him against driving in the snow.
   Warn can also be used with *of* or *about* + noun.
   Posters have been put up warning people of the dangers of smoking.

Unit 14

Hypothetical situations

A *Wish* and *if only*

W*ish* or *if only* can express how we would like things to be different if we had the power to change them.

1 Present states
   We use *wish/if only* + past simple to express wishes about present states. Stative verbs such as *be, have, know* and *understand* are used.
   I wish I was/were taller.
   If only I knew how to play the guitar.

2 Present actions
   We use *wish/if only* + *would* when we want something to happen or someone to do something. Active verbs (verbs describing actions) are used.
   I wish you would turn your music down.
   If only this wind would stop blowing.
   Wish/If only + *would* is used if we want to express irritation at other peoples' actions or behaviour.
   I wish you would stop tapping your foot.
   Wish/If only + past simple can also be used if the action occurs habitually.
   I wish you didn't (or wouldn't) smoke so much.

3 Present ability
   Wish/If only + *would* is used for events which are outside of our control. Consequently, we do not normally say 'I wish I would…'. Instead, we use 'I wish I could…' to indicate our inability to change things.
   I wish I could remember where I put my keys.

4 Wishes for the future
   Wish/If only + *would* or *could* can be used to express wishes for the future. This use of *wish* suggests that the action will probably not happen.
   I wish I could go on holiday with you in summer. (I know that I can't go with you).
   If there is more possibility that the action will happen, we use *hope*.
   I hope I can go on holiday with you in summer. (I don't know if I can or not).

5 Past situations
   We use *wish/if only* + past perfect to express wishes and regrets about the past.
   I wish I hadn't left school when I was 16.
   The following structures can also be used to express wishes and regrets about the past.
   a Third and mixed conditionals (see Unit 11)
      If I hadn't been so tired, this wouldn't have happened.
   b *should have* + past participle
      We should have got the train. This traffic's terrible.

B *Would rather*

We use *would rather* + past simple when we want someone else to do something in the present or future.

I'd rather you went to get some bread now.

He said he'd rather we didn't arrive too early tomorrow.

If the subject of *would rather* and the following verb is the same, we usually use the infinitive without *to* (see Unit 7).

We'd rather sit in the garden than go to the beach.

C *It's time*

We use *it's (high/about) time* + past simple when we want something to happen or be done now. It implies that the action should have been done already.

It's time you went to bed. You've got school tomorrow.

Unit 15

Expressing purpose

There are several different ways of expressing purpose (saying why people do things).

1 Infinitive with *to*
   *I'm writing **to thank** you for the lovely present you sent.*
   The negative infinitive, *not to do something*, cannot be used to express purpose.

2 *In order (not) to* + infinitive
   *She wore dark glasses **in order not to be recognized.***

3 *So as (not) to* + infinitive
   *We set off early **so as to avoid** the traffic.*

4 *So (that)* + clause
   a Future meaning: *so (that)* + *can/will*/present simple
      *I'm going to save some money **so I can go** away on holiday.*
      *I'll take an umbrella **so that I don't/won't get** wet.*
   b Past meaning: *so (that)* + *could/would*
      *I sat near the front **so that I could see** the board better.*

5 *In case* + clause
   If we do something to prepare for a possible situation or problem we use *in case* + present simple/past simple.
   a Future meaning: *in case* + present simple
      *Here are some crisps **in case you get** hungry later on.*
   b Past meaning: *in case* + past simple
      *He made a copy **in case he lost** the original.*

6 *In case* and *if*
   Note the difference in meaning between *in case* and *if*:
   I'll take my umbrella if it rains. (= I'll take my umbrella only if it is raining when I leave the house.)
   I'll take my umbrella in case it rains. (= I'll take it as a precaution, even if it isn't raining when I leave the house.)

Tapescripts

Unit 1 (Page 7)

Listening

FCE Part 3 – Multiple matching

Speaker 1

After we got the invitation my mum and I kept having big rows about what I was going to wear for the big event. She's always criticising me for my taste in clothes and she'd bought me this long, bright red dress to wear on the day. Of course, I refused. I went instead in a short black skirt, trainers and a sports top, thinking I'd look really cool and trendy. But of course, when we got to the church and I saw all the other guests in their smart new clothes and expensive hats I just felt really, really stupid and embarrassed. The bride and groom looked quite surprised when they saw me so I spent most of the time at the reception trying to avoid them.

Speaker 2

We really had no other option but to send her home to get changed, dye her hair back and take out the nose stud. We have rules and the rules are there to prepare young people for the reality of the world of work. I don't know of many jobs where you could turn up with shabby old clothes, green hair and a pierced nose. We insist on uniform from the first day until the last, and that includes sitting your GCSE exams. It's unfair on other candidates who respect the regulations, and distracting for them at a time when they need maximum concentration.

Speaker 3

Indeed, attitudes were already beginning to change. In 1919, the young French star Suzanne Lenglen caused a sensation at the British championships by wearing a calf-length, sleeveless dress. Her unconventional, yet practical clothing shocked spectators who were used to seeing women play in the long heavy dresses which were typical of that period. As a result Lenglen attracted the kind of attention from the world's press which was normally reserved for the stars of the silent movies. She silenced her critics, however, by beating her opponents and going on to win several major titles.

Speaker 4

He clearly has ability. You only have to look at his examination results to see that. And he used to live in France which means he probably wouldn't mind changing countries, if we needed him to. No, what concerns me is his appearance. If he's prepared to turn up for something as important as this, wearing what can only be described as casual clothes, what would he be like with our clients? If he really is a serious candidate and we decide to take him on, then he will have to get used to wearing something a little more formal.

Speaker 5

They had to have their little joke, didn't they. "Jane's having a little celebration at her house for her 'coming of age' and she wants everyone to go in fancy dress." That's what they said. So I thought about it for ages, what I was going to go as and everything. I spent more time thinking about my costume than about what present I was going to get for Jane. Of course, when I turned up at the house dressed as Coco the Clown and everybody else was wearing normal clothes, I don't know who was more surprised, me or Jane.

Unit 2 (Page 15)

Listening 1

FCE Part 2 – Blank filling

I = Interviewer   B = Brad Andrews

I: With us today in the studio we have Brad Andrews, one of the most famous names in dance music and club DJ-ing of the moment. Brad, why are club DJs so popular these days?

B: DJ-ing has changed an awful lot since the seventies. People used to go to discos and clubs to drink, talk or pick each other up. Now they come for the music, so whether you have a good time or not depends very much on the skills of the DJ.

I: Do you really need that much skill to put on a few records?

B: It's not that simple. I often operate three turntables at once, sometimes using one or two CD players as well. A lot of DJs are talented musicians, because you need a great deal of co-ordination to play with the records and use these huge decks we have nowadays. The job of DJ-ing is mostly about mixing tracks, using several records at once to create a totally whole new sound. On one record I might use just the high notes and sounds, and combine that with the bass on another record. Then I'll bring in a third one with the bass and treble turned off and use it to mix in vocals or another drum. It's a complex business.

I: And from what I hear, a well paid one, too. Would you mind telling us how much you earn for a single gig?

B: There are probably about three or four DJs in the country earning up to ten thousand pounds for a three-hour gig, that much I can tell you. But you have to understand this is an extremely demanding job. People go to see their favourite DJs like fans go to see bands, except top DJs play live gigs every weekend and not just three or four weeks in the year. Dedicated clubbers will often follow a DJ around the country, or even the world. People come from Paris to London just to spend Saturday night in a club, before going back on the train on Sunday morning.

I: Does a gig require much preparation?

B: You're dead right it does. I arrange and build a set at a club like I would do in a concert on stage, or if I was recording a single in the studio. You're basically composing a three-hour piece of music. It's as if you're taking people on a journey, and you want them to enjoy it. I also need to clear my mind before I get out there and do my stuff, so I use a form of meditation to get myself ready for a gig.

I: Looking ahead now Brad, could you tell us what the future of dance music is. How do you think it will develop in the next few years?

B: Well, it's interesting to think that here we are at the beginning of the twenty-first century, still using the old-fashioned vinyl records on old-fashioned turntables to create sophisticated sounds. But obviously computer programmes can now be used to put together a dance track in the same way that I described earlier, and of course much quicker. That could well be the way ahead for DJs. Another trend now is for established, big-name bands to ask DJs to rearrange their music in order to attract a younger audience.

I: A bright future indeed, then. We'll take a break now, but don't go away. Brad's going to do a bit of live DJ-ing for us here on Radio Perfect …

Unit 2 (Page 21)

Listening 2

FCE Part 4 – Multiple choice

I = Interviewer   L = Liz

I: In today's edition of Sports Showcase we talk to 19-year-old Liz Harris, one of the country's rising stars in the fast-growing sport of snowboarding. How long have you been into snowboarding, Liz?

L: I first did it when I was on holiday with my parents. When I was younger I used to go skiing every year with them and then one year I tried snowboarding, and I haven't skied since then. That was five years ago.

I: And what's the achievement that you're most proud of so far?

L: I suppose it has to be when I entered my first international competition this year. I came first in the Big Air event and won some money.

I: Let's hope you can go on winning! Would you say, Liz, that there are any particular qualities or strengths you need to have to be a snowboarder?

L: Good co-ordination and balance helps, but you don't have to born with it. If you practise for a few days, you'll get it anyway, even if you're not naturally sporty.

I: And have you ever had any nasty falls?

L: I hurt my back a few years ago on a dry slope. I was doing a jump and I fell really badly, but I didn't break anything. So far I've been really lucky, unlike my friends, who've all had bad injuries. Broken limbs, that kind of thing. No doubt I'll break an arm or a leg soon! It's just a question of time.

I: How many boys are there compared with girls who snowboard?

L: There are more guys, that's for sure, but it's a lot more even now. When I first started snowboarding you hardly ever saw any girls, but now there are loads of them. Not as many as the guys, but almost.

I: And how do the male snowboarders treat the girls?

L: Well, as far as my friends are concerned, they couldn't care less what sex you are. But there are certain people that think girls are rubbish, and that they shouldn't get paid as much as guys. On the whole, though, spectators have got used to seeing girls on the slopes.

I: You're professional, aren't you, but you don't get paid.

L: No, I get a few hundred pounds from some of my sponsors just to help me to pay for my lift pass. They also give me a few boards a year and then, you know, when I get photos in a magazine on the board it's basically a free advert for the company. So, yeah, all of my equipment is given to me and that's very useful of course. But I usually just save up the money in the summer and then go and spend it all riding in the winter.

I: What sort of advice would you give to a girl who wanted to take up snow-boarding?

L: If you can't get out to the Alps, then try going along to your local dry slope, where you can get lessons and hire equipment, or you could try the Cardiff Snow Dome, which is like a big indoor fridge with real snow. So wrap up warm because it can get quite cold in there. Anywhere in Britain, though, is fine really. There are dry slopes all over the place.

I: We hear you've been doing some modelling work as well. Is that right?

L: Yes, I have. I was on the cover of a fashion magazine a couple of months ago and I'm hopefully going to get some more work because of that. I didn't actually get paid for doing it. But, of course, it's great exposure, and any part-time modelling work now could be useful for the future.

I: You mean, you might go on to become a full-time model?

L: Who knows? If my luck runs out with the snowboarding, then why not? We'll just have to see.

I: Well, good luck for the moment with the snowboarding, Liz, and we'll certainly be looking out for you on the catwalk.

Unit 3 (Page 31)

Listening 1

FCE Part 3 – Multiple matching

Speaker 1
They last for about eight hours, which is about all you need them for really, even during the winter months when the nights are much longer of course. They're absolutely marvellous. Each one has a solar panel, which stores energy during the day, and then they come on as soon as it gets dark. When we moved into the area, we were a little worried about security, so we put them all along the driveway. They certainly seem to keep the burglars away. They also help you to see your way safely back to the front door if you come back after a good night out.

Speaker 2
An amazing gadget. It's solar powered, so it doesn't need batteries. You just attach it to a box which has solar panels on top and leave it by the window. It'll charge itself in a couple of hours – as long as it's sunny, of course! It's handy to have round the house for when you have a power cut and you can't see what you're doing, and it's ideal for camping too. Just leave it outside the tent in the afternoon and it's ready for you to use when you need it later on.

Speaker 3
We ordered it off the Internet. An American company. They said it was the latest in environmentally-friendly appliances. No batteries, no fuel, just sunlight. Take it on camping trips, they said, and enjoy delicious al fresco meals. Use it outside at home, they said, and keep the kitchen cool. What a waste of money. It keeps the kitchen cool alright, but when you live in a country which hardly sees the sun all year, it keeps the food cool, too. It would have been better to order the fridge.

Speaker 4
This one looks good! Clockwork and solar-powered and it comes in translucent red or blue plastic. There's a photo of one here. Cool! A bit expensive, though – sixty quid. Anyway, it says here: "As well as a handle to wind it up, it comes equipped with a solar panel which automatically takes over when the machine is placed in direct sunlight. Its waterproof beatbox is perfect for the beach." It also says it's got

headphones if you're worried about noise pollution. Can't see why you would be, though, can you?

Speaker 5
Solar-assisted, really. I mean, you still need batteries, but the tiny solar cell means you can use the playback without running them down. Cost an arm and a leg, mind you, but as far as I'm concerned it was worth every penny. I can plug it into my PC and the images are just fantastic. Really clear. Do you want to see where I went on holiday?

Unit 3 (Page 34)

Listening 2

FCE Part 4 – Matching

F = Father   H = Helen   M = Mother

F: Why on earth do you want a mobile phone?

H: Oh come on dad, don't be so old-fashioned. All my friends have got one and they're really handy. And they come in really great colours.

F: But it's not something you can treat lightly, Helen. It's not just a question of what *is* and what *isn't* fashionable. There are other more important issues involved here, which I'm not so sure you're fully aware of. You don't seem very well informed.

H: What do you mean, 'well informed'?

M: Well, I think your father's probably talking about the health risks. You must have heard about what they can do to your brain. The scientists are talking about how they can give you headaches and make you forget things.

F: And stop you sleeping properly.

H: They're talking about it, but they haven't proved it, yet. And anyway, think of the benefits. If I'm out with my friends and I get into trouble, I can use the mobile to call you.

F: But you can always use a phone box.

H: If you can find one! And when you do, nine times out of ten the phone isn't working.

M: I think Helen's got a point. Just imagine if she missed the last bus and she didn't have any money for a taxi. I'd feel a lot happier if I knew she could phone us wherever she was.

F: And then I have to get up in the middle of the night to go and pick her up! OK, fair enough. I can see I'm fighting a losing battle, here. And have you two thought about who is going to pay for this little gadget?

H: But they're really cheap, dad. They're virtually giving them away for nothing.

F: Of course they are. Because they know that teenagers like yourself will be using them to call up their friends every five minutes, and that parents like us will be there to pay the exorbitant bill.

H: You're always complaining about how you can never use the phone because I spend so much time on it. Well, problem solved. Now I can use the mobile.

M: I think as long as you promise only to use it for emergencies, or when one of us needs to use the phone in the house, then we're prepared to pay for the calls. Aren't we, dear?

F: Mmm. I suppose if we're going to benefit from it, then I don't mind so much.

M: And you're not to take it to school, either.

H: Don't worry about that, they've banned them from school.

Tony Bailey's girlfriend phoned him on his mobile during a maths lesson and he answered it. The teacher was really angry, and now they're worried we'll all be ringing each other up during lesson time.

M: I'm not surprised. In fact, if we agree to buy you one I'd be very grateful if you didn't take it with you when you're out with us. It's so irritating when you're having a conversation with someone in a café or some other public place and their phone rings. They ignore you and spend all their time talking to the person who's just called them!

F: And why those same people have to raise their voices and speak so loudly when they're on the phone, I just don't understand. They must think everyone else is deaf.

H: Maybe they are, or maybe they're in another noisy café. Who knows? Anyway, what do you think about these portable video-phones …?

Unit 4 (Page 47)

Listening

FCE Part 1 – Multiple choice

One
I used to think he was so good looking – those sparkling blue eyes and that sexy smile – although now of course the wrinkles have taken over and he's lost it completely. Call me old-fashioned, but I really don't think that somebody of his age should be wearing tight trousers and flowery shirts. It's obscene. And the way he talks to the press! I mean, 'politeness' is just not a word he understands. I'm not surprised they get upset and give him bad reviews.

Two

M = Man   W = Woman

M: So, have you decided which film we're going to see, then?

W: Well, I really wanted to see the new Fiona Miller film which everyone is raving about.

M: Oh, please, no! I couldn't stand another costume drama.

W: No, this one's very different from her others. She plays the part of an out of work spy who decides to turn to crime and begin a life as a jewel thief. But anyway, Katie says it's not her cup of tea, so I'm afraid it's 'get your handkerchief ready for another tear-jerker'. You know the plot already: boy meets girl, girl meets another boy, first boy gets upset – all that kind of nonsense.

Three

SO = Shop Owner   C = Customer

SO: I'm afraid I'm going to have to ask you to pay an extra £3.

C: Why?

SO: Well, you're only supposed to have the video out for two days: it says it on the box – 48 hours only.

C: Right, and I took it out on Saturday.

SO: And today's Tuesday, so that's one day overdue. Hence the extra £3.

C: But you're not open on Sundays, so that day doesn't count. Saturday to Monday, one day, and Monday to Tuesday, two days.

SO: I'm very sorry, sir, but that's not how we work.

Four

Drained, darling, absolutely drained. And have you read what the critics wrote about it? I don't know how anyone could say it was 'disappointing'. I mean, OK, so it's not the most exciting part I've ever had to play but I gave it my all, absolutely everything. One look at my face will tell you just how utterly exhausted I am. I could sleep for a week.

Five

What do you think we should get him? … An atlas! That's not very much … I know he's interested in geography, but he's been with the company for nearly 25 years. I really don't think an atlas would express our appreciation for all he's done for the firm. He's been like a father to us all … I don't know, something that will remind him of us in his retirement, something he can use every day. How about a palm top or something?

Six

M = Man   W = Woman

M: What was it like?
W: Oh, don't ask. I certainly wouldn't recommend it to anyone.
M: Too violent for you, was it?
W: Quite the opposite. I mean, at first there was the usual dose of gratuitous violence – basically what you'd expect from that type of film, and partly why I went to see it. After that, though, not a great deal happened. From what I can remember – when I wasn't falling asleep, that is – the script seemed to focus on an analysis of the protagonist's inner self.
M: A kind of 'non-action film', then.
W: Exactly.

Seven

Hello, yes, it's about a book I bought in your shop last week. A Katharine Adams novel. I just wanted to point out that there were one or two pages missing … No, no, there's really no need to apologize. I mean it's not as if it was the last page or anything. And I got the gist of what was happening without the pages. I just thought you ought to know so you can check the rest of your stock, or talk to the publishers or something … That's OK … Yes, pages 60 to 64 …

Eight

Well, we were born in the same month, but I'm a Leo, as you know, whereas her birthday's at the beginning of July, which makes her a Cancer. I don't know if that's good or bad. We certainly seem to laugh at the same things; the same jokes, the same comedy programmes … Sorry? … Oh, next Friday. We're going to a jazz concert, although I can't say it's my favourite type of music. She's really into it, and she wanted me to go, so …

Unit 5 (Page 59)

Listening 1

FCE Part 4 – True/False

R = Richard   L = Louise

R: Right, let's see, jobs and duties. Where shall we begin?
L: Let's talk about washing up first. Now that's something I really can't stand. My mum makes me do it after every meal at the weekend, and she won't let me go out with my friends until I've done it. I just think that's so unfair. I mean, none of my friends have to do it. I bet you don't either, do you?
R: No, you're right. In fact, no one in my family does. The most I have to do is get the plates out of the dishwasher.
L: Lucky you! I wish we had one. And what about cleaning shoes? You have a machine to do that as well, I suppose.
R: Unfortunately not. If it was left up to me, I wouldn't bother. But my dad says that shoes tell you a lot about a person so he has me brushing and polishing every other day. It's such a pain.
L: Same here. I'm not made to do it that often, but I still dread having to do it.
R: Right, so that could be one of our three. What's next?
L: Well, I honestly can't understand why clothes shopping is there. That's no chore for me. I mean I could spend all day popping in and out of shops. But going to buy food - now that's completely different.
R: I can't bear doing either of them. In fact, even *talking* about them makes me feel funny. Shall we move on?
L: OK. What do you feel about visiting relatives?
R: Oh that's not so bad. I've got a pretty small family so it doesn't happen that often. And I get on really well with my grandparents, the ones that are still alive, that is. In fact, one of my granddads is a real laugh, and I think he enjoys my company when I go to see him, now that he's on his own. How about you?
L: Well, I suppose I'm a bit lazy really. My parents both say I should go and see my grandparents more often, but they live so far away – I always make sure I'm in when they come to see us, and they come round quite a lot, so I don't feel as though I *need* to go and see them. I don't think my mum and dad agree, though.
R: Oh well, that's relatives for you. Let's have a look at the next one.
L: What about looking after animals? Have you got any pets?
R: I've got a couple of fish, but they're not really that much trouble. You just have to change their water once a week, and drop some food into their tank every now and then. But you've got a dog, haven't you?
L: Yeah, don't remind me. Every morning he's there by the front door with his lead in his mouth, looking up at me with his big eyes, as if to say; 'Come on, it's that time again.' And if I ignore him, he starts barking, and my dad gets angry and says, 'He's your dog, no one else wanted one, so you've got to take responsibility for him'. Thanks, dad. You're a great help.
R: Bad luck. Get a fish next time.
L: Oh, I love him really. Anyway, what have we decided so far?
R: Well, we both seem to agree on cleaning shoes, and neither of us likes shopping for food. So that leaves one more. I can't talk about cleaning the car, 'cause we haven't got one.
L: And my dad won't let any of us go anywhere near his. I think he's frightened we might scratch it, or something, so he takes it to the local car wash. That's fine by me.
R: And if you tell me you like tidying your room, I just won't believe you.
L: Well I think we've found the third one – I absolutely …

Tapescripts

Unit 5 (Page 60)

Listening 2

FCE Part 2 – Blank filling

I = Interviewer   AN = Allan Nicholls

I: With us today on "All in a Day's work" we have Allan Nicholls, station officer at Hove Fire Station, who's here to talk about the job of the much-respected fire-fighter. Allan, the first thing I'd like to ask you is about the selection procedure. What do you have to do in order to become a fire-fighter?

AN: Well, as you can imagine, it's a fairly rigorous process, with a variety of different tests. Whilst we don't insist on any academic qualifications, potential recruits do have to undergo a short educational test, aimed at assessing – basic literacy and numeracy, or in other words, reading, writing and arithmetic. Surprisingly for some, you no longer have to be a minimum height. Instead, there are a series of physical tests, designed to measure such things as how tightly they can grip things, or whether their back and legs are sufficiently strong. If they get through this stage they go on to the next one, the practical awareness day which involves fitness tests, checks to see if claustrophobia is a problem and practical tasks such as ladder climbing.

I: And are women accepted into the force?

AN: Ah yes, indeed, though they are still very much in the minority. At the moment here at Hove we have four women on the workforce.

I: Now, fire-fighters are obviously on call 24 hours a day, but perhaps you could tell us how the shift system operates.

AN: Well, there's an eight-day rota. A fire-fighter works two nine-hour day shifts, followed by two 15-hour night shifts. And then of course we get four days off before – starting again. It's a continuous cycle.

I: And what characterises a typical shift?

AN: We always begin with the Watch Parade, which is where one shift finishes and the next begins. This is a fairly formal affair and it's compulsory for everyone to wear full uniform. And then once the various jobs have been detailed for the shift, there are equipment checks. The breathing apparatus, for example, is a vital piece of equipment and lives can depend on it, so, it's essential that this and everything else is maintained in perfect working order. Nothing escapes attention, including of course the fire engines which also have to be checked from top to bottom. And then after that, if we're not called out to a fire there's the routine work which is programmed into the day. That can be anything from training to the more everyday jobs of cleaning and maintenance. Fitness of course is extremely important, so we also have a kind of mini gym where we work out every day.

I: Many listeners have phoned in saying they would like to know when your busiest period is.

AN: Well, we don't really have a 'busiest period,' despite the fact that most people might think it's November 5th, Guy Fawkes night. We do, however, tend to be busier in the evening, rather than during the day. That's the time when shops and other business premises are left unattended and also when most people are at home, cooking and so on, and as you might expect, the majority of fires are domestic ones. It's worth pointing out that the fires themselves often take only minutes to put out, whereas clearing up afterwards can take several hours. We have to do everything necessary to prevent the danger of a fire re-igniting, so that means taking all the floors up, getting flammable things like carpets out of the building, and so on.

I: Fire-fighting is obviously dangerous work, Allan. Do you ever feel fear?

AN: Any fire-fighter who said that he had never felt frightened would be fooling himself and you. But it's all a matter of control. It's what we've been trained for and we learn to control feelings such as fear. But rather than the danger and the drama of the job it's very satisfying being out on the street, knowing that you're helping the public. There's also the camaraderie which goes with working as part of a team. I certainly don't think I'd be able to do any other job.

Unit 6 (Page 70)

Listening 1

FCE Part 3 – Multiple matching

Speaker 1
My sister was always going out alone on her bike and she'd spend hours cycling along the country lanes. She'd come home with blackberries she'd picked and tales of wild rabbits she'd seen. I couldn't understand how anyone could get so excited about a rabbit. She went on to live on a farm and milked cows for a living. I left home when I was 16 and moved into a flat with a boy who played drums in a punk band. My parents were really upset. I had my hair cut really short and wore clothes that got all the neighbours talking. We're still both like chalk and cheese.

Speaker 2
She'd do anything just to be different. That often caused a lot of friction in the family and I know our parents had a really hard time. If the atmosphere got a bit tense I'd try to smooth things over. I was always there for my sister. Mum and Dad used to get really mad about the way she lived her life, but I'd always make excuses for her. And if she ever got into trouble I never told them the whole truth. I don't think they know half of what she got up to.

Speaker 3
During our early years at school the other kids used to tease her all the time and I watched her get called all kinds of names because of her skin colour. I could never understand why it was only her they picked on and not me, and I used to feel angry and guilty that I didn't get teased as well. It didn't seem fair that she had to put up with all the taunts alone.

Speaker 4
We might be twins but a lot of our personality traits are different. We don't share the same taste in clothes and we argue a lot, but then I think most brothers and sisters do, don't they? In our case it's because we want to be better than each other, at sports, at school and even at getting boyfriends. When people see us fighting they immediately think we don't get on with each other, but nothing could be further from the truth.

Speaker 5

She always liked dressing up and putting on loads of make up. When we were kids she always wore the shortest mini-skirts and she smelt like a perfume factory. She used to make fun of me because I was so plain and unconcerned about my appearance, and she laughed openly at my clothes. It never bothered me though. I knew I couldn't compete with her looks so I just laughed back. I called her 'Alexis' after that woman in one of those 70s soap operas on the telly.

Unit 6 (Page 75)

Writing

FCE Part 2 – Descriptions

M = Marion   S = Steven   K = Karen

M: Oh well, that's easy. I know who I'm going to write about.

K: Already?

M: Yes, the mysterious Eilean.

S: Go on then, Marion. What happened?

M: Well, it was last summer. We were driving down to the coast to spend a week with my relatives. All my dad's family live down in Brighton, about a five-hour drive from here. Anyway, just as we coming into the outskirts of the town all this steam started coming out of the engine. So we all got out of the car and mum and dad had a look under the bonnet, but all they could do was scratch their heads. They haven't the faintest idea about cars.

K: So what did you do?

M: Well fortunately this other car stopped and the driver offered to help. And that's how I met Eilean, his daughter. She was ready to sort out the problem herself but her dad told her she'd get herself dirty so *he* did it. I suppose the first thing I noticed about her was her clothes. They were 'hippy-style'– all long and flowing with lots of bright, cheerful colours. And that's how *she* was really – bright and cheerful and we had a real laugh together there on the side of the motorway, and on the one or two other occasions we met as well. She was also incredibly tall, with long flowing hair that seemed to go down as far as her knees.

S: She sounds a bit like one of my ex-girlfriends, Marcia.

K: One of the thousands, no doubt.

S: Actually, come to think of it, I could write about *her*. We were both watching this street entertainer, a magician he was, and he asked for two volunteers to come out onto his 'stage', which was this low wall. So – I went out and so did Marcia, and that's how we met. I remember thinking how soft her features were and when I looked into her eyes I realised I'd fallen for her in a big way.

M: How romantic!

S: And then the magician asked us to focus on this rabbit he had in a box, but I just couldn't keep my eyes off Marcia, so I didn't have a clue what was going on and the magician got quite angry. That's when she smiled at me and I got so nervous I nearly fell off the stage! Brought together by magic, we were.

M: That's almost what Eilean said, only she believed in Destiny, and according to her that's what caused us to meet. She was a bit strange, but I'd still like to have kept in touch with her. I *have* written a few times, but the most recent letters have gone unanswered and she seems to have disappeared off the face of the Earth.

S: Probably that magician again! How about you, Karen?

K: Well, it looks as if I'm going to have to make something up. Nothing like either of your two stories has ever happened to me. But, I often go walking in the mountains so I'm going to write about a rescue when I was trapped in the snow with a broken leg.

M: Sounds good.

K: It gets better. The man who rescued me was a gorgeous, well-built hunk with piercing blue eyes and a beautifully dark complexion, let's say – a – Mediterranean type.

S: Oh dream on!

M: And his gentle manner and soft spoken voice comforted me in the freezing cold and almost made me forget my pain. The best bit though was when he picked me up in his arms and carried me down the mountain – that can be my last paragraph, leaving the reader wondering what happened next.

S: I've just thought of another story – the one of how Marcia and I split up with each other. We were at the theatre one night and one of the actors kept looking at her ...

Unit 7 (Page 83)

Listening 1

FCE Part 2 – Note taking

A = Announcer   M = Matthew

A: And next on 'Consumer Watch' I have with me Matthew Brereton, UK head of the Safebuy supermarket chain. He's here to give away a few secrets on the psychology of supermarkets, and how the big companies design their shops. Matthew.

M: Thanks Barbara. Well, the layout of most major supermarkets is roughly the same, and for more or less the same reasons. You'll notice that the entrance, for example, is usually situated to one side of the building. This is to ensure, of course, that shoppers walk down as many aisles as possible before they leave the store. Ah – if we had it in the middle, then they might visit only one half of the supermarket and as a result only buy half as much. The first thing you often see as you come through the entrance is the fruit and vegetable area. As well as being pleasant to the eye, er, this also gives customers the impression they are coming into an outdoor market. Fresh, colourful products are far more attractive than tins of convenience food so the customer is put in a good mood, from the start.

A: A good mood to buy things, you mean?

M: Exactly. And next to the fruit and vegetable area is the confectionery; umm, crisps, chocolates, sweets and so on. Parents often come shopping with their children and we need to ensure that they are kept happy and interested so that they don't disturb mum and dad from the business of spending money. Then at the back of the supermarket in the corner you'll probably find the fresh meat counter. This is partly to make sure that as little room as possible is taken away from the main display areas by the staff who are serving. But it's also there so as not to distract customers when we have deliveries. Er, they really don't want to see us bringing big carcasses of meat through the store, so, er, it's brought in through the back door. And very close to the fresh meat you can expect to see the pre-packed meat. Ah, people who are put off by the sight of blood and um – dead animals prefer to buy their meat in the form of convenience food to prevent them having to make the connection between the product and the animal. Er, they buy a lamb chop, but they don't think of a baby lamb in the field. The freezer goods are nearby. There's a limited amount of space so the smaller suppliers often find it difficult to get room for their products. Ah, that's why you only tend to see the well-known brands here.

A: And how about those areas at the end of the aisle? How do you decide what to put there?

M: Yes, these are key selling sites, and sales of goods at these points can be as much as five times higher than other areas. So we generally move goods to the end of aisle areas when we want to sell them quickly: goods which have not been selling well, and especially those which are nearing their sell-by date. Bread, too, needs to be sold quickly, but we put the bakery section in the far corner, as far away from the entrance as possible, next to other basic foodstuffs such as milk. This is so that customers have to walk past hundreds of products to reach it. Um, it's expensive to run a bakery but it increases sales of other products. The smell, too, is an important factor as it helps to create a warm, homely atmosphere in the store.

A: And the alcoholic drinks. They're often at the far end too, aren't they Matthew?

M: Yes, very near the exit. Er, by this time the shopper is beginning to enjoy the shopping experience, so he or she will buy more alcohol if it's here than if it's by the entrance. Er, the same is true for those products we put at the checkouts; er, more sweets and chocolates, usually. The kind of things people buy on impulse as they wait to pay – er, a reward they give themselves for doing the shopping.

A: Thank you very much, Matthew, for taking us through that shopping experience. Next week, the department store and we'll be talking to …

Unit 7 (Page 90)

Listening 2

FCE Part 4 – Matching

I = Interviewer   R= Rebecca   G = Greg

I: What made you go and live in the countryside, Rebecca?

R: I suppose my priorities had changed with age. When I first went to London, I used to love the hustle and bustle of the place. But then I gradually became more aware of the planes roaring overhead, car horns beeping all the time, music blaring out at strange hours. I needed a break.

I: Greg, I can see you're smiling.

G: Yes. I remember when I first moved out with my family, we all found it a little too quiet. But we quickly got used to it, and now we prefer living with less noise. We also like the fact that you don't have to worry about the kids so much if they go off on their own.

R: Hmm, I'm not so sure. Some people drive like maniacs on those narrow roads. I feel I have to keep an even closer eye on my two kids than before. And there are lots of wide open spaces for them to get lost in, too.

G: But that's where the neighbours come in. Everyone seems to know everyone else's business in the village. That could be seen as an intrusion, but it's very handy if your kids go wandering off, or you're worried about burglars breaking into your house.

R: You're right there. In fact, we leave everything unlocked, and the neighbours sometimes just come into our house without even knocking on the door. We don't mind, though. It's like having a big extended family.

I: What about the amenities where you live?

G: The basics are within walking distance from us; the school, the shops, even a couple of tennis courts.

R: I wish I could say the same. We have to get the car out just to go and buy a loaf of bread. And you really do need to be able to drive to live where we do; the bus service is just too infrequent.

G: It's better than not having one at all. We're actually trying to get the local authorities to put on at least one bus a day, particularly for the older residents who don't have a car and who sometimes need to go into town.

R: Yes, and I'm actually wondering how my two are going to find it when they become teenagers. Well, they'll want to go into town, too. They'll probably complain of boredom and want us to go and live in the city again.

G: And who can blame them? I know at that age I would have been bored out of my mind! No cinemas, no decent shops, no cafés to sit in, no discos to go to …

I: Do you think either of you will ever go and live in the city again?

G: Naturally, I'd prefer to stay in the village and work at home rather than do a nine-to-five job in an office. I have my computer, e-mail and the phone and a wonderful working environment. However, anything can happen and we'd be prepared to move back to London if we felt it was to our advantage.

I: Rebecca?

R: I'll be going back to work just as soon as my youngest child starts school. Obviously I've thought about it a lot, and the fact that living where I do now will mean spending two hours driving to and from work every day. But I'd rather do that than give up my life in the country.

I: Well, thank you for both coming all that way to speak to us today. We'll have a break for music now and then it's competition time once again …

Unit 8 (Page 99)

Listening

FCE Part 1 – Multiple choice

One

We really didn't expect this. We thought it'd be the typical economy type hotel. You know, nothing special, just a bed, a wardrobe and a shower in the room if you're lucky. Well, the en suite bathroom was a big surprise, I can tell you. It's twice the size of ours at home. And as for the view from the balcony, it's unbelievable. We really can't complain.

Two

… and I think that although my experience running a restaurant may not seem very relevant, it's still a people-orientated job. I am definitely a 'people person'. I like dealing with the public. So whether it's listening to customers and giving them advice on the best places to go, or talking on the phone to tour operators and trying to get the best deal, I think I'd be well suited to the job. I have good people skills and I think that's an important strength.

Three

TG = Tour Guide   W = Woman

TG: Are you sure you had it when you left the hotel?

W: Positive: I didn't want to bring it but my husband made me put it in my bag. He said you should never leave your money or your passport in your room. And then when we
were having a drink and I went to pay, it had gone. Well, someone must have put their hand in when I wasn't looking.

TG: We'll have to report it straight away.

Four

We went there because we wanted to see the stained glass windows. They say they're among the finest in Europe and the colours are supposed to be incredible when the sun shines through them. Unfortunately we couldn't go in because we weren't properly dressed – they won't let you in if you're wearing short trousers. And the next morning when we went back it was Easter Sunday. So of course, we couldn't get to the part where the windows are because there was a special service.

Five

M = Man   B = Boy

M: Yes, your skin is quite badly burnt. How long were you out in the sun for?

B: About an hour, maybe. It was after lunch and I fell asleep on the beach.

M: Do you have any other symptoms – dizziness, a temperature?

B: No, it just really hurts.

M: Well, it doesn't sound like sunstroke. This cream should take away the sting, but if you start to feel sick or dizzy, get yourself to a doctor straight away.

B: Thanks. How much do I owe you?

M: I'll just check. One second.

Six

I shouldn't complain really. I mean, the whole economy of this town is based on tourism and if they stopped coming, then a lot of people would be out of work and on the dole. But I do wish they'd show a little more respect. There are a lot of them who have music blaring out of their cars during the day, and then at night you get big groups coming into the centre for the pubs and clubs. And they don't seem to care that we can't sleep with them making such a racket. Most of them drunk, I shouldn't wonder.

Seven

B = Boy   M = Mother

B: Where are we going?

M: Well, we picked up a leaflet for a nature park just outside the town. They've got all sorts of wild animals and you can drive through and see them in their natural habitat. It looks very good.

B: But you said we were going to go to the Aqua Park.

M: We can't go in this weather. And besides, your father and I want to do something different.

B: But that's not fair. You can't just change your mind like that.

M: Don't be selfish, Steven. It's our turn today.

Eight

No, the 14th ... That's right. Saturday the 14th ... Well my plans have changed and I'm not going to Bristol any more. I couldn't get anywhere to stay there, so I had to find somewhere in the city of Bath ... But I don't see why I have to pick it up two days before. Surely you could just give me the new one the day I travel, on the 14th ... Yes, I appreciate that's the procedure, but it's very inconvenient.

Unit 9 (Page 108)

Listening

FCE Part 4 – True/False

I = Interviewer   A = Alastair Agnew

I: We have in the studio today Alastair Agnew, Chairman of the Ghost Club in London. He's here to give us some advice on how to correctly identify ghosts. Alastair, a see-through figure in white that walks through walls. That's a fair enough description of a ghost, isn't it?

A: Well, only one out of three correct, I'm afraid Jean. Far from having the translucent appearance they do in the films, ghosts look solid, just like real people. The only thing that gives them away is the fact that, as you rightly say, they can walk through walls. And the only reason they do *that* is that when they were alive the wall may not have existed. Indeed, what's interesting is that in many cases you may only see them from the knees upwards, due to the fact that the ground level was lower in their day.

I: And how about the noises we usually associate with ghosts? The footsteps and the moaning sounds we all make when we imitate one ...

A: ... and the sound of laughter, crying and even the noise of music. Yes, these have all been heard when ghosts have been sighted. In fact, in a study carried out in England it was revealed that in 39 per cent of hauntings people claimed to have heard ghostly footsteps. One popular explanation for these sounds is the 'stone-tape theory'.

I: And what does that say?

A: That the brickwork or stones of a building can somehow absorb sounds and later play them back, rather like a tape recorder. And the same theory is used to explain some of the smells which are given off when ghosts are around. Smells such as decaying flesh, baking bread or animal odours are supposedly absorbed into the walls and then later released. So a building that was once used as a church for example may give off the smell of incense.

I: And as Chairman of the Ghost Club you would not agree with that explanation, would you?

A: It may account for some of the phenomena, but it certainly does not prove that ghosts do not exist. Sceptics have yet to put forward a theory to explain why, for example, some people have their hair stroked or sometimes feel a sharp poke in the side of their body when no one else is around.

I: And are there any places where ghosts are more likely to occur than others?

A: If your house is on or near a crossroads, you may well be haunted. That's because these used to be burial places for suicides and many criminals who were hanged nearby. The number of car crashes at crossroads is also presumed to raise the spirit count. And even if you don't live on a crossroads, if you wait at one for a bus, there's a good chance a spirit will follow you and give you a bit of a surprise.

I: And finally Alastair, are we all able to see ghosts?

A: Certainly, yes, though some people are more likely to attract paranormal attention than others. Similarly, some household pets are also good indicators that there's a spirit in the vicinity. Dogs for example may stubbornly refuse to enter one part of a room or start growling without explanation if they sense a ghost. Cats may hiss and spit, while a budgie or a hamster will look on wondering what all the fuss is about.

I: Thank you Alastair. So then, if you or your dog think you might have spotted a ghost, the Ghost Club would love to hear from you. We'll be giving out their address at the end of the programme. Now it's over to Jeremy ...

Unit 9 (Page 109)

Language Focus – Question tags

2

That's a fair enough description of a ghost, isn't it?
And as chairman of the Ghost Club you would not agree with that explanation, would you?

3

You don't believe him, do you?
You won't let me down, will you?
You went away for the weekend, didn't you?
He's not playing very well, is he?
He's already passed First Certificate, hasn't he?
I'm right about that, aren't I?
You can play chess, can't you?
Let's phone Paul, shall we?

Unit 10 (Page 123)

Listening 1

FCE Part 2 – Note taking

P = Presenter   O = Police Officer

P: And now it's time for our regular 'Crimewatch' slot and here with us today is Police Officer Richard Woodcock from the Crime Prevention Unit of the Metropolitan Police. Richard, perhaps you could begin by telling us what characterises a typical burglary.

O: Well, burglary is one of the crimes most people worry about, not so much because of the loss of property, but more because of the sense of invasion it causes – the idea that someone has gone through all your personal belongings. Many residential burglaries occur because of common misconceptions. For example, while people typically worry about night-time thefts, nearly 50 per cent of residential break-ins happen during the day, when homes are vacant because owners are out working . What's more, robbing a house takes less time than many people think. Most burglars get in and out in less than ten minutes.

P: And how does the police go about combating the problem?

O: Police forces all over the country have targeted burglary. Operation Bumblebee, for example, was a major crime-prevention campaign run by the Metropolitan Police and aimed at beating the burglars. The scheme has included raids on criminals who are known to sell stolen goods. At the end of Operation Bumblebee's first year burglaries fell by 13 per cent, a figure which has to be considered a success.

P: And what would you say are the most important measures our listeners can take to protect their own homes?

O: Most householders are aware of the risk of being burgled and the majority have already installed locks on doors and windows. What many of these same people don't do, however, is use them! So rule number one is lock up before you go out. And whatever you do, don't leave spare keys under the doormat, thinking that no one is going to find them. It's the most obvious place for a burglar to look and an open invitation to walk in unchallenged. If you have another set of keys leave them with a trusted neighbour or friend. A home alarm system is another must, and a good deterrent to any would-be burglars, but make sure you have it put in by an installer who works to the British standard. Your local crime prevention officer can give you advice on how to choose an installer. And I mentioned locks earlier, but don't forget about the garage door as well. This can provide easy access for burglars, allowing them to gain access not only to your car, but directly into your home if there's an adjoining door.

P: Thank you, Richard. Now, many listeners have phoned in asking about Neighbourhood Watch Schemes and how to set them up. What information can you give them?

O: Well, the best thing about these schemes is that they bring the community together and provide everyone with the chance to fight local crime. Your neighbours look out for you, your family, your home and your street, and you do the same for them. If you see anyone acting suspiciously near a neighbour's house, you contact the police .It especially enables people to check on vulnerable members of the community, such as the elderly or disabled. The schemes have come a long way since the early view some people held of nosy neighbours interfering in other people's business. There are now more than 155,000 Neighbourhood Watch schemes in the country, with more than ten million residents directly benefiting from them. It's the largest voluntary organisation in the country and one of the most effective for beating crime.

P: And where should listeners go to ask about starting one?

O: The local police station will tell you all about it or you can phone the National Neighbourhood Watch Association on – and I have the number here – 020 72 72 3348.

P: Thank you Richard. We'll give that number again at the end of the programme ...

Unit 10 (Page 131)

Listening 2

FCE Part 3 – Multiple matching

Speaker 1

My mum gave me nearly £100 in cash to pay for a trip to France with my school. When I went to give the money to the French teacher, I couldn't find it anywhere. I knew my mum would be angry with me for losing it – so I told her I'd been mugged by two boys on the way to school. So she phoned the school, who called the police and when they came to the school to interview me the next day, they realised I was lying, because I kept giving different descriptions of my attackers. I've never been told off by so many people – my mum, the teachers, the police. Later that day I realised I needn't have lied after all – I found the money in the bottom of my jacket pocket.

Speaker 2

We were just going shopping, not far away, just to the shopping centre in town. And anyway, I was supposed to check that all the windows were closed upstairs in the house – before we left, like. Well, I forgot, didn't I, and when dad asked me if I'd remembered to 'check the windows were closed' I couldn't be bothered to get out of the car and go back to do it. So I said I had. Well, we were only going to be out for a short while, so I thought we didn't need to worry. That morning we were burgled – we lost £3,000 worth of stuff, including my whole music system. I had to own up – I mean it was obvious they got in through the window, wasn't it? And there was no sign of forced entry.

Speaker 3

We weren't allowed to have parties in our house when I was a teenager, my mum and dad wouldn't let us. They didn't really approve of our friends – they didn't want them smoking in the house and spilling drinks and stuff on the new carpet. So when they went away for the weekend to celebrate their wedding anniversary, me and my brother decided to have a celebration of our own, with some friends, of course. We would have got away with it – if they hadn't phoned up in the middle of the party. They heard all the music and all our friends and everything. They never let us do anything after that.

Speaker 4

I once wrote a note to my teacher, you know, a fake one in my mum's handwriting, so I could get out of doing sport. My mum found out and went mad. I'd written a couple of practice letters before doing the final copy, you know, to practise her writing, and the next day she found them in the bin. I should have burned them or torn them up into pieces. I can still hear her now: "You've let us down, my boy. We've brought you up to be honest and you've let us down." She was really upset. I didn't have to do sport, though.

Speaker 5

All the time I was growing up I don't think I ever told one lie to my parents. There were things I got up to, you know, things I wasn't supposed to do that I did, like most people. I mean I wasn't an angel, by any means. I smoked the odd cigarette with friends, got into trouble at school for not being polite to teachers, that kind of thing. But if I wanted to do something like go to an all night party I knew how to get round my dad so he'd let me go. You know, I'd wash his car or offer to do the gardening or something like that. But telling lies? No, I didn't need to do that.

Unit 11 (Page 137)

Listening 1

FCE Part 2 – Note taking

I = Interviewer   P = Paul Murphy

I: So Paul, how did you get involved with the International Rescue Corps?

P: One of the founder members of the organisation lived near me in the East of England. He helped set up the IRC way back in 1981 after the Italian earthquake. He was a friend of mine but also a fellow fire-fighter. I joined because I've got a skill to offer, and I thought it would be exciting to travel all over the world rescuing people.

I: And how many missions have you been on?

P: Eight abroad – seven earthquakes and a hurricane – and about 10 in the UK. Er, in this country we're often called upon to find missing people, especially in bad weather. Er, if a disaster strikes a foreign country, we sometimes make offers of help to the government there via the British Embassy, but more often than not the country goes to the United Nations and er, asks for rescue teams like ours.

I: And what can IRC offer that other agencies can't?

P: As well as being able to offer our services free of charge, we carry our own specialist equipment for finding and saving people who are trapped in collapsed buildings. That includes fibre optic probes, where we can put a camera into the smallest of holes to see what's happening, microphones to pick up voices or vibrations and thermal imaging to detect heat.

I: Who pays for you to go?

P: IRC is a charity, and none of our members receives any kind of payment. They're volunteers, so they also have to ask for time off work to go abroad.

I: What's the worst weather you've worked in, Paul?

P: Armenia was freezing cold but Nicaragua was bad because of the heat and mosquitoes, which never stopped biting. And the rain was horrendous, too. When we got there the hurricane had been reclassified as a tropical storm, but we had to suffer torrential rain all the time we were there.

I: What's the most amazing survival story you have come across?

P: I suppose it has to be the time we went to Japan after the Kobe earthquake. Er, one woman had been trapped for over 40 hours when we discovered she was there, and it took us another four hours to get her out. The remarkable thing about that is that normally, once people have been trapped for 24 hours after an earthquake, not many come out alive. The thing which saved her was a wardrobe, which had fallen on top of her and protected her from the falling debris. She was partly inside it. And I remember the first thing she said when we finally got her out was that she was bored! Not the kind of emotion you'd expect from an earthquake victim, is it?

I: Certainly not! And what advice would you give to people if they get caught in an earthquake?

P: As soon as you feel the slightest shake, get out of the building and into the open air. That's often easier said than done, of course, especially if you're on the tenth floor when it happens. Um, if it's not possible to get out, then you should take cover in the safest area of the building to stop other things falling on you. But really it's up to the governments of countries in earthquake zones to take the initiative and construct safer buildings. In this way damage is minimised and lives are saved.

I: Thank you, Paul, and the best of luck on your future missions.

Unit 11 (Page 143)

Listening 2

FCE Part 1 – Multiple choice

One
I really can't understand why they put it all the way out there.

They maintained that if they'd built it in the heart of the city there would have been problems getting out to fires in the rural areas. Too far and too much traffic, they said. But that's exactly why it would have made more sense to build it in the centre instead of on the edge. You know, it takes a fire engine nearly 20 minutes to get from that suburb to the other side of the city.

Two

If I was a member of the Council I'd make sure something was done about the mess on the streets. It's an absolute disgrace. Local people need more help to keep them clean, and that help has to come from the authorities. There aren't enough litter bins, for one thing, so the pavements outside my premises are covered with paper, drink cans and cigarette butts. Before I open up in the morning I have to spend about 10 minutes sweeping it all up. I wouldn't sell anything if I didn't.

Three

You have to remember that some species of plants were facing extinction in the area. People would come out to the countryside for a picnic, see all these beautiful flowers and pick them, without realising the effect this was having. If we hadn't made this a conservation area and limited the number of people coming in, then we'd have no flowers at all, and people would be really upset. As it is, we can congratulate ourselves on the action we took and look forward to a brighter future for this patch of countryside.

Four

W1 = Woman 1   W2 = Woman 2

W1: So what was it like?
W2: Marvellous. Just what we were looking for.
W1: And what was that?
W2: Well, if we'd gone to one of the other islands, we'd have had to put up with busy roads and crowded beaches.
W1: So weren't there many tourists where you went?
W2: Oh plenty. More than we expected really. But it didn't seem to matter, because with the vehicle restrictions there was almost a total lack of exhaust fumes, no congestion and very little noise. And because the island's so small, you could walk everywhere anyway.

Five

M = Man   W = Woman

M: I think we should all get together and decide what we're going to do. I can't put up with it any more.
W: Neither can we. The noise of that boy's music makes the whole house shake. My husband says it's just like being in an earthquake, only worse.
M: Of course it's the parents' fault, but it's no good talking to them. They're no better than he is.
W: And his teachers can't control him, either. Apparently, he's as rude to them as he is to all of us.
M: So, let's have a meeting of all the residents in the street and we'll decide how to deal with him.

Six

Violent storms swept across the south coast today, causing widespread damage to property. Torrential rain and gale-force winds lashed seaside towns and several people had to be evacuated from their flooded homes by rescue services. One man in Bognor narrowly escaped death as the car he was driving was crushed by a falling tree, which had been struck by lightning.

Seven

W = Woman   M = Man

W: What's the problem, John?
M: Well, we lost a lot of our plants last night.
W: It wasn't our cat, was it?
M: No, the wind. Pulled up all the roses, it did. Blew down a few bushes, too.
W: I'm sorry to hear that.
M: Oh, not to worry. I'd be grateful if you'd give me a hand to clear up the mess, though.
W: I'd be pleased to.

Eight

Something's got to be done. These massive petrol tankers should just not be allowed to sail so close to our shores. The oil slick has already killed thousands of birds and the beaches are a disaster area. Demonstrating is all very well, but it's not going to clean up the mess, is it? We can't leave it in the hands of the politicians, so we've just got to get down to the coast and get our hands dirty with the rest of the volunteers. You coming?

Unit 12 (Page 147)

Listening 1

FCE Part 3 – Multiple matching

Speaker 1
I tried crash diets, such as one where you just eat cabbage soup, and another where you drink nothing but lemonade with some salt and pepper for about seven days without any food. They worked temporarily, but after a while I put the weight back on. Then I was introduced to these diet pills and my weight went down to 65 kilos. But I wasn't earning a great deal of money and I simply couldn't afford to keep it up. That's when I decided to save my money and join a gym.

Speaker 2
I used to eat a lot of junk food. It was quick, inexpensive and it satisfied my hunger immediately. The problem was, I ate very little fresh food, and this had a serious effect on my health. I became overweight and suffered all sorts of illnesses. The doctor strongly advised me to rethink my attitude to food. If not, he said, the consequences could be very serious. Well, you can't ignore advice like that, can you? So I started to eat more healthily. And now if I get hungry between meals, I have a little cheese or some nuts, just to fill the hole.

Speaker 3
I'm under no real pressure to lose weight, but I take care over what I eat, simply because it makes me feel better. When I want to treat myself I have a piece of cake or a few biscuits. I read a lot about dieting, and most nutritionists seem to agree that as long as you eat sweet things after a meal, then there's no problem. So, for example, I only ever eat chocolates after lunch or dinner. And never too many of course – just one or two.

Speaker 4
I like eating and I'm not at all interested in dieting. But I do

go to see a nutritionist, who helps me maintain a sensible, balanced diet: plenty of fresh fruit and vegetables, meat and fish, carbohydrates such as rice and pasta, several glasses of water a day – and no snacks between meals. She told me to give up cheese, but I ignored her. I enjoy good food and I don't want to deprive myself of the things I love.

Speaker 5

A large number of people follow diets, but very few of them are happier as a result. We are constantly under attack from advertising and the media, who tell us that 'thin is beautiful'. I used to believe this and think that I wouldn't find a boyfriend unless I was really skinny, that I had to weigh under 60 kilos for boys to like me. But of course, now I realise that there's more to it than that. Just being yourself is what counts and I don't pay much attention to what others think or say.

Ready for Listening (Page 158)

Part 1 – Multiple choice

Two

These two sides are very well matched. You'll remember they both met in the semi-finals last year, when the game ended in a draw. This year we've had some heavy showers in the last few days and one or two of the players are finding the playing conditions on the pitch more than a little difficult. But it's a throw-in now. Briggs takes it and passes to Duckham. Duckham tries a shot … and it goes just wide of the post.

Three

I thought at first it was some kind of virus, but now I'm wondering if it might be something more serious … No, it's annoying. I simply can't do any work on it at the moment … Yes, I phoned them, but they said they'd need to have it for three days before they could give me an answer … Well, I was wondering if you wouldn't mind having a look at it for me … Could you come round after work? … No, that's great; the sooner the better as far as I'm concerned, as long as your boss doesn't mind.

Four

M = Man   W = Woman

M: Lots of room for the legs, that's nice.
W: Mm, and so comfortable. It's like my favourite armchair. I could go to sleep here and now.
M: Yes, we should've had a coffee after the meal to keep us awake.
W: We'd never have got a ticket to see this if we had.
M: That's true. The queue was enormous.
W: Anyway, wake me up when it starts, won't you?

Five

You can't fault the food, really. Even my husband was impressed and he's always the first to complain if it's not cooked properly. No, I just felt a little uncomfortable; silver cutlery, antique furniture and everyone dressed as if it was a wedding, including the waiters. And the way they spoke to us! It was 'Sir' and 'Madam' every sentence. I suppose I'm just not used to it, that's all.

Six

W = Woman   M = Man

W: Just look at that. It's incredible.
M: What do you mean?
W: Well, there must be about 20 different types of butter in this section. Low-fat, high-fat, Irish, Dutch, Australian – you name it, they've got it.
M: Confusing, isn't it?
W: That's not the point. I'm sure a lot of people will be disappointed there aren't 20 types of carrots and 60 different varieties of cheese. I just don't see why we need them all. And when you think of the transport costs and the fuel needed to import all this stuff and the effect this has on the environment. It makes my blood boil.

Seven

The play finishes at about 11 … Well, I had at first thought of coming back on the train straight afterwards, but the last one's at 11.05, so I probably wouldn't make it … Are you sure you don't mind? … I could always stay in a hotel. There are plenty of cheap ones in that part of town … OK, well, if you're going to put me up for the night, then you'll have to let me take you out for a meal … No, I insist.

Eight

We all know juvenile crime's on the increase. The police do all they can with very limited resources and then it's up to people like ourselves to sort the problem out. In this school alone we have more than 20 youngsters with a criminal record and we get virtually no support from the parents. Social services come in occasionally to give us advice on how to deal with them, but once they've gone and we close the classroom door, we're very much on our own.

Ready for Listening (Pages 159–160)

Part 2 – Note taking

Before everyone goes off to bed perhaps I could have your attention to run through the programme for the next two days. In fact, tomorrow morning we're actually going *out* of Cardiff. Er, it gets very busy at the Rhondda Heritage Park on a Saturday, so we've decided to go there tomorrow to avoid the crowds. Now, we'll need to make an early start as it takes an hour to get there, so we'd like you to be in the hotel reception at 9 o'clock, straight after breakfast. The Heritage Park has a fascinating exhibition on the Welsh coal-mining industry, which was once so important to Cardiff, and as part of the exhibition there's a tour which actually takes you underground.

After lunch in a restaurant we'll come back to the Cardiff Bay Visitor Centre, where we'll spend some time and go for a very pleasant walk around the freshwater lake which has been created as part of the new development there. As you already know, the weather is very changeable so it's a good idea to have a raincoat with you, just in case.

When you get back in the evening, you might like to hear the wonderful singing of a Welsh male voice choir. If you'd like to go tickets are only £4.50, and if you take your children and they're under 14, they can go in for just over half price.

Now, on Saturday morning we've kept the programme free so you can go and do some shopping in the town centre. The

Saint David's Centre is the large indoor shopping mall, but I'd recommend going first to the area around St Mary Street which has a lovely old covered market and some particularly good bookshops which you can browse in. If you're looking for souvenirs and you can't find any in that part of town, then head for David Morgan's where you'll find a whole souvenir section on the ground floor of this large department store.

Um, for lunch we thought it would be nice to have a picnic in Bute Park, which is situated between Cardiff castle and the river. We'll see you all just outside the castle entrance at one, and if the weather's bad we can make alternative arrangements. What we'll probably do if it's raining is take our lunch with us and have it at Hensol in the Vale of Glamorgan, which is where we're going to spend the afternoon. Believe it or not, you'll have a chance to taste the local wine at one of the vineyards there. The climate in South Wales is relatively mild and they've been growing grapes in the area for many years.

We'll be back at the hotel for dinner at 7.30, and then after that we have one or two cultural suggestions for the evening. Of interest perhaps to the younger members of our group, there's a rock concert at the Cardiff International Arena starting at 9. I have to confess I'm not exactly sure who's playing, but if anyone's interested I can certainly find out. If that doesn't appeal then the Welsh National Opera are performing Bizet's 'Carmen' at their base in the New Theatre.

Now that's rather a lot of information ...

Ready for Listening (Page 160)

Part 3 – Multiple matching

Speaker 1
I've been writing for as long as I can remember, and it's something I want to continue to do for a living when I've finished university. I say 'continue' because I've already had one collection of short stories published and I've just started another. I write mostly late at night and at weekends, always after I've finished my course work. I'm doing a maths degree, which has little to do with writing, but I believe in keeping my options open, just in case my creativity runs out.

Speaker 2
For some strange reason I want to be a tattoo artist; you know, paint people's bodies. I'm doing a course in graphic design at art college, which I've been told will be useful. The brother of a friend of mine has a studio and he lets me go and watch him work when I'm not studying at the college. It's the only way to learn, as there are no official courses and no specific qualifications for tattoo artists. At least, not as far as I know.

Speaker 3
As soon as I leave school I'm going to join the Army. I tried to do it when I was 10 but they told me to go back when I was older – so I will! You can learn a trade and do almost any job you want to, and they let you study while you're working. I'd like to work as a physical training instructor, and then maybe later try and get an engineering qualification or something like that. My granddad's an ex-soldier and he always told such good stories that I knew that was what I wanted to do. My parents just think I'm crazy.

Speaker 4
I hope one day to be a speech therapist. I'll have to get a degree in speech therapy first, and to do that I'll need to get good grades next year in my 'A' levels. It's a job which involves helping people who have difficulty communicating, and I've always known I wanted to work in one of the 'caring professions'. My uncle's a speech therapist, but I learnt all about it from a TV documentary I saw a few years ago. And that's when I thought; "I want to do that". Then last year I did some voluntary work while I was studying for my GCSEs, and I was hooked.

Speaker 5
I haven't made up my mind yet, but I'd quite like to go into teaching. Naturally I've had lots of advice from teachers at school about how to go about it and how hard I'll have to work for my exams. But to be honest my decision is based not so much on my academic abilities but rather on the fact that I just feel I'd be right for the job. The teachers I look up to at school are all dynamic, outgoing people and that's precisely how I like to see *myself*.

Ready for Listening (Page 161)

Part 4 – Multiple choice

I = Interviewer   J = Jenny Hadley

I: On *Youth Matters* today we look at what it's like to have a famous dad. Jenny Hadley's here to tell us about life with her pop star father, Tony Hadley, from the top 1980s band, Spandau Ballet. Ask your mum if you've never heard of them! Jenny, when did you become aware that your dad was famous?

J: One of my earliest memories is from when I was six, at a Spandau Ballet concert in Spain. My mum used to take me and my older brother Tom to go and visit my dad when he was on tour around the world. Tom and I were both asked to go up on stage and I can remember sitting on the shoulders of the saxophonist, looking out at thousands of people, all cheering and clapping after a song.

I: And how do you feel now about having a famous dad?

J: Because I've grown up with Dad being famous, it's never really been an issue. I've never seen him as different from anyone else, but I always knew that his profession was a bit unusual. When my friends see his old pop videos on TV they think it's really exciting, but in the family we're all used to his face being on screen. If we're in the living room, we'll mostly ignore it and carry on with what we were doing.

I: How do other people react when they find out who your father is?

J: I can remember when I started secondary school, my art teacher was reading the register, and when she got to my name she paused, looked up and said; "You're not *the* Tony Hadley's daughter are you?" I got embarrassed and my face went bright red as the rest of the class all stared at me asking, "Who's Tony Hadley?" People of my age are too young to remember Spandau Ballet but their mums tell me they used to have his poster on their wall, or that they have his albums, and I think that's cool. I'm really pleased to know that people feel like that about him.

I: What's it like when you're out with your dad?

J: Dad gets recognised virtually everywhere we go. When someone says "Hi", he always stops to chat, which can get dead frustrating, 'cause he *loves* to talk! He's always been incredibly patient with his fans, but I sometimes wish he'd just say, "Sorry, can't stop," and keep walking. He's always in a good mood – he loves to laugh and mess around and he's great fun to be with.

I: Does he have a *lot* of fans?

J: Oh yes! We get tons of fan mail and presents sent to our house and at Christmas they even send stuff to *me* and the rest of the family: things like chocolates, clothes, make-up… It's nice that they think of us, but it's not so nice when they hang around in front of the house, hoping to catch a glimpse of dad. And very often, if he's not in, they stay there until he gets home. That's one of the drawbacks of it all, I suppose.

I: So you have no desire to be famous yourself, I take it.

J: Actually, the acting profession really appeals to me, so all this is good experience. But he wants me to concentrate on my studies for now and wait until I've done my exams before going to drama school. He's pretty conventional in that sense but I respect his opinions.

I: And have you met many other famous people?

J: Yes I have. I've been lucky enough to meet quite a few, like George Michael, Boy George and Queen. But one of the best things that ever happened to me was when I was taken to Geri Halliwell's birthday party by my Auntie Gail and her friend, Shirlie, from Wham! I've always been a fan of Geri's so it was great to meet her. My friends asked me to get her autograph, but that wouldn't have been very cool. We chatted for ages about her work with young people as a UN ambassador. I'd love to meet her again: we got on really well.

L: Who knows? Maybe one day she'll be asking for *your* autograph.

J: I don't think so, somehow!

Unit 13 (Page 168)

Listening 1

FCE Part 4 – Yes/No

A = Announcer   G = Grace

A: Grace, how long have you had problems with your eyes?

G: Well, I was actually born completely blind and my sight didn't develop until I was about a year old. Ever since that age I've only ever been able to see out of one eye. I kind of got used to that, and thought it was quite normal. Then one day when I was about eight I was having a bit of a laugh with my mum. Just for a joke she covered up my left eye, the good one, and said, "How many fingers?" and I said, "I don't know?" "What do you mean you don't know?" she said. She thought I was playing around, but when she realised I wasn't she took me straight down to the doctor. That's when I found out I have an incurable eye disease, which may or may not get worse, but definitely won't get any better.

A: And *has* it got worse?

G: Not really, no. It's been more or less the same ever since. Though I was having a check-up when I was a bit older and they discovered I had tunnel vision as well.

A: What exactly is that?

G: It means I only have central view. I don't have any lateral view, so I'm unable to see anything which isn't directly in front of me. Not like most people who can see slightly to the side when they look ahead. It sounds a bit weird, but to me it's normal.

A: So did you have to go to a special school when you were younger?

G: I was determined to go to a normal school because I was convinced that if I did it would teach me to cope better. I kind of suspected, and my parents warned me, that it wouldn't be easy. You know how cruel kids of 11 and 12 can be to each other. And sure enough they called me names and bullied me and I must have cried every day for a year. And I did get to the point when I wanted to leave, but my dad told me to carry on and see it through. He said it'd get better – and it did. A lot of those who'd called me names became good friends.

A: You eventually left school at 16 , didn't you?

G: That's right. I guess I got to the point where I felt like I knew that all I wanted to do was sing and play the guitar. My dad said I was too young and tried to put me off the idea. But then when he saw how determined I was, he told me I'd need to get a job if I wanted to save up enough money to record a demo. So I did get a job and very quickly managed to get enough money together to do the demo.

A: And that led to your first record deal.

G: And everything else that went with it – the contacts, the song writing, the touring. I love it all, especially going on tour, though you wouldn't believe the stresses and strains involved. Most people think it's a breeze, like dead easy and no worries. But the way I see it, you have a kind of responsibility when you're up there on stage. Being an entertainer is all about being larger than life and making people feel good.

A: So you've come a long way from your schooldays when the other kids made you cry!

G: Right. But in a way going through that experience at school helped me get over my shyness. So I don't worry any more what people think about my eyes. I'm far too busy worrying about what they think of my music!

A: Well, your first single was a number one hit in America, so you certainly don't seem to have anything to worry about there …

Unit 13 (Page 171)

Listening 2

FCE Part 1 – Multiple choice

One

Of course, I wasn't very happy about him losing his job. We had a few sleepless nights, I can tell you, what with the mortgage to pay and two hungry kids to feed. But no one was to blame for what happened, and thankfully it all worked out in the end. I'm just glad it's all over now. I don't know how we'd have managed to cope if he hadn't been taken on at the power station.

Two

W = Woman   M = Man

W: Dave's done well for himself, hasn't he?

M: Yes, well, it's hardly surprising, is it?

W: Why do you say that?

M: Well, it was the same thing at school. Fortune always smiled on him. He passed exams with the minimum of effort and now he's making money in the same way. He makes a few good decisions, invests in the right companies and bingo! Suddenly he's a millionaire. Still, it

Tapescripts

couldn't happen to a nicer guy. No one deserves it more
than him.

Three

M = Man   W = Woman

M: Looking forward to going rock climbing, Sally?
W: Well, to tell you the truth, I haven't made up my mind
about it. Everyone tells me it's great fun, especially when
you realize that you're quite safe, with all the ropes and
everything. But what if you get stuck and can't go on?
That's what worries me. I can't see I'm going to enjoy
myself, clinging to a rock waiting for someone to come
and pull me off. Still, I won't know if I don't try, will I?

Four

Yes, well, we're very pleased you actually managed to phone
us. At least you've done something right. You may have
noticed, however, that it is now two o'clock in the morning …
Yes, but you said you would be home by 12. If you can't keep
promises then you shouldn't make them … No, we can't come
and pick you up. You're old enough to be able to solve your
own problems now.

Five

Oh come on, you said you'd help me out. I'll pay you back as
soon as I get paid. It's just that it's our anniversary and I want
to take her someone special to celebrate. … I can't ask mum!
You know how she is with money. She didn't lend you any
that time you were broke, so I don't see why it'd be any
different for me.

Six

W = Woman   M = Man

W: How on earth did you manage to get in such a mess?
M: It's toner from the photocopier. I was changing it and it
went all over my clothes.
W: If your mother could see you now, she'd have a fit!
M: Have you got anything to clean it off with?
W: No, you'll have to go next door and get something from
the shop. But don't take too long about it. I've got a few
jobs I want you to do in sales department.

Seven

I'd like to say how flattered I feel to have been invited to open
this magnificent sports centre. And I am particularly proud
of the fact that you voted unanimously for my name to be
given to the centre. If I think back to all my sporting
successes, the medals I have won and records I've broken,
none of them ever gave me as much pleasure as this moment
today. As a child growing up in this area, I never dreamed I
would one day …

Eight

What I like about it is that you're doing things that nobody
else has done before, discovering things about yourself as
well as the world you live in. I've been to places I never knew
existed until I got there, and I've travelled enormous
distances without seeing another living soul. It's not whether
it's the highest, the hottest or the coldest that matters to me,
but being the first person to set foot there. That's why I do it.

Unit 14 (Page 179)

Listening

FCE Part 4 – Multiple choice

P = Presenter   S = Sue

P: Sue, welcome to the studio. Tell us about your recent dive.
How did you come to be in a shark tank?
S: A very good question! I did ask myself that a few times as
well! No, I'd been scuba diving for two years when my
dive club arranged a diving trip at the Deep Sea World
Aquarium near Edinburgh. It sounded really exciting and
a bit different – I mean, there's not much chance of diving
with sharks in British waters. The aquarium lets visitors
come face to face with sharks, rays, eels and hundreds of
fish protected by the world's longest underwater aquarium
tunnel. But a group of friends and I were allowed to go
one step further and actually get into the water with all
the marine life, including the sharks.
P: And what was the reaction to the news that you were
going to be diving with sharks?
S: Well I was probably the most worried of anybody. When I
went through the tunnel beforehand just to have a look at
the sharks, they looked so big, and there seemed to be so
many of them. I have to confess I did feel quite frightened
at that stage. My non-diving friends just thought I was
mad, but diving ones were really quite envious!
P: And did you have to wear any special gear for the dive?
S: Not really – just my usual dive kit, which includes dry suit,
cylinder and mask. However, we weren't allowed to use
flippers in case we accidentally disturbed any of the
fragile marine life in the tank. Instead, we walked very
carefully on the aquarium floor with lead weights in our
pockets to prevent us from floating.
P: Did you receive any training to dive in the aquarium?
S: The aquarium is very strict about who they let dive in
their tanks. Every diver must prove that they're fully
qualified and experienced. We dived in groups of four,
plus a guide from the aquarium.
P: What were the sharks like?
S: Huge – they were all around three to four metres long. It
was amazing watching them swim above our heads,
seeing their rows of razor-sharp teeth. We had to be
careful that the bubbles from our breathing gear didn't get
into the sharks' gills, as that could affect their breathing.
We were also told not to get in the way of their tails,
which are incredibly muscular and could possibly break a
limb.
P: Were you told what to do if attacked?
S: Our guide was in front of us the whole time and watched
the sharks constantly. We were assured there'd be no
danger of attack as it wasn't their usual feeding time. In
fact, shark attacks are very rare and usually occur when
they think they may be attacked themselves or if they
mistake people for a food source.
P: What was it like being in the aquarium?
S: Walking through the water all the time, instead of
swimming, felt very strange at first. We had to watch
where we put our feet as many fish, such as stingrays, live
on the sandy bottom. It was also really weird seeing
friends in the tunnel watching us in the tank. We were in
there for about 30 minutes in total and it passed in a
flash.
P: How did you feel after the dive?
S: Exhilarated! It was one of the most amazing things I've

ever done. The aquarium says its main aim is to increase awareness of the marine environment in an "interactive and entertaining manner", and it certainly did that!

Unit 15 (Page 186)

Listening

FCE Part 3 – Multiple matching

Speaker 1
I never had time to go to the German classes my company arranged for us at work, so I used to put tapes on in the car on the way in every morning and just let the language wash over me. I was completely immersed in it for the whole journey. Then I'd listen to the same section on the way home and that was enough to ensure I learnt what I'd heard in the morning. When I go to Germany on sales trips now I have very few problems understanding people. Business seems to be improving, too.

Speaker 2
I went to Spain twice when I was studying languages at university; once on holiday and the next year to work in a bar. The holiday was a disaster in terms of language learning. I spent most of the time with my English friends and hardly learnt a thing. When I went back there to work, though, I spoke Spanish all day and my speaking and understanding really improved. That experience working abroad helped me pass my final exams just as much as studying, I'm convinced. Oh, and I'm getting married this year to my Spanish girlfriend.

Speaker 3
I spent three years teaching English in Poland with my boyfriend back in the early 90s. It took us both quite a long time to learn any Polish in the beginning, partly because of laziness, but mostly because we were working long hours teaching and speaking English all day. Things got better, though, once we eventually got to know a few Polish people and we had more chance to speak the language. We both became much more integrated after that. We even saw a few films in Polish at the cinema.

Speaker 4
Here in Wales everyone can speak English, but more and more young people are learning Welsh, the real native language. My mum and dad both came to Wales from England, so I only ever spoke in English till I came to this school. But all lessons are in Welsh, see? Right from day one everything has been in Welsh and I've learnt really quickly. So now I've got the two languages. I speak in Welsh with my friends and I speak it at home, too, with my brother. It's great 'cause we can talk about things in front of my mum and dad and they've got no idea what either of us is saying – really useful sometimes!

Speaker 5
When I left university I desperately wanted to work abroad, but all three French-owned companies that I applied to turned me down at the interview stage. I'd only ever learnt grammar when I was at school so when I had to speak French in the interview I couldn't understand the questions and I'm sure the interviewers couldn't understand a word of what I was saying. So I signed up for a two-month course in Paris and when I came back I got the first job I applied for.

Ready for Speaking (Page 197)

Part 1 – Interview

I = Interviewer   **P = Paolo**   **C = Christina**

I: Hello, good morning.
CP: Good morning.
I: Could I have your mark sheets, please? Thank you. Would you like to sit down? Right, my name is Allan Reeves and this my colleague Teresa Riley. She's just going to be listening to us. So, you are Christina and you're Paolo, is that right?
CP: Yes, that's right.
I: OK, well, first of all we'd like to know something about you, so I'm going to ask you a few questions about yourselves. Let's start with you Christina. Where are you from?
C: I'm from Corinth, in Greece. I have lived there all my life. I live there with my three sisters and my parents. I am in my last year at school. My mother works in a shop and my father works in a bank.
I: Thank you, Christina. Can you tell me something about Corinth?
C: Ah well, yes. Erm, it is by the sea, so we can go swimming. Also there are parks, er, and lots of bars and things to do in the evening, so, er, it is very lively, especially in summer. In winter it is more quieter. Many tourists come to Corinth to see the ancient town – they come to see the Apollo's temple and the old market. It's very interesting.
I: And what about you, Paolo? Where are you from?
P: From Italy.
I: Whereabouts in Italy are you from?
P: I'm from a small town near Ravenna.
I: And what's it like living there?
P: It's OK. I mean, it's nothing special. There's more to do in Ravenna.
I: OK, Christina, what subjects do you enjoy most at school?
C: Well, I like languages very much, but my favourite subject is mathematics. I always like it, since I was very young. It is something I can do, working with numbers and usually I get very good marks. I wish my English would be as good!
I: Paolo, do you work or are you a student?
P: I work in my uncle's computer business.
I: And how important in English for your work?
P: Well, yes, it's very important. I have to read a lot of things about computers in English, and sometimes I must talk to foreign customers.
I: Now, let's move on to what you do in your spare time. Paolo, what kind of sports are you interested in?
P: Er, I play football, tennis, and, er, I go swimming.
I: And how often do you play football?
P: Once a week. Yes, every Saturday. I play in a team. It's good fun.
I: And Christina, do you have any hobbies?
C: Well, not really hobbies, but in my free time I like to go to the cinema, going out with my friends and things like that .
I: Which sort of films do you like to watch?
C: Oh, I like action films. I like films where many things happen. I don't like romantic films or historical films. I think they are a little bored.
I: Now, thinking about the future, Christina. What do you hope to do in the next few years?

C: Well, I want to go to the university and study business studies first. Then after that, if it's possible, I'll work in a big company, as an accountant or something like that. Maybe in the future I can use my English, and find a job in another country. That would be very exciting.

I: And what kind of job do you hope to be doing in ten years' time, Paolo?

P: Well, 10 years is a long time, so I'm not sure what will happen. First, I want to help my uncle expanding his business, and then maybe in the future, I could set up my own business.

Ready for Speaking (Page 198)

Part 2 – Talking about photographs

I = Interviewer   C = Christina   P = Paolo

I: Now, I'd like each of you to talk on your own for about a minute. I'm going to give each of you two different photographs and I'd like you to talk about them. Christina, here are your two photographs. They show grandfathers with their grandchildren. Can you Paolo see them? I'll give you your two photographs in a minute Paolo.
Christina, I'd like you to compare and contrast these photographs, and say how important grandparents can be in situations like these. Remember, you have only about a minute for this so don't worry if I interrupt you. OK?

C: Yes, er, in the first picture the girl is playing the piano with her grandfather whereas in the other one the man is teaching his granddaughter to ride a bicycle. In both pictures everybody is smiling and seems to be enjoying themselves. Er, what else? Yes, in the first picture they are indoors whereas in this one they are outside and the girl is wearing a special hat for protect her head if she falls over. I can't make out how old is the man in this picture, but I think he is younger that the other grandfather. Er, let me see, well, I think grandparents can help a lot, especially nowadays, because parents are very busy and often they don't have the time to be with their children.
Grandparents can look after the grandchildren, during the school holidays, er, cook for them and make sure they are not in danger. They can even play with them, like in these pictures. Children can learn many things from their grandparents, maybe not things like use the computer, but more traditional activities, such as riding a bike or making things, er…

I: Thank you. Paolo, has an older relative taught you to do something?

P: Yes, my uncle taught me to play golf.

I: Thank you. Now Paolo, here are your two photographs. They show people in an emergency situation. Please let Christina see them.
I'd like you to compare and contrast these photographs, and say how serious you think each of the situations looks. Remember, Paolo, you have only about a minute for this, so don't worry if I interrupt you. All right?

P: OK. In this picture I can see a television journalist interviewing a policeman. They must be in America because the policeman's uniform is the typical one you see in films and on TV. Also the writing is in English. It's not obvious what has happened but maybe there's been an accident. Or there might have been a crime even. Perhaps a murder or something, I don't know. Er, in this picture it looks as if they are in an ambulance, because the woman's

wearing a thing on her face for air, for oxygen, and the man's writing down the details about the woman. Er, it's difficult to say which is more serious, we don't really know what's happened. Er, in the first picture the television camera is there, and nobody is allowed to cross the, the line, so it must be quite important. It's not just an ordinary crime or accident. In the second one, the woman looks quite relaxed, well, not relaxed, maybe, but she isn't panicking, so I think this situation isn't very serious.

I: Thank you. Christina, do you think you could be a policewoman?

C: Oh, no. I think it's a very difficult job. It's maybe good to meet lots of people and work outside, but it's too dangerous – I wouldn't like to do it, no.

I: Thank you.

Ready for Speaking (Page 199)

Part 3 – Collaborative task

I = Interviewer   C = Christina   P = Paolo

I: Now I'd like you to talk about something together for about three minutes. I'm just going to listen.
I'd like you to imagine that the History Museum in your town would like to attract more visitors. Here are some ideas for improving the museum.
First, talk with your partner about the proposals saying how they might appeal to different people. Then choose two which you think would be the most successful in attracting new visitors.
You have only about three minutes for this. So again, don't worry if I stop you. And please speak so that we can both hear you. All right?

C: Which one shall we start with?

P: Let's talk about the interactive computer programme first. In my opinion it will appeal to a lot of people, because computers are so important in our lives today. Most people know how to use a computer now, don't they?

C: Well, not everyone, no, I don't agree. And anyway, I don't think the people go to the museums to use a computer. They can do that at home or at work. A medieval fair would be something very different, though. That would be interesting for people of all ages. It could be good fun, don't you think?

P: Yes, that's true. The visitors could take part in different activities and eat medieval food. And if the organizers dressed up in costumes, that would make history very colourful and realistic. It sounds like a great idea.

C: So that could be one of the two things we choose. Now, what do you think about the concerts? Visitors to the museum would like to listen music. People who work could come in their lunch break and have a relaxing moment.

P: Yes, but I really don't think it would attract many people who work, particularly if the museum is in a city – everyone is busy all day. Retired people would probably appreciate it and have more time to enjoy it, but that wouldn't increase the number of visitors very much, would it?

C: No, I suppose you're right.

P: Personally, I think we need to have activities which appeal to children, because if children want to come, their parents will have to come too.

C: Yes, I agree. So, let's have a look for something. Well, children could enjoy coin-making, but it wouldn't make

parents say, "we really must take our children to the museum"!
P: You're right. It's a bit dull.
C: But how about the cave painting? That sounds really enjoyable for children. If they have to paint like prehistoric man, then I imagine they will have to use their hands, and make a mess. And children love doing that, don't you agree?
P: Yes, I do. They would enjoy themselves very much. But let's look at the others before we decide. The exhibition of kitchens is nothing special. I mean, you can see things like that in lots of places, can't you?
C: Yes, it isn't the most fascinating idea. I don't know who would want to see that. Maybe some adults, but not many. And the Megascreen, well. That's like the computers. Nobody will go to a museum to see a film. What you think, Paolo?
P: I completely disagree. To my mind that's the kind of thing that will make it different to other museums and would appeal to all types of different people. And the screen would be very big, so it's not the same that watching it on television or at the cinema.
C: Well, I'm really keen on films, but I rather go to a real cinema. I prefer the atmosphere there. And historical films are old and a bit boring, especially for children, so not many people would go.
P: Well, I think that should be one of the two things we choose, personally. I think it would bring people who don't normally go to museums or even who have never been.
C: OK, well we agree on the medieval fair, but not on the Megascreen. I think the cave painting is a better idea. What do you think of the fashion shows?
P: Oh no. I don't know anyone who is interested in fashion shows.
C: Really?
I: Thank you.

Ready for Speaking (Page 199)

Part 4 – Further discussion

I = Interviewer   C = Christina   P = Paolo

I: Christina, what do you think makes a good museum?
C: I don't know really. I suppose that, I think that, in general the museums are a little bored. You only look at objects which are in, in, erm, how do you say? Erm, well, like boxes, in glass boxes or cupboards, so there is nothing to do. I think if you could touch the things in an exhibition, that would make it more interesting, a more enjoyable experience.
I: Uh huh, Paolo?
P: I think ideas like the medieval fair are good because they help you to have a better idea of like in the past. The last year I went to a museum where people in costumes explained how different things were used. Even they cooked with some old saucepans and things. Perhaps they weren't real, but it doesn't matter. The important is that you can imagine how people lived before.
I: How could the teaching of history in schools be improved?
C: I'm not quite sure, but, well, er, at school we just sit and listen the teachers, listen to the teachers, and write what they say. In Greece there are so many ancient monuments so perhaps we could visit more and not just read and write about them all the time.

I: What do you think, Paolo?
P: Er, when I was at school we just listened to the teachers. I think history was the worst subject for many people. I think we need better teachers who are good at making a subject more interesting for pupils. I don't know, but I think it depends on the teacher.
I: What was the most important moment in the history of the twentieth century?
C: Er, I haven't thought about it before, really, but, er, perhaps it was, yes, I think it was when the first man landed on the Moon. I have seen pictures of this, and I think it should, it must have been something quite incredible at the time. Now, going into space is quite normal, but that moment was very different. What do you think, Paolo?
P: Well, I think landing on the Moon was important, but travel in space would not be possible if we did not have computers. The invention of the computer, for me, was the most important moment. It changed the way we live…
C: You only say that because you like computers!
P: No, but almost everything we do needs computers nowadays. Aeroplanes, industries, banks, companies – they all need to have computers. And if the computers break down, there are always many problems for these things. We cannot survive without computers.
C: Maybe, but I think there are more important things that happened in the last century. Things with people and not machines. For example, when people started to think about the environment more. The planet is in a bad condition, and if organizations like Greenpeace didn't exist, it would be worse. Don't you agree?
P: Yes, you're right, but even organizations like Greenpeace need computers to do their work!
I: Paolo, what items from our lives today will be in the history museums of the future?
P: That's a difficult question. Possibly, some things we have in the house, some domestic ap, er, domestic applications? No, well, it doesn't matter, domestic machines we use for cooking or other jobs, things like the cooker, the vacuum cleaner or the iron. I think some of these things will be replaced for robots which do not need people to use them.
C: Do you really think we will have robots?
P: Yes, we already have them now. In only a few years, I think we will be able to use them in the home for doing simple things.
C: Well, I think one thing in the museums of the future will be the money. I think the credit cards will be the only thing we use. Already now, some people never pay for things with cash. In only a few years I think they will stop making the money.
I: Thank you. That is the end of the test.

Macmillan Education
Between Towns Road, Oxford OX4 3PP
A division of Macmillan Publishers Limited
Companies and representatives throughout the world

ISBN 1-405-06744-6

First published 2001
This edition 2004

Designed by Andrew Jones
Illustrated by Mike Atkinson and Phil Healey
Cover design by Andrew Oliver

The author would like to thank his wife, Azucena, for her invaluable help and
constant support. The author also wishes to thank his colleagues at International
House, Madrid, for their encouragement and inspiration, as well as the many
teachers and students who helped with piloting, especially Gail Butler, Steven
McGuire, Andrew Graydon, Joanna Herbert, Anne Horkan, Kuldip Kaur, Stephen
Nicolls, Karen Reeves, Paul Scannell, Katie Smart, Hilary Thomson, Alice Tierney and
Alistair Wood. Thanks also to Helen Holwill for her excellent editorial work and Sarah
Curtis for her faith in the project.

The publishers would like to thank all those who participated in the development of
the project, with special thanks to Sophia Ashton, Helen Barmakellis, Liam Bellamy,
Margarita E. Garraman de Monzani, Vasilis Karalis, Jean Lister, Nick Milner, Jackie
Newman, David Pearce, Joanna Porebska, Lynn Smith, George Vasilakis, Peter
Williamson, Malcolm Wren and Grzegorz Œpiewak.

The author and publishers would like to thank the following for permission to
reproduce their material: Extract from 'Handle with care' by Jess Hallett, copyright ©
The Times 1999, first published in Style Magazine 28.11.99, reprinted by permission
of the publisher; Extract from 'The thrill of it all' by Alison MacArthur, first published
in Focus Magazine July 1999, reprinted by permission of the publisher
(www.focusmag.co.uk); Extract from 'Rodean girl sinks to depths men can't' by Alex
O'Connell, copyright © The Times 1999, first published in The Times 24.09.99,
reprinted by permission of the publisher; Extract from Notes From A Big Country by
Bill Bryson (Doubleday, 1998) reprinted by permission of Transworld Publishers
Limited; Extract from 'Better buy them a book' by Robert Matthews, copyright ©
Telegraph Group Limited 1997, first published in The Telegraph 05.01.97, reprinted by
permission of the publisher; Extract from 'Families switch off television to surf
Internet' by Robert Uhlig, copyright © Telegraph Group Limited 1998, first published
in The Telegraph 18.11.99, reprinted by permission of the publisher; Extract from 'Life
through the lens: Keanu Reeves' first published in Sugar Magazine August 1999,
reprinted by permission of Hachette-Filipacchi UK Limited; Extract from The Hat of
Victor by Adrian Mathews (Fourth Estate, 1996), copyright © Adrian Matthews 1996,
reprinted by permission of A M Heath & Co Ltd; Extract from 'Home is where the
school is' by Alan Road, first published in Reader's Digest April 1999, reprinted by
permission of the publisher; Extract from 'A more commercial tune' by Sara Edgehill,
copyright © The Independent 1995, first published in The Independent 06.11.95,
reprinted by permission of the publisher; Extract from 'Gift of your Gab' first
published in The Daily Mail, reprinted by permission of Solo Syndication Ltd; Extracts
from 'Family feuds – or just lunch?' by Jan Parke, first published in The Independent
20.06.99; Extract from 'She's black, I'm white, but we're twins', first published in
Sugar Magazine November 1999, reprinted by permission of Hachette-Filipacchi UK
Limited; Extract from 'You can't be sisters' first published in Woman's Realm 30.11.99,
reprinted by permission of Rex Features Limited; Extract from 'Rock of the ages' by
Jennifer Rodger, copyright © The Times 1999, first published in Style Magazine
28.11.99, reprinted by permission of the publisher; Extract from 'So you want to get
married' by Jo Carlowe; Extract from 'Addicted to love' by Dickon Ross, first
published in Focus Magazine September 1999, reprinted by permission of the
publisher (www.focusmag.co.uk); Extract from 'Shopaholic pill will put brakes on big
spenders' by Andy Goldberg, copyright © The Times 1999, first published in The
Sunday Times 19.12.99, reprinted by permission of the publisher; Extract from 'It
narrows the mind and distends the stomach, so let's travel less' by John Rentoul,
copyright © The Independent 1998, first published in The Independent 12.01.98,
reprinted by permission of the publisher; Extract from 'Short breaks for every month
of the year', first published in Woman's Weekly 10.08.99, reprinted by permission of
Rex Features Limited; Extract from How To Tell A Ghost Story by Fiona McClymont,
reprinted by permission of author; Extract from 'Why Hallowe'en is hateful' by James
Delingpole, copyright © Telegraph Group Limited 1996, first published in The
Telegraph 26.10.96, reprinted by permission of the publisher; Extract from World
Famous Strange But True by Colin, Damon & Rowan Wilson (Magpie Books Ltd,
1994), reprinted by permission of Constable & Robinson Limited; Extract from 'Is
someone being paid to spy on you?' by Jo Upcraft, first published in Sugar Magazine
July 1999, reprinted by permission of Hachette-Filipacchi UK Ltd; Extract from 'Man
fined £800.00 for not clearing up his dog's mess' by Helen Johnstone, copyright ©
The Times 1999, first published in The Times 03.12.99, reprinted by permission of the
publisher; Extract from 'International rescuer' interview by Caroline Rees, first
published in FHM Magazine February 2000, reprinted by permission of the publisher;
Extract from 'Dad would be proud of what I do' by Daisy Price, copyright © The
Independent 1999, first published in The Independent 06.12.99, reprinted by
permission of the publisher; Extract from 'Choose life: get on your bike' by Andrew
Buncombe, copyright © The Independent 1999, first published in The Independent
09.06.99, reprinted by permission of the publisher; Extract from 'Karaoke rolls those
excess stones – but a drink or two will put them back' by Michael Fitzpatrick,
copyright © Telegraph Group Limited 1999, first published in The Telegraph 05.08.99,
reprinted by permission of the publisher; Extract from 'It's just not natural' first
published in Focus Magazine January 1999, reprinted by permission of the publisher
(www.focusmag.co.uk); Extract from 'Roast Ghost' from 'Bizarre Tales' taken from
New Scientist 12.03.94, reprinted by permission of the publisher; Extract from
'Scooter importer aims to have city buzzing with his success' by Henrietta Lake,
copyright © The Times 1999, first published in The Times 18.12.99, reprinted by
permission of the publisher; Extract from 'He's my river hero' first
published in Woman's Own 22.02.00, reprinted by permission of Rex Features
Limited; Extract from 'Palette of the Apes' by Emma Bayley, first published in Focus
Magazine August 1999, reprinted by permission of the publisher
(www.focusmag.co.uk); Extract from 'Q & A What's it like to scuba dive in a shark
tank' interview with Sue Hall, first published in Best Magazine 22.02.00, reprinted by
permission of The National Magazine Company Limited; Extract from 'Oldest goldfish
Tish has his chips at 43' by Paul Stokes, copyright © Telegraph Group Limited 1999,
first published in The Telegraph 07.08.99, reprinted by permission of the publisher;
Extract from 'Speaking in one tongue' by Dickon Ross, first published in Focus
Magazine April 1999, reprinted by permission of the publisher
(www.focusmag.co.uk); Extract from 'American High' by Victoria Stanley, copyright ©
Telegraph Group Limited 2000, first published in The Telegraph 11.03.00, reprinted by
permission of the publisher; Extract from 'Know your children before sending them
away to learn' by Max de Lotbiniere, copyright © Max de Lotbiniere 2000, first
published in The Guardian 23.02.00; Extract from 'The grateful undead' by David
Lister, copyright © The Independent 1999, first published in The Independent
18.12.99, reprinted by permission of the publisher; Extract from 'Location groupies
force sale of the UK's second most famous door' by Kate Watson Smith, copyright ©
The Independent 1999, first published in The Independent 16.09.99, reprinted by
permission of the publisher; Extract from 'When the heat is on' by Clive Tully, first
published in Country Walking July 1996, reprinted by permission of the publisher;
Extract from 'Internet ends 38 year search' by Nigel Bunyan, copyright © Telegraph
Group Limited 2000, first published in The Daily Telegraph 11.02.00, reprinted by
permission of the publisher; Extract from 'Set your sites high and go surfing' by
Emma Houghton, copyright © The Independent 2000, first published in The
Independent 16.03.00, reprinted by permission of the publisher; Extract from 'My
dad's a pop star' by Jo Upcraft, first published in Sugar Magazine May 2000,
reprinted by permission of the Hachette Filipacchi UK Ltd.

The author and publishers would like to thank the following for permission to
reproduce their photographs:
Collections pp32(tr), 74, 80(red door, carved door, yellow door), 90(l), 91(t), 122(r),
134(tm,ml), Collections / John Callan 60(dustman), Collections / Ashley Cooper 101,
Collections / Richard Davis 32(tml), Collections / Geoff Howard 60(receptionist),
Collections / Scruton 60(waitress), Collections / Shout 61, Collection / Brian Shule
14(ml, mr), Collections / Brian Shule 115; Corbis pp14(tr), 18(mr), 31(tl, ml), 32(mml,
mmr), 46(br), 54, 80(blue door), 100, 103, 108, 134(mm), 150(l), 162(l, tr), 174(l);
Hulton Getty pp32(tmr, ml), 42(ml); Helen Holwill p91(b); Huw Holwill p134; Kobal
pp42(tl, tr, mr); Popperfoto pp18(tl), 32(tl), 60, 98(t), Popperfoto / Steve Price 90(r),
Popperfoto / Reteur 18(tr), Popperfoto / Reteur 43, Popperfoto / Reteur 139,
Popperfoto / Reteur 140, Popperfoto / Reteur 148, Popperfoto / Reteur 179; Sanyo
p31(tr); Frank Spooner p27; Sporting Picture pp18(mr), 21;
Stone pp9, 15, 60(hairdresser), 66, 70, 82, 98(b), 122(l), 123, 134(tl), 150(r), 164, 169,
186, 191, 198, 202; Rex p174(r); John Walmsley p48.

Commissioned photographs by Haddon Davies pp2, 3, 5, 32(mr), 34, 46(br), 87, 108(t),
112, 113, 126, 154, 166, 170, 146, 162(br).

Cover and title page photos provided by Thinkstock, Digital Vision, Photodisk.

Whilst every effort has been made to locate the owners of copyright, in some cases
this has been unsuccessful. The publishers apologise for any omission of original
sources and would be pleased to make the necessary arrangements at the first
opportunity.

Printed and bound in Thailand

2008   2007   2006   2005
10 9 8 7 6 5 4 3 2